Athenian Democracy
and Imperialism

PROBLEMS IN EUROPEAN
CIVILIZATION SERIES

Athenian Democracy and Imperialism

Edited and with an Introduction by
Loren J. Samons II
Boston University

HOUGHTON MIFFLIN COMPANY

Boston   New York

To Dan

Editor-in-Chief: Jean Woy
Assistant Editor: Keith Mahoney/Leah Strauss
Project Editor: Elena Di Cesare
Editorial Assistant: Angela Schoenherr
Associate Production/Design Coordinator: Deborah Frydman
Manufacturing Coordinator: Andrea Wagner
Marketing Manager: Sandra McGuire

Cover Image: Courtesy of the American Numismatic Society, New York.

Cover Design: Sarah Melhado

Library of Congress Catalog Number: 97-72543

ISBN: 0-395-81551-7

123456789-DH-01 00 99 98 97

Contents

Preface

The study of Athenian democracy and imperialism provides a unique opportunity to test modern notions about the form of government now prevailing, in theory if not in practice, throughout the world. Moreover, this study fits well within a series dedicated to *Problems in European Civilization* since no consensus currently exists on such basic questions as whether Athenian government can properly be called "democracy," or whether this "democracy" required the profits of empire for its perpetuation and growth. Athens' extension of political participation to the lower classes while concurrently solidifying her hegemony over fellow Greeks also creates both intellectual and emotional discomfort for the modern scholar or student imbued with democratic ideals.

In the following work I have attempted to provide relevant ancient source material and a selection of modern scholarship that will enable the student to begin addressing questions about the nature of the Athenian empire and democracy. In choosing the modern works I have not attempted to set diametrically opposing views against one another, although at times this has occurred. Rather I have tried to assemble works that argue clearly for positions across the scholarly spectrum, and thus I have necessarily drawn on some works with which I disagree strongly. This area of study elicits as much controversy as any field of ancient history, perhaps more so in view of our own emotional involvement in the issues surrounding Athenian government. Students, therefore, should not be surprised at the widely divergent views canvassed here. They should also beware of any apparent consensus view or current orthodoxy on these issues: two hundred years ago most of the American Founders (as well as other political theorists) considered Athenian democracy a prime example of poor government. Now we talk of the "democratic" principles upon which our modern society is supposedly based.

The focus of this collection is political. Obviously these historical events and political developments occurred within the wider context of Greek society at large; yet I have chosen to provide a more thorough discussion of democracy and imperialism proper rather than a necessarily more superficial treatment of a broader range of issues. A few works on related topics are included in the suggestions for further reading at the end of this book. The selections in each section are arranged in the approximate chronological order of publication. Although at times this may seem illogical because of the subject matter treated (Pericles' reforms appear after Thucydides' evaluation of his career, for example), it allows the reader to perceive the development of the ancient tradition or the modern debate on a given topic. Also, in the interest of providing space for more selections, the reader is occasionally asked to make cross-references to passages included elsewhere in the volume.

Thucydides' history is the fundamental text for the study of Athenian democracy and imperialism. To excerpt his work seems almost impious, and the selections offered here cannot replace a careful reading of his entire (if unfinished and problematic) text. However, if they serve to encourage further study of this great author, perhaps the sacrilege may be forgiven.

The Department of Classical Studies at Boston University granted me a sabbatical during my membership in the University's Society of Fellows in the Humanities, and the University provided a subvention for a trip to Greece in conjunction with current research. I wish to thank both the chairman of the department, Professor Jeffrey Henderson, and the Director of the Society, Professor Katherine T. O'Connor, for their assistance and encouragement. The members of the Society themselves provided useful criticism on a version of the Introduction presented here. The editors of Houghton Mifflin and of its late acquisition D.C. Heath, especially James Miller, Elena Di Cesare, Angela Schoenherr, and Keith Mahoney, have worked with dedication on the project. Professors J. M. Balcer (Ohio State University), Phyllis Culham (United States Naval Academy), Thomas Martin (College of Holy Cross), Paul Rahe (University of Tulsa), Barry Strauss (Cornell University), and Carol Thomas (University of Washington) read the proposals for the press and provided useful suggestions for the work. Of other colleagues and friends who have assisted me during this endeavor I must thank especially Professor Lucia Athanassaki for her generosity and kindness in Greece (and America), and Professors Stephen Esposito, Charles Fornara, James Kennelly, and Bradley Thompson for valuable consultation on points of detail. Professor James Sickinger has been an invaluable resource on numerous historical and epigraphic matters (including the inscriptions translated here). Professors Brendan McConville and Walter Stevenson, and Messrs. Peter Nilsen and Gary Scheller discussed various subjects with me and generously provided additional assistance. Finally, I wish to thank my brother, Dan, whose insights crystallized certain ideas about democracy (among other things) for me, and my wife, Jamie, who not only read the proofs, but also made it all worthwhile.

L. J. S. II

Important Dates

511/10	Overthrow of tyranny at Athens
508/7	*Demokratia* instituted by Cleisthenes
490	First Persian invasion of southern Greece; battle of Marathon
487/6	Lot replaces election for Archons
483/2	Rich silver strike in Attica; money used for Athenian navy
480	Second Persian invasion; Spartan stand at Thermopylae; allies victorious at Salamis
479	Battle of Plataea; allied Greek forces expel Persians from Greece
478/7	"Delian League" founded by Athens and allied Greeks; tribute payments and ship contributions assessed by Athens on allies
477–450	League/Athenian actions versus Persians and disaffected Greek allies
462/1	Reforms of Ephialtes in Athens; Spartan-Athenian alliance broken; Athens allies with former "medizing" states of Thessaly, Argos; Cimon ostracized
460	"First" Peloponnesian War begins; Athenian expedition to Egypt (to 454)
458/7	Long Walls begun; Athenian loss to Sparta at Tanagra
457/6	Archonship opened to *zeugitae* class in Athens
454/3	Athenians move treasury of League to Athens (?); begin inscribing "tribute lists"
451/0	Five Years' Truce (Athens and Peloponnesian League); Pericles' law to restrict Athenian citizenship; pay for jury service instituted (?)
450	Cimon's expedition to Cyprus versus Persian forces
449	Athenians make formal Peace with Persia (?); revolts among allies (?)
448	Pericles' "Congress Decree" (?)
447/6	Parthenon construction begun; Athenian loss at Coroneia in Boeotia
446	Revolt and reconquest of Euboea

446/5	Thirty Years' Peace (Athens and Peloponnesian League)
444/3	Foundation of Thurii; ostracism of Thucydides son of Melesias (?)
440–439	Revolt and reduction of Samos; restrictions on comedy instituted (until 437/6)
435	Battle of Leukimme (Corinth versus Corcyra)
433	Battle of Sybota (Corinth versus Corcyra, Athens)
432	(?) Megarian Decree; revolt of Poteidaea
431	Outbreak of Peloponnesian War; Funeral Oration of Pericles (winter 431/0)
429	Death of Pericles
428/7	Revolt of Mytilene
425	Athenians under Cleon and Demosthenes capture Spartiates at Pylos
421	Peace of Nicias (Athens and Peloponnesian League)
416	"Melian Dialogue"; Athenians reduce island of Melos (winter 416/15)
415–13	Athenian invasion of Sicily (and subsequent disaster)
411	Oligarchical revolution of The Four Hundred in Athens (*demokratia* restored in 410)
404	Fall of Athens; oligarchical revolution of The Thirty (*demokratia* restored in 403)
399	Trial and execution of Socrates

Important Terms

In accordance with most of the works excerpted in this book I have generally used latinized or anglicized versions of the more familiar Greek terms and proper names (thus Pericles instead of Perikles). However, no rigid system has been adopted; direct transliterations (e.g., *strategos*) are sometimes employed, and excerpted passages retain the practice of the original author or translator.

archons ("magistrates") In the most restricted sense the term refers to the nine chief magistrates of Athens, elected before 487 and thereafter chosen by lot, especially the Archon Eponymos, who gave his name to the Athenian year (e.g., the year of Themistocles = 493/2). The remaining Athenian archons consisted of the Polemarch (military commander), the Basileus (primarily a religious official), and six Thesmothetae (see *heliaea*). The term can also be used to refer simply to magistrates (e.g., "the archons in the cities").

Areopagus The ancient council of the Athenian state, named for the "hill of Ares" near the Acropolis and consisting of former archons. Beyond judicial duties it seems originally to have exercised a kind of supervisory role over Athenian magistrates and laws, but after Ephialtes' reforms (462/1) its duties were basically restricted to those of a homicide court.

boule ("council") Usually the Athenian council of 500, created by Cleisthenes and consisting of 50 members (*bouleutai*) from each tribe, which among other duties prepared business for the assembly.

cleruchy An Athenian settlement, often on land seized in another state, in which the settlers retained their Athenian citizenship. In a colony, on the other hand, settlers became citizens of the newly founded and independent polis.

deme One of the 139 or so independent villages of Attica or neighborhoods of the city of Athens which, grouped by Cleisthenes into thirty units (*trittyes*) from the coast (10), interior (10), or city (10), made up the ten tribes. Each tribe contained one group of demes (a *trittys*) from each of the three regions of Attica.

dicasts ("jurors")   The Athenian judicial system in the fifth century was based on a group of courts (*dicasteria*) usually comprised of several hundred citizen "dicasts" who cast ballots to decide the defendant's guilt or innocence and the penalty to be assessed.

dokimasia   Procedure whereby individuals selected for office were examined regarding their Athenian citizenship, family, religious obligations, and military service.

ecclesia ("assembly")   The Athenian citizen body met in assembly during the fourth century on at least forty days per year (perhaps less frequently in the fifth), usually on the Pnyx hill west of the Acropolis. Here the *prytaneis* presented the business of the meeting, speeches were delivered, and the citizens decided policy and issued decrees (*psephismata*) by majority vote.

euthynae ("corrections")   Procedure after tenure of office whereby an Athenian official's actions and books were scrutinized for any misconduct.

graphe paranomon ("indictment for illegal motions")   By this procedure an Athenian making an illegal or improperly formulated proposal in the assembly could be brought to trial.

heliaea   A large Athenian court, probably developed from or consisting of the assemblymen acting as a body of jurors. One form of this court was presided over by the Thesmothetae, six Athenian archons with primarily legal and judicial duties.

hellenotamiae ("treasurers of the Greeks")   Athenian magistracy apparently instituted in 478/7 to manage the collection and stockpiling of allied tribute payments.

hippeis ("horsemen")   The cavalrymen of Greece and, at Athens, the second highest of Solon's property classifications, possessing property capable of yielding at least 300 measures of produce per year. In wealth they were therefore second only to the *pentakosiomedimnoi*, or "five hundred measure men," and were eligible to hold most state offices.

hoplite   The chief infantrymen of the classical Greek army, a hoplite carried a short sword, shield and spear, and wore helmet, greaves, and breastplate. His rectangular unit of battle was called a phalanx and required a high degree of discipline to maintain its formation during battle. Since the hoplite supplied his own arms, he usually possessed at least moderate property, and he most often came from the ranks of the ubiquitous independent Greek farmers.

kaloi kagathoi ("the beautiful and the good")   A phrase used by Athenian aristocrats or oligarchs to describe themselves and separate themselves from the *demos* ("citizen body" or "commoners") at large.

liturgies   Obligations laid on wealthy Athenians to provide support for military matters (e.g., the trierarchy, which required outfitting a trireme for one year), or other affairs (e.g., the *choregia*, requiring payment for equipping and training a dithyrambic or dramatic chorus).

metic   A resident alien at Athens, liable to certain taxes and military service, but without the political rights of a citizen.

nomos, *pl.* **nomoi** ("law")   Greek words also referring to "custom," but in an Athenian political context usually designating the laws of Solon, or other fixed statutes that could not (theoretically) be countervened, and which did not simply result from a vote of the assembly (see *psephisma*). Some uncertainty exists about whether there was a clear distinction between laws and decrees (*psephismata*) in the fifth century.

obol   A small unit of Athenian coinage. 6 obols = 1 drachma, 100 drachmae = 1 mna, 6,000 drachmae = 1 talent. Unskilled workers in the fifth century could earn about a drachma per day in wages.

ostracism Athenian practice whereby a quorum of 6,000 voters could banish any Athenian for ten years. The voters' choices for banishment were written on pieces of broken pottery (*ostraka*).

pentecontaetia ("fifty years") Term used to describe the period between the end of the Persian Wars (479) and the outbreak of the Peloponnesian War (431).

phoros When the Athenians founded the Delian League they required each member state to provide ships or monetary tribute (*phoros*), ostensibly for the continued actions against the Persians.

prytany, prytaneis Each of the ten Cleisthenic tribes provided fifty councillors to the boule, and each group of fifty managed the council and served as a standing committee for one tenth of the year each, a prytany, during which time they were called the *prytaneis* ("presidents").

psephisma, *pl.* **psephismata** ("decree") A measure passed by vote in the Athenian *ecclesia* (compare *nomos*).

stasis ("civil strife") Violent conflict that from time to time broke out within Greek states during the Peloponnesian War (and at other times) between opposing factions, sometimes (at least ostensibly) over issues of domestic or foreign policies.

strategos, *pl.* **strategoi** ("general") At Athens ten *strategoi* were elected annually, initially one from each tribe but eventually (the date is disputed) without regard to tribal affiliation. Along with commanding forces on land and sea, *strategoi* like Pericles and Cleon seem to have wielded considerable political influence.

thetes The lowest Athenian property qualification, designating citizens without property or whose property did not reach the qualification for *zeugitae* status. These citizens were available for military service as rowers or lightly armed troops.

trireme   The standard warship of the classical Greek fleet, a trireme was fitted with three superimposed banks of oars as well as equipment for sailing (which was often left on shore during battle). The ships carried about 200 men (mostly rowers) and were designed primarily for ramming other vessels with their bronze "beaks."

zeugitae   ("yokemen" from their teams of oxen or style of fighting)   The third property class in the Solonian system, ranking below the *hippeis* and above the *thetes*, and requiring the production of 200 measures of produce per year. The *zeugitae* probably consisted mainly of the middle (i.e., "hoplite") class.

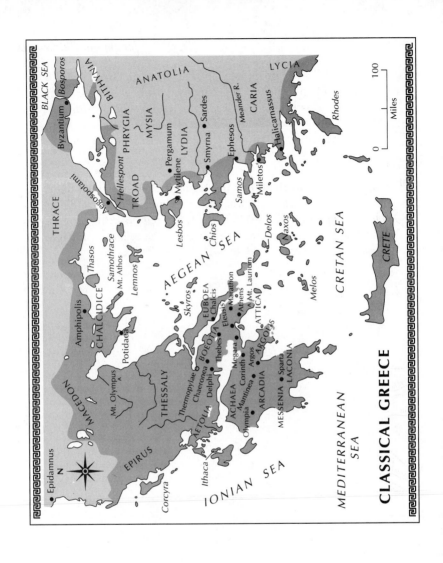

CLASSICAL GREECE

BLACK SEA

BITHYNIA

Byzantium • • Bosporos

ANATOLIA

LYCIA

PHRYGIA

MYSIA

Hellespont

TROAD

Pergamum • • Sardes

Mytilene • Smyrna

LYDIA

Aegospotami

THRACE

Ephesos

CARIA

Meander R.

Miletos

Samos

Halicarnassus

Amphipolis •

Thasos

Samothrace

CHALCIDICE

Mt. Athos

Lemnos

Potidaea •

Skyros

Lesbos

Chios

AEGEAN SEA

Delos

Rhodes

Naxos

Mt. Olympus ∧

THESSALY

EUBOEA

Chalcis

Marathon

BOEOTIA

Eleusis

Mt. Laurium

ATTICA

CRETAN SEA

Thermopylae •

Chaeronea

Thebes •

Athens •

Melos

CRETE

Delphi •

Megara •

AETOLIA

ACHAEA

Corinth • ARGOLIS

Mantinea •

Olympia •

ARCADIA

Argos •

Sparta •

Ithaca

MESSENIA

LACONIA

MACEDON

Epidamnus •

EPIRUS

N

Corcyra

IONIAN SEA

MEDITERRANEAN SEA

0   100

Miles

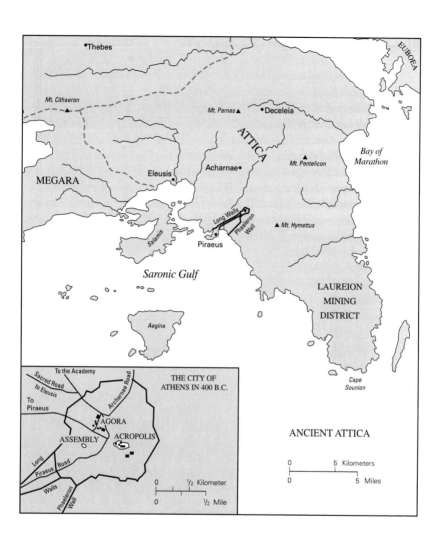

Thebes

EUBOEA

Mt. Cithaeron ▲

Mt. Parnes ▲   •Deceleia

ATTICA

Eleusis   Acharnae•   ▲ Mt. Pentelicon   *Bay of Marathon*

MEGARA

Long Walls

Phaleron Wall

Salamis   Piraeus   ▲ Mt. Hymettus

Saronic Gulf

LAUREION

MINING

DISTRICT

Aegina

Cape Sounion

To the Academy

Sacred Road to Eleusis

Archarnae Road

THE CITY OF
ATHENS IN 400 B.C.

To Piraeus

AGORA

ASSEMBLY   ACROPOLIS

Long Piraeus Road

Walls

Phaleron Wall

0   ½ Kilometer

0   ½ Mile

ANCIENT ATTICA

0   5 Kilometers

0   5 Miles

Introduction: Sources and Problems

Athens, according to the historian Herodotus, became a formidable military force only after the Athenians achieved "equality of speech" (*isegoria*) as a result of the famous reforms of Cleisthenes around 507 B.C.:

> *Thus did the Athenians increase in strength. And it is plain enough, not from this instance only, but from many everywhere, that freedom is an excellent thing; since even the Athenians, who, while they continued under the rule of the tyrants, were not a whit more valiant than any of their neighbours, no sooner shook off the yoke than they became decidedly the first of all. These things show that while undergoing oppression, they let themselves be beaten, since then they worked for a master; but so soon as they got their freedom, each man was eager to do the best he could for himself* (5.78, trans. Rawlinson).

Herodotus, though not an Athenian himself, apparently spent time in the city during its most powerful years, the so-called "golden age" when Pericles was the foremost citizen (Thuc. 2.65) and democratic Athens dominated the Aegean Sea by means of her huge fleet (ca., 460–429). One might conclude from his statement about *isegoria*, therefore, that Herodotus endorsed both the Athenian democracy and the Athenian empire, especially since he chose to defend the admittedly unpopular view that it was the Athenian fleet which had saved all of Hellas from the Persian invasion of 480 (7.139).

It must be conceded, however, that although the so-called "father of history" obviously admired the Athenians, his statements about government betray views probably closer to those of most fifth-century Greek aristocrats than to those of any enthusiastic supporters of *demokratia*. For Herodotus not only praises the Athenian regime, but also expresses admiration for the "good government" (*eunomia*) of oligarchic Sparta (1.66) and of the "free" regime of the Medes after the removal of their Assyrian overlords (1.95–6). Moreover, we are not certain of the precise definition Herodotus attached to the relatively new term *demokratia*, since he uses it only twice: once to describe the Athenian constitution after Cleisthenes (6.131.1) and once to characterize certain regimes established by a Persian official to replace tyrannies in early fifth-century Asia Minor, which at most probably resembled "liberal" oligarchies (6.43.3). Nor does Herodotus employ the term in the famous debate on forms of government (3.80–82), where, in fact, one of his speakers gives the "rule of the many" the

1

epithet *isonomia* ("equality before the law" or "equal distribution of rights," 3.80.6). Such references, combined with his two uses of the verbal form of *demokratia* (4.137.2, 6.43.3), suffice to show that the historian conceived of good government primarily in negative terms: as the absence of tyranny rather than the presence of what we call "democracy." For Herodotus, *demokratia* apparently comprised one possible (but certainly not necessary) form such "good government" might take.

Herodotus is one of our earliest witnesses to the political world of Athens and Greece at large in the fifth century. Yet his narrative and opinions may often seem to create almost as many problems as they solve, and his work clearly demonstrates that even by the late fifth century no generally accepted technical terminology existed for the discussion of either politics or "imperialism." For the latter term, no Greek equivalent exists in the fifth century, and the idea usually seems to be expressed in forms of the Greek noun *arche* (a "sovereignty" or an "empire," but also a "magistracy" and "beginning") and the verbs *archein* ("to rule," also "to begin") and *douloun* ("to enslave"). Thus, as limited (by modern standards) as the fifth-century vocabulary for political theory seems, the terminology for the discussion of inter-state relations was apparently even less developed.

Perhaps this fact may ultimately work to the advantage of the modern student of ancient history and politics. English-speakers of the twentieth century are accustomed to academic disciplines such as philosophy or political science that require the control of an often massive technical vocabulary based not on English words, but rather on languages most have never studied. Thus the term "democracy," which carries numerous connotations and usually positive emotive force, stands for a complex concept—one most individuals learn to identify, if not to define precisely. For the ancient Greeks, the term *demokratia* was simply the combination of the words *demos* ("the people," also "the common people" and "a country district") and *kratos* ("power"), and originally may have had a distinctly negative ring. Likewise *aristokratia* meant "power (or government) of the best" (*aristoi*), while "aristocracy" for us is a conceptual term often carrying negative connotations that have little to do with the root meaning of the word.

By the time Plato composed his dialogues in the early and mid fourth century, and certainly by the time Aristotle composed his treatises on politics and other subjects, intellectuals clearly felt the need for more precise definitions and categorization of terms. From the world of the fifth century, however, we have the opportunity to observe the works of impressive thinkers and writers such as Herodotus and Thucydides, who were free from (or only beginning to grapple with) the construction of formal terminology. Moreover, we also possess actual contemporary documents (such as decrees of the state inscribed on stone), which provide another, more direct insight into the workings and conceptualization of the Athenian government by fifth-century "politicians." For the views of the "common man," the comedies of Aristophanes provide perhaps our best source; through him we can begin to learn what "average" Athenians considered humorous. In a similar way the tragedies of Aeschylus, Sophocles, and Euripides, while commenting on the larger moral issues of their day, may provide us with some insight into the political dilemmas facing the Athenian *demos* in the fifth century. Relevant here also is the ever-increasing archaeological record of this period, especially those excavations ongoing in the Athenian *agora* ("marketplace") and elsewhere in the former Athenian empire.

When examining any of our contemporary or near-contemporary sources on Athenian democracy and imperialism, the modern student must exercise the highest degree of critical analysis. The precise origins of much material, stemming as it does from the "oral tradition," cannot be determined. Often, like the famous Roman jurist Lucius Cassius Longinus, we must ask of the sources; "Cui bono?" ("Who benefits?"). Not all of the fifth-century authors were as candid as the so-called "Old Oligarch," author of a *Constitution of the Athenians*, who stated at the outset that he thought *demokratia* a poor form of government. Even Thucydides, who is still considered by some to be the most even-handed of ancient historians, expressed a perhaps hypercritical attitude toward Cleon, the "demagogue" whom Aristophanes mercilessly and hilariously lampooned. In Herodotus, whose "open-minded" view of the non-Greeks led some in antiquity to denounce him as *philobarbaros* (a "barbarian lover"), some scholars have thought to discern the influence of Pericles or his followers, who wished to defend the statesman's family from charges of treason and collaboration with the tyrants who ruled Athens in the sixth century B.C.

Later sources on Athenian democracy and the Athenian empire, including those of the fourth century, present even further difficulties. Not only are these later authorities dependent (as are we) on what they could read in the fifth-century documents, many were also influenced by the politics of their own day and the (now even more distant) oral traditions passed down from earlier generations, with varying degrees of tendentious addition and subtraction. On the other hand, authorities such as Aristotle in the fourth century B.C. and Plutarch in the second century A.D. had at their disposal numerous works of the fifth and fourth centuries that are no longer extant. When we are lucky, they even refer by name to the authority upon whom they are drawing, and these "fragments" of lost works serve as important sources of otherwise unobtainable information, which must nonetheless be subjected to rigorous criticism.

Any study of fifth-century Athens thus faces numerous problems of "source criticism" as well as the issue of interpretation of the information after its origins and reliability are evaluated. In the arguably inter-related areas of Athenian democracy and imperialism, modern discussions suffer from the additional disability created by our own history and political circumstances. Often this leads to the tendency for students (or even scholars) to treat Greek history as a teleological journey towards "democracy," which moderns sometimes view as the ultimate (if not perfect) form of government. On this view, Athens becomes less the exceptional and indeed iconoclastic state many contemporary Greeks considered her than the perfection of the Greek polis and ultimate expression of Hellenic political development. Thus, although it is true that our ancient sources almost universally looked askance at the democratic polis of Athens, many modern scholars have tended to exhibit the precisely opposite bias. For the consideration of Athenian imperialism in its democratic context, this fact has occasionally encouraged the tendency to minimize the sometimes brutal aspects of Athenian rule while exaggerating the "backward" nature and militarism of the Spartan oligarchy. This modern view, in a way, takes its leave from the Funeral Oration of Pericles as recorded by Thucydides (2.35–46), in which the Athenian statesman dilated on the openness and relative equality of Athenian society as opposed to the closed nature of the Spartan state. But Pericles' words surely cannot be considered an unbiased or even fair depiction of the actual conditions in either polis. The context of his speech, a funeral in Attica for Athenian soldiers fallen in the first year of the war against the Peloponnesians, certainly invites us to read the words of the politician in light of our own experience of political and patriotic oratory, keeping in mind the somewhat different nature of political debate in fifth-century Athens.

Conversely, some recent scholarly work has begun to emphasize those aspects of Athenian society that appear "undemocratic," elitist, slave-dependent or sexist, at least when judged by modern standards. Analysis of this type does help us to place the Athenians on a kind of relative (if anachronistic and ultimately self-congratulatory) scale, but it often also relegates the Spartans and other Greeks to a position of even greater "barbarity," a term as scrupulously avoided as the concept it represents is broadly applied in such work. Too often students and scholars forget that in reprimanding the Spartans (or Athenians) based on our own standards of political or social morality one runs the risk of practicing the self-assured prejudice usually condemned in others. Moreover, the ironies of Greek history are manifold. Few scholars, for example, have emphasized the fact that the rise of "democracy" in Hellas, resulting in the increased power of the middle and lower class male, seems to have carried with it the reduction in the status and power of aristocratic women. It was, after all, oligarchic Sparta that Aristotle criticized for granting too much power to women (*Pol.* 1269b–1270a), and there that young girls received physical training akin to that of their male counterparts (Xen. *Const. of the Spartans* 1.3–4). Likewise, we know of no fifth-century Athenian poetess or female general, whereas Sappho lived and wrote in aristocratic Lesbos of the early sixth century and Artemisia of Halicarnassos (under Persian rule) led a contingent of ships in Xerxes' army (Hdt. 7.99).

Finally, one must confront squarely the fact that the form of government the Western world has seen fit to designate as the appropriate political condition of human beings developed in a state that was concurrently pursuing an aggressive foreign policy aimed at the domination of the Aegean Sea and Hellas. This policy culminated in an attempt to conquer the huge island of Sicily and spread Athenian rule into the central Mediterranean, a move that would have anticipated the Roman conquest of the island and creation of the Roman empire by two centuries. Thucydides, no friend of democracy, described the decision to attack Sicily:

> *All alike fell in love with the enterprise. The older men thought that they would either subdue the places against which they were to sail, or at all events, with so large a force, meet with no disaster; those in the prime of life felt a longing for foreign sights and spectacles, and had no doubt that they should come safe home again; and the idea of the common people and the soldiery was to earn wages at the moment, and*

> *make conquests that would supply a never-ending fund of pay for the future. With this enthusiasm of the majority, the few that liked it not, feared to appear unpatriotic by holding up their hands against it, and so kept quiet (6.24.3–4, trans. Crawley).*

Before the failure in Sicily, the empire provided the Athenians with annual revenues (in the form of tribute payments exacted from "allied" states as well as taxes, tolls, rents, and fines) which, combined with the silver mines of Attica, made ancient Athens the wealthiest Greek state of the fifth century B.C. In such circumstances, the Athenians chose not only to beautify their city with buildings like the Parthenon, but also to institute payment for public service such as jury duty, making active participation in the government a real and not just theoretical possibility for many free Athenians of moderate or lower means. Aristotle, in fact, identified popular control of the courts as the most "democratic" element of Athenian government (*Pol.* 1273b–1274a; cf. *Const.* 9.1), and at Athens the jurors received daily payments that amounted roughly to a day's wage for an unskilled laborer. These payments, in addition to those for the men rowing the warships in the Athenian fleet and working in the state building-program, as well as the grants of land seized from other Greek states to Athenian settlers, mean that Athens created (even if unintentionally) perhaps the first democratic welfare system, though the state required definite, and sometimes dangerous, service in return for payment.

Modern students tend to associate "imperialism" with restrictive regimes such as monarchy or oligarchy, forms of government that we usually think more susceptible to militarism and the desire for expansion Thucydides so clearly attached to his home state of Athens. The selections from Thucydides and other ancient sources included in this volume will hopefully afford each reader the opportunity to test this view and to evaluate carefully the potential relationship between domestic politics and foreign policy in ancient Athens. In the end, we may be forced to admit that the popular (if rarely stated) modern view that democracies tend to be more peaceful than other types of regimes constitutes a theoretical supposition no less in need of proof than the opposite hypothesis. The modern authorities excerpted here will hopefully demonstrate both the breadth of scholarly opinion on these issues and help the student evaluate the ancient sources while stimulating further debate. The problems of definition, as described above, may often appear paramount. What do we mean (and what did the ancient Greeks mean) by "democracy" and *demokratia*? Should we consider Athens "democratic" in the modern sense of the word? How did the Athenians and other Greeks conceive of the Athenian "empire," especially within the context provided by the Peloponnesian "League" led by Sparta on the one hand and the massive Persian empire ruled by the Great King on the other?

We must also examine carefully the political debate that occurred within the city of Athens itself, about which we are admittedly ill-informed, but which must have played a crucial role both in the development of democracy and in the management of the empire. Here the personality of Pericles looms large, both as the central political figure of the fifth century (who apparently withstood significant political opposition) and also as the individual who may have been the primary theoretical apologist for, and exponent of, the form of government his own predominance seemingly belied. Pericles' role as proponent of the building program, as a friend of the leading philosophers and sculptor of his day, as a successful general, and as a leader whose stated policy according to Thucydides was "No concessions to the Peloponnesians" (1.140), makes him both a necessary object of study and a potentially illuminating example for modern democracies.

The recent movement towards more democratic regimes in eastern Europe and elsewhere, celebrated by most in the West, does not seem to have carried with it a concurrent movement toward peace or "civility" in international relations. It seems an appropriate time to re-examine the relationship between democracy and imperialism in the state that created *demokratia*, perhaps with a view toward understanding the perils — as well as we understand the benefits — of freedom.

Variety of Opinion

A scheme unexecuted is with [the Athenians] a positive loss, a successful enterprise a comparative failure. The deficiency created by the miscarriage of an undertaking is soon filled up by fresh hopes: for they alone are enabled to call a thing hoped for a thing got, by the speed with which they act upon their resolutions. Thus they toil on in trouble and danger all the days of their lives, with little opportunity for enjoying, being ever engaged in getting: their only idea of a holiday is to do what the occasion demands, and to them laborious occupation is less of a misfortune than the peace of a quiet life. To describe their character in a word, one might truly say that they were born into the world to take no rest themselves and to give none to others.

Corinthians (describing Athenians: Thuc. 2.70)

[After Athens' victory over the Persians] she experienced a complete reversal of fortune, which was due to the instability of the national character. For the Athenian populace is always more or less in the situation of a ship without a commander.

Polybius 6.44

The people [of Athens], who had been the cause of the acquisition of a maritime empire during the course of the Persian wars, acquired a conceit of themselves; and in spite of the opposition of the better citizens they found worthless demagogues to support their cause.

Aristotle, *Politics* 1274a

In all ages, whatever, the form and name of government, be it monarchy, republic, or democracy, an oligarchy lurks behind the façade. . . .

Ronald Syme, *The Roman Revolution* (1939)

The Aegean world gained considerably from the use made by Athens of the wealth that she drew from the cities and, as the Athenians claimed at Sparta in 432, they made considerably less use of force than imperial powers are expected to use; but they could have made more concessions to the general Greek passion for autonomy without undermining their position.

Russell Meiggs, *The Athenian Empire* (1972)

Prima facie Athenian democracy would seem to have been a perfectly designed machine for expressing the will of the people.

A. H. M. Jones, *Athenian Democracy* (1957)

Under the [democracy] Athens managed for nearly two hundred years to be the most prosperous, most powerful, most stable, most peaceful internally, and culturally by far the richest state in all the Greek world. . . .

If [today] such bitter opponents . . . both claim to be defending real or genuine democracy, we are witnessing a new phenomenon in human history. . . . [A]ll share the belief that democracy is the best form of political organization. The historical aspect of this situation is receiving less attention than it merits. It is not self-evident, I submit,

that there should be such near unanimity about the virtue of democ-
racy when during most of history the reverse was the case.

M. I. Finley, *Democracy Ancient and Modern* (1985)

Sobriety, abstinence, *and* severity, *were never remarkable characteris-*
tics of democracy, or the democratical branch or mixture, in any con-
stitution; they have oftener been the attributes of aristocracy and
oligarchy. *Athens, in particular, was never conspicuous for these qual-*
ities; but, on the contrary, from the first to the last moment of her
democratical constitution, levity, gayety, inconstancy, dissipation, in-
temperance, debauchery, *and a* dissolution of manners, *were the pre-*
vailing character of the whole nation.

John Adams

The celebrated Pericles, in compliance with the resentment of a prosti-
tute, at the expense of much of the blood and treasure of his country-
men, attacked, vanquished, and destroyed the city of the Samnians
[i.e., Samos]. *The same man, stimulated by private pique against the*
Megarensians [i.e., the Megarians], . . . *or to avoid a prosecution with*
which he was threatened as an accomplice in a supposed theft, . . . or to
get rid of the accusations prepared to be brought against him for dissi-
pating the funds of the State in the purchase of popularity, or from a
combination of all these causes, was the primitive author of that fa-
mous and fatal war . . . which, after various vicissitudes, intermissions,
and renewals, terminated in the ruin of the Athenian commonwealth.

Alexander Hamilton, *Federalist* VI

Had every Athenian citizen been a Socrates, every Athenian assembly
would still have been a mob.

James Madison, *Federalist* LV

Throughout most of Western history, Athenian democracy has been in
bad odor.

J. T. Roberts, *Athens on Trial* (1994)

As a matter of fact the [Athenian] demagogues and the popular courts,
possessed by the craze to level downwards—the disease of democra-
cies—found that it was easier to strip the wealthy than to enrich the
poor.

A. Andreades, *A History of Greek Public Finance* (1933)

The charges levelled against the Athenians, the so-called "abuses,"
when assembled to form a single bill of particulars, create a misleading

impression. This assembling of complaints is modern; no one put them together in the fifth century. The truth is that no single imperial practice could be judged gravely oppressive, irritating in individual cases thought it might be.

M. F. McGregor, *The Athenians and their Empire* (1987)

Critics of Plato and Aristotle find their thinking illiberal, reactionary, and backward. But they have not refuted the philosophers' basic connection between agrarianism and the stable Greek state. And they have not shown that the Hellenic character and ethos were the unique products of an urban, democratic, and imperialistic Athens, rather than the earlier bounty of the ten-acre farmer, hoplite, and council member. So if we now object to the view of Plato and Aristotle, it may be because we have lost empathy with the horny-handed farmer himself and his cargo of self-reliance, hard work, and a peculiar distrust of rich and poor alike.

V. D. Hanson, *The Other Greeks* (1995)

Democracy is not only or even primarily a means through which different groups can attain their ends or seek the good society: it is the good society itself in operation.

S. M. Lipset, *Political Man* (1960)

Today, the idea of democracy is universally popular. . . . Yet a term that means anything means nothing. And so it has become with "democracy," which nowadays is not so much a term of restricted and specific meaning as a vague endorsement of a popular idea. . . .

Advocates of democracy sometimes appear to believe that the values of democracy constitute the complete universe of value: if you could have a perfect democracy, they imply, then you would have a perfect political order, maybe even a perfect society.

R. Dahl, *Democracy and Its Critics* (1989)

In short, I say that as a city we are the school of Hellas; and I doubt if the world can produce a man, who where he has only himself to depend upon, is equal to so many emergencies and graced by so happy a versatility as the Athenian.

Pericles (Thucydides 2.41.1)

Index of Sources

A few years after moving the Delian league's treasury to Athens (454/3), the Athenians began to build the Parthenon (pictured). Probably about this time they also began to pay citizens for jury duty. (Greek National Tourist Office)

I The Nature of Athenian Democracy

Herodotus wrote that Athens received its demokratia from the reformer Cleisthenes (6.131), and the Athenians of the fifth century invariably used this term to describe their government. The modern term "democracy" obviously derives from the name of Athens' regime, yet scholars have often been as ready to demonstrate the differences between modern democracy and ancient demokratia as they have been to point out the similarities. Whereas eighteenth-century political theorists like James Madison shuddered at the prospect of a government resembling Athenian democracy, some modern scholars criticize the Athenians for their failure to extend the franchise to women and slaves—that is, for not being "democratic" enough. The following ancient sources and modern works are offered as an attempt to help the reader evaluate the historical circumstances that resulted in demokratia and the principles upon which it may have rested.

Sources

Pseudo-Xenophon

The Constitution of the Athenians

The treatise on the *Constitution of the Athenians* excerpted below was apparently composed in the fifth century (perhaps around 431) by an unknown Athenian commonly called the "Old Oligarch" (from his political views and tone) or "Pseudo-Xenophon" (because the document was preserved among the works of the fourth-century historian Xenophon). The piece contains a sustained polemic against the Athenian form of government and perhaps demonstrates some of the typical criticisms made of democracy in antiquity.

(1.1)   Now, in discussing the Athenian constitution, I cannot commend their present method of running the state, because in choosing it they preferred that the masses should do better than the respectable citizens; this, then, is my reason for not commending it. Since, however, they have made this choice, I will demonstrate how well they preserve their constitution and handle the other affairs for which the rest of the Greeks criticise them.

(2)   My first point is that it is right that the poor and the ordinary people there should have more power than the noble and the rich, because it is the ordinary people who man the fleet and bring the city her power; they provide the helmsmen, the boatswains, the junior officers, the look-outs and the shipwrights; it is these people who make the city powerful much more than the hoplites and the noble and respectable citizens. This being so, it seems just that all should share in public office by lot and by election, and that any citizen who wishes should be

From J. M. Moore (trans.), *Aristotle and Xenophon on Democracy and Oligarchy*. Copyright © 1975 J. M. Moore. Reprinted by permission of the Regents of the University of California and the University of California Press.

able to speak in the Assembly. (3)   On the other hand, there are offices which bring safety to the whole people if they are in the hands of the right people, and danger if they are not; the people demand no share in these — they do not suppose that they ought to be able to cast lots for the post of *strategos* or commander of the cavalry, for they realise that they gain greater advantage from not holding these offices themselves but allowing the most capable to hold them. However, they are eager to hold any public office which brings pay or private profit.

(4)   Again, some people are surprised at the fact that in all fields they give more power to the masses, the poor and the common people than they do to the respectable elements of society, but it will become clear that they preserve the democracy by doing precisely this. When the poor, the ordinary people and the lower classes flourish and increase in numbers, then the power of the democracy will be increased; if, however, the rich and the respectable flourish, the democrats increase the strength of their opponents. (5)   Throughout the world the aristocracy are opposed to democracy, for they are naturally least liable to loss of self control and injustice and most meticulous in their regard for what is respectable, whereas the masses display extreme ignorance, indiscipline and wickedness, for poverty gives them a tendency towards the ignoble, and in some cases lack of money leads to their being uneducated and ignorant.

(6)   It may be objected that they ought not to grant each and every man the right of speaking in the *Ekklesia* and serving on the *Boule*, but only the ablest and best of them; however, in this also they are acting in their own best interests by allowing the mob also a voice. If none but the respectable spoke in the *Ekklesia* and the *Boule*, the result would benefit that class and harm the masses; as it is, anyone who wishes rises and speaks, and as a member of the mob he discovers what is to his own advantage and that of those like him.

(7)   But someone may say: "How could such a man find out what was advantageous to himself and the common people?" The Athenians realise that this man, despite his ignorance and badness, brings them more advantage because he is well disposed to them than the ill-disposed respectable man would, despite his virtue and wisdom.

(8)   Such practices do not produce the best city, but they are the best way of preserving democracy. For the common people do not

wish to be deprived of their rights in an admirably governed city, but to be free and to rule the city; they are not disturbed by inferior laws, for the common people get their strength and freedom from what you define as inferior laws. (9)   If you are looking for an admirable code of laws, first you will find that the ablest draw them up in their own interest; secondly, the respectable will punish the masses, and will plan the city's affairs and will not allow men who are mad to take part in planning or discussion or even sit in the *Ekklesia*. As a result of this excellent system the common people would very soon lose all their political rights.

(10)   Slaves and metics at Athens lead a singularly undisciplined life; one may not strike them there, nor will a slave step aside for you. Let me explain the reason for this situation: if it were legal for a free man to strike a slave, a metic or a freedman, an Athenian would often have been struck under the mistaken impression that he was a slave, for the clothing of the common people there is in no way superior to that of the slaves and metics, nor is their appearance. (11)   There is also good sense behind the apparently surprising fact that they allow slaves there to live in luxury, and some of them in considerable magnificence. In a state relying on naval power it is inevitable that slaves must work for hire so that we may take profits from what they earn, and they must be allowed to go free. Where there are rich slaves it is no longer profitable for my slave to be afraid of you; in Sparta my slave would be afraid of you, but there, if your slave is afraid of me, he will probably spend some of his own money to free himself from the danger. (12)   This, then, is why in the matter of free speech we have put slaves and free men on equal terms; we have also done the same for metics and citizens because the city needs metics because of the multiplicity of her industries and for her fleet; that is why we were right to establish freedom of speech for metics as well.

(13)   The practice of physical exercises and the pursuit of culture has been brought into disrepute by the common people as being undesirable because they realise that these accomplishments are beyond them. However, for the staging of dramatic and choral festivals, the superintending of the gymnasia and the games and the provision of triremes, they realise that it is the rich who pay, and the common people for whom such things are arranged and who serve in the triremes. At all events, they think it right to receive pay for

singing, running and dancing, and for sailing in the fleet so that they may have money and the rich may become poorer. In the courts too, they are as much interested in their own advantage as they are in justice. . . .

[(2.18) The Athenian people] do not allow comedians to attack the people so that they may not be abused themselves; they encourage personal attacks if anyone wishes, knowing that the butts of comedy are not for the most part of the common people nor from the masses, but rich or noble or powerful; only a few of the poor, ordinary citizens are attacked in comedy, and they only because they meddle in everything or try to become too influential; therefore the people do not object even to the ridiculing of such men.

(19)   Therefore it is my view that the common people at Athens know which citizens are respectable and which are wicked; realising that the latter are useful to them and help them, they like them despite their wickedness, but they tend to hate the respectable citizens. They do not think that their virtue exists for the common people's advantage but the opposite. On the other hand, there are some who are truly of the common people, but are not by nature on the side of the common people. (20)   I do not blame the common people for their democracy, for anyone is to be pardoned for looking after his own interests; but a man who is not of the common people and chooses to live in a city that is ruled by a democracy rather than one with an oligarchy is preparing to do wrong, and realises that it is easier to get away with being wicked under a democracy than under an oligarchy. (3.1)   As far as the Athenian constitution is concerned, I do not commend its type; since they chose a democratic form of government, it seems to me that they preserve their democracy well in the manner which I have described.

I notice that people also find fault with the Athenians because there are occasions when it is impossible to get a matter dealt with by the *Boule* or the *Ekklesia* although one waits for a year. This happens at Athens solely because there is such pressure of business that it is not possible to deal with everyone who raises a point. (2)   How could they do so when they have so many obligations? They celebrate more festivals than any other Greek city, during which there is even less possibility of transacting public business; they handle more public and private lawsuits and judicial investigations than the whole of the rest of mankind; the *Boule* has multifarious business to deal with concerning war, revenue, legislation, the day-to-day affairs of the city and matters affecting their allies, and has to receive the tribute and look after the dockyards and shrines. Is it remotely surprising if, with so many matters to deal with, they cannot settle everyone's business? (3)   Some say that if you approach the *Boule* or the people with money, then things get considered. Now I would agree that money plays a considerable part in getting things done in Athens, and it would be even more influential if more people employed it; however, I am absolutely sure that the city could not deal with all the requests that come before it, however much gold and silver were offered. (4)   The courts are also involved if someone does not refit a ship or builds on public land; in addition, every year they have to settle disputes about the provision of choruses at the Dionysia, the Thargelia, the Panathenaia, the Promethia and the Hephaestia. Four hundred trierarchs are appointed every year, and they must judge any appeals which arise. Further, they must examine magistrates and decide on their conduct, examine orphans, and appoint guards for prisoners. (5)   This, then, happens every year. They also have to decide cases of avoidance of military service when they arise, and any other crime which suddenly occurs, such as unusual violence or impiety. I am omitting a great deal of public business, but I have listed the most important items apart from the assessments of the tribute, which generally occur every four years. (6)   Well then, ought one to suppose that all these cases ought not to be dealt with? If so, let someone suggest what ought to be omitted. If then, one must agree that all these matters have to be decided, the courts must sit throughout the year, since even now when they do sit throughout the year they cannot prevent crime because of the numbers involved. . . . (8)   In addition to this, one must consider the fact that the Athenians have to hold festivals, during which no trials can take place, and they have twice as many as other states. However, even if one were to assume for the sake of argument that they only held as many as the state which holds fewest, even then it would be impossible in my view for affairs at Athens to be arranged other than they are now, except for minor changes here and there; significant alterations cannot be made without taking away something from the democracy. (9)   Many suggestions can be made for improving the constitution, but it is not easy to find satisfactory ways of improving it while preserving the democracy intact, except, as I have just said, for minor changes.

Demagogues and Dicasts

Aristophanes (ca. 450–385 B.C.), the comic playwright, wrote some of the most stinging indictments ever penned about the politician Cleon (whom he treated as an ill-bred demagogue), the philosopher Socrates (whom he lumped in with the Sophists), and the tragedian Euripides (who he thought was debasing the art form). His jokes about the Athenian *demos* are equally pointed; yet despite Aristophanes' own insistence that playwrights have something serious to say and should improve the citizens (see, for example, his *Frogs* and the selection from Henderson in Part IV), many scholars still doubt the existence of an identifiable political message in his works.

Aristophanes' play *Knights* was performed at the Lenaea festival around February of 424 and won the first prize. In this parody of the way demagogues trick the Athenian assembly by promising them "goodies," the slaves of a man called Demos (Mr. Peepul) compete for his attentions. A new slave Paphlagon (representing Cleon) has become his master's favorite, but is ultimately bested by the Sausage Seller (in league with the young nobles, the Knights), who uses the demagogue's own methods against him. In *Wasps* (Lenaea, 422, first or second prize), Aristophanes satirizes the Athenian jury system.

Knights

FIRST SLAVE: We two have a master with a farmer's temperament, a bean chewer, prickly in the extreme, known as The Peepul of Pnyx Hill, a cranky, half-deaf little codger. Last market day he bought a slave, Paphlagon, a dresser of hides, an arch-criminal and slanderer. He sized up the old man's character, this rawhide Paphlagon did, so he crouched before the master and started flattering and fawning and brown-nosing and suckering him with odd tidbits of waste leather, saying things like, "Mr. Peepul, do have

From Aristophanes, *Knights*, translated by Jeffrey Henderson. (Cambridge: Harvard University Press).

your bath as soon as you've tried only one case." — "Here's something to nibble, wolf down, savor: a 3-obol piece." — "Shall I serve you a snack?" And then Paphlagon swipes whatever any of the rest of us has prepared and presents it to the master. Why, just the other day I whipped up a Spartan cake at Pylos,[1] and by some very dirty trick he outmanoeuvred me, snatched the cake and served it up himself — the one I'd whipped up! He shuts us out and won't allow anyone else to court the master; no, when master's having supper he stands by with a leather swatter and bats away the politicians. And he chants oracles; the old man's crazy about sibyls. And since he sees that the master's a mooncalf, he's devised an artful technique: he tells outright lies about the household staff; then *we* get whippings, and Paphlagon chases after the servants, shaking us down, shaking us up, demanding bribes, making threats like, "See how I got Hylas that whipping? You'd better be reasonable or you've lived your last day!" And we pay the price, because if we don't, the master will pound on us till we shit out eight times as much. (*to Second Slave*) So now, my friend, let's figure out quickly what path to take and to whom. . . .

[The slaves of Mr. Peepul read an oracle proclaiming that a sausage seller is destined to replace Paphlagon. After finding one, they inform him that he is to become an important person.]

SAUSAGE SELLER: Tell me, just how does a sausage seller like me become a big shot?
FIRST SLAVE: That's precisely why you *are* going to be great, because you're loudmouthed, low down and from down town.
SAUSAGE SELLER: *I* don't even think I deserve great power.
FIRST SLAVE: Uh oh, what makes you say you don't deserve it? You sound as though you've got something good on your conscience. Don't tell me you come from a distinguished family!
SAUSAGE SELLER: Heavens no, they're nothing if not low down.

---

[1]At Pylos in 425 Athenian forces under Cleon and Demosthenes captured over 100 Spartans alive. Cleon claimed credit for the victory, although Demosthenes probably engineered the successful assault.

FIRST SLAVE: Congratulations, what blessed luck! Right there you've got a fine start in politics!

SAUSAGE SELLER: Look, mister, I'm uneducated except for reading and writing, and I'm damn poor even at those.

FIRST SLAVE: The only thing that hurts you there is that you're only damn poor. No, political leadership's no longer a job for a man of education and good character, but for the ignorant and disgusting. Please don't throw away what the gods are offering you in their prophecies! . . .

SAUSAGE SELLER: The prophecies are flattering, but it's an amazing idea, me being fit to supervise the people.

FIRST SLAVE: Nothing could be easier. Just keep doing what you're doing: make a hash of all their affairs and turn it into baloney, and always keep the people on your side by sweetening them with gourmet bons mots. You've got everything else a demagogue needs: a repulsive voice, low birth, marketplace morals—you've got all the ingredients for a political career. Plus, the oracles and Delphic Apollo agree. (*extending the cup and garland*) So put on this garland and pour a libation to the god Dimwit, and see that you settle our enemy's hash. . . .

[Paphlagon and Sausage Seller compete for Mr. Peepul's affections.]

PAPHLAGON: Just how could there be a citizen who cherishes you more than I do, Mr. Peepul? First of all, when I was a Councillor, I showed record profits in the public accounts by putting men on the rack, or throttling them or demanding a cut, without regard for anyone's personal situation, so long as I could gratify you.

SAUSAGE SELLER: Mr. Peepul, that's nothing to brag about: I'll do the same thing for you. I'll snatch other people's loaves and serve them to you. The first thing I'll prove to you is that he isn't your friend or your partisan, save only that he enjoys sitting by your fire. At Marathon you outduelled the Medes in defense of our country, and your victory bequeathed to our tongues matter for minting great phrases. But he doesn't care if you have to sit like that on the hard rocks, unlike me, who bring this cushion I've had made for you. Here, lift up a moment: now sit back down comfortably, so you don't chafe what sat to the oar at Salamis.

THE PEEPUL: Who are you, my man? You're not a descendant of Harmodius' famous family, are you?[2] All I can say is, this act of yours is truly outstanding and Peepul-spirited!

PAPHLAGON: With that paltry bit of brown-nosing you're suddenly his partisan!

SAUSAGE SELLER: Well, you hooked him with much paltrier baits than that.

PAPHLAGON: I say the man has never appeared who stuck up for the Peepul better than me, or cherished you more, and I don't mind staking my head on it!

SAUSAGE SELLER: Just how can you claim to cherish him, when you've seen him living in barrels and shanties and garrets for eight years now and feel no pity, indeed shut him in and rifle his hut? And when Archeptolemus brought a peace-proposal you tore it in pieces, and the embassies that offered a treaty, you kicked their butts and drove them from the city.

PAPHLAGON: Yes, so he could rule over all Greeks! It's right in the oracles: one day this Peepul shall draw five obols to hear cases in Arcadia, if he stays the course; in any event, I'll nourish and cater to him, finding him his three obols by any means, fair and foul.

SAUSAGE SELLER: Yes, though you weren't planning how he can rule Arcadia, by Zeus, but how you can steal and take bribes from the allied cities, and how the Peepul can be made blind to your crimes amid the fog of war, while mooning at you from necessity, deprivation and jury-pay. But if the Peepul ever returns to his peaceful life on the farm, and regains his spirit by eating porridge and chewing the fat with some pressed olives, he'll realize the many benefits you beat him out of with your state pay; then he'll come after you with a farmer's vengeful temper, tracking down a ballot to use against you. You're aware of this, so you keep fooling him and rigging up dreams about yourself. . . .

[The chorus of knights upbraids Mr. Peepul for his gullibility.]

CHORUS: Mr. Peepul, you've a fine sway, since all mankind fears you like a man with tyrannical power. But you're easily led

---

[2]Harmodius was one of the two Athenians credited with slaying Hipparchus, brother of the tyrant Hippias, in 514.

astray: you enjoy being flattered and lied to, and gape after every speechmaker. You've a mind, but it's out to lunch.

THE PEEPUL: There's no mind under your long hair, since you consider me stupid: there's purpose in this foolishness of mine. I relish my daily pap, and I pick one thieving political leader to fatten; I raise him up, and when he's full, I swat him down.

CHORUS: In that case you'll do well; and your character really does contain, as you claim, very deep cunning, if you deliberately fatten these men, like public victims, on the Pnyx, and then when you chance to lack dinner, you sacrifice one who's bloated and have yourself a meal.

THE PEEPUL: Just see if I don't trick them ingeniously, those who think they're smart and I'm a sucker. I watch them at all times, pretending not even to see them, as they steal; and then I make them cough up whatever they've stolen from me, using a verdict-tube as a probe. . . .

[The Sausage Seller has "boiled down" Mr. Peepul, transforming him into the Athens of old.]

THE PEEPUL: Tell me, how did I used to act, and what was I like?

SAUSAGE SELLER: First of all, whenever somebody said in the Assembly, "Peepul, I'm your lover and I cherish you, and I alone care for you and think for you," whenever anybody started a speech with that stuff, you'd flap your wings and toss your horns.

THE PEEPUL: I did?

SAUSAGE SELLER: And then in return he got away with cheating you.

THE PEEPUL: You don't say! They did that to me, and I didn't catch on?

SAUSAGE SELLER: God yes, because your ears would open up like a parasol and flap shut again.

THE PEEPUL: Was I that mindless and senile?

SAUSAGE SELLER: And by god, if two politicians were making proposals, one to build long ships and the other to spend the same sum on state pay, the pay-man would walk all over the trireme-man. Here, why are you hanging your head? Won't you stand your ground?

THE PEEPUL: It's that I'm ashamed of my former mistakes.

SAUSAGE SELLER: But you aren't to blame for them, never think it! The blame's with those who deceived you this way. . . . [After the Peepul describes how his behavior will improve in the future, Sausage Seller presents him with peace treaties (ending the war with Sparta).]

Wasps

[A young nobleman (Bdelycleon or "Cleon-hater") counters his jury-pay loving father's (Philocleon) praise for the Athenian court system (*dicasteria*), which provided payment of three obols per day for himself and the other aged dicasts (the "Wasps").]

PHILOCLEON: Yes, right from the start I'm going to prove as far as our [i.e., the jurors'] power is concerned that it's equal to that of any king. What creature is there today more happy and enviable, or more pampered, or more to be feared, than a juror, and that though he's an old man? First of all, when I come from my bed, there are big men, six-footers, watching out for me at the court railings. Then as soon as I approach, he puts his soft hand in mine, the hand that's been stealing some public money; and they bow down and supplicate me, pouring forth their plea in a piteous tone: "Have mercy on me, father, I beg you, if ever you yourself have nicked anything when you were holding some office or buying food for your mess on campaign." And this a man who wouldn't even have known of my existence if it hadn't been for his acquittal that previous time!

BDELYCLEON: Let me have a note of this, about the suppliants. [*Writes.*]

PHILOCLEON: Then when I've been supplicated and had my anger wiped away, and gone into court, once I'm inside I take no account of all the promises I've made; I just listen to them leaving nothing unsaid to get themselves off. Tell me, what kind of wheedling can't a juror hear there? Some of them bewail their poverty, and exaggerate the misery they are in, until as he goes on he makes it out to be as great as mine. Others tell us stories, others something funny of Aesop's; others again make jokes in the hope that I'll laugh and lay aside my wrath. And if we're not persuaded by these means, straight away

From A. H. Sommerstein (trans.), *Aristophanes' Wasps.* Copyright 1983. Reprinted by permission of Aris & Phillips Ltd.

he drags his little children, the girls and the boys, by the hand up to the platform, and I listen while they all hang their heads and bleat in unison, and then their father beseeches me on their behalf, trembling as if I were a god, to acquit him on his audit: "If thou delightest in the voice of the lamb, I pray thee take pity on my son's cry"—and on the other hand if I enjoy *pork* he asks me to heed the voice of his daughter. And then we lower the pitch of our anger a bit for him. Isn't this a mighty power that allows us to mock at wealth?

BDELYCLEON: That's now the second point of yours I'm writing down. [*Writing*] "Allows us to mock at wealth." And now please mention the benefits you get from your so-called dominion over Greece.

PHILOCLEON: Well then, we get the chance to look at boys' private parts when they're being examined for registration. And if Oeagrus [an actor] comes into court as a defendant, he doesn't get off until he's picked out the finest speech in *Niobe* [a lost play] and recited it to us. And if a flautist wins his case, he rewards us for it by putting on his muzzle and playing a voluntary for us as we leave. And if a father leaves a daughter as heiress and gives her to someone on his deathbed, then we tell the will it can go and boil its head, and the same to the shell that's lying very grandly over the seals, and we give the girl to anyone whose entreaties persuade us. And for doing all this we cannot be called to account—which is true of no other public authority.

BDELYCLEON [*making another note*]: Yes, you know, that *is* grand; on that, what you've mentioned, I congratulate you. But it's wrong of you to unshell the heiress against her will.

PHILOCLEON: Then again, the Council and People, when it's at a loss to decide an important case, votes to hand the criminals over to the jurors. Then Euathlus and that big fellow Flatteronymus, the one who threw away his shield, keep saying they'll never betray us and they'll fight for the masses. And no one ever carries a motion in the Assembly unless he first proposes to discharge the courts after they've tried one case. And Cleon himself, the mighty screamer, we're the only people he doesn't take bites out of; he watches over us, holds us in his arms and keeps off the flies. You've never done anything at all like that for your own father! But Theorus—and he's a man no less important than . . . Euphemius[3]—uses his sponge to black our shoes with pitch from his basin. Look at the sort of blessings you're shutting

[3]An unknown figure, but undoubtedly a comparison meant to insult Theorus.

me off and holding me back from. And you said you were going to prove that it was slavery and subjection! . . .

BDELYCLEON: It is a hard task, calling for formidable intelligence above the level found among comedians, to cure a long-standing malady that is innate in this city. But, O our Father, son of Cronus—

PHILOCLEON [*thinking himself addressed*]: Stop, none of this "father" stuff. If you don't explain it to me quickly in what way I'm a slave, then [*waving his sword*] you will most certainly perish, even if it means I have to keep away from the sacrificial feasts.

BDELYCLEON: Then unknit your brow a little, Daddy, and listen. First of all reckon up roughly, not with counters but just on your hands, the amount of tribute that comes in to us altogether from the allied states, and apart from that the taxes, one by one, and the many one-per-cents, court fees, mines, markets, harbours, rentals, confiscations. We get a total for all these of nearly two thousand talents. Out of this now put down pay for the jurors for a year, six thousand of them (ne'er yet have more this land inhabited): we get, I think, a hundred and fifty talents.

PHILOCLEON: You mean our pay doesn't even come to one-tenth of the revenue!

BDELYCLEON: No, indeed it doesn't.

PHILOCLEON: In that case where does the rest of the money go?

BDELYCLEON: It goes to those "I-will-never-betray-the-Athenian-rabble-and-I'll-always-fight-for-the-masses" people. You're bamboozled, father, by these deft phrases, and you choose them to rule over you. And then they get bribed by the allied states to the tune of fifty talents, by making terrifying threats like this: "You will give me your tribute, or I will overthrow your city with my thunder." While *you* are quite content to nibble at the trotters of your own empire. And since the allies have realized that the common riffraff are being fed a starvation diet from a voting-urn funnel and regaling themselves on zero, they regard you as mere ballot-fodder, while these men they ply with gifts—jars of salt-fish, wine, rugs, cheese, honey, sesame, pillows, libation-bowls, dress clothes, crowns, necklaces, drinking-cups, health-and-wealth. But to *you*, none of the people whom you got to rule by dint of much toil on land and much oar-work on the waters gives so much as a head of garlic for your boiled fish.

PHILOCLEON: No, indeed; only yesterday I had to send out for three cloves from Eucharides. But you're getting on my nerves with not explaining to me what my actual slavery is.

BDELYCLEON: Well, isn't it absolute slavery for all these men, themselves and their bootlickers, to be holding office and drawing salaries, while *you're* quite content if someone gives you those three obols, money that you yourself originally acquired by hard toil, rowing and fighting and besieging? And on top of that, you go to and fro under orders. That's what makes me choke most of all, when in comes a pansy young man, the son of Chaereas, spreads his legs like this, waggles his body voluptuously, and tells you to arrive early and in good time to judge, "because any of you who arrives after the sign goes up won't get his three obols." *He* gets his prosecutor's fee, a drachma, even if he does come late. Then he goes shares with someone else among his colleagues in office, if one of the defendants has offered any bribe, and the two of them organize the business and both speak very earnestly, but then they're like a pair of sawyers, one pulling and the other yielding in turn. You're just agape for the paymaster, and you don't notice what's being done.

PHILOCLEON: Do they do that to me? Heaven help me, what are you saying? How you churn up my deepest sediments, and win over my mind more, and do I don't know what to me!

BDELYCLEON: Consider then how, when it would be possible for you and the whole people to be rich, you've been penned up somehow or other by these men who always say they're for the people. You rule over a vast number of cities, from the Black Sea to Sardinia, but you don't get the least bit of benefit, except that pay you draw, and they drip that into you with a piece of wool, like oil, always a little at a time, just to keep you alive. The reason is that they *want* you to be poor, and I'll tell you why that's so. It's so that you should know your trainer, and then, when *he* hisses to you to set you on one of his ene- mies, you'll leap savagely upon them. If they wanted to provide a living for the people, it would be easy. There *are* a thousand states which now pay us tribute. If one had ordered each of these to main- tain twenty men, then twenty thousand of the common folk would be living in abundance of hare's meat, of crowns of all kinds, of beestings fresh and boiled, enjoying a life worthy of this land and of the trophy at Marathon. As it is you're like olive-pickers, going at the beck and call of the man who has your wages.

PHILOCLEON: Good lord, what's happened to me? A numbness is creeping over my hand, and I can't hold my sword, I've gone all weak.

BDELYCLEON: But when they're frightened themselves, they offer you all Euboea, and promise to supply corn in lots of fifty bushels. But they never gave it to you; except the other day you got five bushels, and that with difficulty, after being charged with not being a citizen; it came in one-quart instalments, and it was barley. That's why I locked you up all that time; *I* wanted to feed you, and I didn't want these men to make a fool of you with their bombastic ranting. And now I'm willing to provide you with absolutely anything you want, except paymaster's milk to drink.

CHORUS LEADER: Truly it seems he was a wise man who said, "Until you have heard the tale of both parties, you should not judge." For now I have made up my mind [*to Bdelycleon*] that you are the clear winner; so that now we slacken off our anger and drop our staffs. . . .

Thucydides

Pericles' Funeral Oration

Thucydides, an Athenian nobleman and general, was born sometime before 455 B.C. and lived to see the end of the Peloponnesian War (404 B.C.). His unfinished history of this war, which breaks off in mid-thought during his account of 411/10, constitutes our best source for Athenian history (and much else) during this period. In the passage below, Thucydides records the Funeral Oration delivered by Pericles after the first year of the war. Great disagreement exists among scholars as to how much of this speech should be attributed to Thucydides and how much to Pericles.

From R. Crawley, *Thucydides*.

There is no doubt, however, that this speech constitutes the only full-fledged defense of Athenian democracy to survive antiquity.

[2.35]   Most of my predecessors in this place have commended him who made this speech part of the law, from the feeling that it is well that it should be delivered at the burial of those who fall in battle. For myself, I should have thought that the worth which had displayed itself in deeds, would be sufficiently rewarded by honours also shown by deeds; such as you now see in this funeral prepared at the people's cost. And I could have wished that the reputation of many brave men were not to be imperilled in the mouth of a single individual, to stand or fall according as he spoke ill or well. For it is hard to speak properly upon a subject where it is even difficult to convince your hearers that you are speaking the truth. On the one hand, the friend who is familiar with every fact of the story, may think that some point has not been set forth with that fulness which he wishes and knows it to deserve; on the other, he who is a stranger to the matter may be led by envy to suspect exaggeration if he hears anything above his own nature. For men can endure to hear others praised only so long as they can severally persuade themselves of their own ability to equal the actions recounted: when this point is passed, envy comes in and with it incredulity. However, since our ancestors have stamped this custom with their approval, it becomes my duty to obey the law and to try to satisfy your several wishes and opinions as best I may.

[36]   I shall begin with our ancestors: it is both just and proper that they should have the honour of the first mention on an occasion like the present. They dwelt in the country without break in the succession from generation to generation, and handed it down free to the present time by their valour. And if they deserve praise, much more do our immediate fathers, who added to their inheritance the empire which we now possess, and spared no pains to be able to leave their acquisitions to us of the present generation. Lastly, there are few parts of our dominions that have not been augmented by those of us here, who are still for the most part in the vigour of life; while the mother country has been furnished by us with everything that can enable her to depend on her own resources whether for war or for peace. That part of our history which tells of the military achievements which gave us our

several possessions, or of the ready valour with which either we or our fathers stemmed the tide of Hellenic or foreign aggression, is a theme too familiar to my hearers for me to dilate on, and I shall therefore pass it by. But what was the road by which we reached our position, what the form of government under which our greatness grew, what the national habits out of which it sprang; these are questions which I may try to solve before I proceed to my panegyric upon these men; since I think this to be a subject upon which on the present occasion a speaker may properly dwell, and to which the whole assemblage, whether citizens or foreigners, may listen with advantage.

[37]   Our constitution does not copy the laws of neighbouring states; but we are rather a pattern to others than imitators ourselves. Its administration favours the many instead of the few; this is why it is called a democracy. If we look to the laws, they afford equal justice to all in their private differences; if to social standing, advancement in public life falls to reputation for capacity, class considerations not being allowed to interfere with merit; while as to poverty, if a man is able to serve the state, he is not hindered by the obscurity of his condition. The freedom which we enjoy in our government extends also to our ordinary life. There, far from exercising a jealous surveillance over each other, we do not feel called upon to be angry with our neighbour for doing what he likes, or even to indulge in those injurious looks which cannot fail to be offensive, although they inflict no positive penalty. But all this ease in our private relations does not make us lawless as citizens. Against this fear is our chief safeguard, teaching us to obey the magistrates and the laws, particularly such as regard the protection of the injured, whether they are actually on the statute book, or belong to that code which, although unwritten, yet cannot be broken without acknowledged disgrace.

[38]   Further, we provide plenty of means for the mind to refresh itself from business. At stated periods of the year we celebrate games and sacrifices; besides which the elegance of our private establishments forms a daily source of pleasure and helps to banish the spleen. While the magnitude of our city draws the produce of the world into our harbour, so that to the Athenian the fruits of other countries are as familiar a luxury as those of his own.

[39]   If we turn to our military policy, there also we differ from our antagonists. We throw open our city to the world, and never by alien acts exclude foreigners from any opportunity of learning or ob-

serving, although the eyes of an enemy may occasionally profit by our liberality; trusting less in system and policy than to the native spirit of our citizens; while in education, where our rivals from their very cradles by a painful discipline seek after manliness, at Athens we live exactly as we please, and yet are just as ready to encounter every legitimate danger. In proof of this it may be noticed that the Lacedæmonians never invade our country with a contingent, but with the whole of their confederates; while we Athenians advance unsupported into the territory of a neighbour, and fighting upon a foreign soil usually vanquish with ease men who are defending their homes. While our united force was never yet encountered by any enemy, through our being at once occupied with our marine and being by land continually despatched upon a hundred different services; so that, wherever they engage with some such fraction of our strength, a success against a detachment is magnified into a victory over the nation, and a defeat into a reverse suffered at the hands of our entire people. And yet if with habits not of labour but of ease, and courage not of art but of nature, we are still willing to encounter danger, we have the double advantage of escaping the experience of hardships in anticipation and of facing them in the hour of need as fearlessly as those who are never free from them.

Nor are these the only points in which our city is worthy of admiration. [40]   Cultivating refinement without extravagance and knowledge without effeminacy, we employ our wealth more for use than for show, and place the real disgrace of poverty not in owning to the fact but in declining the struggle against it. Our public men have, besides politics, their private affairs to attend to, and our ordinary citizens, though occupied with the pursuits of industry, are still fair judges of public matters; for, unlike any other nation, regarding him who takes no part in these duties not as unambitious but as useless, we Athenians are able to judge at all events if we cannot originate, and instead of looking on discussion as a stumbling block in the way of action, we think it an indispensable preliminary to any wise action at all. Again, in our enterprises we present the singular spectacle of daring and deliberation, each carried to its highest point, and both united in the same persons; although usually decision is the fruit of ignorance, hesitation of reflexion. But the palm of courage will surely be adjudged most justly to those, who best know the difference between hardship and pleasure and yet are never tempted to shrink from danger. In generosity we are equally singular, acquiring our friends by conferring not by receiving favours. Yet, of course, the doer of the favour is the firmer friend of the two, in order by continued kindness to keep the recipient in his debt; while the debtor feels less keenly from the very consciousness that the return he makes will be a payment, not a free gift. And it is only the Athenians who, fearless of consequences, confer their benefits not from calculations of expediency, but in the confidence of liberality.

[41]   In short, I say that as a city we are the school of Hellas; while I doubt if the world can produce a man, who where he has only himself to depend upon, is equal to so many emergencies, and graced by so happy a versatility as the Athenian. And that this is no mere boast thrown out for the occasion, but plain matter of fact, the power of the state acquired by these habits proves. For Athens alone of her contemporaries is found when tested to be greater than her reputation, and alone gives occasion neither to her assailants to blush at the antagonist by whom they have been worsted, nor to her subjects to question her title by merit to rule. Rather, the admiration of the present and succeeding ages will be ours, because we have shown our power not by mere representations, but by mighty proofs, and because far from needing a Homer for our panegyrist, or other of his craft whose verses might charm for the moment only for the impression which they gave to melt at the touch of fact, we forced every sea and land to be the highway of our daring, and everywhere, whether for evil or for good, left imperishable monuments behind us. Such is the Athens for which these men, in the assertion of their determination not to part with her, nobly fought and died; and well may everyone of their survivors be ready to suffer in her cause.

[42]   Indeed if I have dwelt at some length upon the character of our country, it has been to show that our stake in the struggle is not the same as theirs who have no such blessings to lose, and also that the panegyric of the men over whom I am now speaking might be by definite proofs established. That panegyric is now in a great measure complete; for the Athens that I have celebrated is only what the heroism of these and their like have made her, men whose fame, unlike that of most Hellenes, will be found to be only commensurate with their deserts. And if a test of worth be wanted, it is to be found in their closing scene, and this not only in the cases in which it set the final seal upon their merit, but also in those in which it gave the first intimation

of their having any. For there is justice in the claim that stedfastness in his country's battles should be as a cloak to cover a man's other imperfections; since the good action has blotted out the bad, and his merit as a citizen more than outweighed his demerits as an individual. But none of these allowed either wealth with its prospect of future enjoyment to unnerve his spirit, or poverty with its hope of a day of freedom and riches to tempt him to shrink from danger. No, holding that vengeance upon their enemies was more to be desired than any personal blessings, and reckoning this to be the most glorious of hazards, they joyfully determined to accept the risk, and making sure of their vengeance to leave their wishes to take care of themselves, and committing to hope the uncertainty of success, to trust to action in the business before them. Thus choosing to die resisting, rather than to live submitting, they fled only from dishonour, but met danger face to face, and after one brief moment, while at the summit of their fortune, were taken away, not from their fear, but from their glory.

[43] So died these men as became Athenians. You, their survivors, must determine to have as unfaltering a resolution in the field, though you may pray that it may have a happier issue. And not contented with a mere hearsay notion of the advantages which are involved in the defence of your country, though these would furnish a valuable text to a speaker even before an audience so alive to them as the present, you must yourselves realise the power of Athens, and feed your eyes upon her from day to day, till love of her fills your hearts; and then when all her greatness shall break upon you, you must reflect that it was by courage, sense of duty, and a keen feeling of honour in action that men were enabled to acquire it, and that no personal failure in an enterprise could make them consent to deprive their country of their valour, but they laid it at her feet as the most glorious contribution that they could offer. For this offering of their lives made in common by them all they each of them individually received that renown which never grows old, and for a sepulchre, not so much that in which their bones have been deposited, but that noblest of shrines wherein their glory is laid up to be eternally remembered upon every occasion on which deed or story shall call for its commemoration. For heroes have the whole earth for their tomb; and in lands far from their own, where the column with its epitaph declares it, there is enshrined in every breast a record unwritten with no tablet to preserve it, except that of the heart. These take as your model, and judging happiness to

be the fruit of freedom and freedom of valour, never decline the dangers of war. For it is not the miserable that would most justly be unsparing of their lives; these have nothing to hope for: it is rather they to whom continued life may bring reverses as yet unknown, and to whom a fall, if it came, would be most tremendous in its consequences. And surely, to a man of spirit, the degradation of his being a coward must be immeasurably more grievous than the unfelt death which strikes him in the midst of his strength and patriotism!

[44]   Comfort, therefore, not condolence, is what I have to offer to the parents of the dead who may be here. Numberless are the chances to which, as they know, the life of man is subject; but fortunate indeed are they who draw for their lot a death so glorious as that which has caused your mourning, and to whom life has been so exactly measured as to terminate in the happiness in which it has been passed. Still I know that this is a hard saying, especially when those are in question of whom you will constantly be reminded by seeing in the homes of others blessings of which once you also boasted: for grief is felt not so much for the loss of what we have never known, as for that to which we have been long accustomed. Yet you who are still of an age to beget children must bear up in the hope of having others in their stead; not only will they help you to forget those whom you have lost, but will be to the state at once a reinforcement and a security; for never can a fair or just policy be expected of the citizen who does not, like his fellows, bring to the decision the interests and apprehensions of a father. While those of you who have passed your prime must congratulate yourselves with the thought that the best part of your life was fortunate, and that the brief span that remains will be cheered by the fame of the departed. For honour alone never grows old; and honour it is, not gain, as some would have it, that rejoices the heart of age and helplessness.

[45]   Turning to the sons or brothers of the dead, I see an arduous struggle before you. When a man is gone, all are wont to praise him, and should your merit be ever so transcendent, you will still find it difficult not merely to overtake, but even to approach their renown. The living have envy to contend with, while those who are no longer in our path are honoured with a goodwill into which rivalry does not enter. On the other hand, if I must say anything on the subject of female excellence to those of you who will now be in widowhood, it will be all comprised in this brief exhortation. Great will be your glory in

not falling short of your natural character; and greatest will be hers who is least talked of among the men whether for good or for bad.

[46] My task is now finished. I have performed it to the best of my ability, and in word, at least, the requirements of the law are now satisfied. If deeds be in question, those who are here interred have received part of their honours already; for the rest, their children will be brought up at the public expense till manhood by their country, which thereby offers a most useful prize both to them and others, who may, like them, thus be left desolate; for where the greatest rewards for merit are given, there also will merit be most common among the citizens. And now that you have brought to a close your lamentations for your relatives, you may depart.

Plato

Protagoras and Socrates on Justice

Plato (ca. 429–347 B.C.) was born into an aristocratic Athenian family and spent his youth in Athens during the Peloponnesian War as a follower of Socrates. After his teacher's death, he established his own school of philosophy in Athens at the Academy and devoted the rest of his life to writing the philosophical dialogues that are our best source for both Plato's and (problematically) Socrates' thoughts. In this selection from the *Protagoras*, the famous sophist Protagoras, who claimed to teach young men success in life through rhetoric, argues that justice and conscience were given equally to all men, a fundamental principle of democratic theory. Following the passage excerpted below, Socrates goes on to demonstrate that pleasure and pain are simply other names for good and bad, and that the skill in determining the greater good (i.e., what is more pleasurable ultimately) is a kind of mathematical technique (356–57) which should be

From Plato, *Protagoras*, translated by C. C. W. Taylor. Copyright © 1976 Oxford University Press. Reprinted by permission of Oxford University Press.

able to be taught (361a–d). The coward, for example, simply lacks the knowledge of what he should truly fear, whereas a courageous man is wise about what is to be feared (360c–d).

[(319) Protagoras:]. . . 'What I teach is the proper management of one's own affairs, how best to run one's household, and the management of public affairs, how to make the most effective contribution to the affairs of the city both by word and action.'

'Have I understood you correctly, then?' I [Socrates] said. 'You seem to me to be talking about the art of running a city, and to be promising to make men into good citizens.'

'That, Socrates,' he said, 'is precisely what I undertake to do.'

'It's a splendid thing to have discovered,' I said, 'if you have in fact discovered how to do it (for I shall not say, particularly to you, anything other than what I really think). I didn't think that was something that could be taught, but since you say that you teach it I don't see how I can doubt you. Why I think that it can't be taught or handed on from one man to another, I ought to explain. I say, as do the rest of the Greeks, that the Athenians are wise. Well, I observe that when a decision has to be taken at the state assembly about some matter of building, they send for the builders to give their advice about the buildings, and when it concerns shipbuilding they send for the shipwrights, and similarly in every case where they are dealing with a subject which they think can be learned and taught. But if anyone else tries to give advice, whom they don't regard as an expert, no matter how handsome or wealthy or well-born he is, they still will have none of him, but jeer at him and create an uproar, until either the would-be speaker is shouted down and gives up of his own accord, or else the police drag him away or put him out on the order of the presidents. That's the way they act in what they regard as a technical matter. But when some matter of state policy comes up for consideration, anyone can get up and give his opinion, be he carpenter, smith or cobbler, merchant or shipowner, rich or poor, noble or low-born, and no one objects to them as they did to those I mentioned just now, that they are trying to give advice about something which they never learnt, nor ever had any instruction in. So it's clear that they don't regard that as something that can be taught. And not only is this so in public affairs, but in private life our wisest and best citizens are unable to hand on to others the excellence which they possess. For Pericles, the father of these young men, educated them very well in those subjects in which there were teachers, (320) but he neither instructs them himself nor has them instructed by anyone else in those matters in which he is himself wise; no, they wander about on their own like sacred cattle looking for pasture, hoping to pick up excellence by chance. Or take the case of Cleinias, the younger brother of Alcibiades here. Pericles, whom I mentioned just now, is his guardian, and no doubt for fear he should be corrupted by Alcibiades he took him away from him and sent him to be brought up in Ariphron's house; and before six months were up he gave him back to Alcibiades, not knowing what to do with him. And I could mention many others, good men themselves, who never made anyone better, either their own families, or anyone else. So when I consider these facts, Protagoras, I don't think that excellence can be taught. But then when I hear you say that you teach it, I am swayed once again and think that there must be something in what you say, as I regard you as someone of great experience and learning, who has made discoveries himself. So if you can show us more clearly that excellence can be taught, please don't grudge us your proof, but proceed.'

'Certainly I shall not grudge it you, Socrates,' he said. 'But would you rather that I showed you by telling a story (as an older man speaking to his juniors) or by going through a systematic exposition?'

Several of those who were sitting around asked him to proceed in whichever way he preferred. 'Well,' he said, 'I think that it will be more enjoyable to tell you a story.'. . .

[Protagoras relates how Prometheus stole technical skill and fire from the gods for man. He then continues. . . . (322)] 'Since man thus shared in a divine gift, first of all through his kinship with the gods he was the only creature to worship them, and he began to erect altars and images of the gods. Then he soon developed the use of articulate speech and of words, and discovered how to make houses and clothes and shoes and bedding and how to till the soil. Thus equipped, men lived at the beginning in scattered units, and there were no cities; so they began to be destroyed by the wild beasts, since they were altogether weaker. Their practical crafts were sufficient to provide food, but insufficient for fighting against the beasts—for they did not yet possess the art of running a city, of which the art of warfare is part—

and so they sought to come together and save themselves by founding cities. Now when they came together, they treated each other with injustice, not possessing the art of running a city, so they scattered and began to be destroyed once again. So Zeus, fearing that our race would be wholly wiped out, sent Hermes bringing conscience and justice to mankind, to be the principles of organization of cities and the bonds of friendship. Now Hermes asked Zeus about the manner in which he was to give conscience and justice to men: "Shall I distribute these in the same way as the practical crafts? These are distributed thus: one doctor is sufficient for many laymen, and so with the other experts. Shall I give justice and conscience to men in that way too, or distribute them to all?"

' "To all," said Zeus, "and let all share in them; for cities could not come into being, if only a few shared in them as in the other crafts. And lay down on my authority a law that he who cannot share in conscience and justice is to be killed as a plague on the city." So that, Socrates, is why when there is a question about how to do well in carpentry or any other expertise, everyone including the Athenians thinks it right that only a few should give advice, and won't put up with advice from anyone else, as you say—and quite right, too, in my view—but when it comes to consideration of how to do well in running the city, (323) which must proceed entirely through justice and soundness of mind, they are right to accept advice from anyone, since it is incumbent on everyone to share in that sort of excellence, or else there can be no city at all. That is the reason for it, Socrates.

'Just in case you still have any doubts that in fact everyone thinks that every man shares in justice and the rest of the excellence of a citizen, here's an extra bit of evidence. In the case of the other skills, as you say, if anyone says he's a good flute-player or good at anything else when he isn't, they either laugh at him or get angry at him, and his family come and treat him like a madman. But in the case of justice and the rest of the excellence of a citizen, even if they know someone to be unjust, if he himself admits it before everyone, they regard that sort of truthfulness as madness, though they called it sound sense before, and they say that everybody must say that he is just whether he is or not, and anyone who doesn't pretend to be just must be mad. For they think that everyone must possess it to some extent or other, or else not be among men at all.

'On the point, then, that they are right to accept advice from any-one about this sort of excellence in the belief that everyone shares in it, that is all I have to say. I shall next try to show that they think that it does not come by nature or by luck, but that it can be taught, and that everyone who has it has it from deliberate choice. In the case of unde-sirable characteristics which people think are due to nature or chance, nobody gets annoyed at people who have them or corrects or teaches or punishes them, to make them any different, but they pity them; for instance, is anyone silly enough to try treating the ugly or the small or the weak in any of those ways? No, that sort of thing, I think, they know comes about, good and ill alike, by nature and by chance. But when it comes to the good qualities that men acquire by deliberate choice, and by practice and teaching, if someone doesn't have them, but the opposite bad qualities, it's then that people get annoyed and punish and correct him. One such quality is injustice and impiety and in a word whatever is the opposite of the excellence of a citizen. (324) There everyone gets annoyed with anyone who does wrong, and cor-rects him, clearly because it's something which you acquire by delib-erate choice and learning. For if you care to consider, Socrates, the effect which punishment can possibly have on the wrongdoer, that will itself convince you that people think that excellence is something which can be handed on. For no one punishes a wrongdoer with no other thought in mind than that he did wrong, unless he is retaliating unthinkably like an animal. Someone who aims to punish in a rational way doesn't chastise on account of the past misdeed—for that would-n't undo what is already done—but for the sake of the future, so that neither the wrongdoer himself, nor anyone else who sees him pun-ished, will do wrong again. This intention shows his belief that excel-lence can be produced by education; at least his aim in punishing is to deter. Now this opinion is shared by everyone who administers chas-tisement either in a private or in a public capacity. And everyone chas-tises and punishes those whom they think guilty of wrongdoing, not least your fellow citizens, the Athenians; so according to this argument the Athenians are among those who think that excellence can be handed on and taught. It seems to me, Socrates, that I have now ade-quately shown that your fellow citizens are right to accept the advice of smiths and cobblers on political matters, and also that they regard excellence as something that can be taught and handed on.'

Aristotle

On Athenian Politics

In the *Politics*, Aristotle (384–322 B.C.), provided his answer to Plato's theories on government expounded in the *Republic* and the *Laws* along with his own theories about polis government and society. Somewhat more practical than his famous teacher, Aristotle praised a moderate regime he called simply a "polity" (*politeia*), which was essentially a limited democracy or moderate oligarchy (depending on one's point of view). Emphasizing the need for a large, property-owning middle group in society (see the selection from Hanson at the end of Part I), Aristotle also commented on certain failings of the more radical democracy practiced at Athens.

[1273b, 2.12.2]. . . Solon is held, by one school of thought, to have been a good lawgiver, who may be credited with a triple achievement. He swept away an oligarchy which was far too absolute; he emancipated the people from serfdom; and he instituted that 'ancestral democracy' under which the constitution was so admirably tempered—with the Council of the Areopagus standing for oligarchy, the method of electing the executive magistrates for aristocracy, and the system of popular law courts for democracy. (3)   In actual fact, (1274 a) however, it would appear that two of these elements—the council and the method of electing the executive magistrates—existed before his time and were simply continued by him. But he certainly introduced the principle of democracy by making membership of the law-courts open to every citizen; and that is the reason why he is blamed by some of his critics, who argue that he really destroyed the other elements by making these popular law-courts, with their members appointed by lot, supreme in every case.

(4)   Later, as these courts grew in strength, the successors of Solon, seeking to flatter the people in the way that men flatter a tyrant,

From Ernest Barker (editor and translator), *The Politics of Aristotle*. Copyright © 1962 Oxford University Press. Reprinted by permission of Oxford University Press.

transformed the constitution into its present form of extreme democracy. Ephialtes and Pericles curtailed the Council of the Areopagus; Pericles introduced the system of paying the members of the lawcourts; and thus each demagogue, in his turn, increased the power of the people until the constitution assumed its present form.

(5) This development, however, appears to be due to accident rather than to any deliberate design on the part of Solon. The people, who had been the cause of the acquisition of a maritime empire during the course of the Persian wars, acquired a conceit of themselves; and in spite of the opposition of the better citizens they found worthless demagogues to support their cause. Solon himself would seem to have given the people only the necessary minimum of power. He gave them simply the rights of electing the magistrates and calling them to account; and if the people do not enjoy these elementary rights, they must be a people of slaves, and thus enemies to the government.

(6) [Even in giving these rights, he instituted a check]: only the notable and the well-to-do were made eligible for any office; and the magistrates were exclusively drawn from the Pentecosiomedimni [the class with an income, from landed property, of 500 measures of produce], the Zeugitae [the class with an income of 200], and the Hippeis [the class with an income of 300]—while the lowest class, that of the Thetes [with an income of less than 200], was ineligible for any office. . . .

[The general citizenry must be given some share in the government . . . (1281b, 3.11.8)] and we thus find Solon, and some of the other legislators, giving the people the two general functions of electing the magistrates to office and of calling them to account at the end of their tenure of office, but *not* the right of holding office themselves in their individual capacity.

(9) [There is wisdom in such a policy.] When they all meet together, the people display a good enough gift of perception, and combined with the better class they are of service to the state (just as impure food, when it is mixed with pure, makes the whole concoction more nutritious than a small amount of the pure would be); but each of them is imperfect in the judgements he forms by himself.

(10) But this arrangement of the constitution [which gives the people deliberative and judicial functions] presents some difficulties. The first difficulty is that it may well be held that the function of judging when medical attendance has been properly given [a function

analogous to that of the people in judging the conduct of magistrates]
should belong to those whose profession it is to attend patients and
cure the complaints from which they suffer—in a word, to members
of the medical profession. The same may be held to be true of all other
professions and arts; (1282a) and just as doctors should have their conduct examined before a body of doctors, so, too, should those who follow other professions have theirs examined before a body of members
of their own profession. . . .

(12)   When we turn to consider the matter of election [as distinct from examination], the same principles would appear to apply.
To make a proper election, it may be argued, is equally the work of experts. It is the work of those who are versed in geometry to choose a
geometrician, or, again, of those who are acquainted with steering to
choose a steersman; and even if, in some occupations and arts, there
are some non-experts who also share in the ability to choose, they do
not share in a higher degree than the experts.

(13)   It would thus appear, on this line of argument, that the
people should not be made sovereign, either in the matter of the election of magistrates or in that of their examination.

(14)   It may be, however, that these arguments are not altogether
well founded. In the first place we have to remember our own previous argument of the combination of qualities which is to be found in
the people—provided, that is to say, that they are not debased in character. Each individual may indeed, be a worse judge than the experts;
but all, when they meet together, are either better than experts or at
any rate no worse. In the second place, there are a number of arts in
which the creative artist is not the only, or even the best, judge. These
are the arts whose products can be understood and judged even by
those who do not possess any skill in the art. A house, for instance, is
something which can be understood by others besides the builder: indeed the user of a house—or in other words the householder—will
judge it even better than he does. In the same way a pilot will judge a
rudder better than a shipwright does; and the diner—not the cook—
will be the best judge of a feast.

(15)   The first difficulty which confronts our argument about the
rights of the people would appear to be answered sufficiently by these
considerations. But there is a second difficulty still to be faced, which
is connected with the first. It would seem to be absurd that persons of a
poor quality should be sovereign on issues which are more important

than those assigned to the better sort of citizens. The election of magistrates, and their examination at the end of their tenure, are the most important of issues; and yet there are constitutions, as we have seen, under which these issues are assigned to popular bodies, and where a popular body is sovereign in all such matters.

(16) To add to the difficulty, membership of the assembly, which carries deliberative and judicial functions, is vested in persons of little property and of any age; but a high property qualification is demanded from those who serve as treasurers or generals, or hold any of the highest offices. This difficulty too may, however, be met in the same way as the first; and the practice followed in these constitutions is perhaps, after all, correct.

(17) It is not the individual member of the judicial court, or the council, or the assembly, who is vested with office: it is the court as a whole, the council as a whole, the popular assembly as a whole, which is vested; and each individual member—whether of the council, the assembly, or the court—is simply a part of the whole.

(18) It is therefore just and proper that the people, from which the assembly, the council, and the court are constituted, should be sovereign on issues more important than those assigned to the better sort of citizens. It may be added that the collective property of the members of all these bodies is greater than that of the persons who either as individuals or as members of small bodies hold the highest [executive] offices.

(19) This may serve as a settlement of the difficulties which have been (1282b) discussed. But the discussion of the first of these difficulties [whether expert skill or general knowledge should be the sovereign authority] leads to one conclusion above all others. Rightly constituted laws should be the final sovereign; and personal rule, whether it be exercised by a single person or a body of persons, should be sovereign only in those matters on which law is unable, owing to the difficulty of framing general rules for all contingencies, to make an exact pronouncement.

(20) But what rightly constituted laws ought to be is a matter that is not yet clear; and here we are still confronted by the difficulty stated at the end of the previous chapter—that law itself may have a bias in favour of one class or another. Equally with the constitutions to which they belong [and *according to* the constitutions to which they belong] laws must be good or bad, just or unjust.

(21)   The one clear fact is that laws must be constituted in accordance with constitutions; and if this is the case, it follows that laws which are in accordance with right constitutions must necessarily be just, and laws which are in accordance with wrong or perverted constitutions must be unjust.

The Aristotelian *Constitution of the Athenians*

Most of the surviving text of the *Constitution of the Athenians* (*Athenaion Politeia*) attributed to Aristotle was discovered in London among some Egyptian papyri in 1890. Although scholars continue to debate whether Aristotle himself (or perhaps one of his students) authored the treatise, most agree that the fourth-century work constitutes an invaluable source for the study of Athenian government. In the following passage the author provides a brief history of the development of Athenian democracy from Cleisthenes' revolution (ca. 507 B.C.) to Pericles' citizenship law of 451/0 B.C.

(20.1)   When the tyranny had been overthrown, strife broke out between Isagoras son of Tisander, a friend of the tyrants, and Cleisthenes of the Alcmaeonid family. As Cleisthenes was getting the worse of the party struggle, he attached the people to his following, by proposing to give political power to the masses. (2)   Isagoras then fell behind in power, so he called back Cleomenes [King of Sparta], with whom he had a tie of hospitality, and since it appeared

From Aristotle, *The Athenian Constitution*, edited and translated by P. J. Rhodes, pp. 63–65, 67–70 (Harmondsworth: Penguin, 1984). Reproduced by permission Frederick Warne & Co.

that the Alcmaeonids were among those who were under a curse, persuaded Cleomenes to join him in driving out the accursed. (3) Cleisthenes withdrew; and Cleomenes came with a few men and solemnly expelled seven hundred Athenian households. After doing this he tried to dissolve the council and make Isagoras and three hundred of his friends masters of the city. However, the council resisted and the common people gathered in force; the supporters of Cleomenes and Isagoras fled to the Acropolis; the people settled down and besieged them for two days, but on the third made a truce to release Cleomenes and all the men with him, and recalled Cleisthenes and the other exiles. (4) Thus the people obtained control of affairs, and Cleisthenes became leader and champion of the people. The Alcmaeonids bore the greatest responsibility for the expulsion of the tyrants, and had persisted in opposition to them for most of the time. . . .

(21.1) For these reasons the people placed their trust in Cleisthenes. Then, as champion of the masses, in the fourth year after the overthrow of the tyrants, the archonship of Isagoras [508/7], (2) he first distributed all the citizens through ten tribes instead of the old four, wanting to mix them up so that more men should have a share in the running of the state. This is the origin of the saying 'Don't judge by tribes', addressed to those who want to inquire into a man's ancestry. (3) Next he made the council a body of five hundred instead of four hundred, fifty from each tribe (previously there had been a hundred from each old tribe). He refused to divide the Athenians into twelve tribes, to avoid allocating them according to the already existing thirds: the four tribes were divided into twelve thirds, and if he had used them he would not have succeeded in mixing up the people. (4) He divided the land of Attica by demes into thirty parts—ten parts in the city region, ten in the coast and ten in the inland—and he called these parts thirds [*trittyes*], and allotted three to each tribe in such a way that each tribe should have a share in all the regions. He made the men living in each deme fellow-demesmen of one another, so that they should not use their fathers' names and make it obvious who were the new citizens but should be named after their demes: this is why the Athenians still call themselves after their demes. . . . (6) He left the clans, brotherhoods and priesthoods each to retain their traditional privileges. He appointed ten eponymous heroes for the tribes, chosen by the Delphic priestess from a pre-selected list of a hundred founding heroes.

(22.1) When this had been accomplished, the constitution was much more democratic than that of Solon. Many of Solon's laws had been consigned to oblivion by the tyranny, through not being used, and Cleisthenes enacted other new laws in his bid for popular support, among them the law about ostracism. (2) First, in the eighth year after this settlement [501/0], the archonship of Hermocreon, the Athenians imposed on the council of five hundred the oath which it still swears today. Then they appointed the generals by tribes, one from each tribe; but the leader of the whole army was the polemarch. (3) In the twelfth year after this, the archonship of Phaenippus [490/89], they won the battle of Marathon. They waited two years after their victory, and then [488/7], now that the people were confident, they used for the first time the law about ostracism: this had been enacted through suspicion of men in a powerful position, because Pisistratus from being popular leader and general had made himself tyrant. (4) The first man to be ostracized was one of his relatives, Hipparchus son of Charmus, of Collytus: it was because of him in particular that Cleisthenes had enacted the law, since he wanted to drive Hipparchus out. The Athenians, with the tolerance normally shown by the people, had allowed those friends of the tyrants who had not joined in their crimes during the disturbances to continue living in the city, and Hipparchus was the leader and champion of these. (5) Immediately afterwards, in the next year, the archonship of Telesinus [487/6], for the first time since the tyranny the nine archons were appointed by lot on a tribal basis, from a short list of five hundred elected by the members of the demes: all the archons before this were elected. Also Megacles son of Hippocrates, of Alopece, was ostracized. (6) The Athenians continued for three years to ostracize the friends of the tyrants, on account of whom the law had been enacted; but after that, in the fourth year [485/4], they took to removing anyone else who seemed too powerful: the first man unconnected with the tyranny to be ostracized was Xanthippus son of Ariphron. (7) In the third year after that, the archonship of Nicodemus [483/2], when the mines at Maronea were discovered and the city had a surplus of one hundred talents from the workings, some men proposed that the money should be distributed to the people, but Themistocles prevented this. He refused to say what he would do with the money, but urged the Athenians to lend the hundred richest citizens one talent each: if they were satisfied with the way in which the money was spent, it should be put down to the city's account, but if not, the money should be reclaimed from those to whom it had been lent. When he had obtained the money on these terms, he had a hundred triremes built, each of the hundred men taking the responsibility for one; and with these ships the battle of Salamis was fought against the barbarians. At this time Aristides son of Lysimachus was ostracized. (8) In the third year [481/0], the archonship of Hypsichides, all those who had been ostracized were recalled, on account of Xerxes' invasion: and for the future it was resolved that anyone who was ostracized should live within the limits of Geraestus and Scyllaeum, or else was to be absolutely oulawed.

(23.1) Up to this point there had been a gradual development and increase in the city and in the democracy. After the Persian Wars, however, the council of the Areopagus recovered its strength and administered the city. It acquired its predominance not by any formal decision but through being responsible for the battle of Salamis. When the generals were unable to handle the crisis, and proclaimed that each man should save himself, the Areopagus provided money, gave the men eight drachmae each, and enabled them to embark on the ships. (2) For this reason the Athenians bowed to its authority, and the city was well governed at this time. During this period they trained themselves for war, gained a good reputation among the Greeks, and acquired the leadership at sea despite the opposition of the Spartans. (3) The champions of the people at this time were Aristides son of Lysimachus and Themistocles son of Neocles: Themistocles practised the military arts, while Aristides was skilled in the political arts and was outstanding among his contemporaries for his uprightness, so the Athenians used the first as a general and the second as an adviser. (4) The two men were jointly responsible for the rebuilding of the walls [of Athens, destroyed by the Persians], in spite of being personal opponents; and it was Aristides who saw that the Spartans had gained a bad reputation because of Pausanias and urged the Ionians to break away from the Spartan alliance. (5) For that reason it was he who made the first assessment of tribute for the cities, in the third year after the battle of Salamis, the archonship of Timosthenes [478/7], and who swore the oaths to the Ionians that they should have the same enemies and friends, to confirm which they sank lumps of iron in the sea. . . .

(25.1)   For about seventeen years after the Persian Wars the constitution in which the Areopagus was dominant persisted, though it gradually declined. As the masses increased, Ephialtes son of Sophonides became champion of the people, a man who appeared to be uncorrupt and upright in political matters. He attacked the council of the Areopagus. (2)   First he eliminated many of its members, bringing them to trial for their conduct in office. Then in the archonship of Conon [462/1] he took away from the council all the accretions which gave it its guardianship of the constitution, giving some to the council of five hundred and some to the people and the jury-courts. . . .

(4)   . . . Afterwards Ephialtes and Themistocles attacked the Areopagus at a meeting of the council of five hundred, and then in the assembly in the same way, and persisted until they had taken away its power. Ephialtes too was removed by assassination not long afterwards, through the agency of Aristodicus of Tanagra.

(26.1)   In this way the council of the Areopagus was deprived of its responsibility. Afterwards the constitution was further slackened through the men who devoted themselves eagerly to demagogy. At this time it happened that the better sort had no leader, but their champion was Cimon son of Miltiades. . . .

(2)   In other respects the Athenians in their administration did not abide by the laws as they had done before, but at first they did not interfere with the appointment of the nine archons. However, in the sixth year after Ephialtes' death they decided that the rankers [*zeugitae*] should be admitted to the short list from which lots were drawn for the nine archons, and Mnesithides was the first of these to hold office [457/6] . Previously all the archons had been from the cavalry and the five-hundred-bushel class, and the rankers had held only the routine offices, except when some stipulation of the law was disregarded. (3)   In the fifth year after that, the archonship of Lysicrates [453/2], the thirty justices called deme justices were instituted again. (4)   In the third year after that, under Antidotus [451/0], on account of the large number of citizens it was decided on the proposal of Pericles that a man should not be a member of the citizen body unless both his parents were Athenians.

Analysis

A. H. M. Jones

The Economic Basis of Athenian Democracy

A. H. M. Jones, late Professor of Ancient History at Cambridge University, was one of the most prolific and versatile scholars of the last generation, publishing influential works on subjects ranging from the late Roman Empire to the Greek city. One of the strongest champions of Athenian democracy, Jones in this passage surveys the actual workings of the regime, and then challenges the view that Athenian democracy was to some degree dependent on imperial revenues and slavery.

Prima facie the Athenian Democracy would seem to have been a perfectly designed machine for expressing and putting into effect the will of the people. The majority of the magistrates were annually chosen by lot from all qualified candidates who put in their names, so that every citizen had a chance to take his turn in the administration. In the fifth century the military officers, of whom the most important were the ten generals, were elected by the assembly. In the fourth, when finance became a difficult problem, a few high financial officers were also elected. This was an inevitable concession to aristocratic principles: for the Greeks considered popular election to be aristocratic rather than democratic, since the ordinary voter will prefer a known to an unknown name—and in point of fact the generals usually tended to be men of wealth and family, though a professional soldier or two were usually members of the board in the fourth century. But the assembly, of which all adult male citizens were members, kept a strict control over the generals, who received precise instructions and departed from them at their peril. The assembly was in a very real sense a sovereign body, holding forty regular meetings a year and extraordinary sessions as required, and not merely settling general questions of policy, but making detailed decisions in every sphere of government—foreign affairs, military operations, finance.

The administrative lynch-pin of the constitution was the council of five hundred, annually chosen by lot from all the demes (wards or parishes) of Athens and Attica in proportion to their size, and thus forming a fair sample of the people as a whole. It had two main functions, to supervise and co-ordinate the activities of the magistrates, and to prepare the agenda of the assembly. No motion might be put to the assembly unless the question had been placed on the order paper by the council and duly advertised; snap divisions were thus precluded. On uncontroversial issues the council usually produced a draft motion, which could however be freely debated and amended in the assembly by any citizen; in this way much formal business was cleared away. On controversial issues the council normally—and naturally in view of its composition—forebore to express an opinion, and merely put the question before the people, leaving it to any citizen to draft the motion during the actual debate. The presidents of the council and the assembly were chosen daily by lot from the council to preclude any undue influence from the chair.

Finally, as ultimate guardians of the constitution, there were the popular law courts. Juries were empanelled by lot for each case from a body of 6,000 citizens annually chosen by lot, and decided not only private cases but political issues. These juries as a regular routine judged any charges of peculation or malfeasance brought against magistrates on laying down their office; they decided the fate of any citizen accused of treason or of "deceiving the people" by his speeches in the assembly; they could quash any motion voted in the assembly as being contrary to the laws, and punish its author. Political trials were frequent in Athens, and in the fourth century in particular the indictment for an illegal motion [the *graphe paranomon*] was constantly employed for political purposes, often on very technical grounds. The result was that the popular juries—in such cases sometimes thousands strong—tended to become a Supreme Court.

In general all citizens who were not expressly disqualified for some offence, such as an unpaid debt to the treasury, had equal political rights: in particular all could speak and vote in the assembly. For membership of the council and of the juries and probably for all magistracies there was an age qualification of 30 years. For offices, or at any rate some of them, there were also qualifications of property: but these were mostly moderate and, by the late fourth century, at any rate, and probably by the fifth, were in practice ignored. To make the system work truly democratically it was further necessary that every citizen, however poor, should be able to afford the time for exercising his political rights, and from the time of Pericles pay was provided for this purpose. Magistrates were paid at varying rates according to the nature of their duties; members of the council received 5 obols a day by the fourth century—the rate may have been lower in the fifth; and members of the juries were given a subsistence allowance of 2 obols, raised in 425 B.C. to 3. Finally from the beginning of the fourth century citizens who attended the assembly—or rather the quorum who arrived first, for a limited sum of money was allocated to each assembly—were paid a subsistence allowance of 1, then 2, then 3 obols. Later the rate was more liberal. . . .

Two charges have been brought against the Athenian democracy, one both by ancient and by modern critics, the other in recent times only. The first is that the pay, which was an essential part of the system, was provided by the tribute paid by Athens' allies in the Delian League, and that the democracy was therefore parasitic on the empire: the second, that Athenians only had the leisure to perform their political functions because they were supported by slaves—the democracy was in fact parasitic on slavery.

To the first charge there is a very simple answer, that the democracy continued to function in the fourth century when Athens had lost her empire; the Second Athenian League, which lasted effectively only from 377 to 357, was never a paying proposition, the contributions of the allies by no means covering the cost of military and naval operations. And not only did the democracy continue to function, but a new and important form of pay, that for attendance in the assembly, was introduced early in the century. This being so it is hardly worth while to go into the financial figures, particularly as there must be many gaps in our calculations. . . .

[Jones goes on to conclude that Athens' internal revenues, estimated at some 400 talents per year, were more than enough to cover the payments for public service.] That Athens profited financially from her empire is of course true. But these profits were not necessary to keep the democracy working. They enabled Athens to be a great power and to support a much larger citizen population at higher standards of living. One oligarchic critic emphasises the casual profits incidental on Athens' position as an imperial city; the imperial litigation which brought in more court fees, the increased customs revenue, the demand for lodgings, cabs and slaves to hire. Advocates and politicians made money by pleading the legal cases of the allies, and promoting measures in their favour. But these were chicken-feed compared with the solid benefits of empire, the tribute amounting to 400 talents a year and other imperial income raising the annual total to 600 talents, and the acquisition of land overseas, mainly by confiscation from rebellious allied communities or individuals.

The land was utilised either for colonies, which were technically separate states, but being composed of former Athenian citizens were virtually overseas extensions of the Athenian state, or for cleruchies, that is settlements of Athenians who remained full citizens, liable to Athenian taxation and military service, though in practice they naturally would rarely exercise their citizen rights at Athens. Both types of settlement were normally manned from the poorer citizens. Most will have come from the lowest property class, thetes, who possessed property rated under 2,000 drachmae and were liable only for naval service or as light-armed troops on land. The allotments were (in the one case where figures are given) of sufficient value to qualify the owner to rank as a zeugite, liable to military service as a heavy-armed infantry-man or hoplite. By her colonies and cleruchies Athens raised more than 10,000 of her citizens from poverty to modest affluence, and at the same time increased her hoplite force by an even larger number, the cleruchs with their adult sons serving in the ranks of the Athenian army and the colonists as allied contingents.

The tribute was partly spent on the upkeep of a standing navy, partly put to reserve. Pericles is stated to have kept sixty triremes in commission for eight months in the year, and he maintained a fleet of 300 in the dockyards. The dockyards must have given employment to an army of craftsmen, as well as to 500 guards, and the crews of the cruising triremes would have numbered 12,000 men, paid a drachma a day for 240 days in the year. Not all the dockyard workers will have been citizens, nor all the naval ratings, but many thousands of Athenian thetes enjoyed regular well-paid employment thanks to the empire. Of the money put to reserve a part, probably 2,000 talents, was spent on public works, notably the Parthenon and the Propylaea, which again, as Plutarch explains, gave employment to the poorer classes. The remainder formed a war fund of 6,000 talents, which was ultimately spent during the Peloponnesian war on pay to hoplites and sailors.

In response to the favourable economic conditions provided by the empire the population of Athens seems to have risen by leaps and bounds during the half-century between the Persian war (480–479) and the opening of the Peloponnesian war (431). The figures are unfortunately very incomplete and not altogether certain, but . . . [they] suggest a total population of 30,000 citizens, a figure given elsewhere by Herodotus, divided 1 : 2 between hoplites and thetes [ca. 480. . . . By 431, there were about 20,000 hoplites, while] the thetes must have certainly maintained and probably considerably increased their numbers. Otherwise it would be hard to account for the radical tone of the fifth century democracy, and the predominance, noted with disfavour by oligarchic critics, of the 'naval masses' in its councils.

The Peloponnesian war caused great losses both by battle casualties and by the plague: 1,000 hoplites fell at Delium and 600 at Amphipolis, and 2,700 hoplites and 130 triremes carrying perhaps 13,000 citizen sailors, if half the crews were Athenians, were sent to Sicily, of whom only a remnant ever saw Athens again, while in the plague 4,700 men of hoplite status and an uncounted number of thetes perished. Towards the end of the war (411) there seem to have been only 9,000 hoplites resident in Attica, and after the war the cleruchs were all dispossessed. . . . The loss of the empire and the fall of Athens in 404 must have compelled many thousands of citizens, dispossessed cleruchs and unemployed sailors and dockyard workers, to emigrate or take service as mercenaries abroad. A general decrease in prosperity caused the population to sink to a level well below that of the Persian wars, and in particular reduced the thetic class. Hence the increasingly bourgeois tone of the fourth century democracy.

The second charge against the Athenian democracy, that it was parasitic on slavery, is more difficult to answer with any certainty. It will be as well first to make plain the elements of the problem. The

Athenians, like all Greek peoples, regarded themselves as a kinship group, and citizenship depended strictly on descent (always on the father's side and, by a law passed in 451 and reenacted in 403, on the mother's side also) and not on residence, however long. The population of Attica therefore consisted not only of citizens but of free aliens, mainly immigrants who had settled permanently and often lived at Athens for generations, but also including freed slaves and persons of mixed descent; and of slaves, mainly imported but some home-bred. It is unhistorical to condemn the Athenian democracy because it did not give political rights to all residents of Attica; it was the democracy of the Athenian people. It is however relevant to enquire whether the Athenian people was a privileged group depending on the labour of others. Sparta might be called technically a democracy (though the hereditary kings and the council of elders balanced the power of the people) inasmuch as the whole body of Spartiates chose the ephors, in whose hands the government effectively lay, but the Spartiates were a body of rentiers supported by native serfs, the helots, who far outnumbered them. Was the Athenian democracy of this order? The resident aliens (metics) do not concern us here. They made a great contribution to Athenian prosperity, particularly in the fields of industry, commerce and banking—indeed they seem to have dominated the two latter. They were voluntary immigrants and could leave when they wished (except in time of war). That so many domiciled themselves permanently in Attica—a census taken at the end of the fourth century showed 10,000 metics as against 21,000 citizens—is a testimony to their liberal treatment. They enjoyed full civil (as opposed to political) rights, except that they could not own land—hence their concentration on industry and commerce—and were subject to all the duties of citizens, including military and naval service and taxation at a slightly higher scale. They were a contented class, and many demonstrated their loyalty to their adoptive city by generous gifts at times of crisis.

What of slaves? . . . Is it true, as we are still too often told, that the average Athenian, in the intervals between listening to a play of Sophocles and serving as a magistrate, councillor or juror, lounged in the market place, discussing politics and philosophy, while slaves toiled to support him? . . .

Slaves were employed in many capacities—as domestic servants, as clerks and agents in commerce and banking, in agriculture, and in industry and mining. All well-to-do Athenian families had several servants, and no doubt wealthy men kept large households of a dozen or more—precise figures are lacking—but the domestic servant probably did not go very far down the social scale. . . .

We have no reliable evidence for the total number of slaves in Attica at any time. . . . But whatever their numbers their distribution is fairly clear. They were owned in the main by the 1,200 richest families and in decreasing numbers by the next 3,000 or so. It is unlikely that any slaves were owned by two-thirds to three-quarters of the citizen population. The great majority of the citizens earned their living by the work of their hands, as peasant farmers, craftsmen, shopkeepers, seamen and labourers; so contemporary witnesses state, and so the detailed evidence, so far as it goes, suggests. . . .

The majority of the citizens were then workers who earned their own livings and whose political pay served only to compensate them in some measure for loss of working time. Agricultural and industrial slaves in the main merely added to the wealth of a relatively small rentier class, whose principal source of income was land; this same class employed most of the domestic slaves. It only remains to ask how far the Athenian State drew its revenue, directly or indirectly, from slaves. The State owned a certain number of slaves. Most famous are the 1,200 Scythian archers who policed the assembly and the law courts and enforced the orders of the magistrates. There were a number of others ranging from the workers in the mint to the city gaoler and the public slave *par excellence* who had custody of the public records and accounts. Athens thus ran her police force and her rudimentary civil service in part by slave labour—the clerks of the magistrates were mostly salaried citizens. There was apparently a tax on slaves, . . . but it can hardly have been an important item in the revenue to receive so little notice. The mines, which were mainly exploited by slave labour, also brought in revenue to the State, but less than might have been expected seeing that concessionaires sometimes made large fortunes. . . .

The charge brought by fifth-century oligarchic critics (and thoughtlessly repeated by many modern writers), that the Athenian democracy depended for its political pay on the tribute of the subject allies, was brought to the test of fact when Athens lost her empire in 404, and was proved to be a calumny when the democracy continued to pay the citizens for their political functions out of domestic revenues. The modern charge that the Athenian democracy was dependent on slave labour was never brought to the test, since the Athenians never freed all their slaves. This is not surprising, for slavery was an established institution, which most people accepted without question as "according to nature," and to abolish it would have meant a wholesale disregard of the rights of property, which the Athenians throughout their history were careful to respect. It is more surprising that on some occasions of crisis motions for a partial or wholesale freeing of slaves were carried. In 406 all male slaves of military age were freed and granted the citizenship to man the ships which won the battle of Arginusae. After the expulsion of the Thirty in 403, Thrasybulus, the left-wing leader of the restored democracy, carried a measure, later quashed as illegal by the moderate leader Archinus, to free and enfranchise all slaves who had fought for the democracy. In 338, after the defeat of [Athens at] Chaeronea, the left-wing politician Hypereides proposed and carried a motion to free all (able-bodied male) slaves to resist the Macedonians; this motion was again quashed as illegal by a conservative politician.

These facts suggest that there was no bitterness between the mass of the citizens and the slaves, but rather a sense of fellow-feeling. This was a point which shocked contemporary Athenian oligarchs. The "Old Oligarch" speaks bitterly of the insolence of slaves at Athens, and complains that it is illegal to strike them—the reason, he explains, is that the people are indistinguishable in dress and general appearance from slaves, and it would be easy to strike a citizen by mistake. . . .

Though the Athenians treated their slaves with a humanity which was exceptional according to the standards of the time, they never abolished slavery, and the charge that Athenian democracy was dependent on their labour was never brought to the test of fact. But had Hypereides' motion been allowed to stand, and extended to slaves of all ages and both sexes, it would not seem, on the basis of the evidence cited earlier in this article, that its effects would have been catastrophic. All wealthy and well-to-do citizens (or rather their wives and unmarried daughters) would have been incommoded by having to do their own housework. A very small number of wealthy or comfortably off men who had invested all their money in mining and industrial slaves would have been reduced to penury, and a larger number, but still a small minority, would have lost the proportion of their income which derived from industrial slaves, and would have had to let their farms instead of cultivating them by slave labour. A number of craftsmen would have lost their apprentices and journeymen. But the great majority of Athenians who owned no slaves but cultivated their own little farms or worked on their own as craftsmen, shopkeepers or labourers would have been unaffected.

Raphael Sealey

The Athenian Republic

Raphael Sealey, Professor of History at the University of California, Berkeley, has published numerous works on Greek history, politics, law, and society, including a popular textbook entitled A *History of the Greek City States.* In the following selection from *The Athenian Republic,* Sealey treats several important technical problems relevant to any attempt to analyze the nature of the Athenian regime. Sealey first argues that the Athenians ultimately saw their laws (*nomoi*) as immutable rules handed down from Solon, which could only be amended with difficulty. He then discusses the problematic meaning of the word *demokratia*, arguing that the term originally carried "deprecatory force" and thus needed to be defended; ultimately Sealey concludes that by the fourth century *demokratia* came to be understood as the "rule of law," as opposed to the arbitrary rule of a tyrant or oligarchy.

[Between 410 and 403 the Athenians undertook to revise and reinscribe on stone the "laws of Solon." This was followed by a similar republication of the sacrificial calendar (403–399).]

The *graphē paranomōn* throws further light on the view which Athenians held in the late fifth century about the nature and authority of law. Moreover, it promises to throw decisive light on that topic, since it is not a mere opinion expressed by some Athenians but a feature of public law. It is first attested for 415, when it was employed successfully against a decree which the council had passed. In 411 the [oligarchic] revolutionaries persuaded the assembly to suspend the *graphē paranomōn* as a first step toward further changes. . . .

From these occurrences it is clear that the *graphē paranomōn* was an established part of Athenian procedural law well before 403/2. How old it was can only be conjectured. So a problem arises. The body of law current in Athens in the late fifth century included not only laws [*nomoi*] which Solon had written . . . long before but also a great multitude of decrees [*psēphismata*]. If a newly passed decree contravened an earlier decree and was accordingly indicted by way of *graphē paranomōn*, how could one tell which of the two decrees had higher authority and was to be dignified with the title of *nomos*? A possible solution to this problem would say that the *nomoi* of the late fifth century comprised both the laws of Solon and some, but not all, among current decrees. But this solution would only be tenable if there had been a criterion recognizable in the late fifth century for determining which decrees were *nomoi*. There is no trace of any such thing.

A more attractive solution may be suggested by contrast with the Roman principle that whatever the people had last ordered was valid. The modern student may be inclined to take this principle for granted, since he is familiar with the notion of [popular] sovereignty. But in the fourth century the Athenians did not accept this principle in relation to laws. They held, on the contrary, that a new law should be declared invalid if it conflicted with an older law which it did not explicitly repeal. . . .

It is better to recognize in the problem an anomaly of fifth-century law. On the one hand, the Athenians had a concept of law as a set of permanent rules capable of serving as a framework within which resolutions could be passed by a majority in the assembly; so much is implied by the existence of the *graphē paranomōn*. On the other hand, the assembly was in the habit of passing resolutions without regard to any supposed limitations. The work of codification [of Athenian law] in 410–399 was required, not only because many and multifarious decrees had been passed, but also because the Athenians needed to clarify their concept of law and in particular to distinguish between rules of greater and of lesser authority. By 399 they had accomplished the task and its achievement was summed up in the "supplementary" measure saying that no decree should have greater authority than a *nomos.* But in reaching this achievement the Athenians developed ideas of which the germs had been present in their system of law ever since Solon first codified it. . . .

[This] development of legislative procedures and safeguards . . . reveals a protracted and careful series of attempts to bring about the rule of law, that is, to ensure that the law should be the same for everyone. The concept of law current among the Athenians was somewhat different from the modern concept. . . .

First, the Athenians thought that different kinds of material were proper for laws and decrees, even though they may not have pursued the difference to a clear contrast. Aristotle tried to formulate the difference by saying that laws are general, but decrees regulate particular occurrences. Recognition of a difference in proper content accounts for the precept that decrees ought only to be proposed within the framework set by the laws. . . .

[Second,] the classical Athenians believed that their laws had been issued by Solon long before, and although in the fourth century they instituted a regular procedure of amendment, the procedure was weighted against innovation, since concern for evenhanded justice, as understood by the Athenians, made them reluctant to change the laws. Constitutionally governed states of the present day have a legislature, and one of the primary tasks of the legislature is to make laws (in the Athenian sense of general rules). Statute-law is conceived today primarily as expressing the will of the legislator. This belief springs in part from the ideas developed by political theorists, who drew in turn on the Roman notion that government derives its authority from the consent of the governed. The concept of consent and the ideas of the theorists might be subjected to critical scrutiny and perhaps be found wanting. But the modern notion of statute-law as expressing the will of the legislator has a consequence so clear as to stand up to all scrutiny. If statute-law expresses the will of the legislator, it can be changed when the legislator, however constituted, changes his mind. For modern man law is something made and so it can be unmade. For the Athenians law was something already there. A law is a law is a law. . . .

[Sealey now passes on to a discussion of *dēmokratia.*]

Democracy is not an object whose presence or absence can be recognized readily by observation. Questions about the nature of democracy in Athens, about its origin and development, are markedly different from such questions as "Were there olive trees in ancient

Athens?" and "When did silver currency come to be adopted by the Athenians?" . . .

Some historians have spoken of democracy in a Greek context as if their readers knew without explanation what they meant. Others have offered a definition so vague as to have little value, for example, "The Greek word *demokratia* is the name of a form of government— government by the people." Such a statement needs to be supported with an account of those institutions which, in the writer's opinion, do and those which do not amount to "government by the people," and the account of institutions must in turn be supplemented with a study of the Greek usage of the word *dēmokratia* to show whether that usage conformed to the chosen set of institutions. Others have made decision by the vote of a majority in a primary assembly the criterion of democracy. Yet others have been more cautious. They have recognized that cities which contemporaries called *oligarchiai* had a primary assembly, which took decisions by the vote of a majority. They have suggested that a property qualification for voting in the assembly constitutes the essential difference.

The validity of such views can only be determined by looking into the history of the word *dēmokratia*. In this section three preliminary points will be made. The first can be stated in the following dictum, in which each phrase will require explanatory comment:

> As far as is known, in the classical period every Greek city had a primary assembly, which took final decisions on questions of policy by vote of a majority.

[Sealey proceeds to support this statement, then continues.]

. . . Enough has been said to defend the dictum under consideration about the rule of the assembly in the Greek city. Rule by the assembly, in the sense defined, does not characterize only some Greek cities, to be called on that account *dēmokratiai*. It characterizes all Greek cities. The only exception is irregular and arbitrary regimes, such as the rule of the Thirty, and these did not last; either they were overthrown or, if they survived, they developed into more regular governments and they tended to spawn primary assemblies on the way. If anyone wishes to maintain that the constitutional development of Athens was distinctive among Greek cities because it achieved *dēmokratia*, then by *dēmokratia* he must mean something other than the rule of the assembly of citizens.

The other preliminary points to be noted here can be treated more briefly. The first concerns differences between ancient and modern meanings. As noted above, some present-day historians have spoken of "democracy" in Athens as if the meaning were known and as if the word meant the same thing both in ancient and in modern contexts. It is not possible at this point in the present inquiry to say whether "democracy" in modern English means the same as *dēmokratia* in Attic Greek. Before saying that one would have to discover what each word means. Although something will be said below about the meaning of *dēmokratia*, it would not be profitable to ask what the English word "democracy" means. It scarcely needs to be shown that the English word is used to mean many different things, often in a tendentious manner; the only secure generalization is that any foreign government supported by the United States will be declared by some journalist to be "undemocratic."

It would accordingly be nugatory to say that ancient democracy differed from modern democracy. On the other hand, it is informative to note that some ancient republics differed from modern republics in a manner pertinent to understanding their forms of government. A modern republic has a legislature and the tasks of the legislature include making laws. But as argued [above], the Athenians did not regard the laws as things to be made from time to time by a competent authority. They thought that the laws were already there. When challenged to say where the laws came from, they told of an ancient lawgiver. In the fourth century they admitted that the laws might sometimes need to be amended, but they insisted that this should only be done in a reluctant and circumspect manner. If modern democracy, whatever it may be, is characterized by a habit of making laws, it differs in its concept of law from the ancient Athenians. . . .

The history of Herodotos is the earliest extant work in which the word *dēmokratia* occurs. In his usage *dēmokratia* is a critic's term, uttered by someone who finds fault with the thing designated as *dēmokratia*. It is also a narrator's term, employed by Herodotos in a relatively neutral way. But it is not an advocate's term. When such a man as [the Persian] Otanes advocates a condition which others call *dēmokratia*, he prefers a beautiful word for it. In the Persian debate [see Part VII] the word *oligarchia* behaves in a similar way. Dareios (3.82.3 and 5), criticizing the proposal of Megabyxos, calls it a proposal for *oligarchia*, and Herodotos as narrator (3.81.1) calls it a proposal for *oli-garchia*. But Megabyxos avoids the word *oligarchia* and says (3.81.3): "Let us select a company of the best men and entrust them with control." By drawing together "the best" (*aristoi*) and "control" (*kratos*) Megabyxos almost says *aristokratia*.

In the pages of Thucydides *dēmokratia* and *oligarchia* behave in a similar way. In an important observation (3.82.8) [see Part VII] the historian says that in the internal conflicts exacerbated by the Peloponnesian War the watchwords used by the two sides in conflict degenerated into empty slogans, as each side tried ruthlessly to overcome the other. The watchwords which Thucydides names are not *dēmokratia* and *oligarchia* but *isonomia politikē* [political equality] of the multitude (*plēthos*) and *aristokratia sōphrōn* [moderate aristocracy]. . . .

The deprecatory force of *dēmokratia* is illustrated by a remark of Perikles in the funeral speech. He says (2.37.1):

> . . . *Admittedly, since our constitution is administered not for a few but for the majority, it is called* dēmokratia. *Nevertheless as regards the laws everyone gets equal treatment in private disputes, and as regards public esteem, in so far as each has a claim to recognition, he is not honored for the most part because of his class-affiliation but because of his merits, and on the other hand in a case of poverty, if a man can do the state some service, he is not debarred by obscurity.*

This translation employs "admittedly," "nevertheless," and "as regards" in an attempt to reproduce the force of the repeated [Greek] particles *men* and *de*. Those particles are crucial for understanding the passage. Once their force is recognized, it becomes clear that Perikles cannot disclaim the name *dēmokratia* for the Athenian constitution, to which it had stuck, but he insists that the constitution has great merits in spite of its name. . . .

The complex implications of the word *dēmokratia* in its early history cannot be recovered in full, but they should not be neglected, as they are by those who assume that *dēmokratia* was nothing but a neutral term for a defined form of government. It should not be doubted that the value of the word in political discourse derived from its complexity. That complexity had developed in lost chapters of the political history of the fifth century. It also sprang in part from the earlier history of the word *dēmos*, for that too reveals ambiguity. In Homeric and archaic verse *dēmos*, is often a neutral term for the whole community, but sometimes it has pejorative force. . . .

[Moreover, in] the fifth century *oligarchia*, like *dēmokratia*, had little factual meaning. Such factual connotation as it had derived from its opening element *olig-* = "few." An arbitrary *junta* embodied the rule of the few *par excellence*. So as time passed *oligarchia* came to have the factual and restricted meaning which had once been borne by *dynasteia* ["power, domination" of a narrow group]. By contrast and by consequence *dēmokratia* came to express one of the deepest convictions of the Athenians, their belief in the rule of law. . . .

[Sealey summarizes his argument.] If a slogan is needed, Athens was a republic, not a democracy. But slogans lend themselves to distortion. The negative argument of the foregoing chapters has been that calling Athens democracy or *dēmokratia* says nothing. Both the ancient and the modern word are treacherous.

The positive thesis is that the Athenians strove through the centuries to achieve the rule of law. The term, though not wholly precise, is serviceable. It approximates in meaning to *isonomia*, a word which may have been coined to express the ideal pursued when the tyrants were overthrown in archaic Athens. The notion of the rule of law gains in resonance if one notices the institutions through which the Athenians tried to achieve it. One of these was codification. It has been argued above that the first comprehensive code for the Athenians was that of Solon, even though some isolated measures may have been put in writing before. A new codification was carried out at the end of the fifth century, and the revised laws were inscribed on walls in the *stoa basileios* [a building in the Agora] "so that anyone who wishes may inspect them," as the decree of Teisamenos provided. The notion of law as a science requiring professional study never occurred to the Athenians. Consequently, they were not strong on legal memory, but they were not afflicted with an order of experts bent on enlarging its own privileges. Once their code had been revised, they achieved a high degree of sophistication in preserving it. Although they insisted that the laws were not the creation of a still available authority but something given in the past, they instituted a procedure of amendment, and they developed judicial procedures to protect the code both against decrees of the assembly and against ill-considered use of the procedure of amendment.

Josiah Ober

The Ideological Hegemony of the Masses

Josiah Ober, David Magie Professor of Ancient History and Chairman of Classics at Princeton University, has written extensively on Greek politics and history, including a recent collection of essays entitled *The Athenian Revolution.* In his *Mass and Elite in Democratic Athens* Ober argues against the "elitist theory" of democracy, which holds that the masses require and benefit from the direction of governing "elites." Ober maintains that the Athenian people in fact controlled their leaders, who were compelled to adopt and employ the ideology of the *demos* in their speeches before juries and the assembly.

The Athenian democratic "constitution" (a convenient, if imprecise term to describe the formally recognized principles and practices of Athenian government) was undergirded by a belief system that stressed the innate wisdom and binding nature of group decisions, the freedom of the citizen, and the equality of all citizens. Freedom and equality were both limited and conditional, however: individual freedom was constrained by the necessity that the individual subordinate himself to group interests, and equality was limited to the political sphere. The Athenians never developed the principle of inalienable "negative rights" (freedom from governmental interference in private affairs) of the individual or of minorities vis-à-vis the state—a central tenet of modern liberalism. Nor were they convinced that social advantages would result from the equalization of property—an idea discussed by Greek philosophers and a cornerstone of Marxist sociopolitical theory. In addition to inequalities in property-holding, the Athenians continued to live with inequalities of status on the basis of birth—the result of an aristocratic tradition—and of ability—the result of differences in natural gifts and educational opportunity. There were elites in Athens, and elite Athenians tended to compete with one another over anything they thought might enhance their personal standing. These contests were hard fought, because for every winner whose status was enhanced, there were inevitably losers whose standing was lowered. Hence, there remained significant and unresolved tensions within Athenian political society which might have resulted in divisive conflict between community and individual, between mass and elite, between elite and non-elite individuals, and between members of the elites. The political power of the group threatened the liberty of the individual and the property of the wealthy; the wealth, status, and abilities of the elites threatened both the non-elite individual and the masses collectively; intra-elite contests threatened to undermine the stability of the entire society. . . .

[Ober goes on to criticize certain ways of explaining the stability of the Athenian regime.]

M. I. Finley cited de Laix's study [arguing that sovereignty rested in the Athenian Council] as an example of "falling into the constitutional-law trap": the fundamental error of imagining that it is possible to understand politics "by a purely formal . . . analysis of the 'parliamentary' *mechanics* alone." M. H. Hansen . . . concludes . . . that, due to the division of powers between the Assembly and people's courts elaborated in the later fifth and early fourth centuries, the Assembly lost its ultimate sovereignty. The sovereignty issue has generated a good deal of discussion. Martin Ostwald agrees with Hansen that as a result of constitutional reforms in the late fifth century, the "sovereignty of law" replaced the political sovereignty of the people. R. Sealey has argued that *dēmokratia* never implied popular sovereignty but rather meant "rule of law"; according to Sealey, Athens was therefore a republic, not a democracy. . . . [S]uffice it to say here that much of the recent discussion seems to have fallen into the "constitutional-law trap." Attempts to define divisions of powers, to find a unitary locus of sovereignty, and to enunciate a "rule of law" that was exterior, superior, and in opposition to the will of the people will not, I think, help us to understand the nature of Athenian democracy, because the Athenians themselves never acted nor thought along those lines. Laws and constitutional forms are indeed important, . . . because they both reflected and subsequently influenced the political attitudes of the Athenian populace. But the laws themselves may be less significant than the thought process that led to decisions about when laws should be enforced and when they should be ignored. A constitution remains, in Finley's words, "a surface phenomenon," and if we are to understand the reasons for Athenian sociopolitical stability, we must get beneath the surface, to the level of the society. . . .

[Ober associates the stability of the Athenian democracy with the control of the elites by the masses.]

The ideological hegemony of the masses effectively channeled the fierce competitiveness of elites, a legacy of the aristocratic code, into patterns of behavior that were in the public interest. The vital shift occurred in the late sixth and early fifth centuries, when the elite competitors began to compete for the favor of the masses, rather than—or in addition to—the respect of their elite peers. The effect of the shift was that the abilities, wealth, and birthright of the elite politician (and to a lesser degree of all elites) were only valorized when he received public recognition by the demos. Thus, the continuing strength of the aristocratic code of competition and *philotimia* served the interests of the democracy.

Athens' political leaders and advisers were unable to avert the Macedonian victory in 338 B.C. at Chaeronea or the subsequent loss of Athenian freedom of action in foreign policy. But that failure need not be laid at the door of the political organization of the state. Perhaps some solution to the "Macedonian problem" could have been found, perhaps the problem was insoluble given the inequality in resources. In any event, the mistakes the Athenians may have made in assessing and reacting to the military threat posed by Macedon were not the result of fatal flaws in the constitution, the gullibility of the people, or the treachery of the politicians. . . .

Athens is an example of a direct democracy that achieved genuine, long-term, stable methods of decision making by the masses and that was not coopted by the growth of an internal ruling elite. The Athenian example may therefore be used to challenge the universality of Michels' Iron Law of Oligarchy [i.e., that all human organizations tend toward oligarchy]. Michels would, perhaps, respond that the Athenian politicians were merely play-acting; he noted that the elite "aristocrat" in modern society must appeal to the masses by seemingly democratic methods, hide his true motives, persuade the masses that his interests and theirs were identical: "He dissembles his true thoughts, and howls with the democratic wolves in order to secure the coveted majority." This, I think, underestimates the power of ideology and rhetoric to define the values not only of the led but of the leaders themselves. The actions of the Athenian politician were so carefully scrutinized, the privileges granted him so provisional, that he was constrained to act and speak in the best interests of the masses or not at all. No orator was given much of a chance to "howl with the democratic wolves" unless he could also sing a pleasant tune with a meaningful libretto. No orator was delegated true power before he had proved the sincerity of his patriotic adhesion to the principles of the democratic state.

The Athenian system for controlling elite politicians worked precisely because it was based on a series of contradictions. The orator had to be simultaneously of the elite and of the mass, and he was expected to prove his membership in both on a regular basis. The contradictions implicit in Athenian mass-elite ideology are exemplified in the intertwining meanings of *charis* ["gratitude, kindness, goodwill"]: the wealthy orator gave material gifts to the people, protected them by attacking their enemies, worked hard to provide them with good advice, and hence they were grateful to him. But he was also grateful to them: every time they gave him their attention when he spoke in public, voted for him in a political trial or for a proposal he supported in the Assembly, or allowed him to profit materially by his political position, the orator was put in the demos' debt. *Charis* bound orator and audience together by reciprocal ties of obligation. But *charis* and the bonds it engendered could be dangerous. The orator who spoke only in order to please and win *charis* betrayed his function and *harmed* the people by binding them to himself: hence Aeschines' and Demosthenes' reiteration of the pun on *charis* (and its cognates) and *cheiroō*: to take someone prisoner.

The contrariness of the expectations placed on the political orator clearly benefited the demos. Politicians competed for popular favor in public contests which were played according to certain conventions, but the details of the rules remained vague: when was *charis* good and when was it bad? when would an elitist claim be suitable and when would it constitute evidence of secret demos-hating tendencies? when should one praise the citizens and when should one castigate them? None of the answers were spelled out, and so politicians always operated from a position of uncertainty. When the rules of a contest are ill defined, its judge is given a wide interpretive scope. The masses set the rules and always acted as combined referee and scorekeeper; the vague and internally contradictory rules they devised for those who would play the game of political influence allowed the demos to reserve for itself the right to cast its own judgments according to its own lights—and hence to keep control of the state. . . .

The most obvious manifestation of the power of the Athenian citizenry was the franchise. But ballot power was not the ultimate key to the success of the Athenian democracy. The modern world offers examples of states run by narrow elites in which a very high percentage of the citizenry votes in elections: voting is relatively meaningless when there are no genuine choices or when the results of the decision are unimportant. As noted above, it is unlikely that more than one- or two-fifths of the Athenian demos voted upon even the most important matters, and the demos itself remained "imagined" in that all franchise holders never assembled together in one place. On the other hand, every citizen who communicated with other citizens participated, directly or indirectly, in the creation and maintenance of the political ideology of the state. Consequently, the will of the entire "imagined" demos was manifest in the decisions of Assemblies and juries.

A democratic constitution creates an environment in which the masses *may* be presented with real alternatives and so have the chance to make real decisions. But only mass control of political ideology will ensure that elite advisers and leaders present to the voters real alternatives on important issues. Even in the direct democracy of Athens, many decisions, some of them very important (e.g., by ambassadors and by generals in the field), were in fact made by elites. Voting in the Assembly and courts may, therefore, have been most important as an enforcement mechanism, a means of reward and punishment, by which the masses reined in the tendency of elite political experts to diverge from the interests of the masses. The control of ideology was the key, voting merely the means of maintaining that control.

The overriding importance of the popular control of the ideological climate of opinion, along with the ambivalent and contradictory nature of Athenian political ideology, render futile any attempts to explain the Athenian polity in terms of law and constitution alone. The processes of social and political control described here were orderly and efficient only in the long run; they were not rational in origin. Consequently, ancient political philosophers tended to scorn the democracy as based on irrational principles. Much of the confusion in modern debates over the Athenian conception of freedom and the locus of sovereignty in the state seems also to be the result of misguided attempts to find an ordering principle that would render Athenian thought and governmental practice rational and internally consistent. Most Athenians were burdened by no such obsession. They tolerated a degree of inconsistency in their legal and political systems, because too much order was inimical to continued mass rule.

Some important "checks and balances" existed within the Athenian legal and political systems, but of more fundamental importance was the sociopolitical balance achieved on the symbolic plane. The demos ruled, not so much because of its constitutional "sovereignty," as because of its control over significant aspects of the symbolic universe of the Athenian political community. Athenian democracy—like all other forms of political organization—was predicated on and functioned through a network of symbols. At Athens, the key symbols were both revealed and generated through the two-way communication of public speech. Rhetorical communication between masses and elites, expressed through an increasingly rich vocabulary of topoi and images, was a primary means by which the strategic ends of social stability and political order were achieved. Communication was the tool the political equals used to exert their ideological hegemony over both social and political elites.

Athenian public rhetoric—with its complex mix of elitist and egalitarian tactics—was a key form of democratic discourse. It stood in the place of an abstract theory of democracy and made theory unnecessary to the participants. It was arguably the failure of the elite to control political ideology that led them to devise and write formal political theory which would explain what was wrong with the system they failed to dominate. The thesis that the masses controlled the upper classes through ideological means also inverts the traditional Marxist approach to ideology and raises the possibility that lower classes can achieve major changes in the organization of society without overt struggle on the material plane. Hence, the assessment of the nature of Athenian democracy offered here may present an alternative to both ancient and Marxist—as well as to modern elitist—conclusions on the fundamental relationship between politics and society.

Finally, the conclusions arrived at in this book may be seen as challenging the view that democracy never achieved a language or conceptual system independent of aristocratic ideas. Democracy did, I

believe, have its own language, created by the invention of new words
(e.g., *dēmokratia, isonomia*), transvaluation of existing terms (*isēgoria,
plēthos* ["mass, majority"]), subversion and appropriation of the terminology and ideals of the aristocrats (*kalokagathia* ["nobility"], *aretē*
["excellence"]), but above all by the elaboration of the vocabulary of
rhetorical topoi and images described in the preceding chapters. As
long as the demos remained arbiter of public opinion and policy, the
word *dēmokratia* was a name for a political society and culture in
which the most basic and elemental human power—the power to as-
sign meanings to symbols—belonged to the people.

Mogens Herman Hansen

Democracy as an Ideology

Mogens Herman Hansen, Reader in Greek at the University of Copenhagen
and Director of the Copenhagen Polis Centre, has published numerous
works on the subjects of Athenian government and legal procedure, including a treatment of *The Athenian Democracy in the Age of Demosthenes*. In
the following selection from that work, Hansen argues for the "close affinity"
ideologically between Athenian *demokratia* and modern democracy. Using
evidence drawn from fifth- and fourth-century sources (including the fourth-
century orators Isokrates, Aischines, and Demosthenes), Hansen maintains
that the Athenians did possess the concepts of personal liberty and political
equality usually associated with modern democratic regimes.

Nowadays democracy is both a political system and a political ideology. What links the two is the conviction that democratic ideals are
promoted by democratic institutions more than by any other kind of

government. Exactly the same two facets are to be seen in the ancient concept of democracy, which meant on the one hand "government of the people" in the political sense and on the other the ideals characteristic of such a "government of the people" (Arist. *Pol.* 1310a 28–33). The democratic institutions of Athens supplied the framework for a democratic ideology centred, as both supporters and opponents unanimously admitted, on the notions of freedom, equality and the pursuit of happiness. Where the two sides differed was in their *valuation* of this ideology, as two quotations make clear.

In Perikles' funeral speech Thucydides gives him the . . . famous characterization of the Athenian constitution [see Thuc. 2.37.1–3, above]. . . . Two generations later Isokrates in his *Areopagitikos* supplies a sour gloss to those same idealizing sentiments: the ancestors, he says, didn't have a *politeia* that "brought up the citizens to think that unrestraint was democracy and lawlessness liberty and saying what you please equality, and that the licence to do all those things was happiness" (7.20). Comparison of the two texts shows that the "pursuit of happiness" in Isokrates corresponds to what Thucydides says about freedom in the pursuits of daily life. The three ideals are thus in fact two: liberty (subdivided into liberty in the political sphere and liberty in the personal sphere) and equality.

Another concept often treated separately from liberty and equality in modern discussions is the "rule of law." Democrats, in open polemic against supporters of the other two types of constitution, tried to monopolize that particular high ground, as can be seen from a passage in Aischines:

> It is acknowledged that there are three kinds of politeia in all the world, tyranny and oligarchy and democracy. Tyrannies and oligarchies are governed at the whim of the rulers, but democratic states are governed by the established laws. And as you are well aware, Athenians, in a democracy it is the laws that protect the individual and the politeia, whereas the tyrant and the oligarch are protected by mistrust and armed bodyguards. Oligarchs, and those who run unequal states, have to guard themselves against those who would overthrow the state by force: you who have an equal state based on the law have to punish those who speak or have led their lives contrary to the laws (1.4–5).

What Aischines says shows that the "rule of (democratic) law" is conceived as an aspect of democratic equality, so it remains the case that the basic ideals are really just two, freedom and equality. *Demokratia, eleutheria* and *to ison* ["the equal, equality"] were a kind of trio (Plato *Rep.* 563B; Isoc. 7.20; Arist. *Pol.* 1310a 28–33) in Athenian political ideology like democracy, liberty and equality in the liberal-democratic ideology of the nineteenth and twentieth centuries.

Liberty

The fundamental democratic ideal, then, was *eleutheria*, liberty, which had two aspects: political liberty to participate in the democratic institutions, and private liberty to live as one pleased. The dual nature of *eleutheria* is most clearly described by Aristotle in the *Politics*:

> A basic principle of the democratic constitution is liberty. That is commonly said, and those who say it imply that only in this constitution do men share in liberty; for that, they say, is what every democracy aims at. Now, one aspect of liberty is being ruled and ruling in turn. . . . Another element is to live as you like. For this, they say, is what being free is about, since its opposite, living not as you like, is the condition of a slave. So this is the second defining principle of democracy, and from it has come the ideal of not being ruled, not by anybody at all if possible, or at least only in turn (Arist. Pol. 1317a40–b17).

Aristotle's description of democratic liberty is stated in general terms and there is no explicit reference to Athens, but all the sources show that in this respect the Athenians conformed to the norm (Plato *Rep.* 557B; *Def.* 412D; Isoc. 7.20). The ideal "to live as one pleases" is praised as a fundamental democratic value by Otanes in the Constitutional Debate in Herodotos (3.83.2–3: see Part VII), by Athenian statesmen in Thucydides' speeches (2.37.2, 7.69.2), and by the orators in the speeches they delivered before the People's Court (Lysias 26.5). And "to rule in turn" is singled out by King Theseus in Euripides' *Suppliant Women* as an essential feature of Athenian democracy (*Supp.* 406–8: see Part IV; Isoc. 20.20). . . .

[However, it] is often said that *eleutheria* was basically different from modern liberty because the principal aspect of being *eleutheros* was to be free as opposed to being a slave. That is true, and modern studies confirm that *eleutheria* in the sense of self-determination was rooted in the opposition free/slave, whereas the modern concept of liberty does not have slavery as its antonym (except in a metaphorical sense). But *eleutheria* had different shades of meaning according to context; at least three different meanings are attested in the sources in three different contexts, social, political and constitutional.

> 1   *Eleutheros* in the sense of being free as opposed to being a slave applied both to citizens and to foreigners, and it applied to all types of city-state, since slaves existed in all poleis independent of their constitutions (Arist. *Pol.* 1326a 18–20).

> 2   *Eleutheros* in the sense of autonomous as against being dominated by others was of course esteemed in both oligarchies and democracies. Of the thirty-one poleis that fought for freedom against the barbarians in the Persian Wars (Meiggs–Lewis 27; Hdt. 7.178.2), most were oligarchies. . . . *Eleutheria* in the sense of *autonomia* was the freedom of the polis, which is different from freedom *within* the *polis*.

> 3   As a constitutional concept, however, *eleutheria* was associated both with political participation in the public sphere and with personal freedom in the private sphere. Two considerations will suffice to show that *eleutheria* in the constitutional sense was different from *eleutheria* in the social sense (free versus slave) and in the political sense (city autonomy). First, as a constitutional ideal *eleutheria* was specifically democratic and not a value praised in oligarchies or monarchies. . . . Second, as a democratic ideal eleutheria (in the sense of personal freedom) applied not only to citizens, but also to metics and sometimes even to slaves [see Ps. Xen. *Const.* 1.8, 12, above]. . . .

To sum up, the social, political and constitutional meanings of *eleutheros* were interconnected and the idea of self-determination lies behind them all (Democritus DK 68 fr. 251), but the sources show that Greek democrats distinguished constitutional liberty from liberty in the two other senses and imposed the distinction on the rest, by inducing aristocrats and oligarchs to hate *eleutheria* as a mistaken democratic value.

Another alleged difference between individual liberty in ancient Athens and in modern liberal thought lies in the principles and arguments used to justify it. In modern democratic thought liberty is about the protection of individual rights against infringements by the state or by other people, whereas, it is held, Athenian liberty was not based on a clear notion of individual rights. Again, the sources support a rather different view.

Several of the orators state with approval the rule that no citizen could be executed without due process of law (Isoc. 15.22; Lys. 22.2). . . . Another rule forbade torture of Athenian citizens (Andoc. 1.43). It was warranted by a decree (*psephisma*) probably passed immediately after the expulsion of the tyrants in 510/9 before the introduction of the democracy. It was nevertheless adopted by the democrats and, like the expulsion of the tyrants, was later associated with democracy. The principle that free men are exempt from corporal punishment is closely connected with democracy in Demosthenes' speech against Androtion (Dem. 22.55).

The Athenian democracy further provided some protection of a citizen's home. Demosthenes was severely criticized by Aischines for breaking into a house and arresting the alleged traitor, Antiphon, without a warrant, i.e., a *psephisma* of the people (Dem. 18.132), and in the Assembly Aischines got his way and secured the man's release. . . .

Finally in Aristotle's *Constitution of Athens* we are told that, "as soon as the archon enters upon his office, he proclaims through the public herald that whatever a person possessed before he entered upon his archonship he will have and possess until the end of his term" (Arist. *Const.* 56.2). Like the ban on torture of citizens, this is probably a survival from the sixth century . . . [and was] understood as a guarantee that no redistribution of property would take place in Athens, as happened in other Greek *poleis*.

In addition to the protection of person, home and property, the most treasured of individual rights is freedom of speech, cherished by democrats but suppressed by supporters of authoritarian rule. Once more we find the same ideal in democratic Athens (Eur. *Hippolytos* 421–3; Dem. 45.79; *Ep.* 3.13), as in Demosthenes' remark that a basic difference between Spartan oligarchy and Athenian democracy is that in Athens you are free to praise the Spartan constitution and way of life, if you so wish, whereas in Sparta it is prohibited to praise any other constitution than the Spartan (Dem. 20.105–8). The trial of Sokrates is evidence that the Athenians, for once, did not live up to their owns ideals (Hyp. fr. 59; Aischin. 1.173), but the sentence passed on Sokrates is unparalleled in the history of Athenian democracy. A decree prohibiting the ridiculing of individuals in comedies was passed in 440 but abrogated four years later (Schol. Ar. *Ach.* 67; Schol. *Av.* 1297), and the decree of Diopeithes, of about the same date, which laid down that there should be a criminal prosecution of "atheists or astronomers" (Plut. *Per.* 32.2) may have led to a trial of Anaxagoras (Diod. 12.39.2; Diog. Laert. 2.12ff.; Plut. *Per.* 32.5; see Part VI). The evidence for the other public prosecutions of philosophers for impiety—the trial of Protagoras, for instance—is anecdotal and dangerous to rely on without confirmation, and even the trial of Anaxagoras is not above suspicion (Arist. fr. 67; Timon fr. 3): after Sokrates it was an accolade for a philosopher to be charged with impiety, and the Hellenistic biographers were eager to bestow the honour on quite a few of Sokrates' contemporaries.

It is not enough, however, to have laws and regulations protecting the citizens: there must also be ways of enforcing them when infringed by the democratic *polis* itself and its officials. Consequently the Athenians provided for both public and private prosecution of magistrates [through methods including private suits against magistrates and *euthynae*]. . . .

The champions of Athenian democracy emphasized that citizens were protected by the rule of law, and preferred to blame cases of violation on the magistrates and political leaders rather than the *demos* or the *polis* itself. An obvious example is Aischines' praise of the rule of law in democratic Athens quoted above (1.4–5). . . . In oligarchies and tyrannies citizens are exposed to the whims of their rulers; in democracies the laws protect the citizens. Against whom? Obviously against the political leaders and the magistrates, who must respect the democratic laws in their dealings with the citizens.

Public and Private

Like modern liberty, ancient democratic *eleutheria* had two sides: it was both freedom to participate in political life and freedom from political oppression. As has often been noted, these two aspects of liberty are mutually exclusive, for "to rule in turn" implies being sometimes ruled, so that if we maximize the principle of "not being ruled" there is no room left for political decision-making in which to participate. The two opposed aspects of freedom are, however, compatible, but only if combined with a distinction between a public sphere, in which political freedom operates, and a private sphere, in which personal freedom is protected against interference by the state as well as by other people. The separation between a public and a private sphere is well known in the modern world, where it is a basic condition of democratic liberty; but did the Athenians recognize a private sphere in which the *polis* did not interfere but allowed the citizens to live as they pleased? . . .

Athenian sources debating about society regularly contrast the public and the private: what is *idion* ["private"] is set off against what is *demosion* ["public"] or *koinon* ["common"] (Thuc. 2.37.1–2; Dem. 20.136). The dichotomy of public and private is apparent in all aspects of life. The private person (*idiotes*) is opposed to the politically active citizen (Aischin. 1.195; Hyp. 3.27); citizens' homes to public buildings (Dem. 3.25–9, Arist. *Pol.* 1321b 19–23), the national interest to private profit (Xen. *Hell.* 1.4.13; Dem. 19.1); public finance to private means (Isoc. 7.24; Din. 2.18); private litigation to administration of justice in public actions (Pl. *Euthphr.* 2A; Dem. 46.26 [quoting a *nomos*]). Finally, the laws of the city are often subdivided into private (regulating the relations of private persons) and public (concerning the activities of government agencies: Dem. 24.192–3; 18.210).

Thus, the Athenians did distinguish a public sphere from a private sphere; but a note of warning is in order: the Athenian distinction is between the private (*to idion*) and the public (*to koinon* or *demosion*), which is not quite the same as our opposition between the individual and the state. . . . [I]n the Greek sources, the public sphere is most identified with the *polis* (Is. 7.30; Dem. 20.57), whereas the private sphere is sometimes a social sphere without any emphasis on the individual: family life, business, industry and many types of religious association belonged in the private and not in the public sphere. The Athenians distinguished between the individual as a private person and the individual as a citizen rather than between the individual and the state. Thus, instead of *individual* freedom, it is preferable to speak about *personal* or *private* freedom, which was often individual in character, but not invariably so.

The point was made earlier that the public sphere (i.e., the *polis* sphere) was specifically a *political* sphere: the *polis* did not regulate all matters but only a limited range of social activities, and matters such as education, industry, agriculture and trade were left to private enterprise. But, further, Athenians were regularly allowed to think and say what they liked about anything, as long as they did not, for example, profane the Mysteries, or, without due permission, form new cults and religious societies (Hyp. frr. 202–10). That is not denied by those historians who emphasize the omnipotence of the *polis*, but they counter it by another observation: if the Athenians in their Assembly *decided* to interfere with education, production, or whatever, they were entitled to do so, and no one could plead that it was a violation of individual rights. Similarly, the people could at any time impose restrictions on freedom of speech, and sometimes did. So "there were no theoretical limits to the power of the state, no activity, no sphere of human behaviour, in which the state could not legitimately intervene" [M. I. Finley]. But that correct observation ought not to be invoked to establish a difference between ancient and modern democratic ideology, because precisely the same observation applies, for example, to modern Britain: no aspect of human life is *in principle* outside the powers of Parliament and there is no constitutional protection of individual rights, though in practice they are highly regarded and mostly respected.

Not only was the public sphere a political sphere; the majority of the inhabitants of Attica were excluded from it, for the Greek *polis* was a community of citizens only. Metics and slaves lived in the *polis* without being members of it. Freedom to participate in the democratic institutions applied only to citizens and only in the political sphere. Private freedom, however, to live as one pleased, applied to all who lived in Athens, including metics and sometimes slaves. According to the critics of democracy that kind of freedom was extended even to women (Pl. *Rep.* 563A–C), but that shocking charge was, of course, denied by the champions of the Athenian constitution (Thuc. 2.45.2).

Equality

For equality the Athenians had several terms, all compounds beginning with *iso-*. They include *isonomia* (equal political rights: Isoc. 7.20), *isegoria* (equal right to address the political assemblies: Dem. 15.18), *isogonia* (equality of birth: Pl. *Menex.* 239A) and *isokratia* (equality of power: Hdt. 5.92.1a). Historians agree that equality in Athens was a purely political concept that never spread to the social and economic spheres. Equal distribution of land and cancellation of debts, for example, were hotly debated questions in other Greek city-states, but never in democratic Athens (cf. Dem. 24.149). Once again, it is worth noting, a basic democratic value was restricted to the political sphere and did not apply outside it.

But what did political equality mean to the Athenians, and what does it mean today? In Western political thought there is a conflict between two different views of political equality. One view is that all men *are* essentially and by nature equal—that is, alike—and therefore all are entitled to an equal share of everything; the other is that all men *should* have equal opportunities—that is, should be all in a line at the starting-point. The first view is partly descriptive, i.e., an equality of nature is asserted in order to justify an equality of rights; the second view is purely prescriptive and claims on moral grounds an equality of opportunities, which—by the way—is perfectly compatible with an inequality of nature. . . . Historians discussing equality in democratic Athens hardly ever raise the question of whether the Athenian ideal was natural or normative equality; but the sources show that the Athenians were well aware of the distinction and that it was one of the main points in the debate for or against democracy. Critics of democracy, especially the philosophers, imputed to the democrats a descriptive interpretation of equality, as in Book 5 of Aristotle's *Politics*: "Democracy arose from the idea that those who are equal in any respect are equal absolutely. All are alike free, therefore they claim that all are free absolutely. . . . The next is when the democrats, on the ground that they are all equal, claim equal participation in everything" (*Pol.* 1301a 28–35; Pl. *Menex.* 239A). Democrats themselves, however, stressed the other aspect of equality: that all men must have equal rights in order to have equal opportunities, as in the passage from Perikles' funeral speech quoted above; and the same thought is expressed by Euripides in *The Suppliant Women* (see Part IV). . . .

Admittedly, the democratic principle of "one man one vote," the *isopsephos polis* as Euripides says (*Supp.* 353), implies some kind of natural equality: all Athenians are so intelligent and valuable as human beings that they can (and ought to) be given an equal share in political decision-making. Hence, modern historians tend to emphasize *isonomia* as the central aspect of democratic equality and of democratic ideology altogether. But the term *isonomia* is poorly attested in classical Athens. . . . [Hansen notes that *isonomia* is only mentioned by one Athenian orator (Isoc. 7.20–21), was not used as a name for Athenian warships (as were *Demokratia*, *Eleutheria*, and *Parrhesia* ["free speech"]) and was not represented as a goddess (as was Demokratia), then continues . . .] When Herodotos describes the birth of Athenian democracy it is *isegoria* and not *isonomia* that he singles out as the principal form of democratic equality (5.78.1), and his account conforms with what we find in Athenian sources: the aspect of equality most cherished by the Athenian democrats was *isegoria*, not *isonomia*. Now, whereas *isonomia* may imply natural equality as well as equality of opportunity, *isegoria* is really about equality of opportunity. No Athenian expected that every one of the 6000 citizens who attended a meeting of the Assembly could—or would—address his fellow citizens. *Isegoria* was not for everyone, but for anyone who cared to exercise his political rights. Each citizen must have equal opportunity to demonstrate his excellence, but he deserved reward according to what he actually achieved. That is the argument in Perikles' funeral speech (Thuc. 2.37.1) and in the speech given to Athenagoras, the democratic leader in Syracuse (Thuc. 6.39.1), and it is abundantly attested in the innumerable honorary decrees: in the Athenian democracy the indispensable political initiative was stimulated by ambition (*philotimia*: Dem. 10.71) and competition (*hamilla*: Dem. 20.108, 18.320), neither of which is compatible with natural equality. For the Athenians competition was an essential aspect of life in politics as well as in sport, and the quality that mattered was, as in sport, that all must start in line, not that all were essentially equal.

Selection by lot was believed to be a more "democratic" method of appointment than election. Modern historians often connect the democratic preference for sortition with the democratic belief in equality: but, once again, it is only the critics of democracy who connected sortition with equality (Isoc. 7.21–2; Pl. *Lg.* 757B), whereas the democrats themselves seem to have preferred sortition not because of its being the obvious method of selection when all are alike, but because it safeguarded the powers of the people, prevented conflict and counteracted corruption.

There is one more aspect of political equality to discuss: equality before the law (Thuc. 2.37.1; Eur. *Supp.* 429–34). That is sometimes overlooked by historians, or only briefly described, perhaps because no slogan was coined for it as in the case of *isegoria* and *isonomia*. Equality before the law is mostly described in langauge using the adjective *isos* instead of an abstract noun. It is, however, a very important concept for the understanding of the Athenian democratic ideology and is a matter of normative, not natural, equality. The essence of it is that, however men may differ in wealth, power, social status, cleverness or eloquence, all ought to be equally treated by the laws (Dem. 23.86) and by the jurors responsible for the meting out of justice (Dem. 18.6–7). In clear opposition to oligarchy, the emphasis of democrats is regularly on the distinction between the rich and the poor, who are said to deserve the same legal protection as the rich (Dem. 51.11; Isoc. 20.20). Equality before the law is closely connected with the rule of law as the distinguishing mark of democracy as against oligarchy or monarchy (Aischin. 1.5; Dem. 21.188; 25.16).

The upshot of our discussion is that equality of nature was never an integral aspect of Athenian democratic ideology. It was imputed to the democrats by philosophers, but the various aspects of equality invoked by democrats themselves were conceived of as equality of rights, by which all citizens might obtain equal opportunities and equal legal protection.

Liberty and Equality

In political theory there is often an inherent opposition between equality and liberty. But conflict develops only if equality is taken descriptively: if all, because they are by nature alike, ought to be treated equally in all respects, there is no longer liberty for anybody to develop and assert his personal merits. If, on the other hand, equality is understood in the sense of "equality of opportunity," there is no opposition between liberty and equality; all men must be free and have equal opportunity to develop their talents.

The connection between liberty and equality can also be established in another way. An analysis of equality inevitably leads to the question: equality of what? The answer given by liberal democrats in modern Europe has been "equality of liberty": the two concepts have tended to coalesce. A similar convergence of liberty and equality can be found in Greek democratic political theory. Rotation, for example, "to rule and be ruled," is connected sometimes with liberty but sometimes with equality (Arist. *Pol.* 1317a 40, 1332b 25). In Euripides' *Suppliant Women* everyone's right to address the people is described first as liberty but a few lines later as equality (438, 441). Similarly, *isegoria* is linked with *eleutheria* in Herodotos' description of Kleisthenes (Hdt. 5.78.1), and everyone's right to say what he believes (*parrhesia*) is linked with liberty in Plato's *Republic*, but with equality in the pamphlet of the Old Oligarch (Pl. *Rep.* 557B; Ps.-Xen. *Const.* 1.12). The constant interplay of the two concepts is characteristic of Athenian democratic ideology and shows, once again, the close affinity between

modern democracy and Athenian *demokratia* looked at as a political
ideology rather than as a set of political institutions.

Paul Rahe

Athens' Illiberal Democracy

Paul Rahe, who holds the J. P. Walker Chair in American History at the
University of Tulsa, has argued for the "primacy of politics" in classical
Greek society. He recently authored the massive tome *Republics Ancient
and Modern*, which traces the idea of republicanism from the Greek polis
through the modern age. In this selection from that work, Rahe emphasizes those aspects of Athenian democracy its supporters often minimize
or neglect, including its litigious, martial, and "illiberal" nature.

Plato was not the first to judge Athens deficient in reverence, shame,
and *philía* ["friendly love"]. In the last years of the Peloponnesian
War, Pericles' like-named son appears similarly to have lost faith in the
democracy. His father had been prepared to compare his own city favorably with Sparta. He had celebrated her openness to the world, the
absence of a civic regimen, and the citizens' penchant for overlooking
one another's foibles, and he had asserted that his countrymen displayed on the battlefield an inborn valor in no way inferior to the
courage which the Lacedaemonians learned through military drill
and incessant toil. The great statesman had even argued that the city's
comparatively tolerant demeanor in no way prevented a salutary dread
from governing his compatriots' conduct in the public realm. But
where the older Pericles had been inclined to exalt the city of Athena,

his son seems to have despaired of the Athenians' lack of *homónoia* ["likemindedness"]. "Instead of working together for what is of advantage to themselves," he reportedly complained, "they are more abusive of each other and more envious among themselves than they are towards other human beings. In both public and private gatherings, they are the most quarrelsome of men; they most often bring each other to trial; and they would rather take advantage of each other than profit by cooperative aid. They treat public affairs (*tà koiná*) as matters foreign to themselves, and yet fight battles over these concerns and take the greatest pleasure in processing the faculties for such strife" [Xen. *Mem.* 3.5.16–17].

There is every reason to take this description of the ethos of late fifth-century Athens at face value. In the elder Pericles' day, Thucydides tells us, the city was extraordinarily well governed, for that statesman was a man of "rank, intelligence, and evident integrity" who proved capable of "restraining the people in the manner of a free man." Because his motives were known to be worthy, Pericles had no need to say anything solely in order to please the *dêmos* . . . But Pericles died not long after the war had begun. In that regard, he betrayed a lack of [foresight], for he made no provision for his own replacement. Among those who sought to fill his place, there was no one of comparable stature, intelligence, and integrity. They were, in fact, "more or less equal to one another"; and in the contest for preeminence, they conducted the city "in accord with popular pleasure and turned affairs over to the *dêmos*." These men were driven by "private ambition and a concern for personal profit," and in pursuing "private vendettas arising from their struggle for the leadership of the people," they brought harm to the city and its allies, impairing the Athenians' capacity to resist the Peloponnesian foe, inspiring *stásis*, and ultimately bringing the city to its knees [Thuc. 2.65].

In their private affairs, the Athenians were as quarrelsome and combative as they were in public. Among other things, they were notoriously ready to drag one another into court. And, as Theophrastus intimates, this is precisely what one would expect, for there is a connection between slander and backbiting on the one hand and freedom of speech, democracy, and liberty on the other. It would be easy to suppose that the city of Athena had somehow become an open society . . . and it is not at all surprising that, in the wake of the French Revolution, Athens was romanticized and came to represent in the eyes of many the modern, liberal democratic ideal. In our own day, especially among students of the classics, this vision retains considerable force. Athens has even been represented as the primitive, premodern prototype of a working-class democracy.

And yet nothing could be further from the truth. The ancient democracies were, as Tocqueville remarked, "aristocracies of masters," and Athens was no exception. . . . The "universal suffrage" which Athens extended to all adult, male citizens did not decisively set her apart from the less democratic regimes. The difference was simply a matter of degree. In the end, Athens's acceptance of slavery and its prevalence there made of that ancient city "an aristocratic republic"—albeit one "in which all the nobles had an equal right to the government." Despite the growth of the market economy and the concentration of population in the town of Athens and in the port community that grew up at the Peiraeus, the ordinary Athenian remained a peasant smallholder caught up in village life and intent on achieving a measure of self-sufficiency; and partly as a consequence of the campaigns against Persia, the incessant wars elsewhere, and the plentiful supply and low price of slaves, he seems to have been at least as well situated to become a slaveowner as his counterpart the dirt farmer of the American South. Whether slavery dominated the productive sector of the economy or not is and will remain an open question. But, in the end, the answer is of no great importance, for there is no reason to suppose that the mode of production is the only or even the most important force shaping the ethos of a society. What matters in this case is that, like their counterparts among the free white population in the American South, ordinary Athenians could and did take their own measure by comparing themselves favorably with the multitude of slaves in their midst.

Democracy stood, in antiquity, for a limited extension of the circle of loyalty, not for a principled abandonment of the aristocratic sense of inborn superiority. The Athenians not only owned barbarian slaves in considerable numbers and excluded them from all participation in self-determination; they did so without any indication that they doubted the justice of their subjection. Furthermore, by the second half of the fifth century, they had transformed into a great empire of their own a league originally founded to defend the Greeks against Persia's appetite for dominion. The citizens of Athens ruled—and even boasted that they ruled—over an extraordinary number of their fellow Hellenes. As they were more than willing to acknowledge, this, too, involved a form of mastery and servitude. No Athenian would have denied the accuracy of James Madison's claim that "the money with which Pericles decorated Athens, was raised by Aristides on the confederates of Athens for common defence, and on pretext of danger at Delos which was the common depository, removed to Athens, where it was soon regarded as the tribute of inferiors instead of the common property of associates, and applied by Pericles accordingly." Few seem to have worried that their dominion was unjust. The very fact that their allies tolerated this appropriation of the league monies was proof positive that these confederates were, indeed, inferiors and deserving of subjection. In short, the exercise of imperial dominion had much the same effect on Athenian morals and manners as slavery itself. . . .

There were, to be sure, other, more egalitarian influences on the ethos of Athens. Some Athenians did owe their livelihood to the despised professions of trade and industry. But, for the most part, these bourgeois pursuits were left in the hands of metics—and like the Jews of medieval Europe, these immigrants were kept on the periphery of the community: they were denied participation in politics, were refused the privilege of owning landed property, and were subjected to a resident alien's tax as a reminder of their low status. Circumstances and the atmosphere created by democracy rendered the city of Athena somewhat more cosmopolitan than the other cities of Greece. At Athens, in the classical period, as at Sparta, even the rich were plainly dressed. On the streets, we are told, one could hardly distinguish a citizen from a metic or slave, and the Athenians tolerated in both a freedom of speech purportedly unknown even to citizens in other communities. But Athens's openness to the outsider should not be exaggerated: it was the radical democracy of the elder Pericles that tightened the requirements for citizenship, reacting to the permanent presence of immigrants in large numbers by insisting on the exclusion of their offspring from the political community and by reasserting with redoubled fervor the traditional emphasis on purity of blood. . . .

In the enforcement of morals, Athens was, at least when compared with other Greek *póleis*, quite notably lax. But the spirit that animated her regime was identical to that found elsewhere. Manliness and courage, public-spiritedness and piety—these were the standards by which the citizens as such were ultimately judged. James Madison summed up the difference between Sparta and Athens much as Plutarch had done: by juxtaposing not the goals but the approach taken by those who had framed laws for the two cities. "Lycurgus," he remarked, was "more true to his object," and he therefore placed himself "under the necessity of mixing a portion of violence with the authority of superstition; and of securing his final success, by a voluntary renunciation, first of his country, and then of his life." In contrast, "Solon . . . seems to have indulged a more temporising policy," for he "confessed that he had not given to his countrymen the government best suited to their happiness, but most tolerable to their prejudices.". . .

Like other cities, Athens gave women short shrift, relegating them almost entirely to the domestic sphere and, where economically feasible, confining them indoors. In recording a universally acknowledged matter of fact, one client of Demosthenes told a jury, "For the sake of pleasure, we have courtesans; for the body's daily care, we have concubines; and for bearing legitimate children and faithfully guarding what lies within our homes, we have wives." There was even a law at Athens disallowing wills made by those mentally incapacitated by insanity, old age, drugs, illness, or the influence of a woman.

Similarly, despite her much-touted love of novelty and her notorious openness to foreign cults, customs, and ways, Athens was by our standards quite conservative. Prior to the scientific revolution, what was fresh and new was but rarely thought improved: in Attic Greek, the word *néos*, when applied to an event, actually connotes that which is unexpected, strange, untoward, and evil. As one would then expect, Athens was intolerant of religious infractions: this was the *polis* that sentenced the popular general Alcibiades to death for parodying the Eleusinian Mysteries in a private home; this was the community that condemned the commanders victorious at Arginusae for failing to bury the citizen dead; and this was the city that executed Socrates for not believing in the city's gods and for corrupting the youth by teaching them the same doctrine.

It does not matter one whit that these particular prosecutions were politically motivated, as they all were. Nor does it matter that the contest for public offices and honors generally accounted for charges being brought against those such as Demosthenes' ally Timarchus who had continued to exercise their rights as citizens after purportedly allowing themselves to be used as women by other men. What counts above all else is that the rivals of Alcibiades, the opponents of the Arginusae generals, the enemies of Socrates, and the prosecutor of Timarchus had the religious and moral weapons ready to hand. No one—not even Socrates—ever dared to suggest that a man's religious beliefs and behavior were of no concern to the body politic, and no one argued that the city should concede full sexual freedom to all consenting adults. Not even in an emanation from its penumbra can one discern in the constitution of Athens a fundamental right to privacy. In that city, there were no effective institutional constraints on the exercise of popular will against those whose private demeanor had inspired public distrust; and to the best of our knowledge, none were ever even contemplated. Nor can one argue that these trials were isolated incidents. . . .

As citizens, the Athenians exercised collective sovereignty, but they were not endowed with guarantees of civil liberty. Indeed, the body politic possessed in ostracism an instrument specifically designed to provide for the decade-long banishment of men guilty of no crime but the arousal of popular envy, fear, and distaste. And when ostracism fell into abeyance, the popular courts remained fully capable of rigorously enforcing the citizen morality dictated by public opinion. . . .

It should not be surprising that Athenian defendants and plaintiffs displayed an almost obsessive penchant for introducing into their forensic orations matter extraneous to the issue in dispute but pertinent to the defense of their conduct in general. It made perfect sense for them to recount in detail the services that they had performed on the community's behalf. Under Athenian law, any citizen could lay charges, and political disputes often played themselves out as contests in court. Moreover, by the late fifth century, malicious prosecution was quite common; and rich men, because they were envied and because many were suspected of harboring a sympathy for oligarchical rule, were easy marks. Given the fact that orators were vulnerable to prosecution for accepting bribes and for making unlawful proposals and that the generals and the lesser magistrates were subject to an audit and judicial reckoning (*eúthuna*) at the end of their term of office, prudence dictated that the wealthy think hard before entering the political arena. In anticipation of the day when a sycophant could not be bought off, the prosperous were well advised to perform liturgies and other services designed to curry popular favor. For, given the great size of the juries, to go on trial before a court was, in effect, to be judged as a citizen by the city itself.

Benjamin Constant's analysis of the Athenian regime deserves heed. Athens did fail in practice to complete "the subjection of individual existence to the collective body"; she provided her citizens with much "greater individual liberty than Rome and Sparta"; and this phenomenon was intimately linked with the important role played by "commerce" and trade in her development. But by the same token, other aspects of Athenian life—the size of the polity, the laws and customs she inherited, the central importance accorded piety, the prevalence of slavery, the subjection of women, and the possession of an empire—served to make her illiberal not just in principle, but quite often in practice as well. . . . Athens was not a liberal democracy occasionally subject to fits of aberrant behavior; she was a military, moral, and religious community reduced by circumstances and by conscious decisions to an advanced state of disarray and decay.

Of course, one might wish to argue, as scholars caught up in the populist currents of our egalitarian age are wont to do, that the criticism leveled at Athens by Thucydides, the students of Socrates, Aristotle, and the other great thinkers of antiquity should be discounted as the antidemocratic posturings of embittered aristocrats deprived of what they take to be their birthright. Moreover, from the funeral oration of the elder Pericles, one could easily enough construct a defense of Athens' democracy against that critique. This defense would, however, give cold comfort to those tempted to envisage Athens as a liberal regime. If Thucydides' report is to be trusted, Pericles did project a vision of an Athenian people tolerant of unorthodox and hedonistic behavior in private life. But in the same breath he asserted that they were still governed by dread (*déos*) and by shame (*aischúnē*) in their conduct of public affairs. He acknowledged their cultivation of the arts but denied that it resulted in extravagance, and he praised them for their love of intellectual speculation, but only because this never reduced them to cowardly softness.

Pericles' Athens was, by his own later admission, a tyrant *pólis*—the unwanted mistress of a great empire. . . . This Athens was a community of soldiers, not a bourgeois society of men "absorbed in the pursuits of gain, and devoted to the improvements of agriculture and commerce." Pericles' Athenians did not disguise their disdain for men of this stripe. "We do not think that a man who takes no part in politics is 'a man who minds his own business (*apragmon*),'" the statesman observed. "Alone we judge him utterly worthless."

This contemptuous aside was not just a passing remark. On a later occasion, Pericles discussed the *aprágmōn* once more and made his reasoning clear. "Men of this sort," he argued, "would quickly destroy a city—here, if they persuaded others; elsewhere, if they set up an independent town for themselves. For 'the man who minds his own business' is saved only where posted with the man of action; and to seek safety in servitude, while it might suffice in a subject community, would not be of advantage in an imperial city." Empire defined the Athens of Pericles. Empire constituted its greatness. Empire enabled it to become what Homer had once been: "the education of Hellas.". . .

The emphasis on honor and shame runs through the entire [Funeral Oration]. Yet on the closely related subject of piety, Pericles is strangely silent. Despite the solemnity of the occasion, he apparently made no mention of the gods and heroes of the land; and though the circumstances were propitious, he neglected the opportunity for reasserting the ancestral and religious foundations of the community's solidarity in the war then under way. When Pericles did allude to the public sacrifices and to the festival games, he treated these religious events as entertainments adding to the dignity and pleasure of citizen life, not as ceremonies constituting the city's divine service. There is much to link Pericles' celebrated address with the orations delivered in Athens on similar occasions. But in its disdain for tradition and in its celebration of all that is recent in Athenian life, the great statesman's speech stands in stark contrast to the conventional rhetoric with which the Athenians were familiar. . . .

Pericles [in a later speech] was willing to contemplate the city's demise; he contended that even the annihilation of Athens would leave intact and unimpaired the golden memory of what her citizens had done [see Thuc. 2.64 in Part III below]. . . .

One would be hard pressed to imagine an address more warlike in tone. It is no wonder that Alexander Hamilton denounced the republics of antiquity as "an infinity of little jealous, clashing, tumultuous commonwealths, the wretched nurseries of unceasing discord." No modern liberal, acting in a manner consistent with liberal principles, could ever choose to defend a democratic regime in Periclean terms. And yet, as David Hume points out, the great statesman's panegyric of the city was, at least in this respect, typically Athenian.

The illiberal character of the vision which Pericles projected cannot be gainsaid, but one must wonder whether Athens ever actually achieved that at which her greatest statesman evidently aimed. It is characteristic of human affairs that deeds nearly always fall short of the aspirations advertised in speech. If the women of that city were little noticed in public, the position of prominence they occupied within the comparatively invisible world of the household should generally have given them an emotional leverage enabling them to counter in some measure the Athenian fascination with public affairs, and it may have conferred on them a certain indirect, covert influence over the political behavior of their fathers, brothers, husbands, and sons. And yet, the natural allure of the domestic sphere seems to have counted for little when in competition with the erotic politics preached by Pericles—for if the ancient writers had been able to compare the politics of antiquity with those of our own time, there is one point on which they would have been agreed: the development of Athens' empire, the simultaneous and parallel elaboration of her democratic institutions, and the concomitant decay of the traditional ethos of reverence and shame really did unleash a mad and uncontrollable passion for dominion, for power, and for glory, one not just wholly foreign to the bourgeois temper of modern liberal democracy but, in fact, excessive even by the standards of ancient Greece.

Victor D. Hanson

Athens and Agricultural Government

Victor D. Hanson, Professor of Greek at California State University, Fresno, has written extensively about hoplite battle (see, e.g., his *The Western Way of War*), and on the role of the hoplite-farmer in Greek politics. In the middle-class Greek farmer, Hanson finds both the origins of the polis and of the egalitarian thought that has been so influential in the western tradition. In *The*

Other Greeks, Hanson argues for the agrarian nature and origins of the broad, property-based regimes ruling Greek *poleis.* At one end of this political spectrum ranging from democracy to moderate oligarchy, Athens eventually extended the franchise to all free citizens, whether they owned property or not. Meanwhile they excluded perhaps a larger number of non-citizens than other, ostensibly less democratic regimes. Hanson begins by discussing the property-based regimes ruling Greece before the fifth century B.C.

Besides the social protocols and occasional legal sanctions against the accumulation of land, early farmers quite soon sought more formal political power to ensure that the owners of small plots, the *klêroi* of the *polis,* could set the policies and direction of their agrarian communities. The ideology of and social pressure for small, equal-sized farms were transformed into formal law. As we have seen, throughout seventh and sixth century Greece, there was a gradual retrenchment on the part of the old landed aristocracies, themselves anachronisms from the pastoral baronies of the Dark Ages. In their place, broad-based timocracies, governments of property owners, based on wealth rather than absolutely on blood, gradually appeared. We must remember that the birth of constitutional government in the West was *not* an Athenian invention of the fifth century. It was a much earlier outgrowth of agrarianism, a prior effort to formalize and protect a landed egalitarianism. . . .

At the end of the seventh century in Athens, the career of Solon and his so-called legislation, as we have seen earlier, reflects a society in the midst of transition. It is difficult to generalize about the totality of agrarian reform attributed to Solon—laws regulating the export of olive oil, the planting of olive trees, the distribution of landed inheritance, and the like. But the traditional stories of his program do reveal comprehensive shifts in the Athenian economy, the planting of diversified crops, the plight of small farmers, the creation of nonaristocratic wealth, along with the necessary and concurrent efforts to broaden the political basis of an evolving society along nonaristocratic lines. To Solon, the *"dêmos"* was now to be the large group of citizens, quite distinct from the aristocratic elite. This new agrarian majority was to form the backbone of the *polis.* . . .

What should we call early agrarian governments of the seventh, sixth and early fifth centuries? Oligarchies? Timocracies? Democracies? Hoplite constitutions? Agrarian governments? Ancestral constitutions? Aristotle, writing late in the fourth century, was also perplexed by this admittedly gray (and changing) area between broad-based farm-owning "polities" and the later more radical democracies of his own time. After correlating the rise of hoplite infantry with the development of early Greek representative government, he writes: "Therefore, what we now label constitutional governments (*politeias*), the men of the past called democracies, but the early constitutional governments were of course oligarchical and royal, for, since populations were small, the middle class was not large" (*Pol.* 4.1297b24–7).

Even though Aristotle thought Solon had founded Athenian democracy, these original evolving polities, based on the expansion of a rural middle group, were never in truth democracies in the fifth-century Athenian sense. At least they were not popular constitutions where rule was by the entire *dêmos*, propertied and propertyless citizens alike. Instead, the native-born under "constitutional government" (*politeia*) who held no land were without much right to political participation. . . .

For some flavor of the politics of the Greek agrarian movement, we can return briefly to Aristotle, who, as we have seen, took up the question at length in his *Politics*. Although his purposes were philosophical, rather than historical or even ideological, his is nevertheless a gifted analysis of three centuries of earlier Greek political development. At least at one point Aristotle felt there had been among the city-states *four* different spectra of democracies, and also *four* distinguishable forms of oligarchy. From his lengthy discussion, it seems clear that when middling farmers were in control of a Greek *polis*, government was broad-based: it was representative of the economic interests of most of the citizenry; it was designed to follow the dictates of law; its legislation was primarily concerned with preservation of static, fixed plots among the landholding population. That was the entire principle behind agrarian constitutions.

Aristotle must hedge in defining precisely the differences between the inexact rubrics, "oligarchy" and "democracy." Either word could at times describe the agrarian government that he called "polity" (*Pol.* 4.1292b11–12). . . .

Perhaps to the modern mind, especially in the 1990s when the triumph of democracy appears to be widespread and enduring, agricultural government, agrarian "timocracy" with a property qualification, seems illiberal in its restrictiveness and discrimination against the landless poor. This exclusionary nature of agrarian government is quite undeniable. It is entirely in line with our portrait so far of the rise of intensive agriculture and the accompanying creation of a new chauvinistic class of agriculturalists. These were farmers neither extremely wealthy nor poor, who often composed only a third to half the citizen population.

But envision agrarian "democracy" within the context of the times. If representative government is defined merely by the requirements of voting and participation in officeholding—forgetting for the moment such legislative rights as free and unlimited speech, an absence of censorship, juries, fiscal accountability, subsidies for governmental participation, and the use of lots in magistracy selection—then the only form of government *more* representative of the people seems to be radical democracy of the type that emerged at Athens in the late fifth and fourth centuries. There every Athenian born to citizen parents who were Athenians (regardless of wealth or property holding) was entitled to participate in the assembly. But herein also rises a paradox in our discussion of the comparative equality of ancient governments. Under Athenian democracy, as under agrarian democracy, slaves, resident aliens, and women were also disenfranchised.

In the case of Athens, discrimination was very, very widespread indeed. Given the nature of the Athenian economy, restrictions may have affected three-fourths of the *adult resident* population. Citizens at Athens numbered between 40,000 and 50,000 persons during the fifth century, whereas adult resident aliens (about 10,000?), slaves (about 80,000–150,000?), and adult women born to two Athenian parents (about 40,000–50,000) totaled well over 150,000 persons. No more than 40,000–50,000 adult *citizens* directed affairs out of a total of perhaps nearly 200,000 adult *residents* of Attica.

On the other hand, it is conceivable that in many agrarian city-states where there were few, if any, resident aliens engaged in commerce, where manufacturing was rare, where slaves were primarily agricultural (i.e., not more than 15,000 chattels in all of Boeotia), and thus not needed for manufacture or mining, *as great* a proportion of the adult resident population participated in government as under so-called radical democracy at Athens. Could agrarian government be as democratic as "radical" Athenian democracy? . . .

How could a property qualification at Boeotia still result in as egalitarian a society as that at democratic Athens? Clearly, we must look at the actual social and economic conditions under which the Greek agrarian city-states operated before we label them less egalitarian than more radical democracy at Athens. The conservative character of the agrarian economy, its closed, insular nature, must be considered in any discussion of Greek constitutional government. Agrarian "democracy" in theory was not quite democracy as defined by the Athenian model. But because it did not encourage the presence of disenfranchised resident aliens (metics) or slaves engaged in workshops, trade, or mine work, agrarian governments may have been about as representative of its surrounding adult resident population—citizen and noncitizen—as radical democracies. Agrarian economies without large navies and merchant ships simply did not draw in foreign residents and nonfarm slaves in large numbers, populations who by any Greek standard were always shut out from participation in government. . . .

Although the degree of agrarian participation in Athenian democracy is hotly contested by modern scholars, the ancients at least were aware that farmers were reluctant to undergo time-consuming, bureaucratic governmental responsibilities in Athens proper. Aristotle makes the point that farmers live scattered throughout the countryside "and do not meet or feel so much the need for meeting in the assembly" (*Pol.* 6.1319a30–36). Apparently "they have more pleasure in their work than in taking part in politics" (*Pol.* 6.1318b9–27). Once there was established a constantly politically active body of poor at Athens, agrarians' reluctance to trudge into the *polis* might explain the feeling in Greek literature that the landed hoplites at Athens had not the same say in assembly decisions as their roughly equal-numbered counterparts, the landless *thêtes* who rowed in the fleet. . . .

Agrarian egalitarianism throughout all the Greek city-states was the foundation of Athens' innovative step in enfranchising her landless native-born residents. The Athenians were *not* creating *ex nihilo* a new democratic ideology as has been argued recently—the year 1993 was, after all, the 2,500-year anniversary and celebration of Cleisthenes' democratic reforms of 507 B.C. Instead, democracy in the Athenian sense was a modification of prior broad-based, agricultural timocracy. It was a moderate extension of a long tradition of agrarian values to an additional group who did not hold land—a move itself not nearly revolutionary enough to transform the *polis* to meet the complex economic and social challenges of the fourth-century Mediterranean. . . .

Athenian imperialism hastened the democratization process begun by Cleisthenes (507 B.C.). It enhanced social groups who held no land. Twenty thousand citizens now worked outside of agriculture (e.g., Arist. *Ath. Pol.* 24.3; Ar. *Wasps* 709). Beside conferring prestige on landless *thêtes* who had served so well against Persian ships, the formal creation of a vast navy from the tribute of allied states turned Athenian attention permanently seaward away from purely landed aspirations. The erection of the long walls and the fortification of the Athenian port at Piraeus only cemented this new reliance on naval, rather than infantry power alone. Citizens of Athens in a psychological sense walled themselves off from their own farmland to connect with the sea. . . .

[Moreover,] the exploitation of the silver mines at Laurion in southern Attica, the growth of some small factories in Athens, and the manning of a huge Aegean fleet drew nonagricultural slaves into Athens proper in enormous numbers. With them came the metics. They were an unblinkered and gifted group of resident alien businessmen, bankers, and traders, a shadow city of outsiders who had no part in the functioning of democracy, no formal political rights in the *polis*. Surely that demographic reality made the traditional notion of a city-state of agrarian peers problematic. . . .

Athens went farther than any other community in transforming the old agrarian *polis*. But the Greek city-state was not saved by Athens—as the decades after the battle of Chaironeia show (338 B.C.). This "failure" of Athenian democracy—if we can dare label the inability of a state to obtain perpetual autonomy a "failure"—was due to two reasons. First, Athens still found no way to incorporate the resident aliens, wealthy foreigners (metics) or any others not born to native Athenian parents. Those were often just the people so vital to the economy of the fourth-century Greek world. The marginalized were every bit as important—in fact, they were more vital—to the city as the enfranchised native *thêtes*. Even when the poorer landless were brought into the Athenian *polis*, the total number of adult residents outside the city-state's citizen rolls may have been as great at Athens as at other more conservative agrarian communities—rural communities who were far less engaged in trade and overseas contacts. In this political sense, if continued survival, autonomy, and independence within the dangerous world of the fourth century were the simple goals of the

Greek *polis*, Athenian democracy did not go far enough in redefining the relationship of citizen and noncitizen. It did not end the importance of land in the new environment where far greater capital could be made away from the farm; it did not jettison the cumbersome baggage of agrarian prestige and landed egalitarianism. Was it not suicidal to transform the economic and cultural foundations of the Greek *polis*, without a simultaneous and *complete* overhaul of the political framework of the city-state itself? . . .

Athens, as the most powerful of the Greek city-states, essentially had two choices in the widening horizons of the fifth century. She could have retained her agrarian traditions, by foregoing active participation in the eastern Mediterranean in the wake of the Persian defeat. She might have played a prominent role in Greek unification around agrarian principles, creating some federated fortress Greece, a defensive alliance of autonomous agricultural city-states, a democratic and Ionian mirror image of the Peloponnesian League under Sparta.

Alternatively, after taking up an activist and internationalist stance, Athens, like Rome later, could have moved beyond all resemblance to her agrarian genesis, a landed tradition that was so inimical, so disadvantageous to her new cosmopolitan position. Instead, . . . she did neither. She wished to have it both ways: to be a *polis* and simultaneously a commercial and military force in the affairs of the Mediterranean, to give land prestige and yet host thousands of landless.

That was impossible. The two were inherently contradictory. The status of locally owned property still lingered at democratic Athens; the restrictions on citizenship to the native-born were normally in force; the veneer of agrarian egalitarianism and envy of the more successful were only enhanced under democracy. All that was the cargo of the old agricultural Greek *polis*. It should have had no logical place in a new, greedier world, where foreign trade and capital acquisition were necessary elements of state policy, not targets of moral censure.

Athens in the fifth century had forcibly exposed the fragile and parochial agrarian ideals of Greece to the storm of the Mediterranean at large. Through her complex financial and commercial interests, Athens simultaneously sought to extend, to transform, to improve on, and so to preserve the egalitarian heritage of agrarian ideology. Is it not tragic that in that very process she also hastened on the destruction of the entire economic, military, and political premises of the traditional Greek city-state?

Two fragments of Cleinias' decree on tribute collection (see pp. 127–129). The inscription does not have the three-barred sigma, but other letters are thought (by some) to indicate a date before 430. (Courtesy National Epigraphical Museum, Athens)

PART

II From League to Empire

While describing the attempt to install an oligarchy at Athens in 411, Thucydides commented that it was a difficult thing to take away the liberty of the Athenians, who had enjoyed freedom since the overthrow of the tyranny, and who (moreover) had been "accustomed for beyond half that time to rule (archein) others" (8.68.4). This passage, combined with some of those excerpted in this section, would seem to indicate that Thucydides thought the Athenian empire developed at a fairly early stage—at least as early as the 460s. By that time, the allies had become subjects and would be compelled to remain in an alliance they had joined voluntarily in 478/7, when the Athenian Aristeides assessed the amount of tribute or ships each state was to provide for the continued operations against the Persians.

Yet scholars have long disputed or even denied Thucydides' apparent judgment. Early in the twentieth century the dating of certain Athenian inscriptions to the 420s suggested to some that Cleon and the other successors of Pericles bore the responsibility for their strict imperial tone. Later, the redating of many of these documents to the mid-fifth century led to the orthodox conception that Athenian rule became harsh around 450 or so, about the time (it was maintained) that Athens made peace with Persia and abandoned the ostensible justification for the league and the allies' tribute payments. Recent work would seem to have placed all these views (and others) back on the table for consideration. It should be *kept in mind, however, that both the terms "Athenian empire" and "Delian league" are to some degree modern inventions, and that the ancients may have been perfectly capable of justifying either idea in a given context.*

Sources

Pseudo-Xenophon

The Democratic Empire

Pseudo-Xenophon's *The Constitution of the Athenians*, first introduced in Part I, also contained much of interest on the Athenian empire.

(1.14)   As to their relation with their allies, it is clear that they sail out and bring charges against the respectable elements among them, as they seem to do, and hate them. They realise that it is inevitable that an imperial power will be hated by its subjects, but that if the rich and respectable elements in the subject states are strong, the rule of the Athenian people will only last for a very brief period; that is why they disfranchise the respectable elements, and fine, exile and kill them, but support the masses. Respectable Athenians, however, protect the interests of the respectable people in the allied cities, realising that it is always in their interests to do so. (15) Some might maintain that the strength of Athens lies in the allies being wealthy enough to pay tax, but to the common people it seems more advantageous for individual Athenians to possess the wealth of their allies and for them to retain enough to live on, and to work without being in a position to plot.

(16)   There is a feeling that the Athenians are ill advised to compel their allies to sail to Athens for legal proceedings. In reply, the Athenians enumerate the resulting benefits for the Athenian people: first, the legal deposits finance state pay for the year; secondly, they control the allied cities while staying at home without the necessity of going on voyages, and in the lawcourts they support the democrats and destroy their opponents, while if each state held its trials in its own city, because of their hostility towards Athens they would ruin those of their own citizens who appeared to be particularly in favour with the ordinary people of Athens. (17)   There are also other benefits which the Athenian people reap from the fact that cases involving the allies are heard at Athens: first, the 1% tax levied in the Peiraeus brings in a greater revenue; then, individuals who own rooms to let, a carriage, or have a slave for hire make a greater profit; thirdly, the heralds make more because of the visits of the allies. (18)   In addition to this, if the allies did not come for trials, they would only respect those Athenians who go abroad—the *strategoi*, the trierarchs and the ambassadors; but as it is, each individual ally is compelled to flatter the common people of Athens, realising that, having come to Athens, the penalty or satisfaction that he receives at law depends solely upon the common people; such is the law at Athens. Therefore he is compelled to plead humbly in the courts and to seize people's hands as a suppliant as they enter. This situation has increased the subjection of the allies to the people of Athens.

(19)   Moreover, because the Athenians own property abroad and public duties take them abroad, they and their attendants have learnt to row almost without realising it; for it is inevitable that a man who goes on frequent voyages will take an oar, and learn nautical terminology, and the same is true of his servant. (20)   Experience of voyages and practice makes them good helmsmen, some learning in smaller boats, others in merchantmen, and others graduating to triremes; the majority are competent rowers as soon as they board their ships because of previous practice throughout their lives.

(2.1)   Their hoplite force, which seems to be the least effective arm at Athens, is based on the following principle: they realise that they are inferior to their enemies in skill and numbers, but compared with their tribute-paying allies they are the strongest by land as well as by sea, and they think that their hoplite force is sufficient if they maintain this superiority. (2)   There is a further factor which happens to affect them: it is possible for small subject cities on the mainland to unite and form a single army, but in a sea empire it is not possible for those who are islanders to combine their forces, for the sea divides them, and their rulers control the sea. Even if it is possible for islanders to assemble unnoticed on one island, they will die of starvation. (3)   Of the mainland cities which Athens controls, the large ones are ruled by fear, the small by sheer necessity; there is no city which does not need to import or export something, but this will not be possible unless they submit to those who control the sea.

(4)   Further, it is possible for the rulers of the sea to do what land powers cannot always do; they can ravage the land of more powerful states. They can sail along the coast to an area where the enemy forces are few or non-existent, and if the enemy approach they can embark and sail away; in this way they get into less difficulty than those operating on land. (5)   Then again, the rulers of the sea can sail as far as you like from their own land, but land powers cannot make lengthy expeditions from their own territory, for marching is slow, and it is not possible to take provisions for a long period when travelling on foot. Also, a land force must march through friendly territory or win a passage by force, but a naval force can disembark where it is stronger and not do so where it is not, but sail on until it reaches friendly territory or a less powerful state. (6)   Further, the strongest land powers are badly affected when disease strikes their crops, but sea powers are not troubled, for the whole world is not affected simultaneously, and they can import from a prosperous area. . . .

(14)   There is one weakness in the Athenian position: as rulers of the sea, if they lived on an island, it would be open to them to harm their enemies if they wished while remaining themselves immune from devastation of their land or invasion as long as they controlled the sea; in the present situation the farmers and the wealthy Athenians are more inclined to make up to the enemy, but the common people live without fear and do no such thing because they know that none of their property will be burnt or destroyed. (15)   In addition to this, if they lived on an island, they would also be freed from the fear of the city being betrayed by oligarchs, or the gates opened, or the enemy being let in; for how could this happen if they lived on an island? Again, there would be no chance of anyone's staging a coup against the common people; in the present situation, if anyone planned a coup, he would do so in the hope of bringing in the city's enemies by land; if

Athens were an island, this fear also would be removed. (16)   Since it happens that the city was not founded on an island, they handle the situation as follows: they deposit all their property on islands, relying on their control of the sea, and they disregard any devastation of Attica, realising that if they allow themselves to be moved by this, they will be deprived of other greater benefits. . . .

(3.10)   There seems to be a further way in which the Athenians are ill advised, in that they support the lower classes in cities involved in civil strife. There is, however, a reason for what they do: if they supported the more reputable citizens, they would not be supporting those with the same views as their own, for there is no city where the aristocrats are well disposed to the common people, but in each city the lowest element is well disposed to them. After all, like favours like; therefore the Athenians support those sympathetic to themselves. (11)   Whenever they tried to support the aristocrats it was not to their advantage; it was not long before the people were enslaved in Boeotia, and when they supported the aristocrats in Miletus, within a short time they revolted and massacred the common people; again, when they supported the Spartans instead of the Messenians, within a short time the Spartans had overcome the Messenians and were at war with the Athenians.

Herodotus

The League
Against Persia

Herodotus (ca. 484–ca. 415 B.C.) was born in the city Halicarnassus of Asia Minor and travelled extensively throughout the eastern and central Mediterranean, visiting Athens and ultimately settling in the Athenian-sponsored colony of Thurii in southern Italy. An undoubted admirer of

From G. Rawlinson (translator), *The History of Herodotus*, VII, Fourth Edition. Copyright © 1880 Scribner and Welford.

Athens, and perhaps associate of the Periclean circle, Herodotus wrote a vast work that culminated in an account of the wars between Greece and Persia, and contained much else of historical, literary, and anthropological interest. His work was published some time during the 420s or 410s (the date is controversial), and its portrayal of Sparta and Athens as (relatively) united against the Persian menace must have seemed highly ironic in the environment of the Peloponnesian War. In the following (unconnected) passages, Herodotus not only provides background for both Athens' takeover of the leadership of the league against Persia and the foundation of the Delian league, but also gives us some insight into the kinds of things said about the Athenians' earlier relations with Persia and Sparta (ca. 480–479) at the time Herodotus was collecting his material.

(7.132)   Among the number of those [Greek states] from whom earth and water were brought [as a symbol of submission to the Persian King Xerxes in 480], were the Thessalians, Dolopians, Enianians, Perrhæbians, Locrians, Magnetians, Malians, Achæans of Phthiôtis, Thebans, and Bœotians generally, except those of Platæa and Thespiæ. These are the nations against whom the Greeks that had taken up arms to resist the barbarians swore the oath, which ran thus—"From all those of Greek blood who delivered themselves up to the Persians without necessity, when their affairs were in good condition, we will take a tithe of their goods, and give it to the god at Delphi." So ran the words of the Greek oath. [The authenticity and date of this oath are disputed.] . . .

(139)   And here I feel constrained to deliver an opinion which most men, I know, will mislike, but which, as it seems to me to be true, I am determined not to withhold. Had the Athenians, from fear of the approaching danger, quitted their country, or had they without quitting it submitted to the power of Xerxes, there would certainly have been no attempt to resist the Persians by sea; in which case, the course of events by land would have been the following. Though the Peloponnesians might have carried ever so many breastworks across the Isthmus, yet their allies would have fallen off from the Lacedæmonians, not by voluntary desertion, but because town after town must have been taken by the fleet of the barbarians; and so the Lacedæmonians would at last have stood alone, and, standing alone, would have displayed prodigies of valour, and died nobly. Either they would have

done thus, or else, before it came to that extremity, seeing one Greek state after another embrace the cause of the Medes, they would have come to terms with King Xerxes; and thus, either way Greece would have been brought under Persia. For I cannot understand of what possible use the walls across the Isthmus, could have been, if the King had had the mastery of the sea. If then a man should now say that the Athenians were the saviours of Greece, he would not exceed the truth. For they truly held the scales; and whichever side they espoused must have carried the day. They too it was who, when they had determined to maintain the freedom of Greece, roused up that portion of the Greek nation which had not gone over to the Medes; and so, next to the gods, *they* repulsed the invader. Even the terrible oracles which reached them from Delphi, and struck fear into their hearts, failed to persuade them to fly from Greece. They had the courage to remain faithful to their land, and await the coming of the foe. . . .

(144)   Themistocles had before this [480] given a counsel which prevailed very seasonably. The Athenians, having a large sum of money in their treasury, the produce of the mines at Laureium [in 483/2], were about to share it among the full-grown citizens, who would have received ten drachmas apiece, when Themistocles persuaded them to forbear the distribution, and build with the money two hundred ships, to help them in their war against the Eginetans. It was the breaking out of the Eginetan war which was at this time the saving of Greece; for hereby were the Athenians forced to become a maritime power. The new ships were not used for the purpose for which they had been built, but became a help to Greece in her hour of need. And the Athenians had not only these vessels ready before the war, but they likewise set to work to build more; while they determined, in a council which was held after the debate upon the [meaning of the Delphic] oracle, that, according to the advice of the god, they would embark their whole force aboard their ships, and, with such Greeks as chose to join them, give battle to the barbarian invader. . . .

(8.2)   . . . The captain [of the Greek fleet at Artemisium, in 480], who had the chief command over the whole fleet, was Eurybiades, the son of Eurycleides. He was furnished by Sparta, since the allies had said that, "if a Lacedæmonian did not take the command, they would break up the fleet, for never would they serve under the Athenians."

(3)   From the first, even earlier than the time when the embassy went to Sicily to solicit alliance, there had been a talk of intrusting the

Athenians with the command at sea; but the allies were averse to the plan, wherefore the Athenians did not press it; for there was nothing they had so much at heart as the salvation of Greece, and they knew that, if they quarrelled among themselves about the command, Greece would be brought to ruin. Herein they judged rightly; for internal strife is a thing as much worse than war carried on by a united people, as war itself is worse than peace. The Athenians therefore, being so persuaded, did not push their claims, but waived them, so long as they were in such great need of aid from the other Greeks. And they afterwards showed their motive; for at the time when the Persians had been driven from Greece, and were now threatened by the Greeks in their own country, they took occasion of the insolence of Pausanias to deprive the Lacedæmonians of their leadership. This, however, happened afterwards. . . .

[The following events, according to Herodotus, occurred after the battle of Salamis (480), when the Spartans learned that an envoy from the Persians had been sent to the Athenians.]

(141) Now the Lacedæmonians, when tidings reached them that Alexander [King of Macedon] was gone to Athens to bring about a league between the Athenians and the barbarians, and when at the same time they called to mind the prophecies which declared that the Dorian race should one day be driven from the Peloponnese by the Medes and the Athenians, were exceedingly afraid lest the Athenians might consent to the alliance with Persia. They therefore lost no time in sending envoys to Athens; and it so happened that these envoys were given their audience at the same time with Alexander: for the Athenians had waited and made delays, because they felt sure that the Lacedæmonians would hear that an ambassador was come to them from the Persians, and as soon as they heard it would with all speed send an embassy. They contrived matters therefore of set purpose, so that the Lacedæmonians might hear them deliver their sentiments on the occasion.

(142) As soon as Alexander had finished speaking, the ambassadors from Sparta took the word and said,

"We are sent here by the Lacedæmonians to entreat of you that ye will not do a new thing in Greece, nor agree to the terms which are offered you by the Barbarian. Such conduct on the part of any of the Greeks would be both unjust and dishonourable; but in you it would be worse than in others, for divers reasons. It was by you that this war was kindled at the first among us—our wishes were in no way considered; the contest began by your seeking to extend your empire—now the fate of Greece is involved in it. Besides, it were surely an intolerable thing that the Athenians, who have always hitherto been known as a nation to which many men owed their freedom, should now become the means of bringing all other Greeks into slavery. We feel, however, for the heavy calamities which press on you—the loss of your harvest these two years, and the ruin in which your homes have lain for so long a time. We offer you, therefore, on the part of the Lacedæmonians and the allies, sustenance for your women and for the unwarlike portion of your households, so long as the war endures. Do not be seduced by Alexander the Macedonian, who softens down the rough words of Mardonius. He does as is natural for him to do—a tyrant himself, he helps forward a tyrant's cause. But you, Athenians, should do differently, at least if you are truly wise; for you should know that with barbarians there is neither faith nor truth."

(143)   Thus spake the envoys. After which the Athenians returned this answer to Alexander:

"We know, as well as you, that the power of the Mede is many times greater than our own: we did not need to have *that* cast in our teeth. Nevertheless, we cling so to freedom that we shall offer what resistance we may. Seek not to persuade us into making terms with the barbarian—say what you will, you will never gain our assent. Return rather at once, and tell Mardonius that our answer to him is this:—'So long as the sun keeps his present course, we will never join alliance with Xerxes. Nay, we shall oppose him unceasingly, trusting in the aid of those gods and heroes whom he has lightly esteemed, whose houses and whose images he has burnt with fire.' And come not again to us with words like these; nor, thinking to do us a service, persuade us to unholy actions. You are the guest and friend of our nation—we would not want you to receive hurt at our hands."

(144)   Such was the answer which the Athenians gave to Alexander. To the Spartan envoys they said,

"It was natural no doubt that the Lacedæmonians should be afraid we might make terms with the Barbarian; but nevertheless it was a base fear in men who knew so well of what temper and spirit we are. Not all the gold that the whole earth contains—not the fairest and most fertile of all lands—would bribe us to take part with the Medes and help them to enslave our countrymen. Even could we anyhow have brought ourselves to such a thing, there are many very powerful motives which would now make it impossible. The first and chief of these is the burning and destruction of our temples and the images of our gods, which forces us to make no terms with their destroyer, but rather to pursue him with our resentment to the uttermost. Again, there is our common brotherhood with the Greeks: our common language, the altars and the sacrifices of which we all partake, the common character which we bear—did the Athenians betray all these, truly it would not be well. Know then now, if you have not known it before, that while one Athenian remains alive, we will never join alliance with Xerxes. . . .

[Not long after the negotiations recounted above, the Persians marched into Attica again (in 479). When Spartan aid did not arrive, the Athenians took refuge on Salamis.]

(9.6) At the same time [the Athenians] sent ambassadors to Lacedæmon, who were to reproach the Lacedæmonians for having allowed the Barbarian to advance into Attica, instead of joining them and going out to meet him in Bœotia. They were likewise to remind the Lacedæmonians of the offers by which the Persian had sought to win Athens over to his side, and to warn them that, if no aid came from Sparta, the Athenians must consult for their own safety. . . .

(11) [The Athenian ambassadors] therefore addressed the Ephors in these words:—"Lacedæmonians, as you do not stir from home, but keep the Hyacinthian festival, and amuse yourselves, deserting the cause of your confederates, the Athenians, whom your behaviour wrongs, and who have no other allies, will make such terms with the Persians as they shall find possible. Now when terms are once made, it is plain that, having become the King's allies, we shall march with the barbarians whithersoever they choose to lead. Then at length you will perceive what the consequences will be to yourselves.". . .

(106) [After the victory at Mycale in Asia Minor in 479], when they had burnt the rampart and the [Persian] vessels, the Greeks sailed away to Samos, and there took counsel together concerning the Ionians, whom they thought of removing out of Asia. Ionia they proposed to abandon to the barbarians; and their doubt was, in what part of their own possessions in Greece they should settle its inhabitants. For it seemed to them a thing impossible that they should be ever on the watch to guard and protect Ionia; and yet otherwise there could be no hope that the Ionians would escape the vengeance of the Persians.

Hereupon the Peloponnesian leaders proposed, that the seaport towns of such Greeks as had sided with the Medes should be taken away from them, and made over to the Ionians. The Athenians, on the other hand, were very unwilling that any removal at all should take place, and misliked the Peloponnesians holding councils concerning their colonists. So, as they set themselves against the change, the Peloponnesians yielded with a good will. Hereupon the Samians, Chians, Lesbians, and other islanders, who had helped the Greeks at this time, were received into the league of the allies; and took the oaths, binding themselves to be faithful, and not desert the common cause. Then the Greeks sailed away to the Hellespont, where they meant to break down the bridges [used by the Persians to cross into Europe], which they supposed to be still extended across the strait. . . .

(114) On arriving here, they discovered that the bridges, which they had thought to find standing, and which had been the chief cause of their proceeding to the Hellespont, were already broken up and destroyed. Upon this discovery, Leotychides, and the Peloponnesians under him, were anxious to sail back to Greece; but the Athenians, with Xanthippus their captain, thought good to remain, and resolved to make an attempt upon the Chersonese. So, while the Peloponnesians sailed away to their homes, the Athenians crossed over from Abydos to the Chersonese, and there laid siege to Sestos.

Thucydides

The Growth of Athenian Power

In the following passages Thucydides briefly describes the period between the Persian and Peloponnesian Wars (479–432 B.C.), and the growth of Athenian power during those years. In an appended passage, he recounts

From R. Crawley (translator), *The Growth of Athenian Power.*

the Mytilenians' complaints against the Athenians raised to the Spartans in 428, when Mytilene (on the island of Lesbos) revolted from Athens.

---

[89]   The way in which Athens came to be placed in the circumstances under which her power grew was this. After the Medes had returned from Europe, defeated by sea and land by the Hellenes, and after those of them who had fled with their ships to Mycale had been destroyed [479], Leotychides, King of the Lacedæmonians, the commander of the Hellenes at Mycale, departed home with the allies from Peloponnese. But the Athenians and the allies from Ionia and Hellespont, who had now revolted from the king, remained and laid siege to Sestos, which was still held by the Medes. . . .

[Thucydides recounts how, despite opposition from Sparta's allies, the Athenians rebuilt their walls by means of a ruse of the Athenian leader Themistocles. He then continues.]

[93] . . . Themistocles also persuaded them to finish the walls of Piræus, which had been begun before, in his year of office as archon; being influenced alike by the fineness of a locality that has three natural harbours, and by the great start which the Athenians would gain in the acquisition of power by becoming a naval people. For he first ventured to tell them to stick to the sea and forthwith began to lay the foundations of the empire. . . .

[94]   Meanwhile Pausanias, son of Cleombrotus, was sent out from Lacedæmon as commander-in-chief of the Hellenes, with twenty ships from Peloponnese [in 478]. With him sailed the Athenians with thirty ships, and a number of the other allies. They made an expedition against Cyprus and subdued most of the island, and afterwards against Byzantium, which was in the hands of the Medes, and compelled it to surrender. This event took place while the Spartans were still supreme.

[95]   But the violence of Pausanias had already begun to be disagreeable to the Hellenes, particularly to the Ionians and the newly liberated populations. These resorted to the Athenians and requested them as their kinsmen to become their leaders, and to stop any attempt at violence on the part of Pausanias. The Athenians accepted their overtures, and determined to put down any attempt of the kind and to settle everything else as might seem best to them. In the mean-

time the Lacedæmonians recalled Pausanias for an investigation of the reports which had reached them. Manifold and grave accusations had been brought against him by Hellenes arriving in Sparta; and, to all appearance, there had been in him more of the mimicry of a despot than of the attitude of a general. As it happened, his recall came just at the time when the hatred which he had inspired had induced the allies to desert him, the soldiers from Peloponnese excepted, and to range themselves by the side of the Athenians. On his arrival at Lacedæmon, he was censured for his private acts of oppression, but was acquitted on the heaviest counts and pronounced not guilty; it must be known that the charge of Medism formed one of the principal, and to all appearance one of the best founded articles against him. The Lacedæmonians did not, however, restore him to his command, but sent out Dorkis and certain others with a small force; who found the allies no longer inclined to concede to them the supremacy. Perceiving this they departed, and the Lacedæmonians did not send out any to succeed them. They feared for those who went out a deterioration similar to that observable in Pausanias; besides they desired to be rid of the Median war, and were satisfied of the competency of the Athenians for the position, and of their friendship at the time towards themselves.

[96]   The Athenians having thus succeeded to the supremacy by the voluntary act of the allies through their hatred of Pausanias, fixed which cities were to contribute money against the barbarian, which ships [477]; their professed object being to retaliate for their sufferings by ravaging the king's country. Now was the time that the office of "Treasurers for Hellas" [hellenotamiae] was first instituted by the Athenians. These officers received the tribute, as the money contributed was called. The tribute was first fixed at four hundred and sixty talents. The common treasury was at Delos, and the congresses were held in the temple. [97]   Their supremacy commenced with independent allies who acted on the resolutions of a common congress. It was marked by the following undertakings in war and in administration during the interval between the Median and the present war, against the barbarian, against their own rebel allies, and against the Peloponnesian powers which would come in contact with them on various occasions. My excuse for relating these events, and for venturing on this digression, is that this passage of history has been omitted by all my predecessors, who have confined themselves either to

Hellenic history before the Median war, or to the Median war itself. Hellanicus, it is true, did touch on these events; but he is somewhat concise and not accurate in his dates. Besides, the history of these events contains an explanation of the growth of the Athenian empire.

[98] First the Athenians besieged and captured Eion on the Strymon from the Medes, and made slaves of the inhabitants, being under the command of Cimon, son of Miltiades. Next they enslaved Scyros the island in the Ægean, containing a Dolopian population, and colonised it themselves. This was followed by a war against Carystus, in which the rest of Eubœa remained neutral, and which was ended by surrender on conditions. After this Naxos left the confederacy [ca. 470], and a war ensued, and she had to return after a siege; this was the first instance of the engagement being broken by the subjugation of an allied city, a precedent which was followed by that of the rest in the order which circumstances prescribed. [99] Of all the causes of defection, that connected with arrears of tribute and vessels, and with failure of service, was the chief; for the Athenians were very severe and exacting, and made themselves offensive by applying the screw of necessity to men who were not used to and in fact not disposed for any continuous labour. In some other respects the Athenians were not the old popular rulers they had been at first; and if they had more than their fair share of service, it was correspondingly easy for them to reduce any that tried to leave the confederacy. For this the allies had themselves to blame; the wish to get off service making most of them arrange to pay their share of the expense in money instead of in ships, and so to avoid having to leave their homes. Thus while Athens was increasing her navy with the funds which they contributed, a revolt always found them without resources or experience for war.

[100] Next we come to the actions by land and by sea at the river Eurymedon, between the Athenians with their allies, and the Medes, when the Athenians won both battles on the same day under the conduct of Cimon, son of Miltiades, and captured and destroyed the whole Phœnician fleet, consisting of two hundred vessels. Some time afterwards occurred the defection of the Thasians [ca. 465], caused by disagreements about the marts on the opposite coast of Thrace, and about the mine in their possession. Sailing with a fleet to Thasos, the Athenians defeated them at sea and effected a landing on the island. . . .

[101]   Meanwhile the Thasians being defeated in the field and suffering siege, appealed to Lacedæmon, and desired her to assist them by an invasion of Attica. Without informing Athens she promised and intended to do so, but was prevented by the occurrence of the earthquake, accompanied by the secession of the Helots and the Thuriats and Æthæans of the Periœci to Ithome. Most of the Helots were the descendants of the old Messenians that were enslaved in the famous war; and so all of them came to be called Messenians. So the Lacedæmonians being engaged in a war with the rebels in Ithome, the Thasians in the third year of the siege obtained terms from the Athenians by razing their walls, delivering up their ships, and arranging to pay the monies demanded at once, and tribute in future; giving up their possessions on the continent together with the mine.

[102]   The Lacedæmonians meanwhile finding the war against the rebels in Ithome likely to last, invoked the aid of their allies, and especially of the Athenians, who came in some force under the command of Cimon [462/1]. The reason for this pressing summons lay in their reputed skill in siege operations; a long siege had taught the Lacedæmonians their own deficiency in this art, else they would have taken the place by assault. The first open quarrel between the Lacedæmonians and Athenians arose out of this expedition. The Lacedæmonians, when assault failed to take the place, apprehensive of the enterprising and revolutionary character of the Athenians, and further looking upon them as of alien extraction, began to fear that if they remained, they might be tempted by the besieged in Ithome to attempt some political changes. They accordingly dismissed them alone of the allies, without declaring their suspicions, but merely saying that they had now no need of them. But the Athenians, aware that their dismissal did not proceed from the more honourable reason of the two, but from suspicions which had been conceived, went away deeply offended and conscious of having done nothing to merit such treatment from the Lacedæmonians; and the instant that they returned home they broke off the alliance which had been made against the Mede, and allied themselves with Sparta's enemy Argos; each of the contracting parties taking the same oaths and making the same alliance with the Thessalians. . . .

[Having renounced their alliance with Sparta, the Athenians sent an expedition to Egypt to aid in a revolt against Persia and began open hostilities with the Corinthians and other allies of Sparta (460–59).]

[107]   About this time [458/7] the Athenians began to build the long walls to the sea, that towards Phalerum and that towards Piræus. Meanwhile the Phocians made an expedition against Doris, the old home of the Lacedæmonians, containing the towns of Bœum, Kitinium, and Erineum. They had taken one of these towns, when the Lacedæmonians under Nicomedes, son of Cleombrotus, commanding for Pleistoanax, son of Pausanias, who was still a minor, came to the aid of the Dorians with fifteen hundred heavy infantry of their own, and ten thousand of their allies. After compelling the Phocians to restore the town on conditions, they began their retreat. The route by sea, across the Crissæan gulf, exposed them to the risk of being stopped by the Athenian fleet; that across Geraneia seemed scarcely safe, the Athenians holding Megara and Pegæ. For the pass was a difficult one, and was always guarded by the Athenians; and, in the present instance, the Lacedæmonians had information that they meant to dispute their passage. So they resolved to remain in Bœotia, and to consider which would be the safest line of march. They had also another reason for this resolve. Secret encouragement had been given them by a party in Athens, who hoped to put an end to the reign of democracy and the building of the long walls. Meanwhile the Athenians marched against them with their whole levy and a thousand Argives and the respective contingents of the rest of their allies. Altogether they were fourteen thousand strong. The march was prompted by the notion that the Lacedæmonians were at a loss how to effect their passage, and also by suspicions of an attempt to overthrow the democracy. Some cavalry also joined the Athenians from their Thessalian allies; but these went over to the Lacedæmonians during the battle.

[108]   The battle was fought at Tanagra in Bœotia. After heavy loss on both sides victory declared for the Lacedæmonians and their allies. After entering the Megarid and cutting down the fruit trees, the Lacedæmonians returned home across Geraneia and the isthmus. Sixty-two days after the battle the Athenians marched into Bœotia under the command of Myronides, defeated the Bœotians in battle at Œnophyta, and became masters of Bœotia and Phocis. They dismantled the walls of the Tanagræans, took a hundred of the richest men of the Opuntian Locrians as hostages, and finished their own long walls. This was followed by the surrender of the Æginetans to Athens on conditions; they pulled down their walls, gave up their ships, and agreed to pay tribute in future. . . .

[The Athenian expedition to Egypt ended in complete disaster (454).]

[112] Three years afterwards [in 451] a truce was made between the Peloponnesians and Athenians for five years. Released from Hellenic war, the Athenians made an expedition to Cyprus with two hundred vessels of their own and their allies, under the command of Cimon. Sixty of these were detached to Egypt at the instance of Amyrtæus, the king in the marshes; the rest laid siege to Kitium, from which, however, they were compelled to retire by the death of Cimon and by scarcity of provisions. Sailing off Salamis in Cyprus, they fought with the Phœnicians and Cilicians by land and sea, and being victorious on both elements departed home, and with them the returned squadron from Egypt. After this the Lacedæmonians marched out on a sacred war, and becoming masters of the temple at Delphi, placed it in the hands of the Delphians. Immediately after their retreat, the Athenians marched out, became masters of the temple, and placed it in the hands of the Phocians.

[113] Some time after this, Orchomenus, Chæronea, and some other places in Bœotia, being in the hands of the Bœotian exiles, the Athenians marched against the above-mentioned hostile places with a thousand Athenian heavy infantry and the allied contingents, under the command of Tolmides, son of Tolmæus. Having taken Chæronea, and left a garrison in the place, they commenced their return. On their road they were attacked at Coronæa, by the Bœotian exiles from Orchomenus, with some Locrians and Eubœan exiles, and others who were of the same way of thinking, were defeated in battle, and some killed, others taken captive. The Athenians evacuated all Bœotia by a treaty providing for the recovery of the men; and the exiled Bœotians returned, and with all the rest regained their independence.

[114] This was soon afterwards followed by the revolt of Eubœa from Athens. Pericles had already crossed over with an army of Athenians to the island, when news was brought to him that Megara had revolted, that the Peloponnesians were on the point of invading Attica, and that the Athenian garrison had been cut off by the Megarians, with the exception of a few who had taken refuge in Nisæa. The Megarians had introduced the Corinthians, Sicyonians, and Epidaurians into the town before they revolted. Meanwhile Pericles brought his army back in all haste from Eubœa. After this the Peloponnesians marched into Attica as far as Eleusis and Thrius, ravaging the country under the conduct of King Pleistoanax, the son of Pausanias, and without advancing

further returned home. The Athenians then crossed over again to Eubœa under the command of Pericles, and subdued the whole of the island: all but Histiæa was settled by convention; the Histiæans they
expelled from their homes, and occupied their territory themselves.

[115] Not long after their return from Eubœa, they made a
truce with the Lacedæmonians and their allies for thirty years [446/5],
giving up the posts which they occupied in Peloponnese, Nisæa,
Pegæ, Trœzen, and Achaia. In the sixth year of the truce, war broke
out between the Samians and Milesians about Priene. Worsted in the
war, the Milesians came to Athens with loud complaints against the
Samians. In this they were joined by certain private persons from
Samos itself, who wished to revolutionise the government. Accordingly the Athenians sailed to Samos with forty ships and set up a
democracy; took hostages from the Samians, fifty boys and as many
men, lodged them in Lemnos, and after leaving a garrison in the island returned home. But some of the Samians had not remained in
the island, but had fled to the continent. Making an agreement with
the most powerful of those in the city, and an alliance with Pissuthnes,
son of Hystaspes, the then satrap of Sardis, they got together a force of
seven hundred mercenaries, and under cover of night crossed over to
Samos. Their first step was to rise on the commons, most of whom
they secured, their next to steal their hostages from Lemnos; after
which they revolted, gave up the Athenian garrison left with them and
its commanders to Pissuthnes, and instantly prepared for an expedition against Miletus. The Byzantines also revolted with them. . . .

[Thucydides goes on to recount how the Athenians eventually
ended the Samian revolt (439). He then notes that the events which
led to the Peloponnesian War, including the affairs of Poteidaea and
Corcyra (see Part VI), began a few years after this. . . . In the following
selection from Book III, Thucydides reports a speech made by the
Mytilenians, who were seeking Spartan aid in their revolt from Athens
(in 428). For the consequences of their failed revolt, see Part V.]

[10] "Justice and honesty will be the first topics of our speech,
especially as we are asking for alliance; because we know that there
can never be any solid friendship between individuals, or union between communities that is worth the name, unless the parties be persuaded of each other's honesty, and be generally congenial the one to
the other; since from difference in feeling springs also difference in
conduct. Between ourselves and the Athenians alliance began, when

you withdrew from the Median war and they remained to finish the business. But we did not become allies of the Athenians for the subjugation of the Hellenes, but allies of the Hellenes for their liberation from the Mede; and as long as the Athenians led us fairly we followed them loyally; but when we saw them relax their hostility to the Mede, to try to compass the subjection of the allies, then our apprehensions began. Unable, however, to unite and defend themselves, on account of the number of confederates that had votes, all the allies were enslaved, except ourselves and the Chians, who continued to send our contingents as independent and nominally free. Trust in Athens as a leader, however, we could no longer feel, judging by the examples already given; it being unlikely that she would reduce our fellow confederates, and not do the same by the rest, if ever she had the power.

[11] "Had we all been still independent, we could have had more faith in their not attempting any change; but the greater number being their subjects, while they were treating us as equals, they would naturally chafe under this solitary instance of independence as contrasted with the submission of the majority; particularly as they daily grew more powerful, and we more destitute. Now the only sure basis of an alliance is for each party to be equally afraid of the other: he who would like to encroach is then deterred by the reflexion that he will not have odds in his favour. Again, if we were left independent, it was only because they thought they saw their way to empire more clearly by specious language and by the paths of policy than by those of force. Not only were we useful as evidence that powers who had votes, like themselves, would not, surely, join them in their expeditions, against their will, without the party attacked being in the wrong; but the same system also enabled them to lead the stronger states against the weaker first, and so to leave the former to the last, stripped of their natural allies, and less capable of resistance. But if they had begun with us, while all had still their own resources, and a centre to rally round, the work of subjugation would have been found less easy. Besides this, our navy gave them some apprehension: it was always possible that it might unite with you or with some other power, and become dangerous to Athens. The court which we paid to their commons and its leaders for the time being, also helped us to maintain our independence. However, we did not expect to be able to do so much longer, if this war had not broken out, from the examples that we had had of their conduct to the rest. . . ."

The Aristotelian Constitution of the Athenians

Benefits of Empire

In the midst of describing the development of the Athenian democracy, the author of the *Constitution of the Athenians* discusses the advantages that the payments from the allied states brought to Athens. It is perhaps unlikely (though not impossible) that *tribute* collected from the allies was utilized for public payment as soon after 478/7 as this passage implies. The Athenians did not begin inscribing on stone the quota of one-sixtieth of the tribute paid to Athena until 454/3, and most scholars infer that the treasury of the league at that time had been transferred from Delos to Athens. After 454/3, some argue, the Athenians began to draw on this reserve for public payments and the building program.

(24.1) After this [the foundation of the Delian league in 478/7], now that the city was confident and a large amount of money had been collected, Aristides advised the Athenians to assert their leadership, and to leave the fields and live in the city: there would be maintenance for all, some on campaign, some on guard duty, others attending to public affairs; and by living in this way they would secure their leadership. (2) The Athenians were persuaded. They took control of the empire, and became more domineering in their treatment of the allies, apart from Chios, Lesbos and Samos: these they kept as guardians of the empire, accepting their existing constitutions and allowing them to retain the subjects over whom they ruled. (3) In accordance with Aristides' proposal, they provided ample maintenance for the common people, so that more than twenty thousand men were supported from the tribute, the taxes and the allies. There were 6,000 jurors; 1,600 archers, and also 1,200 cavalry; the council of 500; 500 guards of the dockyards, and also 50 guards on the Acropolis; about 700 internal officials and about 700 overseas. In addition to these, when the Athenians sub-

From Aristotle, *The Athenian Constitution*, edited and translated by P. J. Rhodes, pp. 68 (Harmondsworth: Penguin, 1984). Reproduced by permission Frederick Warne & Co.

sequently organized their military affairs, they had 2,500 hoplites; 20 guard ships; other ships sent out for the tribute, carrying 2,000 men appointed by lot; also the town hall; orphans; and guardians of prisoners. All these were financed from public funds.

Plutarch

Treatment of the Allies

Plutarch (ca. A.D. 50–120), priest of Delphi, biographer, and philosopher, wrote numerous treatises on both historical and philosophical subjects. His works apart from the well-known biographies of famous Greeks and Romans are known collectively as the *Moralia,* but it is upon the *Lives* that his reputation today mainly rests. Although he is often criticized on historical grounds, Plutarch himself was careful to draw a distinction between the writing of history and his own task of composing biography, which was more concerned with showing the character of the man than with the chronology of his career. Nonetheless, he is invaluable as a historical source since he often draws on earlier works and documents no longer extant. The following passages from Plutarch's life of Pericles may tell us something about the Athenians' attitudes toward the allies and the tribute-payments, although the historicity of these reports has been questioned (see the selection from Frost in Part III).

(12)   But there was one measure above all which at once gave the greatest pleasure to the Athenians, adorned their city and created amazement among the rest of mankind, and which is today the sole testimony that the tales of the ancient power and glory of Greece are no mere fables. By this I mean his construction of temples and public buildings; and yet it was this, more than any other action of [Pericles],

From Plutarch, *The Rise and Fall of Athens,* translated by I. Scott-Kilvert, pp. 178–182, 184–185 (London/New York: Penguin, 1960). Reproduced by permission of Frederick Warne & Co.

which his enemies slandered and misrepresented. They cried out in the Assembly that Athens had lost her good name and disgraced herself by transferring from Delos into her own keeping the funds that had been contributed by the rest of Greece, and that now the most plausible excuse for this action, namely, that the money had been removed for fear of the barbarians and was being guarded in a safe place, had been demolished by Pericles himself. "The Greeks must be outraged," they cried. "They must consider this an act of barefaced tyranny, when they see that with their own contributions, extorted from them by force for the war against the Persians, we are gilding and beautifying our city, as if it were some vain woman decking herself out with costly stones and statues and temples worth millions of money."

Pericles' answer to the people was that the Athenians were not obliged to give the allies any account of how their money was spent, provided that they carried on the war for them and kept the Persians away. "They do not give us a single horse, nor a soldier, nor a ship. All they supply is money," he told the Athenians, "and this belongs not to the people who give it, but to those who receive it, so long as they provide the services they are paid for. It is no more than fair that after Athens has been equipped with all she needs to carry on the war, she should apply the surplus to public works, which, once completed, will bring her glory for all time, and while they are being built will convert that surplus to immediate use. In this way all kinds of enterprises and demands will be created which will provide inspiration for every art, find employment for every hand, and transform the whole people into wage-earners, so that the city will decorate and maintain herself at the same time from her own resources."

Certainly it was true that those who were of military age and physically in their prime could always earn their pay from the public funds by serving on Pericles' various campaigns. But he was also anxious that the unskilled masses, who had no military training, should not be debarred from benefiting from the national income, and yet should not be paid for sitting about and doing nothing. So he boldly laid before the people proposals for immense public works and plans for buildings, which would involve many different arts and industries and require long periods to complete, his object being that those who stayed at home, no less than those serving in the fleet or the army or on garrison duty, should be enabled to enjoy a share of the national wealth. . . .

(13)   . . . The director and supervisor of the whole enterprise was Pheidias, although there were various great architects and artists employed on the individual buildings. . . .

But it was Pheidias who directed the making of the great golden statue of Athena, and his name is duly inscribed upon the marble tablet on the Acropolis as its creator. Almost the whole enterprise was in his hands, and because of his friendship with Pericles all the artists and craftsmen, as I have said, came under his orders. The result was that he himself became the victim of envy and his patron of slander, for the rumour was put about that Pheidias arranged intrigues for Pericles with free-born Athenian women, when they came on the pretext of looking at the works of art. The comic poets took up this story and showered Pericles with all the innuendoes they could invent, coupling his name with the wife of Menippus, a man who was his friend and had served as his second in command in the army. Even Pyrilampus's fondness for keeping birds was dragged in, and because he was a friend of Pericles, he was accused of using his peacocks as presents for the women who granted Pericles their favours. The fact is that men who know nothing of decency in their own lives are only too ready to launch foul slanders against their betters and to offer them up as victims to the evil deity of popular envy. . . .

(14)   Thucydides and the other members of his party were constantly denouncing Pericles for squandering public money and letting the national revenue run to waste, and so Pericles appealed to the people in the Assembly to declare whether in their opinion he had spent too much. "Far too much," was their reply, whereupon Pericles retorted, "Very well then, do not let it be charged to the public account but to my own, and I will dedicate all the public buildings in my name." It may have been that the people admired such a gesture in the grand manner, or else that they were just as ambitious as Pericles to have a share in the glory of his works. At any rate they raised an uproar and told him to draw freely on the public funds and spare no expense in his outlay. Finally, Pericles ventured to put matters to the test of an ostracism, and the result was that he secured his rival's banishment and the dissolution of the party which had been organized against him. . . . [For this Thucydides (not the historian), see Part III.]

(17)   When the Spartans began to be vexed by the growing power of Athens, Pericles, by way of encouraging the people to cherish even higher ambitions and making them believe themselves capable of great achievements, introduced a proposal that all Greeks, whether living in Europe or in Asia, in small or in large cities alike, should be invited to send delegates to a congress at Athens. The subjects to be discussed were the Greek sanctuaries which had been burned down by the Persians; the sacrifices owed to the gods on behalf of Hellas to fulfil the vows made when they were fighting the Persians; and the security of the seas, so that all ships could sail them without fear and keep the peace. Twenty men were chosen from the citizens above fifty years of age to convey this invitation. Five of these invited the Ionian and Dorian Greeks in Asia and the islands, as far as Lesbos and Rhodes; five visited the regions on the Hellespont and those of Thrace as far as Byzantium; five others proceeded to Boeotia, Phocis, and the Peloponnese, passing from there by way of the Ozolian Locrians to the neighbouring mainland, as far as Acarnania and Ambracia, while the rest travelled through Euboea to the Oetaeans and the Maliac gulf, and to the Achaeans of Phthia and the Thessalians; urging them all to attend and join in the deliberations for the peace and well-being of Greece. However, nothing was achieved, and the delegates never assembled because of the covert opposition of the Spartans; at least this is the reason generally given, since the Athenian overtures were first rejected in the Peloponnese. I have mentioned this episode, however, as an illustration of Pericles' lofty spirit and of the grandeur of his conceptions.

Inscriptions and the Controversy over Three-barred Sigma

The Athenians of the fifth century inscribed certain of the *ecclesia*'s decrees and other official records on stone tablets called *stelai* and set them up publicly in Athens. Many of these stones have survived into the present age, some far more preserved than others. Greek historians and modern students of the inscriptions, or epigraphists, spend much of their time attempting to determine what letters are left on the stones we have (and what letters might have been on the lost portions). The reading, dating, and supplementation of these stones has led to extreme controversy, almost (it would sometimes seem) in inverse proportion to the number of letters remaining on a given stone. In the following selections I have attempted to err in the direction of conservatism rather than endorsing more speculative restorations.

The translations are based on the texts and restorations published in the third and most recent edition of *Inscriptiones Graecae*, D. Lewis, editor, excepting the Standards Decree, which derives from *A Selection of Greek Historical Inscriptions*, R. Meiggs and D. Lewis, editors. I have attempted to provide literal translations that reproduce the order of thoughts and phrases in the original texts (if at the expense of idiomatic English). Regular text represents certain or virtually certain words or letters on the stone; italics represents probable words or terms that are partially restored; words or letters in square brackets do not appear on the stone and are wholly supplementary. In cases where one or two letters have been carried over to the next line of the inscription, I have usually chosen not to divide the word in the translation. At the beginning of each text I provide a list of possible dates for the document.

The present orthodox view of the historical context for these inscriptions places most of them under the earliest possible date, largely based on the form of letters inscribed, especially the sigma, which many scholars believe was not cut with three bars (as opposed to four) after about 445. This view has been challenged in numerous publications by H. B. Mattingly, now collected in his work *The Athenian Empire Restored*. Recent work (to some scholars) seems to have confirmed certain of Mattingly's contentions. Thus the orthodox view—that the Athenian regime became "imperial" and issued many of the decrees included here in the early or mid-440s after formally renouncing the war against Persia by negotiating the Peace of Callias—may now require some revision. If, as Mattingly has maintained, many of these decrees belong to the 420s, some may adopt his conclusion that the "imperialism" found in them is a relatively late phenomenon. Based on this view, the process of reducing the allies to the status of subjects began in Pericles' last years and was completed during Cleon's career. Conversely, some scholars who agree with Mattingly about the late date of certain documents (such as Fornara and myself) maintain that Athenian imperialism appeared almost immediately after the formation of the Delian league, and that the bureaucracy of empire documented in the decrees should not be confused with the long-standing exercise of Athenian compulsion and power noted by Thucydides (compare the view of Finley below).

Regulations for Erythrae (460s–450s)

Erythrae, a city opposite the island of Chios on the coast of Asia Minor, apparently underwent some disaffection from the Athenian empire in the late 450s, perhaps involving an Erythraean faction favorable to the Persians (see R. Meiggs, *The Athenian Empire*, pp. 112–115). This is the context favored by most historians for this decree. Athenian actions towards Erythrae potentially tell us much about Athens' reactions to trouble in allied states and her willingness to interfere in their internal politics.

The text is based on a copy made (probably) by a French traveler in the early nineteenth century. The stone and the nineteenth-century copy are both lost, and readings are correspondingly tenuous in many cases. The first seven lines are omitted; although very little of them are preserved, they apparently concerned regulations for the bringing of sacrifices to Athens during the Great Panathenaea, an especially grand celebration held every four years of the annual Panathenaic festival.

. . . of the meat . . . to (anyone) wishing. Of Erythraeans *by*
lot a boule shall be (chosen) of 120 men. And the
. . . in the boule and . . . [someone shall not?] *serve* in the   10
   boule,
[no]r (someone) less than thirty *years old*. And there shall
   be prosecution [against]
those examined (if found guilty). And they shall not serve
   on the boule (again) within four years . . .
Both the choice by lot and establishment of the *present*
   boule (shall be handled by) the *inspec-*
tors (episkopoi) and [the] commander of the garrison
   (phrourarch), but in the future by the boule and the
   [garrison]
commander, not less than thirty days *before* the dissolution   15
   of [the (old) boul]e.

Inscriptiones Graecae, 3rd ed., vol. I, ed. D. Lewis (Berlin: De Gruyter, 1981), no. 14, trans. L. J. Samons II.

And let there be an oath sworn, by Zeus and Apollo and
    Demeter, (by those chosen) calling down *dest-*
ruction [upon themselves if swearing falsely . . .] *and destruction*
    on their children . . .

(Lines 18–20 are omitted, in which mention is made of sacrifices and
a fine.)

[And the] boule shall swear the *following*: "I will serve on   21
    the boule to the best of my *ability* [and]
as justly as (I am able) for the people (plethos) of the
    Erythraeans and (that) of the Athenians and of the
allies and I will not *revolt* from the people of the Athenians
    nor
[the] allies of the Athenians, neither I myself nor will I be
    persuaded by another
nor . . . neither I myself nor will I *be persuaded* by   25
    another . . .
. . . and I will not receive (any) one of the *fugitives*, neither . . .
    (I myself nor?)
will I be persuaded *by another* (to receive any) [of those]
    fleeing [to] the Medes, without the *boule of the*
Athenians and the *demos*, nor shall I banish (any of those)
    remaining (in Erythrae) *without* the
boule of the Athenians and the demos. And if any
    [Erythraean] slays
another *Erythraean*, let him be executed if he be *found*   30
    guilty . . . [But if banishment (?)]
is the judgment, let him flee the *entire* Athenian alliance
[and] let *the* property (of him) become public property of
    the Erythraeans. But if anyone . . .

Lines 33–46 are very difficult to restore and have been omitted. They
contain further mention of property or money (36), the *demos* of the
Athenians (38), the allies (41), ten archers (42), and probably a guard
or garrison (42, 46).

A Proxeny Decree for Acheloion
(ca. 450–49 or 426/5)

The Athenians passed decrees granting the status of *proxenos* (a kind of official friend in a foreign state) to their supporters or benefactors throughout the empire. An interesting aspect of this status is the added penalties for any city in which one of Athens' *proxenoi* was murdered, perhaps an indication that the status of "friend of the Athenians" did not come without some risk. In the following decree, a certain Acheloion is declared a *proxenos*, and the cities of the Delian league are apparently referred to as "the cities which the Athenians rule." Some scholars believe this phrase was not employed until the Peloponnesian War, and on this (and other) grounds would date the decree to the 420s despite its early letter-forms (including the three-barred sigma).

And *he* [shall be a proxenos of the Athenians and a] benefactor. [And if by anyone]
Acheloion is do[ne an injustice, suits may be brought in] accordance with this (measure) in A[thens before
   (the court of) the]
polemarch, [and] a court [fee shall not be paid]   5
of more than five drachmas [by the one bringing
suit.] And if someone *slays* [Acheloion
or of] his children any (one) [in any of the cit-
ies] which the Athenians [rule, the city
shall owe] *five* talents [just as if an Athe]-   10
nian by someone is *slain*. [And the court case in Athens
shall] be in accordance with *the* [same (procedure) as (in
   the case of any) Athenian]
having been killed . . .
   (nothing more of the stone remains)

Inscriptiones Graecae, 3rd ed., vol. I, ed. D. Lewis (Berlin: De Gruyter, 1981), no. 19, trans. L. J. Samons II.

The Standards (or "Coinage") Decree
(ca. 450–446, or 420s, or before 414)

This decree is known from fragments of several copies found across the former Athenian empire. One fragment, from the island of Cos, was written in Attic script and contained the three-barred sigma, and primarily on this basis many scholars have dated the decree to the years just before 445. Recently another fragment in Attic script has been identified; it does not contain the three-barred sigma and comes from a city which apparently was not under Athenian control until the 420s. Whatever the date of these regulations, this decree shows a remarkable Athenian willingness to institute uniform (i.e., Athenian) standards for weights, measures, and coinage, a move that probably had some economic advantages but was an undoubtedly unpopular infringement on the cities' sovereignty. Aristophanes parodies the decree in *Birds* 1040–41 (414). Because of the composite nature of the text, the decree is conventionally divided into clauses and no line numbers are given. For missing portions of the text longer than about 15 spaces approximations of the number of lost letter spaces have been provided.

---

(1) [This clause is extremely fragmentary; there is apparently mention of "(local?) ma]gistr[ates (archons) in the] *cities* or ma[gistrates (from Athens?)".] (2) And [the] hellenotamiae [(ca. 24 empty spaces) . . . shall] make a record. [And] *if* [not . . .] any of the cities, let [those malefactors] be *brought* [to trial immediately by anyone wishing into] the heliaea (a court) of the [thesmothetae]. And *the* thesmothetae *within five* [days shall] *submit* [the matter for judgment for those] *indicting* in each case. (3) But if [anyone besides] the magistrates [in] the cities does not act *in accordance with the decrees,* either (anyone) of the *citizens* or of the foreigners, [let him be without] *citizen rights* [and his] *property* shall *become* public and a [tithe (shall be given)] to the goddess (Athena). (4) [And if] there are *no* Athenian magistrates

A Selection of Greek Historical Inscriptions to the End of the Fifth Century B.C., eds. R. Meiggs and D. Lewis (Oxford: Oxford University Press, 1988), no. 45, trans. L. J. Samons II.

(present), the magistrates [of each city] *shall* [carry out the matters in the] decree. [And] if they do not act in accordance with the [decrees, let there be prosecution against] these *magistrates* [in Athens] on pain of [loss of citizen rights (?)]. (5) [And in] *the* mint [having received] the *silver* [they shall mint not] *less* than half and [... (ca. 31 spaces) ...] the cities. [The commissioners (epistatai) shall always] *exact* [three] drachmas per *mna* [(minted, i.e., 3%) ... (ca. 23 spaces) ... they shall] *convert* (the money) or [be] liable ... (6) And what is left [over of the exacted] silver [they shall mint and] *give* either to the *generals* [or to the ...] (7) And when it is given ... (ca. 29 spaces) ... and to (the god) Hephaistos ... (8) [And if] *anyone* makes a motion [or] puts it to a vote concerning [these things that it should be permitted] to use or *loan* [out foreign] *coinage* [let him be immediately indicted (or brought?) before] the Eleven.[1] And the [Eleven shall punish (him)] *by death*. But [if] he disputes the charge, [let the case be heard by the] *dicasterion*. (9) Heralds shall be elected by the [demos (?) ... (ca. 25 spaces) ... the] *things decreed*, one to the *Islands*, [and one to Ionia, and one to the] *Hellespont*, and one [to the area] *around* Thrace. [The generals, having prescribed the journey for each (?) shall] dispatch [these men. If not, let each be called to account at his (?)] *euthynae* (and liable to a fine of) *ten thousand* [drachmas]. (10) And *this* decree [the] magistrates in the cities shall [place] in the marketplace of [each] *city* [having inscribed it on a] *stele* of stone, and (it shall also be placed) by the *commissioners* (epistatai) [in front of] the mint. And these matters shall be *carried* [out by the Athenians,] *if* (those in the cities) themselves are not willing. (11) And the herald going (to the cities) shall ask them (to carry out) whatever the Athenians have bid (them). (12) The secretary of the [boule for the future] shall make an addition to the oath of the boule as *follows*: "If anyone mints coins of silver in the *cities* and does not use the *coins* [of the] *Athenians* or the weights or *measures* [(of the Athenians) but (uses) foreign] *coins* and measures and weights, [I shall exact vengeance on an]d p[unish (him) in accordance with the] *earlier* decree which Klearchos [proposed]." (13) [And it shall be permitted for anyone to turn in] the foreign coin [which he may have and to exchange (it) in accordance

---

[1]A board of Athenian officials overseeing executions, the jail, and certain court cases.

with these same (measures)] whenever he wishes. And the *city* [shall give in return our native coin(?)]. But he, his own (coins) [shall convey to Athens (?) and take them to the] *mint*. (14) [And] *the* commissioners having written [up everything given to them from each source (upon a stele)] shall *place* [the stele of stone in front of the] *mint* for the one *wishing* to view (it). [They shall write up both the total of coins (that are)] foreign, *separately* [(listing) the silver and gold, and the total of native] silver . . .

Cleinias' Decree on Tribute Collection (ca. 447 or ca. 424)

In the following decree the Athenians sought to "tighten-up" the collection of tribute, which had apparently sometimes been subject to fraud or theft while en route to Athens. The earlier date for the decree is based primarily on the letter forms and the name of the proponent, Cleinias. A Cleinias, the father of Alcibiades, was killed at the battle of Coroneia in Boeotia in 447/6. Yet a strong case has been made that the reference to the "cow and panoply" must come after the (apparently first) order to bring these to Athens in a decree of 425, and that Cleinias' decree shows a more developed system of tribute collection than that of a similar measure passed in 426.

Gods.
Resolved by the boule [and the]
demos. (The tribe) Oineis *held the prytany, Spou-*
dias was secretary, [. . .]on
presided, Cleini[as made the motion:] *The*   5
boule and the *magistrates* (archons) [in] the
cities and the [inspect]ors (episkopoi) shall
take care that [there may be] *collect-*
ion of tribute *in* [the course of the] *year*
annually and that it is *brought* to Athens.   10
Seals *shall be made*

Inscriptiones Graecae, 3rd ed., vol. I, ed. D. Lewis (Berlin: De Gruyter, 1981), no. 34, trans. L. J. Samons II.

for the cities, *so that* it may not be possible to commit injustice for those *bringing* the
tribute. *And the* city, having written in
a tablet whatever amount of *tribute* it may send, shall close   15
up (the tribute) with the seal and send it to Athens. And
   those
bringing (the tribute) shall present the tablet in the boule
for reading whenever they give the tribute. And the
prytaneis, after the Dionysia shall convene an ecclesia for the
hellenotamiae [to] show to the Athenians (which) of the ci-   20
ties have given [the tribute] completely and which have fall-
en short, in separate (lists), however many [these may be.
   The] *Athenians*, having sel-
ected men, *four* [in number, shall send them out to] the cities
   to confirm
in writing *the* [tribute brought] *and* to demand the part not [given from those who fell] *short*;   25
two shall sail *to* [the (cities) in the Island (district) and those
   in Ionia upon] a
swift trireme, [while the two others (shall sail) to the (cities)
   in the Hellespont (district) and]
(those) toward Thrace. [Let the prytaneis bring these things
   before the (?)]
boule and before the [demos immediately after the Dionysia
   festival (?) and let them take]
counsel concerning t[hese matters continuously until they   30
   are completed.]
But if any *Athenian* [or ally commits an injustice (?)
   concerning]
the tribute, which it is necessary [for the cities, having
   written (it) in a tab-]
let for those *bringing* [(it), to send to Athens, let him be]
indicted before [the prytaneis by the one] *wishing*, [an
   Athen-]
ian or an *ally*. [And the] *prytaneis* shall *bring*   35
before the boule [the case which] *anyone* brings, [or at
   their] *euth-*
ynae each (will be liable for a fine) [of ten thousand]
   drachmas for bribery. [Whoever may]

be changed by *the* [boule, let their decision in his case
   not] be final [but let it be]
brought before *the* [heliaea immediately]. And whenever it
   seems [an injustice has been done,]
decisions *shall be made* [by the] *prytaneis* as to what *seems*   40
   [best for] *him*
to suffer or *pay.* [And] *if* anyone concerning the *bringing*
of the cow or [the panoply] does an injustice, there shall be
   indictments
against him *and* [punishment] *in* accordance with these
   things. And the [hellen-]
o[tamiae, after they have written (them) up] *on* a board that
   has been *whitened*
[shall publish both the assessment] of the tribute and [the   45
   cities]
[which have paid completely (?)] *and* they shall *inscribe*
   [(?) . . .

The last 21 lines of the inscription are omitted; they are extremely
fragmentary and may contain additional stipulations about late payment of, or disputes over, tribute.

An Athenian Treaty with Colophon
(ca. 447/6 or 427)

Located somewhat inland from the coast of central Asia Minor,
Colophon may have been in revolt from Athens in the early 440s. At any
rate, her tribute payment was reduced from 3 to 1.5 talents per year
sometime between 450 and 446, and the Athenians apparently often reduced the tribute of a rebellious state after placing an Athenian settlement there (see Meiggs, *Athenian Empire*, pp. 161–163, 530). This
reduction, disaffection in other cities during the same period, and the
nature of the document translated here make such a revolt at Colophon
a possibility. Nonetheless, the earlier dating of this decree still rests
heavily on the three-barred sigma found on the stone, and the early
Peloponnesian War provides another very satisfactory context (see Thuc.

Inscriptiones Graecae, 3rd ed., vol. I, ed. D. Lewis (Berlin: De Gruyter, 1981), no. 37,
trans. L. J. Samons II.

3.34). The first 37 lines (omitted here) are very poorly preserved and difficult to restore. They may contain some mention of colonists (from Athens or other cities in Ionia?) chosen to settle in Colophon, but little more can be said about them.

[This] decree [and the oath shall be inscribed by the] *secretary* of the *boule* [on a stele of stone on the Acropolis at the expense]

of the Colophonians. [And at Colophon these things and   40
the oath,]

having inscribed [them on a stone stele, those (sent) into Colophon]

as colonists shall *place* [in whatever place is fitting according to Coloph-]

onian law. [The Colophonians shall swear: "I shall act and]

speak and counsel (in the boule) [to the best of my ability (what is) beautiful and good] *concerning* the demos of the [Athenians and concerning the   45
colony]

and I shall not *revolt* [from the demos of the Athenians either]

in word or in deed, [neither I myself nor shall I be persuaded by another]

and I shall love the [demos of the Athenians and I shall not] *desert*, and the demo[kratia in Colophon / demos of the Colophonians (?) I shall not destroy (?), neither]

I myself nor [shall I be persuaded by another, nor . . .   50
(something in/to another?)]

city *nor* [shall I foment stasis there (?), but in accordance with the] *oath*

these things as true (?) [I shall establish, without guile and harm, (swearing by)]

Zeus and *Apollo* [and Demeter, and if these things]

I transgress, [may both I myself be utterly destroyed and the]

children of mine [for all time, (but) remaining true to my   55
oath, may there be]

for me many and [good things (?) . . .]

Regulations for Chalcis (446/5 or 424/3)

Located on the western coast of the great island of Euboea, Chalcis was an extremely important city to Athens even before the creation of the empire (Hdt. 5.77). The island provided a great source of food (and land) for the Athenians, and its loss late in the Peloponnesian War was bemoaned in Athens (Thuc. 8.95-6). After the Athenians were defeated at Coroneia in Boeotia (447/6), many cities of Euboea revolted, and Pericles led an expedition to recover the island for the empire. The main terms of the settlement for Chalcis were inscribed in a decree (now lost) attached to the one translated below. Arguments for the earlier date of this well-preserved inscription are based both on letter forms (in this case the *rho*) and historical considerations. However, Mattingly notes imperial language here that he finds more fitting to the period of the Peloponnesian War, and this (along with other factors) has led him to prefer the later date for the decree.

Resolved by the boule and the demos, Antiochis held the prytany, Dracontides presided, Diognetos made the motion:
On the following terms an oath shall be sworn by the
    Athenian
boule and dicasts: "I shall not expel Chalcidians from Chalcis, nor the city (of Chalcis) shall   5
I move (or, destroy), nor any private citizen shall I deprive
of his citizen rights nor shall I punish (him) by exile nor
    seize
(him) nor slay (him) nor (his) property shall I take
away without trial, without (the approval of) the demos of
    the Ath-
enians, nor shall I put (anything) to a vote against a party   10
    that has not been summoned to trial,
either against the government or against any private citizen
whatever, and an embassy arriving I shall lead before

Inscriptiones Graecae, 3rd ed., vol. I, ed. D. Lewis (Berlin: De Gruyter, 1981), no. 40, trans. L. J. Samons II.

the boule and demos within ten days whenever
I am one of the prytaneis, to the best of my ability. And
   these things I shall est-
ablish firmly for the Chalcidians (if they are) obedient to the   15
demos of the Athenians." The oath shall be administered by
   an embassy
coming from Chalcis along with the oath commissioners
to the Athenians, and they shall list (the names of) those
   swearing
the oath. That all swear the oath shall be the responsibility of the generals. (empty space)   20
On the following terms the Chalcidians shall swear: "I shall
   not rev-
olt from the demos of the Athenians by any arti-
fice or any contrivance at all, neither by word nor
by deed, nor shall I be persuaded by anyone in revolt,
and if anyone revolts I shall denounce him to the Athenians,   25
and I shall pay the tribute to the Athenians, which
I may persuade the Athenians (to assess?), and an ally shall I
be, the best and most just possible,
and the demos of the Athenians I shall assist
and defend, if anyone does an injustice to the demos of the   30
Athenians; and I shall be obedient to the demos of the Athenians." This oath shall be taken by the Chalcidian adults,
all of them. Whoever does not swear the oath, (his) citizen
   rights
shall be lost and his property become public and
a sacred tithe to Olympian Zeus   35
shall be (paid) from this property. The oath shall be administered
   by an emba-
ssy of Athenians coming to Chalcis with
the oath-commissioners in Chalcis, and they shall list
(the names of) the Chalcidians who swear.
(empty line)
Anticles made the motion: With good fortune for the   40
   Athenians
shall the oath be made by the Athenians and Chalcidians, just as for the Eretrians it was decreed

by the demos of the Athenians. That as swiftly as possible it may happen will be the responsibility of the generals.
(As) those who shall administer the oath after arriving in   45
Chalcis, the demos shall elect five men
immediately. And concerning the hostages, let there be an
answer given to the Chalcidians, that at present the Athenians are resolved to allow matters (to remain) as voted.
And whenever it seems good, having taken counsel there   50
  shall be made
an agreement, just as it may seem suitable
to the Athenians and Chalcidians. And (as for) the
foreigners (xenoi) in Chalcis, except for however many
  dwelling (there)
pay taxes in Athens, and any to whom has been given
immunity from taxes by the demos of the Athenians, the   55
  others
shall pay taxes in Chalcis, just as the other
Chalcidians. And this decree and the
oath shall be inscribed at Athens by the secretary of the boule on a stone stele and (he) shall
place (the stele) on the Acropolis at the expense of the   60
  Chalcidians;
and in Chalcis, in the temple of Zeus the
Olympian the boule of the Chalcidians having inscribed
  (the same things)
shall place (the stele). These things were decreed for the Chalcidians. (empty spaces) And the sacrifices (required by) the
  oracles
for defence of Euboea shall be made as swiftly as possible by   65
Hierokles[1] with three men who may be elected by
the boule from its own (members). That as swiftly as possible
  the sacri-
fices may occur shall be the joint responsibility of the
  generals, and

---

[1]Probably the expounder of oracles lampooned by Aristophanes in his *Peace* 1046–1126
(in 421).

the silver (payment) for them they (the generals) shall furnish.
(empty spaces)

Archestratos made the motion: The other matters (shall be)   70
just as

Anticles (moved). But the euthynae[2] for the Chalcidians,
among

themselves in Chalcis shall be (carried out), just as in Athens for Athenians, except (in cases involving) exile, death,
and loss of citizen rights. Concerning these (cases) the
appeal shall be

in Athens in the heliaea of the thesmoth-   75
etae, in accordance with the decree of the demos. And
concerning the

guard of Euboea the generals shall have the responsibility, to the best of their ability, that it be
the best possible for the Athenians.

                    (THE) OATH   80

Analysis

David Stockton

The Peace of Callias

David Stockton, Fellow and Tutor in Ancient History at Brasenose College, Oxford University, has published widely on both Greek and Roman
history, including his book *Cicero: A Political Biography*. In the article
from which the following excerpt derives, Stockton begins by surveying
the diverse, inconsistent, and scattered fourth-century references to the
Peace of Callias—which many scholars believe to have been made be-

---

[2]Here the term *may* refer to punishments generally rather than to the examinations of
officials after their year of office.

From David Stockton, "The Peace of Callias," *Historia*, 8. Copyright © 1959. Reprinted
with permission of Franz Steiner Verlag.

tween Athens and Persia ca. 449—including its mention by the orator
Isocrates. On the other hand, Stockton notes, fragments from the lost
works of Theopompus and Callisthenes indicate that they denied the existence of a formal peace between Athens and Persia. Theopompus claimed
that the stele in Athens bearing the peace treaty was a forgery because it
was inscribed with Ionic letters (instead of Attic), not a regular Athenian
practice until 403/2. In the passage excerpted here, Stockton argues that
the silence about the peace in Thucydides and Herodotus should be
taken as strong evidence that Theopompus and Callisthenes were right—
no Peace of Callias was made. The issue is seminal to our characterization
of the Athenian empire since Athens' hegemony over the Delian league
was based originally on hostility to the Persians (Thuc. 1.96, above). While
the Athenians might have been able to hold out the threat of the "Persian
menace" during a de facto cessation of hostilities, any formal treaty with
Persia not only took away the Athenians' primary justification for their empire and tribute collection, but also potentially exposed them to the
charge of "medizing" (joining the Medes and Persians).

We must face squarely the bald fact that the anti-Athenian Theopompus and the pro-Athenian Callisthenes both denied the authenticity of
the Peace of Callias, and denied it at a time when its reality was a
rhetorical commonplace, and when it seems that there was in existence a stele . . . bearing what was said to be the text of that Peace. It
seems to me that in all these circumstances Theopompus and Callisthenes would not have stuck their necks out in this way unless they
were pretty sure that it was on others that the axe would fall. . . .

Now, the really disquieting thing is that the fifth century in fact offers no explicit evidence either for or against the Peace. Whatever the
terms of the Peace are conjectured to have been, whether they were
creditable to Athens or rather disappointing, it is remarkable that not
one fifth-century authority should allude to it. For, whatever the exact
terms, it is generally agreed that the Persians covenanted (if they
covenanted anything) to keep their ships of war out of the Aegean. In
490 B.C., Persia had launched her strength against Athens. She had
strong bases in the Aegean. If, some forty years later, the Great King so
humbled himself to a small Greek state ("Who are these Athenians?,"
asked King Darius) that he undertook, and publicly, to keep his fleet
out of the Aegean, and publicly ceded the province of Ionia, was not

this something for Athenians to shout about? To beat Persia at Eurymedon, to liberate large areas from Persian suzerainty, that is one thing: to extract from the Great King a formal and public acceptance of defeat is quite another. Yet, far from a shout of triumph, we strain our ears in vain for a whisper.

The obvious people to have told us about Callias and his peace are Herodotus and Thucydides.

The silence of Thucydides is very difficult to explain, if we suppose that the peace was a reality. It is not of much use to stress the sketchy nature of the *Excursus* on the Pentecontaëtia [1. 89–117], and to make a list of all the other events which fail to find a place therein. It does not help to say that, after all, the Peace of Callias was not all that one-sided, and acquired a rather meretricious glitter only after (and in contrast with) the base surrender made to Persia in the Peace of Antalcidas [in 387/6]. There is no escaping the fact that, brilliant achievement or half-confession of failure, the Peace is more relevant to the *Excursus* than any of the other omissions; and that its omission must therefore cast strong doubts on its existence.

For the *Excursus* is specifically introduced by Thucydides as a brief survey of the history of the Pentecontaëtia, designed to illustrate the growth of Athenian power during this period. This purpose is again emphasized at the close of the *Excursus*. In discussing the growth of Athenian power, Thucydides naturally tells his readers about the formation and subsequent development of the Confederacy of Delos: we read of the fixing of the original tribute; of secessions and revolts; of synods and organization—not a great deal, of course, since this is only a recapitulation, but for the length of the *Excursus* a good deal. We are told that the members of the Confederacy covenanted to contribute ships and money for the pursuance of the war against the Persian. And we read how Athens, at first only *prima inter pares,* slid into a position of scarcely-veiled tyranny.

To this theme, the Peace of Callias, had it been concluded, must have been relevant: so relevant, indeed, that Thucydides could not have passed over it in silence. The Confederates were bound to pay ships and money ["against the barbarian"]. What if the war ["against the barbarian"] was brought to an end by a formal peace? Would not the obligation of the Confederates to contribute to the cost of the war end also? And if Athens none the less continued to enforce payment, is not this a vital stage in the development out of Confederacy into Empire? And is not this development a large part of Thucydides' theme in the *Excursus?* Some champions of the Peace of Callias have indeed regarded it as the turning point of this development: and rightly, if there was such a peace. But is it reasonable to suppose that Thucydides, with his great interest in this development of the Confederacy, intertwined as it is with the growth of Athenian power and the outbreak of war in 431 B.C., failed to take the point, or disregarded it as not sufficiently important to merit inclusion? Three words would have sufficed: ["with Peace made"]. There is not one.

Moreover, I want also to stress that the *Excursus* is not the only place where Thucydides fails to refer to the Peace where a reference would have been apt and timely. Take the speech of the Mytilenean ambassadors to Sparta in Book III. In chapter 10 [see above], they seek to explain the reasons for their dissatisfaction with Athenian leadership: the Athenians started off well, but gradually became tyrannical in their attitude towards their allies. Should we not expect some reference to the decision to continue exacting the *phoros* after the conclusion of peace with Persia? There is no such reference.

Next, let us turn to Book VIII. Let me briefly recall the situation. Athens has lost a great armament at Syracuse [in 413]. Her back is to the wall. Sparta has moved over to the offensive in the Aegean, and Athens' Empire, her very lifeline through the narrows, is threatened. But, by herself, Sparta is unable to deliver the *coup de grace*. The decision rests with Persia: if she joins Sparta, Athens is lost; if she remains neutral, there is a fighting chance. Is it not passing strange (if not passing belief) that in such a situation, throughout his narrative of the negotiations with Persia of both Sparta and Athens, Thucydides should fail to mention the not unimportant fact that Persia was bound by a treaty not to bring a fleet into the Aegean? . . .

There is another very important passage at VIII. 56. 4, a passage which has in fact been regarded as very strong evidence for the authenticity of the Peace of Callias. Gomme, indeed, goes so far to regard it as conclusive evidence. "Alcibiades was trying to win over the Persian King from the Peloponnesian to an Athenian alliance, and reported that the king might be willing, if they surrendered all Ionia and the adjacent islands, and if they would allow him to bring his fleet into the Aegean. . . . Such a demand, coming from one about to accede to a request, could only be based on a written agreement. The treaty is genuine."

I confess, I cannot follow Gomme here. I quite fail to see why this demand "could only be based on a written agreement." Are we to suppose that the Peace of Callias forebade the Great King to build ships, *tout court?* Yet this is what Gomme seems to be saying here. More important, if the demand was based on a written agreement, why on earth does not Thucydides tell us as much? It is not unimportant for the reader to know; and Thucydides has nowhere previously referred to such an agreement, so that he need not remind us of it now. In reality, the language of the King's demand is quite neutral, and could just as well be based on the existing situation. Athens holds Ionia and the adjacent islands. Her fleet is at sea. The Great King demands as his price that Athens cede to him the islands and Ionia, and guarantee not to oppose his fleet if he sends it into the Aegean or to deny him access to Aegean shiptimber. To say that this passage is conclusive for the Peace is quite unjustified. On the contrary, Thucydides' failure to refer to the Peace in this context makes it almost certain that he knew nothing of such a Peace. And, if Thucydides knew nothing of it, it did not exist. . . .

And now, Herodotus. Like Thucydides, he says nothing; and I find his silence just as impressive. After all, Herodotus was the historian of the Persian Wars, and he did not limit himself to the narration of events earlier than 479 B.C. It is hard to believe that he would not, somewhere or other, have found space to refer to the peace which formally brought to an end the war between Athens and Persia.

It has, of course, been held that Herodotus does refer to the Peace of Callias in VII. 151. In this passage he tells us that many years after 480 B.C. "there chanced to be at Susa at the same time on other business some Athenian envoys, Callias son of Hipponicus and his companions." Wade-Gery thinks that it is "likely that the ["other matter"] for which Kallias was at Sousa, is the peace which bears his name." But, leaving aside the question of the date of Callias' visit to Susa, is it really at all likely that the ["other matter"] is the Peace of Callias? If it is, why does not Herodotus say so outright? It is no use suggesting that he was deliberately concealing a fact which he considered discreditable to Athens. If this were his intention, why did he mention Callias' visit at all? Nor would there be any point in trying to cover up what must have been notorious, if it existed. It is secrets men try to keep dark, not common knowledge. It is surely much easier to believe either that Herodotus did not know what business Callias was doing in

Susa, or that if he is trying to muffle up anything in this vague phrase "on other business" it is an unsuccessful attempt to conclude a treaty of peace—or some other discreditable business. The Peace of Callias, I repeat, could not be covered up in this way. Had that Peace really existed, we may be confident that Herodotus would have mentioned it, either here or elsewhere in his work—or I have yet to hear any good reason to the contrary. . . .

Let me now try to draw all these threads together, and briefly to reconstruct the sequence of events as I see it. After the death of Cimon, Pericles felt free to have done with a war which had ceased to be profitable, and which in the light of the situation in Greece might prove embarrassing if pursued further. So the operations against Persia were halted. Persia herself had long been on the defensive, and had no wish to pursue a war in which she could see no prospect of success. So the fighting flickered out. Pericles could now turn his attention to rebuilding Athens' temples and securing the Aegean against Persia. He called for a Hellenic Congress. When this scheme came to grief he decided that Athens must go it alone. The building programme was to be financed from Confederate moneys, and an Aegean fleet maintained from the same source. The *phoros* (which may not have been collected in the year following the cessation of hostilities) was to continue to be paid. To this proposal the enemies of Pericles objected that it was disgraceful that money which was being contributed for the war against Persia should be diverted from its proper use and employed to beautify Athens. Pericles countered with the argument that the allies had no cause to complain, because Athens was keeping the Persians in check. Without an Aegean fleet in being, without the tribute which sustained that fleet, the way would be open at any time to a Persian counter-offensive to recover lost ground. The war had not ended: it was simply that hostilities had ceased.

Understandably, then, we find in all our authorities down to and including Lysias in the *Epitaphius*, no mention of a peace with Persia; although there are several passages, as we have seen, where we should expect it to be mentioned if it did exist, and which therefore strongly suggest that it did not. But after the Peace of Antalcidas we begin, with Isocrates in 380 B.C., to be told of such a peace. We are not surprised to find that there are differences about the date, the author, the scope of the peace: for the peace was a fiction, a product of the years after 387 B.C., when Sparta was held to have betrayed Greece. During these years Athens was going all out to rebuild an Aegean confederacy in order that, as the charter of the Second Athenian Confederacy has it, "the Lacedaemonians may allow the Greeks to be free and autonomous." These were years of vigorous propaganda directed to show what great services Athens had rendered to Greek liberty; how, where Sparta had betrayed Greece and kow-towed to Persia, Athens had humbled the Great King. The theme is already clearly stated in the *Epitaphius*, around 390 B.C. In the *Panegyricus*, the jingoist Isocrates is in fine voice, declaring boldly that Athens has a *right* to the mastery of the sea. How great the temptation to exaggerate the Athenian achievement, and to oppose to the degradation of the "King's Peace" not merely naval and military triumphs over Persia but a great and glorious peace imposed by Athens on a shattered enemy. Indeed, it was a temptation that proved irresistible. Already in 380 B.C. Isocrates has set the two side by side, and there were others to follow eagerly where he led. Ephorus was taken in. Perhaps a stele had already been erected which purported to give the terms of this "Peace of Callias" (the choice of name would not be difficult). . . .

But *could* such a public forgery as this be committed in fourth century Athens? Some have thought not, decidedly. Yet Andocides, as we have seen, could expect to get away with a whole parcel of lies. Apart from the consideration that for many, or nearly all, Athenians it would be no forgery at all but only a republication of an important and heartening document that had got lost or perhaps broken, I cannot see how we can discount *a priori* a public forgery of this kind. There were no back numbers of *The Times* to which men could turn to verify their facts. Theopompus thought such a forgery possible, for he roundly declared that it had happened. And only recently, Mr. Harrison has again underlined the scrappy nature of Athenian fifth century public records. Lysias declared that Nicomachus produced public decrees from the archives to order; and even if his charges are exaggerated, the suggestion is clearly not implausible.

The Peace of Callias came to be accepted as a reality, a rhetorical commonplace, until Theopompus and Callisthenes declared that it was all a lie. But the lie had had a good run for its money, and in its course had gathered sufficient accretions of testimony to its truth to impose itself on posterity. As Plato appreciated, you can do a lot with a lie if it is a really big one.

Russell Meiggs

The Peace of Callias

Russell Meiggs was for many years Fellow and Tutor in Ancient History at Balliol College, Oxford University, and University Lecturer. Among many other works on such diverse topics as *Roman Ostia* and *Trees and Timber in the Ancient Mediterranean World*, Meiggs wrote what has become the standard history of *The Athenian Empire*. In the following selection from that work, Meiggs argues for the authenticity of the Peace of Callias while noting some problems with the theory supporting the peace. The voluminous controversy over the treaty and the development of Athenian imperialism is linked closely to that over the dating of the inscriptions translated above. So great a scholar as M. I. Finley belittled the controversy over the inscriptions (see the selection that follows), though Meiggs retorted that Finley was making a "molehill out of a mountain." Meiggs himself wrote that "Statistically an article on the Peace of Callias can be expected every two years," and since his own publication the debate has continued unabated. In the following passage Meiggs attempts to counter the arguments of those like Stockton, who place such emphasis on the failure of Herodotus and Thucydides to mention the alleged treaty.

After Cimon's campaign in Cyprus [ca. 450/49], no further League operations against Persia are recorded. No Persian ships are known to have sailed west of Pamphylia and no Greek triremes sailed east. Fourth-century Athenian orators knew the reason; it was the famous peace, whose main terms were familiar to them and were repeated with minor variations to their audience when an emotional appeal to past glories suited their argument. The first clear surviving reference comes in Isocrates' *Panegyricus* of 380, when he contemptuously compares the humiliating Peace of Antalcidas dictated by Persia with the terms imposed on Persia by Athens when she was at the height of her power. The next clear references come from Demosthenes in 351 and 343, and he is followed by Lycurgus in 328. At some point in this complacent chorus Theopompus introduced a sour note. The peace, he insisted, was one of many fabrications invented for the greater glory of Athens. Only one of his arguments survives: it must be a forgery because the letters on the stele were Ionic, and Ionic letters were not adopted by Athens until the archonship of Euclides in 403/2.

The orators were not the only purveyors of the "myth" against which Theopompus was protesting. He had probably already read the detailed account of the peace in Ephorus which survives in Diodorus. Another historian may have reached the same conclusion as Theopompus, whether independently or following his lead. According to Plutarch Callisthenes denied that there was a formal peace after the victory of the Eurymedon, though the practical effect of the victory was to keep the Persians east of the Chelidonian isles. Without the full context we cannot be sure what points Callisthenes was making. Though he was probably denying the existence of any peace at any time in the fifth century his actual argument applies only to the sixties and he could possibly be refuting the confused versions of the later orators who associated the peace with this climax of Athenian success. With this confusion we need not be seriously concerned. If there was a peace the only convincing context is after the death of Cimon, where Diodorus records it [449/8]. . . .

Theopompus' acid attack would probably not by itself have weighed heavily against the concordance of Ephorus, the orators, and Craterus. What has influenced sceptics much more strongly is the silence of Thucydides and of all other fifth-century sources. If the Cyprian campaign was followed by a peace Thucydides should have recorded it, for, however much he compressed his review of the fifty years [between the Persian and Peloponnesian Wars], a peace with Persia was too important to omit. His main theme was the development of Athenian power; a peace with Persia would have provided a much more stable background for the concentration of Athenian resources on the control of the Aegean than a mere cessation of hostilities. Hardly less surprising would be Thucydides' failure to mention the peace, if peace there was, in the speech of the Mytilenaeans at Olympia in 428. The Mytilenaeans were attempting to justify to Sparta's allies their revolt from Athens. They speak of Athens relaxing her hostilities against Persia and being more concerned with the suppression of the allies; they do not claim that Athens had made peace, though this would have been a stronger argument in their favour than any they use. We might also have expected a reference when Pissuthnes, satrap at Sardis, intervened at the time of the revolt of Samos in 440, or when Thucydides reviewed in considerable detail the resources of both sides at the outbreak of the Peloponnesian War. It is only in his last book that any evidence for an Athenian peace with Persia has been found; this evidence convinced Gomme, but it cannot be regarded as decisive against this silence in places where the context would seem to demand a reference.

The silence of Herodotus would be less puzzling, for he deliberately ended his story of the Persian wars with the siege of Sestus; but digressions form a large part of his history and there are several contexts, as for instance in his description of Egypt, where he might have been expected to comment on the effects of a peace between Greeks and Persians. A reference has indeed often been seen in a passage which has already been discussed. Callias was with an Athenian embassy at Susa "on other business" when some Argives went up to renew with the new King Artaxerxes the friendly relations that had been established with his father Xerxes. But there is no good reason why Herodotus should have referred so obliquely to a peace which, if made, was publicly accepted at Athens and well known throughout the Aegean world, and the natural context for the Argive embassy is soon after the new king was known to be firmly established.

A further strong argument against a peace can be derived from a passage in Plutarch's *Pericles*, in which he is describing the opposition in the Assembly to Pericles' building policy by the followers of Thucydides son of Melesias. [See Plutarch *Pericles* 12, above.] . . .

This vivid passage has generally been considered to be an authentic echo of a real scene, and the date can be fixed within narrow limits. The first year of the Parthenon accounts was 447–446 and the main annual grants to the commissioners both of the temple and the chryselephantine cult statue were from the outset paid by Athena's treasurers; this implies that the Delian League reserve had been amalgamated with Athena's treasury before the Parthenon was begun. The critical debate on the use of the allies' money should therefore have taken place between Cimon's death in 451 and 447. In Plutarch's version there is no hint of a peace with Persia; the natural inference from the speeches of both sides is that the allies still think that they are paying tribute for operations against Persia and that a state of war still exists. If peace had been made, it should have been at the centre of the argument on both sides and some clear hint should have survived even in a short summary. . . . It remains for those who believe in the peace to explain Plutarch's version.

The silence of the surviving sources of the fifth century combined with Theopompus' criticism makes a strong case against the Peace of Callias, but the reasons for accepting it, though not yet decisive, are stronger. If we could agree with Schwartz that this was a literary rather than a historical problem we could relegate the discussion to an appendix in small type; but one's view of the forties depends to a considerable extent on one's attitude to the peace. If no peace was made there can have been no public decision to abandon operations against Persia, and the allies cannot have known in the early forties that there would be no more League expeditions. If, on the other hand, peace was made it must surely have been publicly made, accepted by the Athenian Assembly, and known throughout the Greek world. It will have at once raised acute problems for Athens and for the allies. The pattern of events in the forties strongly supports the case for a peace but such argument, if unsupported, could reasonably be resented as circular. The firmer starting-point is the peace made by Athens with Darius, Artaxerxes' successor, in 423. . . .

[Meiggs goes on to argue that a peace probably made with Persia in 424/3 should be understood as a renewal of an earlier treaty.]

The treaty of 424–423 is a strong argument in favour of an earlier treaty, and, as Wade-Gery has pointed out, there may be a further link. Another decree of 424–423 is concerned with the payment of her annual dues to the priestess of Athena Nike. It is inscribed on the back of a stele which records the decision to appoint a priestess and build a temple of Athena Nike, and is also concerned with the payment to be made to the priestess. The two decrees are closely associated and the second was proposed by a Callias. The proposer of the first is not known, for the early part of the decree is missing—but the three-bar sigma implies a date before 445, and the frieze along the south wall of the temple of Nike depicted scenes of fighting between Greeks and Persians. It is tempting to believe that the decision to build the temple followed the making of peace and was intended to represent it as a victorious settlement.

A further ground for accepting the peace is the evidence of Theopompus that it was publicly recorded for all to see. If it was a forgery it was a publicly accepted forgery set up officially. As has been suggested above there would be no sting in Theopompus' criticism if the stele had been put up recently, for the date of the copy would be adequate explanation of the Ionic letters. . . .

A more widely accepted view is that the Peace of Callias was invented after and because of the King's Peace of 386 and was designed to emphasize the humiliating contrast between Athens' past pride and her present subservience, which Isocrates himself stresses. The fatal objection to this view is that the determining factor is the public policy of the Athenian state and not the personal views of Isocrates. In the eighties the Athenians, publicly at least, were supporting the King's Peace. When the Athenians made an alliance with Chios in 384 the decree, which sanctions the alliance and praises the Chian envoys who have come to Athens, recognizes the assurance of the Chians "that they will uphold, like the Athenians, the peace and friendship and oaths and terms of agreement which the king swore and the Athenians and the Spartans and the rest of the Greeks," and the Chian envoys have brought with them from Chios "assurances of goodwill to the people of Athens and all Greece and the king." Such language is quite inconsistent with the public sponsoring of a forged peace imposing very restrictive terms on Persia. . . .

The problem raised by Plutarch's account of the building debate is also not insuperable. We could believe that the account has passed through other hands before it is used by Plutarch and that some of the original arguments have been obscured or forgotten. The passage may also have suffered some rhetorical inflation in transmission. The statement, for instance, in Pericles' defence of his policy, that the allies contribute not a single horse, nor ship, nor hoplite, is not accurate. Allies, as we have seen, fought on sea at the battle of Aegina and on land at the battle of Tanagra; later, the regulations imposed in 450–449 on Miletus almost certainly provided for hoplite service. It looks like a typical rhetorical elaboration of a simple argument. The long and detailed analysis of the social and economic advantages of a public-works policy, with its carefully balanced clauses, reads more like the fourth than the fifth century. The whole section may indeed have approached its present form in the late fourth century when Athens had again embarked on a public-building policy. Cicero, for instance, tells us that Demetrius of Phalerum attacked the extravagance of the Propylaea.

This does not deny that the debate in Plutarch may have an authentic nucleus, though it is difficult to identify the original source. . . . [But] whether his ultimate source be genuine or spurious, Plutarch's account of the building debate is not decisive evidence against a Peace of Callias.

Thucydides' silence is more embarrassing. No convincing explanation has been given even by the strongest advocates of the peace and the best that can be offered here is a palliative. It has been held by some that Thucydides' omission of the treaty with Darius [in 424/3] is easily explained if this was a mere renewal of an earlier treaty, and in fact the omission has been used more than once as an argument in favour of the Peace of Callias. But this surely is special pleading. If Thucydides records an Athenian embassy that set out for Susa in 425–424 and returned when it reached Ephesus because it heard that the Persian king had died, there is no good reason why he should not have recorded the embassy on which Epilycus served in 424–423 that took over and completed the mission of the previous year. . . .

A further anomaly in Thucydides' treatment of Athenian relations with Persia intensifies the general problem. Andocides mentions the Athenian decision to abandon their treaty with the Persian king and support the revolt of Amorges. Thucydides introduces Amorges for the first time in his narrative of 412, as "Amorges, the bastard, who had revolted from the king." The Athenian decision to support this rebel is not mentioned in its proper context, probably some three years earlier, and it is never explained, but it is a very surprising step and had a significant bearing on the course of the war. There are then three silences and not only one in Thucydides to explain, and since two known events of some importance are unrecorded, the omission of the third is a rather less strong argument against its existence than it seemed at first. And since Thucydides introduces Amorges without having mentioned the decisive point in his relations with Athens, we may think it not impossible that Thucydides should have shown a knowledge of a treaty without having mentioned it at the two points where it was most relevant to his history.

Such knowledge has been thought to be implied in Thucydides' account of the negotiations of 411. Alcibiades, hoping to secure his recall to Athens, held out the hope that he could secure Persian help. Athenian envoys were sent to negotiate with him but he soon realized that he had considerably less influence with the Persian satrap, Tissaphernes, than he had alleged. To avoid exposure he put forward in the name of the satrap terms which he assumed would be unacceptable in order to throw the responsibility for the breakdown on the Athenians. To his surprise the Athenians seem to have been prepared to sacrifice the whole of Ionia and the offshore islands; what they were not prepared even to consider was the demand that the King should be allowed to build ships and sail along his own coast wherever he wished and with as many ships as he wished. No such clause is included in any of the quick succession of treaties made in 411 between the Spartans and Tissaphernes and it is considerably easier to understand if Persia had, under a previous treaty with Athens, accepted limits for her warships.

The arguments against the Peace of Callias are not strong enough to destroy confidence. That confidence rests partly on the firm evidence for the treaty with Darius but no less on the pattern of events in the early forties which are most easily explained by the assumption that the tradition [of a peace treaty] preserved by Diodorus is basically right. . . .

The fighting against Persia could be ended because the climate of opinion in Athens and in the Aegean had changed sufficiently since 478 to make the new policy acceptable. In 479 when Mardonius sent peace proposals to Athens a councillor who proposed that they should be put before the people was lynched. The victories of Salamis and Plataea exalted the national spirit but did nothing to lessen the hatred. When the Athenians returned to their homes after Plataea the city had been twice occupied and sacked. A few buildings which had served to house Persian officers had been spared, but all their temples had been burnt to the ground and very little else remained standing. Against this background it was difficult to think dispassionately of Persians. They were the national enemy, the barbarians, a subservient race ruled by an arrogant and cruel court. Something of this feeling remains in Aeschylus' *Persae*, produced in the spring of 472, but there emerges also in the tragedy something of the finer side of the Persian character. . . .

The military situation [ca. 450] provided a favourable context for negotiations. The Athenian attempt to reverse the balance of power in the eastern Mediterranean had not been an unqualified success. The ships detached from his fleet by Cimon to look for opportunities in

Egypt had not provoked a general rising against Persia. In Cyprus some successes had been gained, but when Cimon died the fleet returned to Athens without consolidating the ground they had won. As for the Persians, their lack of success in Cyprus must have weakened the confidence that came from the recovery of Egypt, and the final sea battle of the campaign had shown that Greek fleets were still superior to the Phoenicians. More important, Megabyzus, the hero of the Egyptian campaign, had fallen out with the King and was establishing a powerful independent base in Syria. . . .

The Peace of Callias gave rise to crisis in the League and in Athens. With the end of hostilities against Persia the League had lost its original function; but Athens had no intention of relaxing her hold on the organization she had built up. There was widespread protest throughout the Aegean world but Athens made no attempt at compromise. The League would not be allowed to dissolve, the allies would continue to pay yearly tribute. These were the vital years of transition from League to Empire. Even the language changes; the "alliance," becomes "the cities which Athens controls." Athens was able to maintain a firm policy and weather the storm, thanks to the means of control she had already developed. In the fifties, if not earlier, she had learnt to send out constitutional advisers, to install political residents and garrisons. The tools of empire had already been forged.

M. I. Finley

The Athenian Empire: A Balance Sheet

Sir Moses Finley, late Master and Honourable Fellow of Darwin College, and Professor of Ancient History, Cambridge University, was born and educated in America though he spent most of his scholarly career in Eng-

From P. D. A. Garnsey and C. R. Whittaker, *Imperialism in the Ancient World.* Reprinted with the permission of Cambridge University Press.

land. There he became one of the twentieth century's most influential students of Greek history and society, publishing on a wide range of topics from the Homeric world to slavery and the ancient economy. Although himself a great admirer of Athenian democracy, Finley never palliated what he considered the essential preconditions for the development of Athens' regime: slavery and empire. In the following essay, Finley details the benefits Athens received from her empire and here (as elsewhere, see his *Democracy Ancient and Modern*) connects the development of democracy with the imperial revenues and the new political power of the Athenian rowers.

"Every doctrine of imperialism devised by men is a consequence of their second thoughts. But empires are not built by men troubled by second thoughts."[1]

I start with that aphoristic formulation, the truth of which has been demonstrated in the study of modern imperialisms, as an antidote to the familiar practice of *beginning* a discussion of the Athenian empire with aims and motives and quickly sliding over to attitudes and even theory, thereby implying that the men who created and extended the empire also began with a defined imperialist programme and theories of imperialism. An outstanding current example of the procedure I have in mind is the attempt to date a number of Athenian laws and decrees (or to support a proposed date) by what may be called their imperialist tone. If they are "harsh," it is argued, they smack of Cleon and should be dated in the 420s B.C., and not in the time of the more "moderate" Periclean leadership, the 440s or 430s. In so far as the argument is not circular, it implies the existence of an identifiable programme of imperialism, or rather of both successive and conflicting programmes, and that requires demonstration, not assumption.

A second source of confusion is the unavoidable ambiguity of the word "empire." Stemming from the Latin *imperium*, "empire" becomes entangled with the word "emperor," and much of the extensive discussion throughout the Middle Ages and on into modern times ends in a tautological cul-de-sac: an empire is the territory ruled by an emperor. Everyone knows that there are, and have been in the past,

---

[1]A. P. Thornton, *Doctrines of Imperialism* (New York: Wiley, 1965), p. 47.

important empires not ruled by an emperor, and I see no purpose in playing word-games in order to get round that harmless linguistic anomaly. To suggest, for example, that we should abandon "empire" as a category in Greek history and speak only of "hegemony" does not seem to me helpful or useful. It would have been small consolation to the Melians, as the Athenian soldiers and sailors fell upon them, to be informed that they were about to become the victims of a hegemonial, not an imperial, measure.

This is not to question the legitimacy of efforts to differentiate among empires. All broad classificatory terms—"state" is the obvious analogy—embrace a wide spectrum of individual instances. The Persian, Athenian and Roman empires differed among themselves in important ways, as do modern empires. It then becomes necessary, as with all classifications, to establish the canons for inclusion or exclusion. Those who play with "hegemony" seem to me to give excessive weight to purely formal considerations, which, if adopted rigorously, would fragment the category "empire" so much as to render it empty and useless. . . .

A notable example of the formalistic approach is the concern of some historians to define and date the point at which a voluntary association of states was converted into an Athenian empire. The year 454 is a favourite date, because, it is generally believed, the "league treasury" was then transferred from Delos to Athens. At most, such an action was a symbol, a brutal statement of the reality, but not the reality itself. The word "voluntary" is not even a good symbol. . . .

Thucydides, with his incomparable eye for reality, did not confuse it with the symbols and the slogans. "First," he writes in opening his narrative of the half-century between the Persian and Peloponnesian wars (1.98.1), "they (the Athenians) besieged Eion on the Strymon River," still in Persian hands, and then the island of Skyros in the north Aegean. Their populations were enslaved and *their territories were colonised by Athenian settlers.* Next Athens compelled Carystus on Euboea to join the league; clearly the "voluntary" principle had had a very short run. Soon Naxos tried to withdraw from the league (the precise date is uncertain), only to be besieged and crushed by Athens. Naxos "was the first allied city to be enslaved against established usage," comments Thucydides (1.98.4), employing his favourite metaphor for Athenian interference with the autonomy of the subject-cities in the empire.

Of course the Athenian empire underwent significant changes in the more than half a century of its existence. So has every other empire of similar (or longer) duration in history. To establish and explain the changes is a valid historical concern, but I find it a misconceived enterprise to seek one point along a continuous line which permits us to say that there was no empire before and that there was an empire thereafter. Carystus refused to join the alliance and was forced in; Naxos sought to leave and was forcibly prevented. And they were only the first of many city-states in that position, subject to the authority of another state which acted to advance its own interests, political and material.

I do not dispute that the "Delian league" (a modern name for which there is no ancient authority) was welcome when it was created in 478 B.C., both because of the popularity of the vengeance appeal and, fundamentally, because of the need to clear the Aegean Sea of Persian naval forces. The Persians had twice invaded Greece unsuccessfully, and no one in 478 could have had the slightest confidence that the Great King would accept the defeats passively and would not return in a third attempt. Control of the Aegean was the most obvious protective measure, and Athens successfully won the leadership of such an undertaking. An Athenian, Aristides, was given the task of fixing the amount of money or the number of ships equipped and manned which each member-state would provide for the combined league fleet. The Athenians supplied the league treasurers *(Hellenotamiai)* and the military-naval command. Within a dozen years (the exact number depends on the date of the battle of Eurymedon, which no scholar dates later than 466 B.C.), the league's formal objective was achieved. The Persian fleet of 200 triremes, most of them Phoenician, was captured and destroyed in a great land-and-sea battle at the mouth of the Eurymedon River in southern Asia Minor. Yet the "league" remained in existence without a moment's faltering and its membership grew, willingly or by compulsion as the case may have been in each instance, exactly as before Eurymedon.

The chief executant of Athenian policy in those years and the commander-in-chief at Eurymedon was Cimon. . . . And Cimon, of course, far from being a "radical democrat" or "demagogue" like Pericles, let alone Cleon, represented the traditional, oligarchically inclined, landowning aristocracy of Athens. Had he lived longer, he no doubt would have opposed many of the policies adopted by both

Pericles and Cleon with respect to the empire. However, his opposition would not have been on moral grounds. There is no difference in "harshness" between the treatment of the people of Eion and Skyros in Cimon's day and Cleon's proposal nearly half a century later to massacre the people of Mytilene. Our sources, in fact, do not reveal a single Athenian who opposed the empire as such, not even Thucydides son of Melesias or his kinsman and namesake, the historian. [See the selection from Frost in Part III below.] . . .

The present essay will focus on the economics of imperial power. . . . Because of the paucity and one-sidedness of the sources, no narrative is possible, and that means no adequate consideration of development and change. If what follows therefore has a static appearance, that is not because I hold the improbable view that the relations between Athens and her subjects were fundamentally unchanged from 478 to 404 but because I know of no way to document significant change, and no other way to avoid falling into the harshness-of-Cleon trap I have already discussed. We have the impression, for example, that over the years Athens interfered with increasing frequency and toughness in the internal affairs of some or all of the subjects: certain criminal cases had to be tried in Athens before Athenian juries, the right to coin money was taken away for a period, and there were other measures. What little we know about these actions rests almost entirely on epigraphical finds, and although it is usually possible to offer a plausible reason for the introduction of a particular measure at the time of a particular inscription, there has been too much unhappy experience with the crumbling of such logic upon the discovery of a new inscription. Besides, the dates of some of the most critical measures, such as the coinage decree [see above], remain the subject of open controversy.

We know, too, that the Athenians developed a considerable administrative machinery for the empire, 700 officials, says Aristotle (*Constitution of Athens* 24.3), about as many as the number for internal affairs. Apart from suspicion about the duplication of the figure 700, there is no valid reason to question his accuracy. "We do not know enough to say that 700 is an impossible figure" is needlessly sceptical. And again the sources let us down: the evidence for the administration is almost entirely epigraphical; it does not take us back earlier than the Erythrae decree [see above], probably of the mid-450s; it allows barely a glimpse into the division of functions. Nothing can be deduced from silence here: there are virtually no Athenian inscriptions (other than dedications) before the mid-fifth century, and even the tribute drops from site between the original assessment by Aristides and 454. We may safely assume, I believe, that administrative officials (both military and civilian, in so far as that distinction has any meaning in this context) other than the *Hellenotamiai* began to appear at least as soon as there was resistance to membership, that their numbers increased and so did their duties and powers as the years went on. No long-range or systematic Athenian planning is implied in that assumption. What is indisputable is the existence and scale of this administration in the end, not only very large by Greek standards but also, as has apparently not been noticed, relatively larger than the formal administration in the provinces of the Roman empire. . . .

[After discussing the annual collection of hundreds of talents of tribute from the "allies" and the seizure of mines from Thasos by the Athenians, Finley continues.]

It was in the area of private enrichment, not public, that land played a major role in the Athenian empire. The number of Athenian citizens, usually from the poorer strata, who were given either allotments of confiscated land or, at least in Lesbos after the unsuccessful revolt there in 428, a substantial, uniform (and therefore arbitrary) "rent," roughly equivalent to a hoplite's pay for a full year, on holdings retained and worked by the islanders, may have totalled 10,000 in the course of the imperial period. The most naked kind of imperial exploitation therefore directly benefited perhaps 8–10 per cent of the Athenian citizen body. Some confiscations were in places from which the defeated population had been totally expelled, but many were in areas in which the local people remained as a recognised community, and there the settler pattern that has dominated so much of the history of later imperialism was evident, though rather in embryo because the settlements were short-lived.

Colonies and cleruchies are not the whole story, though most accounts of the empire rest with them, "too preoccupied in studying the misdeeds of Athenian imperialism through official institutions and collective decisions" to give due weight to "the action of individuals who played their part in the general concert." Individual Athenians, most of them from the upper end of the social and economic spectrum, acquired landed property in subject territories where there were neither colonies nor cleruchies. The evidence is scarce, but one piece is remarkable enough for a closer look. In the surviving fragments of the very detailed record, inscribed on stone, of the sale by public auction of the property confiscated from men convicted of participation in the double sacrilege of 415 B.C., the profanation of the mysteries and the mutilation of the herms, there are included a few landed estates outside Attica, in Oropus on the Boeotian border, on Euboea and Thasos, and at Abydos on the Hellespont and Ophryneion in the Troad. . . .

They had acquired their holdings by "private enterprise," though we have no idea how that was achieved. Throughout the Greek world in this period, land ownership was restricted to citizens, unless a *polis* by a sovereign act granted special permission to a noncitizen, which it appears to have done rarely and then only for notable services to the state. . . .

As I have already said, we do not know how these acquisitions were brought about. Were they obtained "legally" or "illegally"? Only the Athenian answer is clear: the Athenian state accepted the legitimacy of the title and sold the estates as the property of the condemned men. That the Athenian empire was the operative element seems certain to me: I need not again note the ambiguity of the concept of "voluntary action"; we are here concerned with men who had influence and power inside Athens, men to be courted by subjects. It is even more certain that there was a great resentment in the empire over this breach of the principle of citizen monopoly of the land, hence the Athenian concession in the decree founding the so-called second Athenian league in 378/7 B.C. that neither the Athenian state nor any of its citizens will be permitted "to acquire either a house or land in the territories of the allies, whether by purchase or by foreclosure or by any other means whatsoever" (*IG* II² 43.35–41). . . .

The moment we turn to [another] category of my typology, "other forms of economic exploitation or subordination," we are immediately plunged into the contentious field of Greek "trade and politics." . . .

The problem can be stated in this way. Control of the Aegean was for Athens an instrument of power. How was that instrument employed to achieve ends beyond collection of tribute, land settlement, interference in internal political arrangements, suppression of petty wars and the more or less complete elimination of piracy? More precisely, was it in fact employed for any ends other than those I have just listed, and, in particular, for commercial ends? . . .

The evidence is notoriously slight, almost to the point of nonexistence. In the second chapter of his *Constitution of the Athenians,* Pseudo-Xenophon hammers the point, repeated in blunt words in the next century by Isocrates (8.36), that imperial Athens "did not permit others to sail the sea unless they were willing to pay the tribute." These two writers are so notoriously tendentious that any of their generalisations is suspect, but not *ipso facto* false. Not so easily dismissed is the provision in the Athenian decree of 426 B.C. allowing Methone on the Thermaic Gulf to import a fixed amount (lost) of grain annually from Byzantium, upon registering with Athenian officials there called *Hellespontophylakes* (Hellespont Commissioners). Similar permission was given in the same period to Aphytis (near Potidaea). Only two texts, but they go some way towards documenting Pseudo-Xenophon and Isocrates. The inscriptions do not say that Methone and Aphytis could not sail the sea without paying tribute; they say both less and more; both cities were guaranteed the right to "sail freely" but neither could purchase Black Sea grain without Athenian permission. . . .

I do not suggest that the *Hellespontophylakes* were introduced early in the history of the empire. They were, after all, only the capstone of the structure, an organisation designed to bring about a closed sea. What I do suggest is that such an aim was the automatic consequence of naval power, within the Greek *polis* system, and that steps in that direction would have been taken by the Athenians when and as they were able, and found it advantageous, to do so. Short of going to war, there was no more useful instrument for punishing enemies, rewarding friends, and persuading "neutrals" to become "friends." And if employment of the instrument meant going to war, *tant pis.* The revolt of Thasos, Thucydides writes (1.100.2), arose from a quarrel "about the *emporia* on the Thracian coast and about the mines the Thasians exploited." That was as early as 465 B.C. and, though we do not know the issue dividing Athens and Thasos over the *emporia,* it can scarcely be unrelated to the "closed sea" ambitions of the imperial state, which then simply took over the *emporia* after Thasos was defeated. Of course Athens did not yet have the ability to close the sea which she was to have later, but it is surely wrong to say that the aim itself was *unthinkable* in the 60s and 50s. That is to commit the hegemony-into-empire error once again.

The question, in sum, is not when or whether the "closed sea" was thinkable but when and how Athens was able to close the sea to suit herself. And why. As we shall see in a moment, Athenian purposes did not require total control, even if that were within their reach. The Corinthian warning, in 432, that inland states would soon learn what maritime states already knew, that Athens was able to prevent them from bringing their produce to the sea and from buying what they required in turn (Thucydides 1.120.2), is meaningful but must be understood correctly in practical terms. So is the "Megarian decree." Not even the most monumental special pleading has succeeded in diluting the plain words, repeated three times by Thucydides (1.67, 1.139, 1.144.2), that a decree, moved by Pericles in 432, among other provisions excluded the Megarians "from the harbours of the Athenian empire" [see Part VI below]. All the elaborate arguments about the impossibility of blockade by triremes and about the ease of "sanction-busting," founded in fact though they are, are irrelevant. The Athenians claimed the right to exclude the Megarians from all harbours, and they could have enforced that claim *had they wished*. The long story that began with Eion and Skyros was known to every state which had a harbour, and there were Athenian officials (as well as *proxenoi* and other Athenian friends) in every important harbour-town.

That Athens did not wish to *destroy* Megara is patent, and significant. What she wished, and accomplished, was to hurt Megara and at the same time to declare openly and forcefully that she was prepared to employ the "closed sea" ruthlessly as an instrument of power. The coinage decree, whenever one dates it, was precisely the same kind of declaration. . . .

"Athens" is of course an abstraction. Concretely, who in Athens benefited (or suffered) from the empire, how and to what extent? . . . The traditional Greek view is well known, as it was "quantified" by Aristotle (*Constitution of Athens* 24.3): the common people of Athens, the poorer classes, were both the driving force behind, and the beneficiaries of, the empire. Their benefits are easily enumerated. At the head of the list is the extensive land confiscated from subjects and distributed in some fashion among Athenians. Perhaps as important is the navy: Athens maintained a standing fleet of 100 triremes, with another 200 in drydock for emergencies. Even 100 required 20,000 men, and, though we do not know how many ships were kept at sea regularly on patrol duty and for practice, or how many ships campaigned for how long through all the fighting of the periods 478–431 and 431–404, there seems little doubt that thousands of Athenians earned their pay for rowing in the fleet through the sailing-season annually, and that tens of thousands (including many non-Athenians) were engaged for longer or shorter periods on campaigns in many years. Add the work in the dockyards alone and the total cash benefit to poor Athenians was substantial though not measurable; to a large percentage of all the poor, furthermore.

To be sure, Athens maintained a navy before she had an empire, and continued to do so after the loss of the empire, but the later experience demonstrates that, without the imperial income, it was impossible to pay so large a body of crewman regularly. Similarly with corn supply: Athens succeeded in maintaining imports in the fourth century, too, but in the fifth century everyone knew how imperial power guaranteed those imports (as it supported the navy), even if not everyone knew the text of the Methone decree or had heard of the *Hellespontophylakes*. And it is always the poor who are most threatened by shortages and famines.

Finally, there was pay for office, on which Aristotle laid his greatest stress in his attempt at quantification. No other Greek state, so far as we know, made it a regular practice to pay for holding public office or distributed the offices so widely. That was a radical innovation in political life, the capstone of "Periclean" democracy, for which there was no precedent anywhere. Fundamental radical measures require powerful stimuli and unprecedented necessary conditions. I believe that the empire provided both the necessary cash and the political motivation. "Those who drive the ships are those who possess the power in the state," wrote Pseudo-Xenophon (1.2), and I have already indicated that this unpleasant writer did not always miss the mark with his gnomic propaganda statements.

What, then, of the more prosperous Athenians in the upper classes, the *kaloi kagathoi* ["beautiful and good"]? The paradox, in modern eyes, is that they both paid the bulk of the domestic taxes and constituted the armed forces. Yet, as we have already seen, they also supported the imperial advance of Athens, surely not out of idealistic or political interest in the benefits to the lower classes. How did they benefit? Did they? There is total silence in the literary sources of this question, save for a remarkable passage in Thucydides (8.48) [see Part VII]. . . . The puzzle is that we are unable to specify how the upper classes could have been the chief beneficiaries. Apart from the acquisition of property in subject territories, I can think of nothing other than negative benefits. That is to say, the imperial income enabled the Athenians to construct splendid public buildings and to float the largest navy of the day without adding to the taxpayers' financial burdens. How much of a burden the navy could impose became clear in the fourth century. That is something, but it is hardly enough to resolve the puzzle. . . .

Be that as it may, the conclusion seems to me compelling that the empire directly profited the poorer half of the Athenian population to an extent unknown in the Roman empire, or in modern empires. There was a price, of course, the costs of constant warfare. Men were lost in naval engagements and sometimes in land battles, most shatteringly in the Sicilian disaster. Athenian farmers suffered from periodic Spartan raids in the first stage of the Peloponnesian War, and even more from the permanent Spartan garrison at Decelea in the final decade of the war. The connection between those evils and the empire was obvious, but what conclusions were drawn? War was endemic: everyone accepted that as fact, and therefore no one seriously argued, or believed, that surrender of the empire would relieve Athens of the miseries of war. It would merely relieve them of certain particular wars, and the loss of empire and its benefits did not seem worth that dubious gain. Athenian morale remained buoyant to the bitter end, reflecting their calculus of the profits and the losses. . . .

In Thucydides' account of the debates at Sparta that ended with a declaration of war against Athens, the historian attributes the following words to an Athenian spokesman (1.76.2):

> We have done nothing extraordinary, nothing contrary to human practice, in accepting an empire when it was offered to us and then in refusing to give it up. Three very powerful motives prevent us from doing so — honour, fear and self-interest. And we were not the first to act in this way. It has always been a rule that the weak should be subject to the strong; besides we consider that we are worthy of our power.

There is no programme of imperialism there, no theory, merely a reassertion of the universal ancient belief in the naturalness of domination. Looking back, the historian is free to make his own moral judgments; he is not free to confuse them with practical judgments. Too much of the modern literature is concerned, even obsessed, with trying to determine whether Athens "exploited her allies in any extensive way" or "how much exploitation and oppression took place." Such questions are unanswerable, when they are not meaningless. Athenian imperialism employed all the forms of material exploitation that were available and possible in that society. The choices and the limits were determined by experience and by practical judgments, sometimes by miscalculations.

In this Roman copy of an original Greek bust, Pericles is depicted with his warrior's helmet. Political success in fifth-century Athens depended in part on military accomplishments. (Courtesy Trustees of the British Museum)

Pericles and Athenian Politics

Ancient opinion on Pericles was sharply divided. Thucydides saw him as an incorruptible and determined leader, who as "first citizen" chose "to lead the people rather than to be led by them." The contrast he observed between Pericles and later demagogues like Cleon was not echoed by all sources, many of which characterized Pericles as one of those who had corrupted the demos and purchased his own power through measures such as pay for jury service. Pro-Spartan conservatives could also blame him for the Peloponnesian War and compare him with the tyrant Peisistratus. For the most part, Plutarch took the middle ground, dividing Pericles' career into an early "demagogic" period and a later period of true statesmanship. On any estimation Pericles dominated Athens for at least two decades (ca. 451/0–429), and perhaps best exemplified the complex character that led the Athenians to pursue both democracy and empire.

Sources

Thucydides

The First Citizen

In the following selections, Thucydides first reports the substance of Pericles' speech to the Athenians just before the first Spartan invasion of Attica (summer, 431). The address included a detailed account of Athens' resources for war. Following this, a surprisingly frank speech purportedly made by Pericles before the Athenian assembly about a year later (in 430) is excerpted, along with Thucydides' own analysis of the statesman's position and career.

[2.13]   While the Peloponnesians were still mustering at the Isthmus, or on the march before they invaded Attica, Pericles, son of Xanthippus, one of the ten generals of the Athenians, finding that the invasion was to take place, conceived the idea that Archidamus, who happened to be his friend, might possibly pass by his estate without ravaging it. This he might do, either from a personal wish to oblige him, or acting under instructions from Lacedaemon for the purpose of creating a prejudice against him, as had been before attempted in the demand for the expulsion of the accursed family. He accordingly took the precaution of announcing to the Athenians in the assembly that, although Archidamus was his friend, yet this friendship should not extend to the detriment of the state, and that in case the enemy should make his houses and lands an exception to the rest and not pillage them, he at once gave them up to be public property, so that they should not bring him into suspicion. He also gave the citizens some advice on their present affairs in the same strain as before. Preparing for the war, and carrying in their property from the country, they were

From R. Crawley (translator), *Thucydides II.*

not to go out to battle, but to come into the city and guard it, and get ready their fleet in which their real strength lay. They were also to keep a tight rein on their allies, — the strength of Athens being derived from the money brought in by their payments, and success in war depending principally upon conduct and capital. Here they had no reason to despond. Apart from other sources of income, an average revenue of six hundred talents of silver was drawn from the tribute of the allies; and there were still six thousand talents of coined silver in the Acropolis, out of nine thousand seven hundred that had once been there, from which the money had been taken for the Propylaea (the gates) of the Acropolis, the other public buildings, and for Potidaea. This did not include the uncoined gold and silver in public and private offerings, the sacred vessels for the processions and games, the Median spoils, and similar resources to the amount of five hundred talents. To this he added the treasures of the other temples. These were by no means inconsiderable, and might fairly be used. Nay, if they were ever absolutely driven to it, they might take even the gold ornaments of Athene herself; for the statue contained forty talents of pure gold and it was all removable. This might be used for self-preservation, and must every penny of it be restored. Such was their financial position — surely a satisfactory one. Then they had an army of thirteen thousand heavy infantry, besides sixteen thousand more in the garrisons and on home duty at Athens. This was at first the number of men on guard in the event of an invasion: it was composed of the oldest and youngest levies and the resident aliens who had heavy armour. The Phaleric wall ran for four miles, before it joined that round the city; and of this last nearly five had a guard, although part of it was left without one, viz. that between the Long Wall and the Phaleric. Then there were the Long Walls to Piraeus, a distance of some four miles and a half, the outer of which was manned. Lastly, the circumference of Piraeus with Munychia was nearly seven miles and a-half; only half of this, however, was guarded. Pericles also showed them that they had twelve hundred horse including mounted archers, with sixteen hundred archers unmounted, and three hundred triremes fit for service. Such were the resources of Athens in the different departments when the Peloponnesian invasion was impending and hostilities were being commenced. Pericles also urged his usual arguments for expecting a favourable issue to the war.

[In the summers of 431 and 430 (and several subsequent years) the Spartans invaded Attica and ravaged Athenian territory. (See Part I for Pericles' Funeral Oration, given after the first year of the war.) Moreover, a deadly plague broke out in Athens.]

[59] After the second invasion of the Peloponnesians a change came over the spirit of the Athenians. Their land had now been twice laid waste; and war and pestilence at once pressed heavy upon them. They began to find fault with Pericles, as the author of the war and the cause of all their misfortunes, and became eager to come to terms with Lacedaemon, and actually sent ambassadors thither, who did not however succeed in their mission. Their despair was now complete and all vented itself upon Pericles. When he saw them exasperated at the present turn of affairs and acting exactly as he had anticipated, he called an assembly, being (it must be remembered) still general, with the double object of restoring confidence and of leading them from these angry feelings to a calmer and more hopeful state of mind. He accordingly came forward and spoke as follows:

[60] "I was not unprepared for the indignation of which I have been the object, as I know its causes; and I have called an assembly for the purpose of reminding you upon certain points, and of protesting against your being unreasonably irritated with me, or cowed by your sufferings. I am of opinion that national greatness is more for the advantage of private persons, than any individual well being coupled with public humiliation. A man may be personally ever so well off, and yet if his country be ruined he must be ruined with it; whereas a flourishing commonwealth always affords chances of salvation to unfortunate individuals. Since then a state can support the misfortunes of private persons, while they cannot support hers, it is surely the duty of every citizen to be forward in her defence, and not like you to be so confounded with your domestic afflictions as to give up all thoughts of the common safety, and to blame me for having counselled war and yourselves for having voted it. And yet if you are angry with me, it is with one who is, as I think, second to no man either in knowledge of the proper policy, or in the ability to expound it, and who is moreover not only a patriot but an honest one. A man possessing that knowledge without that faculty of exposition might as well have no idea at all on the matter: if he had both these but no love for his country, he would be but a cold advocate for her interests; while were this last also present but conquered by money, everything would go for that. So that if

you thought that I was even moderately distinguished for these qualities when you took my advice and went to war, I am certainly not open
now to the charge of having injured you.

[61] "For those of course who have a choice in the matter and
whose fortunes are not at stake, war is the greatest of follies. But if the
alternative should come between submission with loss of independence, and danger with the hope of preserving that independence, it is
he who will not accept the risk that deserves blame, not he who will. I
am myself the same man and do not alter, it is you who change, since
in fact you took my advice while unhurt, and waited for misfortune to
repent of it; and the apparent error of my policy lies in the infirmity of
your resolution, since the suffering that it entails is being felt by every
one among you, while its advantage is still remote and obscure to all,
and a great and sudden reverse having befallen you, your mind is too
much depressed to persevere in your resolves. For before what is sudden, unexpected, and least within calculation the spirit quails; and
putting all else aside, this is what you have been certainly confronted
with in the plague. Born, however, as you are, citizens of a great state,
and brought up, as you have been, with habits equal to your birth, you
should be ready to face the greatest disasters and to keep unimpaired
the lustre of your name. For the judgment of mankind is as relentless
to the weakness that falls short of a recognised renown, as it is jealous
of the arrogance that aspires higher than its due. Cease then to grieve
for your private afflictions, and address yourselves instead to the safety
of the commonwealth.

[62] "If you shrink before the exertions which the war makes
necessary, and fear that after all they may not have a happy result, you
know the reasons by which I have often demonstrated to you the
groundlessness of your apprehensions. If those are not enough, I will
now reveal an advantage arising from the greatness of your dominion,
which I think has never yet suggested itself to you, which I never mentioned in my previous speeches, and which has so bold a sound that I
should scarce adventure it now, were it not for the unnatural depres-
sion which I see around me. You perhaps think that your empire extends only over your allies; I will declare to you the truth. The visible
field of action has two parts, land and sea. In the whole of one of these
you are completely supreme, not merely as far as you use it at present,
but also to what further extent you may think fit: in fine your naval resources are such that your vessels may go where they please, without

the king or any other nation on earth being able to stop them. So that although you may think it a great privation to lose the use of your land and houses, still you must see that this power is something widely different; and far from fretting on their account, you should really regard them in the light of the gardens and other accessories that embellish a great fortune, and as, in comparison, of little moment. You should know too that liberty preserved by your efforts will easily recover for us what we have lost, while, the knee once bowed, even what you have will pass from you. Your fathers receiving these possessions not from others, but from themselves, did not let slip what their labour had acquired, but delivered them safe to you; and in this respect at least you must prove yourselves their equals, remembering that to lose what one has got is more disgraceful than to be baulked in getting, and you must confront your enemies not merely with spirit but with disdain. Confidence indeed a blissful ignorance can impart, ay, even to a coward's breast, but disdain is the privilege of those who, like us, have been assured by reflexion of their superiority to their adversary. And where the chances are the same, knowledge fortifies courage by the contempt which is its consequence, its trust being placed, not in hope, which is the prop of the desperate, but in a judgment grounded upon existing resources, whose anticipations are more to be depended upon.

[63] "Again, your country has a right to your services in sustaining the glories of her position. These are a common source of pride to you all, and you cannot decline the burdens of empire and still expect to share its honours. You should remember also that what you are fighting against is not merely slavery as an exchange for independence, but also loss of empire and danger from the animosities incurred in its exercise. Besides, to recede is no longer possible, if indeed any of you in the alarm of the moment has become enamoured of the part of honest unambition. For what you hold is, to speak somewhat plainly, a tyranny; to take it perhaps was wrong, but to let it go is unsafe. And men of these views, making converts of others, would quickly ruin a state; indeed the result would be the same if they could live independent by themselves; for unambition is never secure without vigour at its side; in fine, it is useless to an imperial city, though it may help a dependency to an unmolested servitude.

[64] "But you must not be seduced by citizens like these or angry with me,—who, if I voted for war, only did as you did yourselves,—in spite of the enemy having invaded your country and done what you

could be certain that he would do, if you refused to comply with his demands; and although besides what we counted for, the plague has come upon us—the only point indeed at which our calculation has been at fault. It is this, I know, that has had a large share in making me more unpopular than I should otherwise have been,—quite unde-servedly, unless you are also prepared to give me the credit of any suc-cess with which chance may present you. Besides, the hand of Heaven must be borne with resignation, that of the enemy with fortitude; this was the old way at Athens, and do not you prevent it being so still. Re-member, too, that if your country has the greatest name in all the world, it is because she never bent before disaster; because she has ex-pended more life and effort in war than any other city, and has won for herself a power greater than any hitherto known, the memory of which will descend to the latest posterity, even if now, in obedience to the general law of decay, we should ever be forced to yield—still it will be remembered that we held rule over more Hellenes than any other Hellenic state, that we sustained the greatest wars against their united or separate powers, and inhabited a city unrivalled by any other in re-sources or magnitude. These glories may incur the censure of slow un-ambition; but in the breast of energy they will awake emulation, and in those who must remain without them an envious regret. Hatred and unpopularity at the moment have fallen to the lot of all who have as-pired to rule others; but where odium must be incurred, true wisdom incurs it for the highest objects. Hatred also is shortlived; but that which makes the present splendid and the future glorious remains for ever unforgotten. Deciding, therefore, for glory then and honour now, attain both objects by instant and zealous effort: neither send heralds to Lacedaemon, nor betray any sign of being oppressed by your pre-sent sufferings, since they whose minds are least sensitive to calamity, and whose hands are most quick to meet it, are the greatest men and the greatest communities."

[65]   Such were the arguments by which Pericles tried to cure the Athenians of their anger against him and to divert their thoughts from their immediate afflictions. As a community he succeeded in convincing them; they not only gave up all idea of sending to Lacedaemon, but ap-plied themselves with increased energy to the war; still as private individ-uals they could not help smarting under their sufferings, the common people having been deprived of the little that they ever possessed, while the higher order had lost fine properties with costly establishments and

buildings in the country, and, worst of all, had war instead of peace. In fact, the public feeling against him did not subside until he had been fined. Not long afterwards, however, according to the way of the multitude, they again elected him general and committed all their affairs to his hands, having now become less sensitive to their private and domestic afflictions, and understanding that he was the best man of all for the public necessities. For as long as he was at the head of the state during the peace, he pursued a moderate and conservative policy; and in his time its greatness was at its height. When the war broke out, here also he seems to have rightly gauged the power of his country. He outlived its commencement two years and six months, and the correctness of his previsions respecting it became better known by his death. He told them to wait quietly, to pay attention to their marine, to attempt no new conquests, and to expose the city to no hazards during the war, and doing this, promised them a favourable result. What they did was the very contrary, allowing private ambitions and private interests, in matters apparently quite foreign to the war, to lead them into projects unjust both to themselves and to their allies—projects whose success would only conduce to the honour and advantage of private persons; and whose failure entailed certain disaster on the country in the war. The causes of this are not far to seek. Pericles indeed, by his rank, ability, and known integrity, was enabled to exercise an independent control over the multitude—in short, to lead them instead of being led by them; for as he never sought power by improper means, he was never compelled to flatter them, but, on the contrary, enjoyed so high an estimation that he could afford to anger them by contradiction. Whenever he saw them unseasonably and insolently elated, he would with a word reduce them to alarm; on the other hand, if they fell victims to a panic, he could at once restore them to confidence. In short, what was nominally a democracy became in his hands government by the first citizen. With his successors it was different. More on a level with one another, and each grasping at supremacy, they ended by committing even state affairs to the whims of the multitude. This, as might have been expected in a great and sovereign state, produced a host of blunders, and amongst them the Sicilian expedition; though this failed not so much through a miscalculation of the power of those against whom it was sent, as through a fault in the senders in not taking the best measures after its departure, but choosing rather to occupy themselves with private cabals for the leadership of the commons, by which they not only paralysed operations in the field, but also first introduced civil discord at home. Yet after losing most of their fleet besides other forces in Sicily, and with faction already dominant in the city, they could still for three years make head against their original adversaries, joined not only by the Sicilians, but also by their own allies nearly all in revolt, and at last by the king's son, Cyrus, who furnished the funds for the Peloponnesian navy. Nor did they finally succumb till they fell the victims of their own intestine disorders. So superfluously abundant were the resources from which the genius of Pericles foresaw an easy triumph in the war over the unaided forces of the Peloponnesians.

Plato

Socrates on Pericles

In the *Gorgias,* Plato presents a conversation between Socrates and several interlocutors on the subject of rhetoric and politics. In the following passage Socrates discusses Pericles' success as a statesman with Callicles.

[515c (Socrates)]. . . . recall now those men you were speaking of a little earlier, and tell me about them, whether you still think that they have proved themselves good citizens—Pericles, Cimon, Miltiades, Themistocles.

C: Yes, I do.

S: Then if they were good, it's clear that each of them was making the citizens better from being worse. Was he or not?

C: Yes.

S: Then when Pericles was beginning to speak among the people, weren't the Athenians worse than they were when he was speaking for the last time?

C: Perhaps.

S: No; not perhaps, my good man. They *must* have been, from what we've agreed, if Pericles was a good citizen.

C: So what?

S: So nothing. But tell me this as well:—Is it said that the Athenians became better because of Pericles, or just the opposite—that they were corrupted by him? For that's what I myself hear said, that Pericles has made the Athenians idlers and cowards, chatterers and spongers, by starting them on drawing pay.

C: It's the people with torn ears you hear say that, Socrates.

S: Well, here's something I don't just hear said, but I know it clearly, and so do you:—At first Pericles had a good reputation, and the Athenians never convicted him on any shameful charge, when they were worse. [516]   But when they had been made fine and good by him, at the end of Pericles' life, they convicted him of theft, and nearly condemned him to death, clearly because they supposed he was base.

C: So what? Did that make Pericles bad?

S: Well, a keeper of donkeys or horses or cattle who was like him would be thought bad, if they did not kick or butt or bite him when he took them over, and finally he left them doing all these things from wildness. Or don't you think anyone is a bad keeper of any animal whatever if he takes them over tame and finally leaves them wilder than they were when he took them over? Do you think so or not?

C: Yes, quite—just to gratify you.

S: Then gratify me by answering this too. Is man also one of the animals or not?

C: Of course.

S: Wasn't Pericles a keeper of men?

C: Yes.

S: Well then, shouldn't they, as we were agreeing recently, have become more just through him, after being more unjust, if he was their keeper and was good in politics?

C: Quite.

S: Now aren't the just tame, as Homer said? What do you say? Isn't it so?

C: Yes.

S: But now Pericles left them much wilder than when he took them over, and wilder against him, which he would have wanted least of all.

C: Do you want me to agree with you?

S: Yes, if you think I'm saying what's true.

C: Well, let it be so.

S: Then if they were wilder, weren't they more unjust and worse?

C: Let's say so.

S: Then Pericles was not good in politics, on this argument (*logos*).

C: Well, you say he wasn't.

S: And so do you, from what you were agreeing. But now tell me about Cimon. Didn't those Athenians he was caring for ostracize him so that they wouldn't hear his voice for ten years? And didn't they do the same to Themistocles, and punish him with exile as well? And Miltiades of Marathon — didn't they vote to throw him into the pit, and but for the prytanis wouldn't they have thrown him in? But if these had been good men, as you say they were, that would never have happened to them. Surely good drivers don't avoid being thrown out of the seat at the start, and then — when they take care of the horses, and become better drivers themselves — get thrown out after all that. That doesn't happen in driving chariots or in any other work. Or do you think it does?

C: No, I don't.

[517]   S: Then what we said earlier was true, it seems, that we don't know of anyone who turned out to be a good man in politics in this city. You were agreeing about men now, but not about men of previous times, and you chose these men above others. But these have turned out to be in the same position as men now, so that if they were rhetors, they practised neither true rhetoric — for then they wouldn't have been thrown out — nor flattering rhetoric.

C: But no, Socrates — surely no one now will achieve such works as any one you like of those previous men.

S: My friend, I'm not reproaching them any more than you are, as servants of the city. No; I think they've proved to be better servants than the present people, and more capable of supplying the city with what it had an appetite for. But for forcing change in their appetites, not indulging them, persuading and forcing them towards what will make the citizens better—here they were virtually no different from people now—and that's the only work for a good citizen. But ships, walls, dockyards, and many other things—I too agree with you that the previous people were cleverer than the people now at supplying them. . . .

[518e]   And what you're doing now, Callicles, is . . . eulogizing people who feasted the Athenians, indulging them with what they had an appetite for. It's said that they made the city great; [519]   but that it's swelling and festering because of these earlier people—no one notices this. For without justice and temperance they have left the city full of harbours and dockyards and walls and tribute and that sort of rubbish. And so when that crisis of the disease comes, they'll hold responsible the advisers who are there at the time, and eulogize Themistocles and Cimon and Pericles, the ones responsible for the evils. And perhaps they'll seize on you, if you're not careful, and on my companion Alcibiades, when they lose both their more recent gains and what they had before, though you aren't wholly responsible for the evils, but perhaps partly responsible.

But it's a senseless thing I see going on now and hear about the men of earlier times. For I notice that when the city lays hands on any of the political men for injustice, they're annoyed and scandalized, saying that it's a terrible thing being done to them; they've done much good to the city and now they're being ruined unjustly by it—that's their argument. But the whole thing's false. For not a single leader of a city can ever be destroyed unjustly by the very city he leads.

For it looks as though those who claim to be politicians and those who claim to be sophists are the same. For the sophists too, though they're wise about the other things, do an absurd thing here; they claim to be teachers of virtue, but then they often accuse their pupils of doing injustice to them, depriving them of their fees, and giving no other reward in return when they've benefited from them. Now what could be less reasonable than this argument? They say that men who have been made good and just, when they have lost injustice and acquired justice because of their teacher, do injustice to him, because of what they don't have. Don't you think this is absurd, my friend?

You've really forced me to be a mob-orator, Callicles, when you wouldn't answer.

The Aristotelian Constitution of the Athenians

Pericles' Reforms

In this passage, the author of the Aristotelian *Constitution of the Athenians* describes certain political reforms ascribed to Pericles, apart from his introduction of a law requiring Athenian parentage on both sides for citizenship (in 451/0, see Part I).

27

(1) After this Pericles took on the leadership of the people; he had first distinguished himself when, as a young man, he prosecuted Cimon in the examination after his generalship [463]. The constitution now became still more democratic: Pericles took away some of the powers of the Areopagus, and above all turned the city in the direction of naval power, so that the common people grew confident and increasingly attracted to themselves complete control of the state. (2) In the forty-ninth year after the battle of Salamis, the archonship of Pythodorus [432/1], the Peloponnesian War broke out. During the war the people were shut up in the city, grew accustomed to earning stipends on campaign, and—partly intentionally, partly not—chose to administer public affairs themselves. (3) Moreover, Pericles was the first man to provide payment for jury service, as a political measure to counter the generosity of Cimon. Cimon was as rich as a tyrant: he performed the public liturgies lavishly; and

From Aristotle, *The Athenian Constitution*, edited and translated by P. J. Rhodes, pp. 70–72 (Harmondsworth: Penguin, 1984). Reproduced by permission Frederick Warne & Co.

he maintained many of his fellow-demesmen, for any man of La-ciadae who wished could go to him each day and obtain his basic needs, and all his land was unfenced, so that anyone who wished could enjoy the fruit. (4) Pericles' property was insufficient for this kind of service. He was therefore advised by Damonides of Oe (who seems to have been the originator of most of Pericles' measures, and for that reason was subsequently ostracized) that since he was less well supplied with private property he should give the people their own property; and so he devised payment for the jurors. Some people allege that it was as a result of this that the courts deteriorated, since it was always the ordinary people rather than the better sort who were eager to be picked for jury service. (5) After this judicial corruption began. The way was first shown by Anytus after he had served as general at Pylos: he was brought to trial for losing Pylos, and escaped by bribing the jury.

28

(1) While Pericles was champion of the people the constitution was not in too bad a state, but after his death it became much worse. It was then that the people first took a champion who was not of good repute among the better sort, whereas previously it was always men of the better sort who were popular leaders. . . . (3) After Pericles' death the distinguished were championed by Nicias, who died in Sicily, and the people by Cleon son of Cleaenetus: Cleon, it seems, more than anyone else corrupted the people by his wild impulses, and was the first man who, when on the platform, shouted, uttered abuse and made speeches with his clothes hitched up, while everyone else spoke in an orderly manner. Next, after them, Theramenes son of Hagnon was champion of the others and Cleophon the lyre-maker champion of the people. Cleophon was the first man to provide the two-obol grant: for a while it continued to be paid, then it was abolished by Callicrates of Paeania, after he had first promised to add another obol to the two. Both Cleophon and Callicrates were subsequently condemned to death by the Athenians: the masses generally come to hate those who have led them on to do anything wrong, particularly if they have deceived them. (4) Since Cleophon there has been an unending succession of popular leaders whose

chief desire has been to be outrageous and to gratify the masses, looking only to considerations of the moment.

Plutarch

Pericles

The following passages derive from Plutarch's life of *Pericles*. After an introduction and a brief comparison of Pericles with the Roman general Fabius Maximus (the opponent of the Carthaginian Hannibal in the Second Punic War whose biography was paired with Pericles' in Plutarch's collection), the biographer proceeds to a discussion of the Athenian's family.

---

(3)   Pericles belonged to the tribe of Acamantis and the deme of Cholargus, and he was descended on both sides from the noblest lineage in Athens. His father was Xanthippus, who defeated the Persian generals at Mycale. His mother, Agariste, was the niece of that Cleisthenes who not only performed the noble exploit of driving out the Pisistratids and destroying their tyranny, but went on to establish laws and a constitution that was admirably balanced so as to promote harmony between the citizens and security for the whole state. Agariste once had a dream that she had given birth to a lion, and a few days later she was delivered of Pericles. His physical features were almost perfect, the only exception being his head, which was rather long and out of proportion. For this reason almost all his portraits show him wearing a helmet, since the artists apparently did not wish to taunt him with this deformity. However, the comic poets of Athens nicknamed him "*schinocephalus*" or "squill-head," and Cratinus, for example, in his play *The Tutors* says that "Old Cronos mated with the goddess of party-strife, and their offspring was the biggest

From Plutarch, *The Rise and Fall of Athens*, translated by I. Scott-Kilvert, pp. 167–169, 171–174, 177, 182–183, 205–206 (London/New York: Penguin, 1960). Reproduced by permission of Frederick Warne & Co.

tyrant of all: now the gods call him "The Head-Compeller." And again in his *Nemesis* he refers to "Zeus, the protector of foreigners and heads." Telecleides describes Pericles as sitting on the Acropolis at his wits' end, "at one moment top-heavy with the load of the cares of state, and at another creating all the din of war by himself, from that brain-pan of his, which is big enough to hold eleven couches." And Eupolis in *The Demes* asks questions about each of the great popular leaders as they come up from Hades, and remarks, when Pericles' name is called out last:

> Now you have brought us up the very head
> Of those in the world below.

(4) His teacher in music, most writers agree, was Damon, although according to Aristotle he had a thorough musical training at the hands of Pythocleides. This Damon appears to have been a sophist of the highest order, who used his musical teaching as a screen to conceal his real talents from the world in general; in fact it was he who trained Pericles for his political contests, much as a masseur or trainer prepares an athlete. However, Damon's lyre did not succeed in imposing upon the Athenians, and he was banished by ostracism on the grounds of being a great intriguer and supporter of tyranny, and he also became a target for the comic poets. At any rate Plato, the comic dramatist, makes one of his characters speak these lines to him

> First of all answer my question, I beg you,
> For you are the Chiron, they say, who tutored Pericles.

Pericles also studied under Zeno the Eleatic at the period when, like Parmenides, he was lecturing on natural philosophy. Zeno had perfected a technique of cross-examination which enabled him to corner his opponent by the method of question and answer, and Timon of Phlius has described him as

> Zeno, assailer of all things, whose tongue like a double-edged weapon
> Argued on either side with an irresistible fury.

But there was one man more closely associated with Pericles than any other, who did most to clothe him with a majestic bearing that was more potent than any demagogue's appeal, and who helped to develop the natural dignity of his character to the highest degree. This was Anaxagoras of Clazomenae, whom the men of his time used to call Intelligence personified. They gave him this name either out of admiration for the extraordinary intellectual powers he displayed in the investigation of natural phenomena, or else because he was the first to dethrone Chance and Necessity and set up pure Intelligence in their place as the principle of law and order which informs the universe, and which distinguishes from an otherwise chaotic mass those substances which possess elements in common.

(5) Pericles had an unbounded admiration for Anaxagoras, and his mind became steeped in the so-called higher philosophy and abstract speculation. From it he derived not only a dignity of spirit and a nobility of utterance which was entirely free from the vulgar and unscrupulous buffooneries of mob-oratory, but also a composure of countenance that never dissolved into laughter, a serenity in his movements and in the graceful arrangement of his dress which nothing could disturb while he was speaking, a firm and evenly modulated voice, and other characteristics of the same kind which deeply impressed his audience. It is a fact, at any rate, that once in the marketplace, where he had urgent business to transact, he allowed himself to be abused and reviled for an entire day by some idle hooligan without uttering a word in reply. Towards evening he returned home unperturbed, while the man followed close behind, still heaping every kind of insult upon him. When Pericles was about to go indoors, as it was now dark, he ordered one of his servants to take a torch and escort the man all the way to his own house. . . .

(7) As a young man Pericles was inclined to shrink from facing the people. One reason for this was that he was considered to bear a distinct resemblance to the tyrant Pisistratus, and when men who were well on in years remarked on the charm of Pericles' voice and the smoothness and fluency of his speech, they were astonished at the resemblance between the two. The fact that he was rich and that he came of a distinguished family and possessed exceedingly powerful friends made the fear of ostracism very real to him, and at the beginning of his career he took no part in politics but devoted himself to soldiering, in which he showed great daring and enterprise. However, the time came when Aristides was dead, Themistocles in exile, and Cimon frequently absent on distant campaigns. Then at last Pericles decided to attach himself to the people's party and to take up the cause of the poor and the many instead of that of the rich and the few, in spite of the fact that this was quite contrary to his own temperament, which was thoroughly aristocratic. He was afraid, apparently, of being suspected of

aiming at a dictatorship; so when he saw that Cimon's sympathies were strongly with the nobles and that he was the idol of the aristocratic party, he began to ingratiate himself with the people, partly for self-preservation and partly by way of securing power against his rival. . . .

Pericles, however, took care not to make himself too familiar a figure, even to the people, and he only addressed them at long intervals. He did not choose to speak on every question, but reserved himself, as Critolaus says, like the state galley, the *Salaminia*, for great occasions, and allowed his friends and other public speakers to deal with less important matters. One of these, they say, was Ephialtes, who destroyed the power of the Council of the Areopagus and in this way, as Plato the philosopher puts it, poured out neat a full draught of freedom for the people and made them unmanageable, so that they "nibbled at Euboea and trampled on the islands, like a horse which can no longer bear to obey the rein."

(8) Pericles wished to equip himself with a style of speaking which, like a musical accomplishment, should harmonize perfectly with his mode of life and the grandeur of his ideals, and he often made use of the instrument which Anaxagoras had put into his hand and tinged his oratory, as it were, with natural philosophy. It was from this philosophy that he had acquired, in addition to his natural gifts, what the divine Plato calls "the loftiness of thought and the power to create an ideally perfect work," and by applying this training to the art of oratory he far excelled all other speakers. This was the reason, some people say, for his being nicknamed the Olympian, though others believe that it was on account of the buildings with which he adorned Athens, and others again because of his prowess as a statesman and a general; but it may well have been the combination of many qualities which earned him the name. However, the comic poets of the time, who were constantly letting fly at him either in earnest or in fun, declare that the title originated mainly from his manner of speaking. They refer to him as thundering and lightning when he addressed his audience and as wielding a terrible thunderbolt in his tongue. A saying of Thucydides [not the historian; see Frost in Analysis below] the son of Melesias, has come down to us, which was uttered in jest, but which bears witness to Pericles' powers of persuasion. Thucydides belonged to the aristocratic party and was a political opponent of Pericles for many years. When Archidamus, the king of Sparta, asked him whether

he or Pericles was the better wrestler, Thucydides replied: "Whenever I throw him at wrestling, he beats me by arguing that he was never down, and he can even make the spectators believe it."

The truth is, however, that even Pericles was extremely cautious in his use of words, so much so that whenever he rose to speak, he uttered a prayer that no word might escape his lips which was unsuited to the matter in hand. He left nothing behind him in writing except for the decrees he proposed, and only a very few of his sayings have been handed down. One of these was his appeal to the Athenians to remove "that eyesore of the Piraeus," as he called Aegina, and another his remark that he could already see "war bearing down upon them from the Peloponnese." . . .

(9)   Thucydides characterizes Pericles' administration as having been distinctly aristocratic — "democracy in name, but in practice government by the first citizen." But many other writers maintain that it was he who first led on the people into passing such measures as the allotment to Athenians of lands belonging to subject peoples, or the granting of allowances for the public festivals and fees for various public services, and that because of his policy they fell into bad habits and became extravagant and undisciplined instead of frugal and self-sufficient as they had once been. Let us consider in the light of the facts what may account for this change in his policy.

At the beginning of his career, as we have seen, Pericles had to measure himself against Cimon's reputation, and he therefore set out to win the favour of the people. . . . [B]efore long, what with the allowances for public festivals, fees for jury service, and other grants and gratuities, he succeeded in bribing the masses wholesale and enlisting their support in his attack on the Council of the Areopagus. Pericles was not himself a member of this body, since he had never been appointed by lot to the post either of chief archon or archon thesmothete or king archon or polemarch. These positions had traditionally been filled by lot, and it was only through them that men who had acquitted themselves well in office could rise to membership of the Areopagus. Because he had thus been excluded, Pericles, once he had gathered popular support, exerted himself all the more to lead his party in a campaign against the Areopagus, and he succeeded so well that not only was it deprived of most of its judicial powers through a bill brought forward by Ephialtes, but Cimon himself was ostracized on the charge of being a friend of Sparta and an enemy of the people's interests. Yet this was a man who was second to none in Athens in birth or in wealth, who had won the most brilliant victories over the Persians and filled the city with money and treasure, as has been recorded in his Life. Such was the strength of Pericles' hold over the people. . . .

(11) The aristocratic party had already recognized for some time that Pericles was now the most important man in Athens and that he wielded far more power than any other citizen. But they were anxious that there should be someone in the city capable of standing up to him so as to blunt the edge of his authority and prevent it from becoming an outright monarchy. They therefore put forward Thucydides [son of Melesias], of Alopece, a man of good sense and a relative of Cimon, to lead the opposition. He was less of a soldier than Cimon, but better versed in forensic business and an abler politician, and by watching his opportunities at home and engaging Pericles in debate, he soon succeeded in creating a balance of power in Athenian affairs. He did not allow the aristocrats, the so-called party of the good and true, to become dispersed among the mass of the people in the Assembly, as they had done in the past, with the result that their influence had been swamped by sheer numbers. Instead, by separating and grouping them in a single body, he was able to concentrate their strength and make it an effective counterweight in the scale. Below the surface of affairs in Athens, there had existed from the very beginning a kind of flaw or seam, such as one finds in a piece of iron, which gave a hint of the rift that divided the aims of the popular and the aristocratic parties; but now these two men's rival ambitions and their struggle for power sharply widened this cleavage and caused the one side to be named the party of the many and the other of the few. Pericles therefore chose this moment to hand over the reins of power to the people to a greater extent than ever before and deliberately shaped his policy to please them. He constantly provided public pageants, banquets, and processions in the city, entertaining the people like children with elegant pleasures; and he sent out sixty triremes to cruise every year, in which many of the citizens served with pay for eight months and learned and practised seamanship at the same time. Besides this, he dispatched 1,000 settlers to the Chersonese,

500 to Naxos, 250 to Andros, 1,000 to Thrace to make their homes with the Bisaltae, and others to the new colony named Thurii, which was founded in Italy near the site of Sybaris. In this way he relieved the city of a large number of idlers and agitators, raised the standards of the poorest classes, and, by installing garrisons among the allies, implanted at the same time a healthy fear of rebellion. [For chapters 12–14 and 17, see Part II.]

(15)   From this point political opposition was at an end, the parties had merged themselves into one, and the city presented a single and unbroken front. Pericles now proceeded to bring under his own control not only home affairs, but all issues in which the authority of Athens was involved: these included matters of tribute, the army, the navy, the islands, maritime affairs, the great resources which Athens derived both from the Greek states and from the barbarians, and the leadership she exercised which was buttressed by subject states, friendships with kings and alliances with dynasties. But at the same time Pericles' own conduct took on quite a different character. He was no longer so docile towards the people, nor so ready to give way to their caprices, which were as shifting and changeable as the winds. He abandoned the somewhat nerveless and indulgent leadership he had shown on occasion, which might be compared to a soft and flowery melody, and struck instead the firm, high note of an aristocratic, even regal statesmanship. And since he used his authority honestly and unswervingly in the interests of the city, he was usually able to carry the people with him by rational argument and persuasion. Still there were times when they bitterly resented his policy, and then he tightened the reins and forced them to do what was to their advantage, much as a wise physician treats a prolonged and complicated disease, allowing the patient at some moments pleasures which can do him no harm, and at others giving him caustics and bitter drugs which cure him. There were, as might be expected, all kinds of disorders to be found among a mass of citizens who possessed an empire as great as that of Athens, and Pericles was the only man capable of keeping each of these under control. He achieved this most often by using the people's hopes and fears as if they were rudders, curbing them when they were arrogant and raising their hopes or comforting them when they were disheartened. In this way he proved that rhetoric, in Plato's phrase, is the art of working upon the souls of men by means of words,

and that its chief business is the knowledge of men's characters and passions which are, so to speak, the strings and stops of the soul and require a most skilful and delicate touch. The secret of Pericles' power depended, so Thucydides tells us, not merely upon his oratory, but upon the reputation which his whole course of life had earned him and upon the confidence he enjoyed as a man who had proved himself completely indifferent to bribes. Great as Athens had been when he became her leader, he made her the greatest and richest of all cities, and he came to hold more power in his hands than many a king and tyrant. And in the end he did not increase the fortune his father left him by so much as a single drachma from the public funds, a source of wealth which some men even managed to pass on to their children.

(16)   But despite his unselfishness, there can be no doubt as to his power, which Thucydides describes to us clearly, while even the comic poets testify to it unwittingly in some of their malicious jokes. For example, they nickname him and his associates "the new Pisistratids," and call upon him to take the oath that he will never set himself up as tyrant, as if his supremacy were too oppressive and out of all proportion in a democracy. Telecleides says that the Athenians had handed over to him

> The cities' tribute, even the cities themselves
> To hold or to set free as he thinks fit,
> And the cities' walls to build or to pull down,
> Their treaties and their armies, their power, their peace,
> Their wealth, and all the gifts good fortune brings.

And all this was by no means a sudden harvest, the climax of popularity of an administration which flourished only for a brief season. The fact is that for forty years Pericles held the first place among men such as Ephialtes, Myronides, Cimon, Tolmides, and Thucydides, and after the fall of Thucydides and his ostracism, he exercised for no less than fifteen years a continuous, unbroken authority through his annual tenure of the office of general. During the whole of this period he proved himself completely incorruptible by bribery, although he was not altogether averse to making money. . . .

[Omitted here is a long section treating mainly Pericles' military career, which was extensive, and emphasizing his caution (18), and his desire to consolidate Athenian holdings while keeping the Spartans in check (21). For Plutarch's treatment of the events leading up to the Peloponnesian War, see Part VI.]

(39) Pericles deserves our admiration, then, not only for the sense of justice and the serene temper that he preserved amid the many crises and intense personal hatreds which surrounded him, but also for his greatness of spirit. He considered it the highest of all his claims to honour that, despite the immense power he wielded, he had never given way to feelings of envy or hatred and had treated no man as so irreconcilable an enemy that he could never become his friend. This fact by itself, it seems to me, removes any objection to his otherwise pretentious and childish nickname, and, indeed, gives it a certain aptness: a character so gracious and a life so pure and uncorrupt in the exercise of sovereign power might well be called Olympian, according to our conception of the race of gods who rule over the universe as the authors of all good things and as beings who are by nature incapable of evil. In this we part company from the poets, who confuse us with their ignorant fantasies and contradict themselves with their own fables. . . .

After his death, the course of events soon brought home Pericles' worth to the Athenians and made them sharply conscious of his loss. Those who in his lifetime had resented his power and felt that it overshadowed them turned to other orators and popular leaders as soon as he was out of the way, only to find themselves compelled to admit that no man for all his majesty was ever more moderate, or, when clemency was called for, better able to maintain his dignity. Henceforth the public life of Athens was to be polluted by a rank growth of corruption and wrongdoing, which Pericles had always checked and kept out of sight, thereby preventing it from taking an irresistible hold. Then it was that that power of his, which had aroused such envy and had been denounced as a monarchy and a tyranny, stood revealed in its true character as the saving bulwark of the state.

Analysis

Frank J. Frost

Pericles, Thucydides Son of Melesias, and Athenian Politics Before the War

Frank J. Frost, former Professor of History at the University of California, Santa Barbara, has written extensively on the subjects of Greek history and historiography, including a commentary on *Plutarch's Themistocles*. In the following selection, Frost argues that no concerted oligarchical faction opposing Pericles, democracy, and the exploitation of the "allies" coalesced behind Thucydides son of Melesias as Plutarch would seem to report (*Pericles* 11–12, 14 above). Frost maintains that all Athenians, conservative and democratic alike, supported the empire, that a coalition of powerful forces supported Pericles, and that the statesman's most likely opponents came from the left, i.e., men like Cleon and his followers.

Thucydides, son of Melesias, is traditionally the model of the virtuous aristocrat, representative of the old order, who gathered under his wing the nobles left leaderless by the death of Cimon and created a party of opposition to the democrat, Pericles. That Thucydides was of noble family is certain; that he was virtuous may be conceded. That he underwent a contest of ostracism, probably in 443/2, is proven by the ostraca themselves. But the details of the rivalry between Thucydides and Pericles are found—with minor exceptions—only in Plutarch's life of Pericles, chapters 11–14.

From F. J. Frost, "Pericles, Thucydides Son of Melesias, and Athenian Politics Before the War," *Historia* 13. Copyright © 1964. Published by Franz Steiner Verlag.

In attempting to recreate the political struggles of the period, the biographer has pictured a dramatic setting with the following themes: (1) the rise of Thucydides to political prominence meant class warfare; (2) in this class struggle Pericles was forced to create a welfare state in order to gain the loyalty of the Demos; (3) Thucydides challenged Pericles on the most important aspect of the welfare state—rebuilding of the temples—and this led to his ostracism. A fourth point has from time to time been suggested by modern scholars: further on in the *Pericles*, Plutarch gives a lengthy description of a series of attacks upon the great statesman; H. T. Wade-Gery has said, "we may assume [Thucydides] returned in the spring of 433, and I believe he made himself felt.". . . I hope to show (1) that Plutarch has mistakenly dated these attacks to the period just before the war, and (2) that they occurred earlier and were political maneuvers more typical of a Cleon than of a Thucydides.

The Class War

Cimon died, says Plutarch, and the aristocrats, apprehensive of Pericles' growing power, chose Thucydides to lead their disorganized party. He successfully instilled party discipline and trained them to unite against the Demos. Plutarch's concept of the class system in mid-fifth century Athens and the aggravation it produced is illustrated by the following passage (11.3):

> For there was from the start a concealed fracture, as in a piece of iron, suggesting a variance in popular and aristocratic aims. But the contention and ambition of these men dividing the city most sharply caused one faction to be called the Demos, and the other, the Few.

Neither a proponent of aristocratic government nor a Marxist would have the slightest difficulty accepting such a statement, as it agrees exactly with their preconceptions of the normal situation in all societies. But to identify the Athenian aristocracy of this generation with a political party, or to treat the politics of the period as a contest between two distinct theoretical [policies or programs] is to fall into error.

Plutarch never pretends to have any original insight into the politics of fifth century Athens; he is content to rely on the traditional picture. In this case his assumptions have their origin in the grave logic and brilliant exposition of the fourth century schools: in the Academy's early attempt to establish a canon of political forms, but particularly in Aristotle's endeavor in the *Politics* to apply the methodology of the biological sciences and reduce the entire human political experience to symmetry and order. The distortion inherent in making a "science" of politics is most obvious when political "scientists" try to interpret history—or rather, to jam historical events into tidy patterns necessitated by political "logic." One sees especially in the Aristotelian [*Constitution of the Athenians*] (which Plutarch knew well) the creation of a geometrically correct and therefore logically necessary division of the body politic into Demos and *chrestoi* [the "good," i.e., noblemen] whose ranks go marching, parallel but hostile, through a century of Athenian political development with rival party chieftains neatly labelled for each generation. . . . But is there indeed any reason to believe in the existence of partisan activity based upon political theory in fifth century Athens?

The pamphlet of the Old Oligarch is often thought to be evidence of a strong party of the Right with a well developed political theory. But that gentleman did not really propose an aristocratic polity; what he did was regret the eclipse of a privileged class, as did Theognis before him [see Kagan in Part VII], and his picture of Athens is demonstrably false. Again, it is true that the quaint dialogue of the Persians in Herodotus (III, 80ff.) is evidence for an early appreciation of the theoretical forms of government, but certainly not for partisan activity on this basis (the debate here is close to an elegant spoof of such argument—and was perhaps so intended). [See Part VII.]

There is, on the other hand, more than enough evidence to show that the extraordinary success of Pericles was based on a union of hearts—a system of loyalty to persons rather than to ideas. The political machine of Pericles in fact drew from all elements of Athenian society, but predominantly from those very *chrestoi* in whom we are supposed to see a party of the opposition. The "new Peisistratidae," as the comic poets called them, were no Jacobins; they are best represented by men like the various Calliae: ambassador, financier and general; by Andocides, the orator's grandfather, who traced his family to Hermes and Odysseus; by Metiochus, the perennial office-holder, who is possibly a connection of the Philaid family; by Cleinias the Alcmeonid, and many others of this clan; by Sophocles, of course, whose only qualification for the generalship, so far as we can see, was that he was *kalos k'agathos* ["beautiful and good," i.e., "noble"].

These men are the "Establishment;" they go on embassies, they present financial legislation, they are the generals, magistrates, supervisors of public works. Regardless of their personal relations with Pericles they molded, financed and directed Periclean policy, oblivious to the fact that later generations of doctrinaire theorists would lump them all together, label them *chrestoi*, and thus make their political allegiance theoretically impossible. It is this type of coalition regime: an association of men from the great families, and a handful of new men from the merchant class (about whom, more later) and the army, that is typical of Athens in the fifth century. Such associations were based on practical considerations and lively self-interest rather than ideology. As for right-wing opposition, the day of the *hetairiai* [political clubs] had not arrived (nor the conditions that created them); otherwise, the majority of the *chrestoi* . . . were neither willing nor competent to engage in politics. . . .

Who Attacked Pericles?

Plutarch's interest in the son of Melesias ends after his ostracism. In the biographer's simple scheme the leader of the aristocrats had represented the only disruptive force in Periclean Athens: after his exit all ranks closed and allowed Pericles to rule as the "foremost man" (Thuc. II, 65.9 quoted in *Per.* 9.1). But on the eve of the war (by Plutarch's dating), Pericles was once more threatened by political foes. Although the biographer never identifies the enemy by faction . . . modern scholars have often reasoned that the oligarchic faction had only been awaiting the return of their leader to renew their divisive tactics: "We have therefore to constate that the return of Thucydides coincides with an outbreak of malicious litigation" (Wade-Gery, *Essays*, 260). . . .

But are we sure these are the weapons [i.e., the trials of Pericles' associates and possibly Aspasia—see Part VI], these the subtle plots of an educated and sophisticated aristocracy? I think not. The sophists would not have come to Athens, and no "enlightenment" would have taken place if such a movement had not been enthusiastically welcomed and financially supported by men from the grandest families in Athens. I cannot see how any political maneuver designed to provoke anti-intellectualism and religious bigotry can have failed to be at the same time anti-aristocratic in nature. No aristocrat, with a party of aristocrats behind him, would set afoot such a potentially dangerous and uncontrollable issue; he must always have been aware that the mob would inevitably turn and rend him and his friends as well. And yet, it is undeniable that there *did* occur just such a wave of anti-intellectualism and religious bigotry, that it was also anti-aristocratic in nature, and that it was aimed at the sacrilegious thief Pheidias, the ["ungodly"] Aspasia, the intellectual Anaxagoras, and their friend and protector, the aristocrat Pericles.

In my opinion, the spirit of these prosecutions is to be found in men that had nothing to do with aristocracy: that ambitious new breed from the agora, against whom Aristophanes pitted his Knights [see Part I]. According to the comic poet 128 ff., the first to come into political prominence after the death of Pericles was Eucrates, an "oakumseller." Then came Lysicles. He was a "sheep-seller," a man of humble origin to whom Socrates had to speak in terms of [sheep and fleece] to make himself understood; but Aspasia taught him to speak and he became a successful politician (*Per.* 24.6). Finally emerged the "hideseller" Paphlagon, i.e., Cleon himself.

Eucrates, Lysicles, Cleon and other men who were not *kalos k' agathos* had become rich through the Empire (the futures of hemp and oakum, wool, fleeces and hides can scarcely have failed to improve in a rapidly growing military establishment), and being rich they no doubt wished to become important as well. They found, however, that their way to the most influential positions in the state was barred by what must have seemed to them a rigid gentleman's agreement among the great families to preach democracy, but to preserve an Establishment for their own kind.

Cleon emerged as a politician to be reckoned with in 428/7. But political prominence is not an overnight affair in a democracy. I believe that he may have decided a decade earlier to experiment with methods that were to be so successful in his later career. It is true there is no evidence for Cleon's activities until the first year of the war, when we find a comic poet assisting him by heaping scorn upon Pericles' leadership and accusing the statesman of cowardice (cited in *Per.* 33.8). But this comic poet is the same Hermippus who had earlier brought the indictment of Aspasia. Again, oracle-mongering was well recognized at Athens as one of the weapons of demagogues; and it is the mad [oracle-monger] Diopeithes—later seen as a moving spirit of Cleon's tame dicasts (Arist. *Wasps* 380 with schol.)—who wrote the decree against unorthodoxy aimed at Anaxagoras.

This is no more than a circumstantial case. But motive and method are important in such cases and the evidence for both motive and method are here, establishing a case for a very different ["concealed fracture"] than that assumed by Plutarch, and built upon by some recent historians. If long standing assumptions about "oligarchs" and "democrats" can be discarded, however, there is in fact good reason to believe that the attacks of 438/7 were the handiwork, if not of Cleon, then of someone very much like him, and with the same friends; for the evidence points to a band of pseudo-egalitarians who used the weapons of the agora demagogue—superstitious fear and contempt for intellect—against the ruling elite of Athens.

W. R. Connor

The Indispensable Expert

W. R. Connor, formerly Professor of Classics at Princeton University, is currently Chairman of the Council of the Humanities. He has written extensively on Greek history and historiography and in 1984 published a study of *Thucydides*. In the following selection from his work *The New Politicians of Fifth-Century Athens*, Connor argues that not only Pericles, but also the leaders who followed him like Cleon, succeeded at least in part by making themselves "indispensable experts" in complex public affairs.

[T]he growth of Athens from small town to imperial city imposed new demands upon her politicians—as the city grew the function of the politician changed. In the old quiescent town there were, to be sure, moments of intense and complex difficulties: wars with other states, financial problems, factional strife among the citizens. But these, as best we can tell, were not frequent and could be handled by a kind of

From *The New Politicians of Fifth-Century Athens* (Princeton 1971). Reprinted by Hackett Publishing Co. (Indianapolis 1992).

crisis politics—short periods of intense effort by leaders who were still essentially amateurs. A campaign season or two, perhaps only a few days of concerted effort, could restore tranquil normality.

But as the new century progressed new problems became more common. . . . Athens soon took on the leadership of the confederacy against Persia, the Delian League, and thereby assumed the military and, what was more important, the administrative burden of coordinating defensive and offensive operations in the Aegean. As time went on the treasury of the league was moved to Athens (454 B.C.) and efficiency seemed to demand that Athens exercise more and more direct control over what was rapidly becoming an empire rather than a league. The survival of extensive fragments from the inscriptions recording the annual quotas and divine offerings of this confederacy gives us a good indication of the attention to detail necessary for its proper operation.

But this is only a small part of the story. Treaty negotiations, supervision of religious sites and festivals, and eventually an ambitious building program increased the burden of public administration. And at the same time the growth in the population of Attica created new problems. Yet, although Athens had come to be the ruler of a great empire, . . . the formal political structure under which the city operated was still basically that of the small town that a few generations earlier had cast off tyrannic government and designed a new pattern of civic life. . . . The city was confronted with ever-increasing responsibilities and dangers, which imposed upon her inherited political forms stresses which Cleisthenes and his contemporaries at the end of the sixth century could only dimly have foreseen. The use of lot to fill important state offices, the emphasis on the principle of collegiality, the strictly limited terms of many major officials, might have been effective ways to prevent a recurrence of tyranny or of *stasis,* but they were less likely to meet the needs of a major imperial power. While Athens needed continuity and expertise of leadership, her constitutional procedures provided instead limited tenure of office, collegiality, and frequent changes of personnel.

Yet Athens constantly surpasses our expectations. To be sure, after twenty-seven years of war she lost her empire, her freedom, and her democratic constitution—temporarily. But it is not her eventual defeat which causes wonder. Rather it is the fact that a city with a political organization such as Athens' should have survived so long against such opposition which demands explanation. . . . [P]art of the reason was also, I believe, the skill and competence of her leaders. The growth of the city created a new situation and demanded a new kind of political leadership. The city could not hope to be successful with the old crisis politics. Instead it needed, and found, a new breed of specialized semi-professional politicians who could master and explain the complex details of their city's business.

Pericles is the great and least controversial example. He served repeatedly as general, spoke on major matters in the assembly with care, precision, and rhetorical virtuosity. He supervised the vast building program which transformed the appearance of Athens and which appropriately bears his name. To attain the leisure he needed, he entrusted the management of his farm to an overseer, Evangelus, who ran it with an exactitude that provoked admiration and amazement (Plutarch, *Pericles* 16). His own concentration on duty, reflected in Plutarch's story of his avoidance of all social activity save the marriage feast of Euryptolemus, is probably part of the same pattern of attentiveness to detail and a self-sacrificing determination to master the complicated business of the city.

Pericles' devotion to the city has won recognition both in antiquity and in modern times: it was largely responsible for the ability of Athens' political institutions to survive in an increasingly complex world. But if Pericles is to be praised, so must other less widely admired politicians of the late fifth century. As has recently been pointed out, "Kleon and his like were not simply the people's leaders on the comparatively narrow political front which Thucydides examines: a large part of the point is their mastery of finance and administration. The bulk of business is an important factor. It needed more than a few clear headed experts." The first book of Aristotle's *Rhetoric* outlines the principal topics with which a public speaker must be prepared to deal and the types of problems he is likely to be confronted with (1.4.1359 a 30ff.). It is an impressive, even frightening, array and the burdens of public life are not likely to have been less in the fifth century than they were in the fourth. Politics, in short, had by the period with which we are concerned become a full-time career that demanded from its practitioners "a comprehensive grasp of the resources and interests of their own and other cities," and "a constant readiness to advise on all manner of questions." It created what Professor [Antony] Andrewes has called "the indispensable expert."

Pericles' claim to the title is indisputable. But if we turn from what the ancient authorities *felt* about Cleon and Hyperbolus to the facts that they report about these men, it can be seen that these "demagogues" deserve it as well. . . . [T]hey, like Pericles, devoted themselves to the minutiae of politics as well as to the great issues and the occasions for spectacular oratory. And [this] may lead us to suspect as well that their mastery of public affairs was part of their appeal to a citizenry that recognized its inability to keep fully informed on matters that were often as difficult to understand as they were vital to the city's welfare. Athens needed her experts and found them not so much among her officials as among the *rhetores* who led the *demos*.

Thus part of the significance of Plutarch's story about Pericles' single-minded devotion to business is that it reflects imperial Athens' need for "indispensable experts." Pericles, like Cleon and perhaps many politicians of the last decades of the century, recognized this need and was prepared to fill it.

Charles W. Fornara and Loren J. Samons II

Pericles' Background and Career

Charles W. Fornara, Benedict Professor of Classics and History at Brown University, has published numerous works on subjects ranging from Greek history to the Roman historian Ammianus Marcellinus, and is currently completing one portion of Felix Jacoby's unfinished edition of the fragments of the lost Greek historians. In this selection from *Athens from Cleisthenes to Pericles*, Fornara and I argue that Pericles' connection to the infamous and accursed Alcmeonid family as well as other aspects of his unique background greatly influenced his future political career.

Pericles' mother Agariste came from the aristocratic family of the Alcmeonids, which had incurred a curse for slaying suppliants around 632 B.C. and was then exiled from Athens. After returning sometime later, the family contracted a brief marriage alliance with the tyrant Peisistratus,

Charles W. Fornara, Loren J. Samons II, *Athens from Cleisthenes to Pericles*. Copyright © 1991 The Regents of the University of California.

and the Alcmeonid Cleisthenes served as archon under the Peisistratid tyrant Hippias in 525/4. Although claiming a share in the overthrow of the tyranny in 511/10, the Alcmeonid family was briefly exiled again under Spartan compulsion shortly after Cleisthenes installed *demokratia* ca. 507. During the 480s, the family apparently suffered from a rumor that they had attempted to betray Athens to the Persians (who had brought Hippias with them in apparent hopes of establishing a puppet regime) in 490. Perhaps for this reason Pericles' Alcmeonid uncle Megacles and his father Xanthippus (who had married an Alcmeonid) were both ostracized during this period (see Hdt. 5.71–2, 6.121, 123–26, 131). The Spartans attempted to use the Alcmeonid curse against Pericles himself in the diplomatic machinations just before the Peloponnesian War (Thuc. 1.126–27).

In 432 B.C., just prior to the outbreak of the Peloponnesian War, the Spartans escalated their diplomatic offensive against the Athenians by reminding them that their leader Pericles was polluted by a curse, and they demanded the expulsion from Attica of the sacrilegious family of the Alcmeonids (Thuc. 1.126f.). If their demand were ignored, as they thought it would be, they might thereby at least inject a premonition of supernatural agency into a debate hitherto conducted along pragmatic and rational lines. Dread of the *agos*, the curse, if not sufficient to prompt second thoughts about the propriety of the leadership of Pericles, might introduce a higher level of apprehension in this time of crisis. The background of the *agos* is well known. Two hundred years before, as both Herodotus (5.71) and Thucydides (1.126.3–12) inform us, this family had been stained by the pollution of impious blood-guilt because the head of the house had murdered suppliants after promising them their lives. As a result, the Alcmeonids were twice expelled from Athens, once shortly after the event and again at the time of the revolution of Cleisthenes, himself an Alcmeonid. Pericles, as a direct descendant on his mother's side, was believed to have inherited this stain.

From a modern point of view, the idea that Pericles lay under a curse because of sacrilege committed two hundred years before by maternal relatives seems as implausible as the corollary that the city could itself be polluted by the contamination of his presence. Many features, however, of Athenian judicial practice remind us of the tenacity of this ancient belief. An unclean person, or even an object (Aeschin. 3.244), was held to defile the public places of a city and had to be expelled in order to protect the community from harm. The theme is frequent in drama, an obvious example being Sophocles' play, *Oedipus the King*. . . . There is, in any case, no doubt that the revival of the charge of pollution against the Alcmeonids provoked more psychological stress in the Athenians than Thucydides implies in 1.126. For though, as a rationalist of the new school, which tended to be impatient of supernatural causes, Thucydides may have been disdainful of the superstition, he nevertheless considered it significant enough to be worth mention, making the point more than once that Pericles was held responsible by some Athenians for the onset of the plague (2.59.2, 64.1). The interplay of human and divine, reflected in the charges and countercharges leveled by both sides before the opening of the war, should not be taken by the modern reader as a mere exercise in propaganda.

Family continuity in the matrilineal as well as the patrilineal line of descent is presupposed by the Spartan demand for the expulsion of the Alcmeonids. Not only is it a matter of an ancestral curse "which for almost two centuries continued to be *the* [curse], and which came to the surface in every great crisis"; the *agos* had implications in its own right for the peculiar circumstances surrounding the family and the policies it was compelled to follow or eschew. Although it is impossible as well as improper to explain Pericles' orientation solely or even primarily by way of his family tradition, his possession of a unique heritage remains a vital consideration. His systematic divergence from aristocratic interests and his commitment to the extension of the power of "the many" may, in part, have been inspired by the sense of alienation he inherited from his maternal ancestors; it may even be the case that it played a part in the much-heralded aloofness that characterized his social life (Plut. *Per.* 4–5, 7). . . .

[After an examination of the history of the Alcmeonid family in Athens, the analysis of Pericles' career continues.]

Strictly speaking, to be sure, Pericles was Alcmeonid only on his mother's side, and could point with pride and assurance to the achievements of his father, Xanthippus son of Ariphron, the victor of Mycale, who had been honored by the Athenians with a statue set up by them on the acropolis (Paus. 1.25.1). But *our* definitions of "family" can hardly supersede the impressions and understandings of the contemporary Athenian public. It is plain enough that the special interest devoted to this great family derived from Pericles' association with it, as Herodotus announced in a well-known passage (6.131); and we have already observed the importance ascribed to Pericles' Alcmeonid heritage in the vituperation immediately preceding the outbreak of the Peloponnesian War. The (conjectural) effect on Pericles of his peculiar ancestry can await brief discussion at the conclusion of this chapter; for the moment we may note a suggestive passage in Plutarch where he makes the point that Pericles did not engage in a political career in the normal course of events because he worried how the *demos* would receive him.

> *For he looked very much like the tyrant Peisistratus. Very old men were amazed at the similarity of his voice, which was sweet, and his readiness of tongue and rapidity in conversation. Since he was rich and of splendid birth and possessed friends of great power, he avoided politics in the fear of being ostracized.* (Per. 7.1–2)

Plutarch's assertion seems credible because it appears to be the reflection of sound retrospective analysis of Pericles' career coupled with actual knowledge of the age of his entrance into politics. If accurate, it hints at the stigma attaching to Pericles because of the actions and the fortunes of his mother's family. . . .

[T]he nature of the tradition about Pericles and the alleged alteration of his regime into one of "aristocratic" character [see Plutarch, *Pericles* 15, above] makes clear that it was contrived not from the evidence but from a desire to reconcile two competing views of the statesman. Pericles' career presented a problem to the historical and philosophical critics of the fourth century. His dominance prior to the outbreak of the Peloponnesian War, the ease with which he could be distinguished from the demagogues who succeeded him on his death, and his association with Athens at the apex of its development, something regarded with nostalgia and awe by his fourth-century [successors], required that he be treated with respect. For later writers like Plutarch, Thucydides' famous words in 2.65.5–8 became dogma; in the fourth century it was enough that Pericles guided Athens without a serious rival, was celebrated as the "Olympian" in comic literature, and was well remembered, probably exalted, in the oral tradition. Yet it was also clear to the critics that Pericles had been a demagogue responsible for the radicalization of the city-state. It therefore became desirable to resolve what in essence was an intellectual and literary problem centering on the apparent metamorphosis of the great politician, and the dividing line could plausibly be drawn at the year of the ostracism of Thucydides son of Melesias. The elimination of Pericles' "powerful" rival left him, as it appeared, without opposition, permitting him to rise above faction and, in the words of Thucydides, "to lead the people rather than to be led by them." In this way, the great statesman could be viewed not as a divisive figure but as a leader of the city as a whole. The conservative intellectual establishment of the fourth century could allege that he too had become an elitist, an aristocrat in control over the popular element, and not its creature. The development of the schema should not delude us; we need not suppose, on the basis of the rhetoric, that Pericles underwent a change in the forties. His domestic, imperial, and Spartan policy continued as before. [This policy consisted of the radicalization of the democracy through measures such as jury pay, the extension of Athens' empire in Greece, and "no concessions to the Peloponnesians" (Thuc. 2.140).]

None of this should be taken to imply that Pericles maintained "absolute dominance" at any time. Though he was called so, he was not the tyrant of Athens, and the *demos* could be fickle. His opponents attacked his friends successfully, and the restrictions in comedy applied 440–438/7 suggest pressure and criticism owing to the unpopularity of the Samian War. Since Pheidias went into exile in 438/7 and the comic poets were assailing Pericles for his bondage to "Omphale" at that time, it is likely enough that Pericles faced, and surmounted, a crisis in this period. But, in general, it is hard to believe that the man who survived a catastrophe of the dimensions of the Egyptian Expedition in 454, who dominated the domestic political scene from the 450s to 431, and who had the influence to bring about a war in 431 that posited the destruction of Attica as a matter of course had much to fear from any political opponent from the time he followed Damon's advice and distributed "its own property" to the people.

The career of Pericles, viewed, as it were, from the outside, naturally manifests little sign of the effects on him of his peculiar family tradition. If, after our review, we were to attempt to set down . . . some of the family traditions Pericles inherited on the Alcmeonid side, what features are most likely to have impressed themselves upon him?

If the existence of the curse affected him personally, probably it reinforced his naturally rationalistic turn of mind. The man whose circle included Anaxagoras and Damon, and who evinced qualities that inspired Thucydides, will have greeted traditional ideas skeptically and have discounted supernatural agency as a matter of course. But the inheritance of a curse cuts deep; the experiences of his maternal ancestors cannot but have sharpened his impatience with contemporary representatives of the older ways of thought, making him naturally inclined to disparage their ideas and *ethos*. Cimon and Thucydides son of Melesias inhabited a different world from his; Herodotus and Pericles will have found each other congenial company only if they met very briefly and then but once.

If Pericles scoffed at the *agos*, his contempt for the aristocracy that, in the sixth century at least, isolated his family, would not have been the less real because the superstition was rooted in the conventional religious life of the times, and his sympathies with the class to which he belonged by birth must have been exiguous. We do not believe, today, in the efficacy of curses, but if ever a case history existed of the isolation of a family of wealth and prestige that had incurred a dreadful curse, it is that of the Alcmeonids. A common thread unites the manifestations of their political virtuosity: the absence of fixed and reliable associations with the Athenian nobility. In this respect, one element of his family tradition fused with another, for the absence of common understanding with the nobility was reinforced by the record of the family in championing the *demos*. We have no desire to romanticize Megacles II [the Alcmeonid who married his daughter to Peisistratus], and every reason to suppose that his actions were self-serving. The fact remains that by choosing Peisistratus over the local dynasts, the Athenian citizenry profited greatly. The association of Cleisthenes with the Peisistratids tells the same tale, as does, later, Cleisthenes' establishment of the democracy. Whatever flirting with tyranny there may have been in 490, Pericles' heritage placed him squarely on the side of the *demos*.

There is also the question of Sparta. We should allow for some predetermination of his sympathies in this direction. Cleisthenes had been expelled from Athens by the Lacedaemonians as one polluted by a curse and unfit for Athenian society; the Lacedaemonians had not only been the friends of Cleisthenes' enemies (Isagoras and the [other aristocrats]), but were the proudest and most powerful representatives of a form of government to which Athens, in Pericles' younger days, was becoming the antithesis. Here too it is possible to detect a fusion of attitudes resulting in a powerful controlling idea. Ancestral tradition and fervent patriotism united in an intractable and defiant hostility to Sparta, leading to the wars of the 450s and 431.

The impression conveyed of Pericles in the pages of Plutarch and our other sources is of a man detached from society, indifferent to conventional opinions and devoted, at all cost, to what he conceived to be the role and destiny of his city. It seems indisputable that such a man was the product of his family tradition no less than of the times he shaped so signally.

Donald Kagan

Pericles as Leader and Model

Donald Kagan, Hillhouse Professor of History and Classics at Yale University, has authored a complete four-volume history of the Peloponnesian War, a biography of Pericles, and more recently, an analysis *On the Origins of War and Preservation of Peace*. Although in his works Kagan has criticized Pericles' miscalculations as contributing factors that helped bring on the Peloponnesian War, he remains one of the statesman's many admirers. In the following passage from his biography of Pericles, Kagan champions the Athenian as a possible model for contemporary leaders.

Pericles was one of those extraordinary people who placed his own stamp on his time and shaped the course of history. He was the leading citizen of a great democracy that had a keen sense of its own special role in history and of the special excellence of its constitution and way of life. It had a booming economy producing wealth and prosperity previously unknown, a combined military and naval power made possible only by such wealth, and international responsibilities that stretched its resources to the limit but could not safely be ignored. It was a democracy confronted by an opposing state with an entirely different constitution and character, which regarded the Athenian power and way of life as a deadly menace to its own ambitions and security. The life of Pericles and the democratic society he led indeed have much to teach the citizens of free lands in our own time.

Pericles was an Athenian aristocrat who possessed no great private fortune. The citizen of a democratic republic, he held no office higher than that of general (*strategos*), one of ten, none of whom had greater formal powers than any of the others. He controlled no military or police forces, and he could expend no public money without a vote of the popular assembly of citizens. Unlike the presidents and prime ministers of modern representative democracies, he had no well-established, well-organized political party machinery on which to rely. Each year he had to stand for reelection and was constantly subject to public scrutiny and political challenge.

Pericles also differed from later leaders in the variety of his responsibilities and in his direct and personal execution of them. Elizabeth, Louis, and in our own time such great leaders as Franklin D. Roosevelt and Winston Churchill, were titular heads of their armed forces. But Pericles, like Caesar and, to a lesser extent, Augustus, repeatedly commanded armies and navies in battle. He was also a constitutional reformer who radically expanded Athenian democracy and brought it to fulfillment. As a diplomat, he negotiated public treaties and secret agreements and produced imaginative proposals to advance his city's fortunes. Throughout his career, he managed the public finance with unmatched skill and integrity.

Like Augustus, Lorenzo de' Medici, and Elizabeth, Pericles also sponsored a great outburst of artistic and intellectual activity. It was his idea to crown the Acropolis with the temples and statues that have made it the wonder of the world for two millennia; he also selected the architects and sculptors, and found the vast sums of money to pay for their works. He was the producer of Aeschylus' tragedy *Persians;* the friend and colleague of Sophocles; the friend of Phidias, the greatest sculptor of his day, who devised the master plan of the Parthenon. He commissioned Hippodamus of Miletus, the first city planner, and befriended Herodotus, the father of history. In moments of leisure, he debated with Zeno, Anaxagoras, and Protagoras, the leading teachers and philosophers of his time. His patronage of the arts and his personal support and encouragement of thinkers and their activities made Athens a magnet that drew to it the leading creative talents from the entire Greek world.

Two millennia after the Athenians' defeat we still marvel at what they achieved. But the visible remains, impressive as they are, do not constitute their most important legacy. Pericles confronted the problem that faces any free and democratic society: How can the citizens be persuaded to make the sacrifices necessary for its success? Tyrants and dictators can rely on mercenaries and compulsion to defend their states. Rare states like Sparta—a closed authoritarian society—could inculcate in their people a willingness to renounce their private lives almost entirely. But democracies cannot use such devices. Instead, democratic leadership involves a freer kind of public education. Pericles sought to teach the Athenians that their own interests were inextricably tied together with those of their community, that they could not be secure and prosper unless their state was secure and prosperous, that the ordinary man could achieve greatness only through the greatness of his society. All that he did and all that he sought for Athens was part of that education. Pericles tried to shape a new kind of society and a new kind of citizen, not by the use of force or terror but by the power of his ideas, the strength of his personality, the use of reason, and his genius as a uniquely persuasive rhetorician. . . .

Most democratic politicians are tempted to seek popularity by telling the people only good news, or by appealing to their desires and prejudices. Yet because their opinions have a strong effect on the state's actions, the people in democracies need, more than in other regimes, to understand and face reality. Even so great and powerful a leader as Franklin Roosevelt challenged the popular mood rarely, briefly, and usually indirectly, though protected by a four-year term of office. Winston Churchill, perhaps the most Periclean leader of modern times, paid a price for his political courage. But as prime minister in wartime, even he was shielded by special emergency powers and an extended term of office. Pericles, on the other hand, held office for one year at a time and could be recalled by public vote at least ten times during that year. Yet he refused to flatter the people and appeal to their prejudices. Instead, when the occasion demanded, he informed them of the realities and advised them how to cope; he called upon them to rise above their fears and short-range self-interest, and inspired them to do so. When necessary, he was willing to chastise them and risk their anger.

And provoke their anger he did. Like all democratic leaders, Pericles engaged in the rough and tumble of popular politics and was subject to every kind of attack. Throughout his years in office he confronted political conflict at home and war abroad. Domestic enemies accused him of tyranny on the one hand and demagogy on the other. Comic poets lampooned him in the public theater, made fun of the shape of his head, his Olympian aloofness, and even the woman he loved. He was forced to endure legal actions against her and many of his friends and associates, even seeing some of them driven into exile. He was accused of bringing on war to please his mistress and of imposing an inadequate and cowardly strategy on his people.

Although he successfully overcame all these trials, Pericles' career took a tragic turn, and in the last year he had reason to doubt the value of his life's work. Athens was engaged in a terrible war that he had urged the people to undertake. Then a plague broke out and killed a third of the citizens. The people of Athens held him responsible for all their miseries and removed him from office. The antidemocratic Plato could therefore dismiss him in a way that was both plausible and crushing: Pericles had sought to make the Athenians better, Plato said, yet "they imposed no shameful punishment on him when they were 'worse'; but after he had made them 'noble and good' at the end of his life they condemned him for embezzlement and almost put him to death because they thought he was a scoundrel." [See Plato *Gorgias* above.]

Plato's judgment has influenced all subsequent opinion about Pericles and the democracy he led. Indeed, after Pericles' death, and especially after Athens had lost the war, it was easy to look upon both as a terrible failure. The Athenians lost their empire and the wealth and power that went with it; for a while they even lost their democracy and their liberty. Yet the defeat in war and the loss of empire did not mean the failure of Pericles' enterprise. He had, in fact, foreseen the possibility himself, and in a dark moment of the war urged the Athenians not to be discouraged by the prospect [Thuc. 2.64 above]. . . .

Thucydides reports Pericles' own summary of the qualities necessary for a statesman: "to know what must be done and to be able to explain it; to love one's country and to be incorruptible.". . . It was Pericles' genius to recognize the democratic leader's obligation to educate his people in civic virtue and to have the skills needed to do so. His policies, to be sure, brought the Athenians prosperity and the practical advantages of empire. But his success and that of Athens rested on more than prosperity and rhetoric. He also had a vision for his city that offered the meanest of its citizens the opportunity to achieve, through common effort, personal dignity, honor, and the fulfillment of their highest needs. He used his talents and his character to convey that vision to his people. . . .

In their rational and secular approach, in their commitment to political freedom and individual autonomy in a constitutional, republican and democratic public life, the Athenians of Pericles' day are closer to the values of our era than any culture that has appeared since antiquity. That is why Periclean Athens has such a powerful meaning for us. But if there is much to learn from the similarities, there is at least as much to learn from the differences between the Athenians and ourselves. Although the Athenians valued wealth and material goods as we do, they regarded economic life and status as less noble and important than distinction in public service. Although they were among the first to recognize the dignity of the individual, they could not imagine the fulfillment of their spiritual needs apart from an involvement in the life of a well-ordered political community. To understand the achievements of Pericles and his city we need to be aware of these significant differences, and we must study them with humility. For in spite of their antiquity, the Athenians may have believed things we have either forgotten or never known; and we must keep open the possibility that in some respects, at least, they were wiser than we. . . .

Ancient and modern critics of democracy have shared a basic attitude. Both have distrusted the ordinary person and overridden his autonomy in search of a higher goal: a utopian idea of justice. For Plato, that meant government by a small group of philosophers who would rule in the light of a divine, unchanging knowledge. For Marxian theory, it meant a utopia of equality and total liberty without exploitation or alienation. In its earthly manifestation that came to mean the rule of the "proletariat"—in fact, a small dictatorial "revolutionary vanguard" led by such men as Lenin, Mao, and Castro—governed such utopias as the Soviet Union, Communist China, and Cuba. Both critiques of democracy share the beliefs that individual freedom and self-government are secondary to the construction of a truly just society, and that there is a small class of people who alone know the right goals and how to achieve them.

Most defenders of democracy deny that there is an art or science of government, known or knowable only by some elite group. They believe that good government and the achievement of a good society require the participation of all citizens. The elements of democracy—individual liberty, equality before the law, equal opportunity, the right to vote, and the right to hold office — are not means to a higher end. Rather, the system of democratic self-government is an end in itself. . . .

The story of the Athenians in the time of Pericles suggests that the creation and survival of democracy requires leadership of a high order. When tested, the Athenians behaved with the required devotion, wisdom, and moderation in large part because they had been inspired by the democratic vision and example that Pericles had so effectively communicated to them. It was a vision that exalted the individual *within* the political community; it limited the scope and power of the state, leaving enough space for individual freedom, privacy, and the human dignity of which they are a crucial part. It rejected the leveling principle pursued by both ancient Sparta and modern socialism, which requires the suppression of those rights. By rewarding merit, it encouraged the individual achievement and excellence that makes life sweet and raises the quality of life for everyone. Above all, Pericles convinced the Athenians that their private needs, both moral and material, required the kind of community Athens had become. Therefore, they were willing to run risks in its defense, make sacrifices on its behalf, and restrain their passions and desires to preserve it.

The new and emerging democracies of our time are very fragile, and they all face serious challenges. . . . To succeed, they need a vision of the future that is powerful enough to sustain them through bad times as well as good and to inspire the many difficult sacrifices that will be required of them. They must see that democracy alone of all regimes respects the dignity and autonomy of every individual, and understand that its survival requires that each individual sees his own well-being as inextricably connected to that of the whole community.

This new faith will be especially hard to instill in societies that have learned to be cynical about the use of political idealism. The new democracies will, therefore, need leaders in the Periclean mold, leaders who know that the aim and character of true democracy should be to elevate their citizens to the highest attainable level, and that cutting down the greatest to assuage the envy of the least is the way of tyranny. . . .

Such a vision and such leadership are not readily available in our era. The world has been astounded to see thin shoots of democracy trying to break through the hard surface of oppression. Those who wish to help them grow and flourish could do worse than to turn for inspiration and instruction to the story of Pericles of Athens and his city, where once, against all odds, democracy triumphed.

The author of over 100 plays, Sophocles (here in a restored copy of a fourth-century work) also held the office of imperial treasurer (443/2) and served as general during Athens' war with Samos (440). (Alinari/Art Resource, NY)

PART

 Drama,
Democracy,
and Empire

The works of only three tragic dramatists of the fifth century survive today,
but even in antiquity the plays of Aeschylus, Sophocles, and Euripides
were considered classics and re-performed many times. These three poets,
along with the comic playwright Aristophanes, were all native Athenians,
but fifth-century Athens attracted philosophers, writers, and artists from
all over the Mediterranean, and there can be little doubt that the resul-
tant cosmopolitan and imperial culture of Athens affected these dramatists. To what degree the Athenian tragedians attempted to comment
directly on, or even influence, the domestic or foreign policies of their own
day is a matter of some dispute. The following selections are offered as
possible examples of the way the dramatists introduced topical subjects
into their ostensibly mythical or historical tales.

Sources

Aeschylus

Athens and the Areopagus

The earliest of the surviving dramatists, Aeschylus (525/4–456) is said to have introduced the second actor onto the stage—formerly there had been only one actor and a chorus. In 472 he produced the *Persians*, built around the battle of Salamis and one of the few Greek tragedies to describe historical events. Intriguingly, for this play Pericles served as the *choregos*, a kind of financial backer who provided funds for training the actors and chorus. Aeschylus produced the trilogy *Oresteia*, based on the family of Agamemnon and his son Orestes, in 458. The *Eumenides* formed the last play of the trilogy, and described the mythological creation of the Areopagus Council in Athens. The powers of this council had recently been restricted by Ephialtes (in 462/1, with the help of Pericles, according to some), and at the same time the city had renounced its alliance with Sparta and made an agreement with the medizing Argives. Both events undoubtedly displeased the more conservative elements in Athens—Ephialtes was murdered shortly after the reforms, and, according to Thucydides (1.107, see Part II), an oligarchical plot to betray the city to Sparta was hatched. The fact that Aeschylus seemingly goes out of his way in the *Oresteia* to praise Athens' new ally Argos has thus led some scholars to argue that this play had a specific political message regarding the recent reforms. Nonetheless, no consensus exists about the existence of this message or its precise meaning. In the following passages, Orestes, pursued by the Furies who seek revenge for his matricide, seeks the aid of Athena in Athens. The goddess proposes to create a council (the Areopagus) to hear the case; the new body finds against the Furies, whom Athena ultimately seeks to soothe.

Chorus [of Furies, responding to Athena's proposal.]
    Here is overthrow of all   490
    the young laws, if the claim

From R. Lattimore, "Aeschylus, Eumenides," in D. Grene and R. Lattimore, *The Complete Greek Tragedies*, vol. 1. Copyright © 1992 University of Chicago Press. Reprinted by permission of the publisher.

of this matricide shall stand
good, his crime be sustained.
Should this be, every man will find a way
to act at his own caprice;   495
over and over again in time
to come, parents shall await
the deathstroke at their children's hands.

We are the Angry Ones. But we
shall watch no more over works   500
of men, and so act. We shall
let loose indiscriminate death.
Man shall learn from man's lot, forejudge
the evils of his neighbor's case,
see respite and windfall in storm:
pathetic prophet who consoles   505
with strengthless cures, in vain.

Nevermore let one who feels
the stroke of accident, uplift
his voice and make outcry, thus: 510
"Oh Justice!
Throned powers of the Furies, help!"
Such might be the pitiful cry
of some father, of the stricken
mother, their appeal. Now   515
the House of Justice has collapsed.

There are times when fear is good.
It must keep its watchful place
at the heart's controls. There is
advantage   520
in the wisdom won from pain.
Should the city, should the man
rear a heart that nowhere goes
in fear, how shall such a one
any more respect the right?   525

Refuse the life of anarchy;

refuse the life devoted to
one master.
The in-between has the power
by God's grant always, though   530
his ordinances vary.
I will speak in defence
of reason: for the very child
of vanity is violence;
but out of health   535
in the heart issues the beloved
and the longed-for, prosperity.

All for all I say to you:
bow before the altar of right.
You shall not   540
eye advantage, and heel
it over with foot of force.
Vengeance will be upon you.
The all is bigger than you.
Let man see this and take   545
care, to mother and father,
and to the guest
in the gates welcomed, give all rights
that befall their position.

The man who does right, free-willed, without constraint   550
shall not lose happiness
nor be wiped out with all his generation.
But the transgressor, I tell you, the bold man
who brings in confusion of goods unrightly won,
at long last and perforce, when ship toils   555
under tempest must strike his sail
in the wreck of his rigging.

He calls on those who hear not, caught inside
the hard wrestle of water.
The spirit laughs at the hot hearted man,   560
the man who said "never to me," watches him
pinned in distress, unable to run free of the crests.

He had good luck in his life. Now
he smashes it on the reef of Right
and drowns, unwept and forgotten. . . .   565

[Athena addresses the new Areopagus council.]

Athene
    If it please you, men of Attica, hear my decree
    now, on this first case of bloodletting I have judged.
    For Aegeus' population, this forevermore
    shall be the ground where justices deliberate.
    Here is the Hill of Ares, here the Amazons   685
    encamped and built their shelters when they came in arms
    for spite of Theseus, here they piled their rival towers
    to rise, new city, and dare his city long ago,
    and slew their beasts for Ares. So this rock is named
    from then the Hill of Ares. Here the reverence   690
    of citizens, their fear and kindred do-no-wrong
    shall hold by day and in the blessing of night alike
    all while the people do not muddy their own laws
    with foul infusions. But if bright water you stain
    with mud, you nevermore will find it fit to drink.   695
    No anarchy, no rule of a single master. Thus
    I advise my citizens to govern and to grace,
    and not to cast fear utterly from your city. What
    man who fears nothing at all is ever righteous? Such
    be your just terrors, and you may deserve and have   700
    salvation for your citadel, your land's defence,
    such as is nowhere else found among men, neither
    among the Scythians, nor the land that Pelops held.
    I establish this tribunal. It shall be untouched
    by money-making, grave but quick to wrath, watchful   705
    to protect those who sleep, a sentry on the land.

    These words I have unreeled are for my citizens,
    advice into the future. All must stand upright
    now, take each man his ballot in his hand, think on
    his oath, and make his judgment. For my word is said. . . . 710

Athene [to the defeated Furies]

>   I will bear your angers. You are elder born than I
>   and in that you are wiser far than I. Yet still
>   Zeus gave me too intelligence not to be despised.   850
>   If you go away into some land of foreigners,
>   I warn you, you will come to love this country. Time
>   in his forward flood shall ever grow more dignified
>   for the people of this city. And you, in your place
>   of eminence beside Erechtheus in his house   855
>   shall win from female and from male processionals
>   more than all lands of men beside could ever give.
>   Only in this place that I haunt do not inflict
>   your bloody stimulus to twist the inward hearts
>   of young men, raging in a fury not of wine,   860
>   nor, as if plucking the heart from fighting cocks,
>   engraft among my citizens that spirit of war
>   that turns their battle fury inward on themselves.
>   No, let our wars range outward hard against the man
>   who has fallen horribly in love with high renown.   865
>   No true fighter I call the bird that fights at home.
>   Such life I offer you, and it is yours to take.
>   Do good, receive good, and be honored as the good
>   are honored. Share our country, the beloved of god. . . .

[The Furies, now won over, pray that civil strife may be avoided in Athens.]

Chorus

>   This my prayer: Civil War
>   fattening on men's ruin shall
>   not thunder in our city. Let
>   not the dry dust that drinks
>   the black blood of citizens   980
>   through passion for revenge
>   and bloodshed for bloodshed
>   be given our state to prey upon.
>   Let them render grace for grace.
>   Let love be their common will;   985

let them hate with single heart.
Much wrong in the world thereby is healed.

Sophocles

Ode to Man, Antigone, Law and Justice

Sophocles (ca. 496–406) achieved fame as a playwright when he defeated Aeschylus around 468 (Plut. *Cim.* 8), and continued to write successful tragedies into the last decade of the fifth century. He also served in various political and military positions, holding the offices of general (in 440, with Pericles), imperial treasurer (443/2), and proboulos (413–411). Aristotle considered his *Oedipus Rex* to be a paradigm for good tragedy, and others have maintained that Sophocles achieved a kind of balance between the somewhat archaic grandeur of Aeschylus and the intellectualism of Euripides. A master of treating conflict and personal motivation, in the following passages from *Antigone* (produced ca. 441) Sophocles confronts such issues as the nature of man, the demands of piety, and the rights of the individual versus the state.

Ode to Man

[In the following passage the Chorus praises the capacities of mankind.]

Many are the wonders, none
is more wonderful than what is man.
This it is that crosses the sea   370
with the south winds storming and the waves swelling,

From D. Grene and R. Lattimore (editors), *The Complete Greek Tragedies*, vol. 2. Copyright © University of Chicago Press. Reprinted by permission of the publisher.

breaking around him in roaring surf.
He it is again who wears away
the Earth, oldest of gods, immortal, unwearied,
as the ploughs wind across her from year to year
when he works her with the breed that comes from horses.

The tribe of the lighthearted birds he snares
and takes prisoner the races of savage beasts
and the brood of the fish of the sea,
with the close-spun web of nets.   380
A cunning fellow is man. His contrivances
make him master of beasts of the field
and those that move in the mountains.
So he brings the horse with the shaggy neck
to bend underneath the yoke;
and also the untamed mountain bull;
and speech and windswift thought
and the tempers that go with city living
he has taught himself, and how to avoid
the sharp frost, when lodging is cold   390
under the open sky
and pelting strokes of the rain.
He has a way against everything,
and he faces nothing that is to come
without contrivance.
Only against death
can he call on no means of escape;
but escape from hopeless diseases
he has found in the depths of his mind.
With some sort of cunning, inventive   400
beyond all expectation
he reaches sometimes evil,
and sometimes good.

If he honors the laws of earth,
and the justice of the gods he has confirmed by oath,
high is his city; no city

has he with whom dwells dishonor
prompted by recklessness.
He who is so, may he never
share my hearth!   410
may he never think my thoughts! . . .

Antigone, Law and Justice

[Antigone, who buried her rebellious brother Polyneices and thus de-
fied king Creon's orders to allow his body to remain uncovered, justi-
fies her actions. In the last passage, Creon's son Haemon (Antigone's
fiancé) attempts to soothe his father's wrath.]

Antigone [to Creon]
Yes, it was not Zeus that made the proclamation [that he remain
    unburied];
nor did Justice, which lives with those below, enact
such laws as that, for mankind. I did not believe
your proclamation had such power to enable
one who will someday die to override
God's ordinances, unwritten and secure.
They are not of today and yesterday;   500
they live forever; none knows when first they were.
These are the laws whose penalties I would not
incur from the gods, through fear of any man's temper.

I know that I will die—of course I do—
even if you had not doomed me by proclamation.
If I shall die before my time, I count that
a profit. How can such as I, that live
among such troubles, not find a profit in death?
So for such as me, to face such a fate as this
is pain that does not count. But if I dared to leave   510
the dead man, my mother's son, dead and unburied,
that would have been real pain. The other is not.
Now, if you think me a fool to act like this,
perhaps it is a fool that judges so.

Chorus [of Elders]
>The savage spirit of a savage father
>shows itself in this girl. She does not know
>how to yield to trouble.

Creon
>I would have you know the most fanatic spirits
>fall most of all. It is the toughest iron,
>baked in the fire to hardness, you may see   520
>most shattered, twisted, shivered to fragments.
>I know hot horses are restrained
>by a small curb. For he that is his neighbor's slave cannot
>be high in spirit. This girl had learned her insolence
>before this, when she broke the established laws.
>But here is still another insolence
>in that she boasts of it, laughs at what she did.
>I swear I am no man and she the man
>if she can win this and not pay for it.
>No; though she were my sister's child or closer   530
>in blood than all that my hearth god acknowledges
>as mine, neither she nor her sister should escape
>the utmost sentence — death. For indeed I accuse her,
>the sister, equally of plotting the burial.
>Summon her. I saw her inside, just now,
>crazy, distraught. When people plot
>mischief in the dark, it is the mind which first
>is convicted of deceit. But surely I hate indeed
>the one that is caught in evil and then makes
>that evil look like good. . . .   540

Haemon [to his father Creon, who has condemned Antigone]
>Father, the natural sense that the gods breed
>in men is surely the best of their possessions.
>I certainly could not declare you wrong —
>may I never know how to do so! — Still there might   740
>be something useful that some other than you might think.
>It is natural for me to be watchful on your behalf

concerning what all men say or do or find to blame.
Your face is terrible to a simple citizen;
it frightens him from words you dislike to hear.
But what *I* can hear, in the dark, are things like these:
the city mourns for this girl; they think she is dying
most wrongly and most undeservedly
of all womenkind, for the most glorious acts.
Here is one who would not leave her brother unburied,   750
a brother who had fallen in bloody conflict,
to meet his end by greedy dogs or by
the bird that chanced that way. Surely what she merits
is golden honor, isn't it? That's the dark rumor
that spreads in secret. Nothing I own
I value more highly, father, than your success.
What greater distinction can a son have than the glory
of a successful father, and for a father
the distinction of successful children?
Do not bear this single habit of mind, to think   760
that what you say and nothing else is true.
A man who thinks that he alone is right,
or what he says, or what he *is* himself,
unique, such men, when opened up, are seen
to be quite empty. For a man, though he be wise,
it is no shame to learn — learn many things,
and not maintain his views too rigidly.
You notice how by streams in wintertime
the trees that yield preserve their branches safely,
but those that fight the tempest perish utterly.   770
The man who keeps the sheet of his sail tight
and never slackens capsizes his boat
and makes the rest of his trip keel uppermost.
Yield something of your anger, give way a little.
If a much younger man, like me, may have
a judgment, I would say it were far better
to be one altogether wise by nature, but,
as things incline not to be so, then it is good
also to learn from those who advise well.

Euripides

A "Mythological" Debate

Despite the merciless attacks on him by Aristophanes, more plays of Euripides (ca. 485–ca. 406) have survived from antiquity than of any other fifth-century playwright. Although all the dramatists shaped the myths to their own tastes and purposes, Euripides seems to have taken somewhat more liberties than the others, and his works have an intellectual and rhetorical cast that betrays the influence of the sophists. However, his use of the myths to entertain, and his focus on their more human and emotional elements such as love, excitement, adventure, and surprise makes his works in some way seem more "modern" than those of his fellow tragedians. Euripides also produced works that commented brilliantly on the moral and political problems of his own day, as shown in this passage from *The Suppliant Women* (ca. 420). This play relates how the mothers of the fallen "seven against Thebes" sought aid as suppliants from Theseus in Athens. In this excerpt, a herald from Thebes arrives at Athens, where he and the Athenian hero Theseus proceed to debate the merits of popular government at Athens, here retrojected into the mythical past.

Herald

    What man is master in this land? To whom
    Must I give the word I bring from Creon, ruler   400
    In Cadmus' country since Eteocles
    Fell at his brother Polynices' hand
    Beside the seven-mouthed gates?

Theseus

                           One moment, stranger.
    Your start was wrong, seeking a master here.
    This city is free, and ruled by no one man.   405

The people reign, in annual succession.
They do not yield the power to the rich;
The poor man has an equal share in it.

Herald
    That one point gives the better of the game
    To me. The town I come from is controlled   410
    By one man, not a mob. And there is no one
    To puff it up with words, for private gain,
    Swaying it this way, that way. Such a man
    First flatters it with wealth of favors; then
    He does it harm, but covers up his blunders   415
    By blaming other men, and goes scot-free.
    The people is no right judge of arguments;
    Then how can it give right guidance to a city?
    A poor man, working hard, could not attend   420
    To public matters, even if ignorance
    Were not his birthright. When a wretch, a nothing,
    Obtains respect and power from the people
    By talk, his betters sicken at the sight.   425

Theseus
    What bombast from a herald! Waster of words,
    If it is argument you want—and you yourself
    Have set the contest going—listen. Nothing
    Is worse for a city than an absolute ruler.
    In earliest days, before the laws are common,   430
    One man has power and makes the law his own:
    Equality is not yet. With written laws,
    People of small resources and the rich
    Both have the same recourse to justice. Now
    A man of means, if badly spoken of,
    Will have no better standing than the weak;   435
    And if the little man is right, he wins
    Against the great. This is the call of freedom:
    "What man has good advice to give the city,
    And wishes to make it known?" He who responds   440
    Gains glory; the reluctant hold their peace.
    For the city, what can be more fair than that?

Again, when the people is master in the land,
It welcomes youthful townsmen as its subjects;
But when one man is king, he finds this hateful,
And if he thinks that any of the nobles   445
Are wise, he fears for his despotic power
And kills them. How can a city become strong
If someone takes away, cuts off new ventures
Like ears of corn in a spring field? What use
To build a fortune, if your work promotes   450
The despot's welfare, not your family's?
Why bring up girls as gentlewomen, fit
For marriage, if tyrants may take them for their joy—
A grief to parents? I would rather die
Than see my children forced to such a union.   455
   These are the darts I shoot at what you say.
What have you come to ask of this, our country?
You talk too much; you would regret your visit
Had not a city sent you. Messengers
Should state their mission promptly, then return.   460
I hope that henceforth, to my city, Creon
Sends a less wordy messenger than you.

Chorus

When fortune aids the wicked, how they revel!
They act as if their luck would last forever.

Herald

Now I shall speak. On what has been debated,   465
You may hold your views; I the opposite.
   I and the whole Cadmean people say
Adrastus must not pass into this land.
If he has entered it, you must strip off
His sacred ritual wreaths and drive him out   470
Before the sun-god's flame is down. His dead
Must not be removed by force; the Argives' city
Is no concern of yours. Do what I say
And you will steer your city's course in calm.
If you refuse, there will be much rough water
For us, for you, and for our allies: war.   475
Think now: do not let anger at my words

Goad you to puffed-up answers. You are free;
That does not make you powerful. Hope has driven
Many cities against each other; she stirs
An overreaching heart; she is not to be trusted.   480
When the people vote on war, nobody reckons
On his own death; it is too soon; he thinks
Some other man will meet that wretched fate.
But if death faced him when he cast his vote,
Hellas would never perish from battle-madness.   485
And yet we men all know which of two words
Is better, and can weigh the good and bad
They bring: how much better is peace than war!
First and foremost, the Muses love her best;
And the goddess of vengeance hates her. She delights   490
In healthy children, and she glories in wealth.
But evilly we throw all this away
To start our wars and make the losers slaves—
Man binding man and city chaining city.

Analysis

Simon Goldhill

The Great Dionysia and Civic Ideology

Simon Goldhill, Lecturer in Classics and Fellow of King's College, Cambridge University, has written extensively on Greek tragedy and literary theory, including the work *Reading Greek Tragedy*. In the following passage, Goldhill argues that Athenian drama must be understood within its dramatic setting, the festivals of the god Dionysus held around February (Lenaea) and April (City or Great Dionysia) each year.

There have been numerous attempts to understand the role and importance of the Great Dionysia in Athens, and it is a festival that has been made crucial to varied and important characterizations of Greek culture as well as to the history of drama or literature. Recent scholarship, however, has greatly extended our understanding of the formation of fifth-century Athenian ideology—in the sense of the structure of attitudes and norms of behavior—and this developing interest in what might be called a "civic discourse" requires a reconsideration of the Great Dionysia as a city festival. For while there have been several fascinating readings of particular plays with regard to the *polis* and its ideology, there is still a considerable need to place the festival itself in terms of the ideology of the *polis*. Indeed, recent critics, in a justifiable reaction away from writers such as Gilbert Murray, have tended to emphasize on the one hand that the festival is a place of entertainment rather than religious ritual, and on the other hand that the plays should be approached primarily as *dramatic* performances. This results in the following type of description:

> For the Athenians the Great Dionysia was an occasion to stop work, drink a lot of wine, eat some meat, and witness or participate in the various ceremonials, processions and priestly doings which are part of such holidays the world over. It was also the occasion for tragedy and comedy; but I do not see any way in which the Dionysiac occasion invades or affects the entertainment. . . . To put it another way, there is nothing intrinsically Dionysiac about Greek tragedy. [O. Taplin, Greek Tragedy in Action]

I hope to show in this article how such a characterization of the Great Dionysia provides a fundamentally mistaken view of the festival and its historical context. While there are certain similarities between the Great Dionysia and religious festivals the world over, I shall demonstrate that there are specific ceremonies, processions, and priestly doings that form an essential and unique context for the production of Greek drama and which do indeed importantly affect the entertainment. . . .

It is what happened in the theater itself before the plays . . . that is my main concern, and I want to look in particular at four specific moments of ceremony that are rarely discussed or even mentioned in the context of tragedy. The evidence for the first comes from Plutarch's life of Kimon (*Kim.* 8.7–9):

> When Sophokles, still a young man, entered the lists with his first plays, Apsephion the Arkhōn, seeing that the spirit of rivalry ran high among the spectators, did not appoint judges of the contest as usual by lot, but when Kimon and his fellow-generals advanced into the theater and made the customary libation to the god, he would not allow them to depart, but forced them to take the oath and sit as judges, being ten in all, one from each tribe. So, then, the contest, because of the unusual dignity of the judges, was more animated than ever before.

Plutarch describes how in 468 the *arkhōn*, by a bold stroke, set aside the regular procedure in the theater by appointing the generals as judges. Pickard-Cambridge notes that the probable point in the proceedings was just before the performances of the tragedies, when the judges were about to be chosen. What the passage indicates is that the libations before the tragedies were poured by the ten generals. The nature of the offerings is unclear — "customary," is the only description we have — but it is interesting that for the beginning of the tragic festival's days of drama it was the ten most powerful military and political leaders, the *stratēgoi*, who were actively involved before the whole city. A fourth-century inscription (*IG* II² 1496) confirms that the generals were involved religiously in the dramatic festivals, but also suggests that the number of occasions in the calendar on which all the generals acted together in such a way were very few — no more than four occasions are attested for any one year — and usually it was for some occasion more obviously linked to their civic functions. The inscription mentions, for example, offerings to *dēmokratia*, "Democracy," to *eirēnē*, "peace," and to *agathē tukhē*, "good fortune." On the major state occasion of the Great Dionysia it was, then, the most influential and important representatives of the state who were involved in the opening religious ceremony.

The second element of ceremony can be seen directly in a scholion to Aristophanes' *Akharnians* (on 504):

> It had been ordained that the cities bring their tribute to Athens at the
> Great Dionysia, as Eupolis says in The Cities.

In the Great Dionysia, the tribute of the cities of the Athenian empire was brought into the theater. This ceremony is outlined in more
detail by Isokrates (*De pace* 82, Loeb ed., trans. G. Norlin):

> For so exactly did they gauge the actions by which human beings incur
> the worst odium that they passed a decree to divide the funds derived
> from the tributes of the allies into talents and to bring it onto the stage,
> when the theater was full, at the festival of Dionysos; and not only was
> this done but at the same time they led in upon the stage the sons of
> those who had lost their lives in the war, seeking thus to display to our
> allies, on the one hand, the value of their own property which was
> brought in by hirelings, and to the rest of the Hellenes, on the other,
> the multitude of the fatherless and the misfortunes which result from
> this policy of aggression. And in so doing they counted the city happy.

Here, following Raubitschek's generally accepted analysis, it is evident from the opening sentence that the tribute was divided into talents and displayed in the orchestra. Isokrates' rhetorical use of this
event is interesting, however. As Pearson comments, "Isokrates de-
plores the *aselgeia* [outrageousness, insolence] of their ancestors in
having the tribute publicly presented at the Dionysia." Such a ceremony, Isokrates claims, was a precise way to become hated by other
people. This presumably was not the actual aim of such an event.
Rogers comments in his edition of the *Akharnians*, "the tribute
brought by the allies was spread out talent by talent over the theatrical
orchestra in the sight of the assembled Hellenes"; that is, the display
was not just a piece of pomp and splendor, nor, as Isokrates rhetori-
cally supposes, to show how the Athenians valued the property of the
allies. Rather, it was a demonstration before the city and its many international visitors of the power of the *polis* of Athens, its role as a
force in the Greek world. It was a public display of the success in military and political terms of the city. It used the state festival to glorify
the state.

That this ceremony involved such a projection of self-image, such
a projection of power, may be hinted at in Aristophanes' *Akharnians*
496–509 (Sommerstein, adapted by Goldhill): "Be not indignant with
me, gentlemen of the audience, if, though a beggar, I speak before the
Athenians about public affairs in a comedy. Comedy too knows about

Justice; and what I will say will be shocking but it will be right." Dikaiopolis is preparing to speak to the city as city, to "teach the city." He goes on, "for now at any rate Kleon won't slander me, that I foul-mouth the city when there are *xenoi* ["foreigners"] present. For we're just ourselves and it is the Lenaian contest, and there are no strangers here yet. For the tribute hasn't arrived, and the allies are away from the city." Unlike the Great Dionysia, the Lenaia was a more private affair. Unlike the Great Dionysia, the Lenaia involved no tribute, no allies, no problem about speaking home truths to the city.

A further passage from the *Akharnians* makes this example seem less straightforward. The chorus — also speaking to the city as city — remarks in the parabasis (641–51, Sommerstein):

> For doing that our poet deserves a rich reward at your hands, and also for showing what democracy meant for people of the allied states. That is why they will come now from those states bringing you their tribute, eager to see that superb poet who took the risk of talking justice before the Athenians. So far has the fame of his boldness already spread that even the King, when he questioned the Spartan embassy, first asked them which side was more powerful in ships, and then which side received plenty of abuse from this poet; "for those people," he said, "have been made much better men, and will win the war decisively with him for an adviser."

Again the subject of the speech is the opportunity and license to speak out freely in the democracy. The allies bringing the tribute are said to come because they want to see the best poet — the one who is prepared to speak out *ta dikaia*, "what is just, right," among the Athenians. The Persian King, indeed, in order to test the Spartan embassy, would want to know who had the best navy and against which city the poet had spoken *kaka polla*, which means "many bad things of the city" ("plenty of abuse," as Sommerstein translates), with perhaps also a hint of "many bad things to the city," that is, many foul tales. "That's what gives strength for fighting." It is always difficult to evaluate the balance of joke and serious comment even in the parabasis of an Aristophanic play, but it is interesting that once more Aristophanes, or at least his chorus, seems to be defending the right to free and scurrilous speech, and once more the context for this defense is the occasion of the Great Dionysia when all the *xenoi* ["foreigners"] are there. Many passages from Aristophanes and elsewhere could be used to show the commonplace that poets are the educators of the citizens . . .

but these two passages suggest a more specific awareness of the connection of the Great Dionysia, the ceremony of bringing in tribute in the presence of the *xenoi*, with the city on display, the city aware of its role and image as an international power.

This ceremony moreover can have been introduced only at a relatively late date—after the transfer of the treasury from Delos—and it shows how, with the development of Athenian democracy, the power of the *polis* as such became increasingly emphasized in public ritual and display. (The ceremonies I am discussing were not merely organizational relics from an earlier era.) The public funeral of the war dead and the establishment of the casualty list *stēlai* which I will discuss below, also appear to have been introduced no earlier than the 470s. In both cases, the development of civic ideology is seen in the development of ritual.

The third moment of ceremony I want to discuss is also clearly linked to the authority of the *polis*. Before the tragedies the names of those men who had greatly benefited Athens in some way were read out in front of the whole city, and the honors that had been bestowed on them in the form of a crown or garland were specified. It was a great honor to be singled out in this way before the city, but a passage from Demosthenes, where such crown-giving is discussed, suggests a different kind of reasoning behind such a ceremony (*De corona* 120, Loeb ed., trans. C. Vince):

> But, really now, are you so unintelligent and blind, Aiskhines, that you are incapable of reflecting that a crown is equally gratifying to the person crowned wheresoever it is proclaimed, but that the proclamation is made in the Theater merely for the sake of those by whom it is conferred? For the whole vast audience is stimulated to do service to the city, and applauds the exhibition of gratitude rather than the recipient; and that is the reason why the state has enacted this statute.

The whole audience was stimulated by such a ceremony to do service to the *polis*. . . . Indeed, Demosthenes suggests further that the audience was actually applauding the exhibition of thanks rather than the person being crowned. Demosthenes' rhetoric appeals here to a fundamental and well-known tenet of democratic ideology, namely, that a man acts and should act to benefit the city; so the individual himself and his success were not what was important; it was the city recognizing and being thankful for a contribution to the city that was enacted in such a ceremony. For Demosthenes, this ceremony of announcing the names of civic benefactors was fundamentally connected to the projection and promotion of civic duties and civic self-image. . . .

The fourth ceremonial aspect of the tragic festival is also closely tied to the civic ideology of the Athenian democratic *polis*. Again, the orators provide an important insight into the occasion. The first piece of evidence is Isokrates, *De pace* 82, the passage quoted earlier. Isokrates says that the children of those who died in war were brought onstage. This, he says, was to show the other Greeks how many orphans and what disasters resulted from a policy of aggression. The *De pace* [*On Peace*] is, as its title suggests, something of an anti-imperialist, anti-war tract, and there can be few better examples of a misrepresentative use of a past historical event to further a rhetorical argument. For as we will see, the ideology of this event may imply an attitude quite different from that of Isokrates. I wrote "past historical event" because, as is clear from a fascinating passage of Aiskhines (330 B.C.), this ceremony was already no longer performed by the time of the speech *Against Ktesiphon* [154]. . . .

This passage of Aiskhines . . . gives us . . . a much clearer view of what happened and of its relation to the expected norms of a civic discourse. The young men whose fathers were recognized as heroes of the city because they had died in battle were brought up and educated at the expense of and by the city. When they reached the end of maintained childhood, they were paraded in full military uniform, again provided by the *dēmos*, and they were sent forth to whatever good fortune they might find, and were honored with special places in the theater. The herald proclaimed what the city had done for the boys and what as men they would do for the city . . .

What I hope to have shown so far is this: the four moments of ceremony preceding the dramatic festival were all deeply involved with the city's sense of itself. The libations of the ten generals, the display of tribute, the announcement of the city's benefactors, the parade of state-educated boys, now men, in full military uniform, all stressed the power of the *polis*, the duties of an individual to the *polis*. The festival of the Great Dionysia is in the full sense of the expression a civic occasion, a city festival. And it is an occasion to say something about the city, not only in the plays themselves. The Great Dionysia is a public occasion endowed with a special force of belief. This is fundamentally and essentially a festival of the democratic *polis*.

After such preplay ceremonies, the performances of tragedy and comedy that follow could scarcely seem—at first sight—a more surprising institution (at least if one judges from modern examples of state occasions with a particularly strong nationalist or patriotic ideology). For both tragedy and comedy, in their transgressive force, in their particular depictions and uses of myth and language, time after time implicate the dominant ideology put forward in the preplay ceremonies in a far from straightforward manner; indeed, the tragic texts seem to question, examine, and often subvert the language of the city's order. . . .

Again and again, for example, as has been discussed by critics from Hegel onward, tragedy dramatizes conflicting obligations of household and state—especially emphasized, for example, in the *Septem*, the *Antigone*, or the *Oidipous Tyrannos*. The hierarchical order of family and state is depicted in tragedy as a locus of tension and conflict—tension and conflict between members of the same family and between the duties of civic and familial roles. Again and again, as has been the subject of numerous important studies, tragedy investigates and undercuts the secure meanings of key words in the discourse of social order—*dikē*, "justice," *kratos*, "power" *sōphrosunē*, "right thinking"—and depicts tensions and ambiguities in their sense and usage. Again and again, tragedy portrays the dissolution and collapse of the social order, portrays man reaching beyond the bounds and norms of social behavior, portrays a universe of conflict, aggression, impasse. In part, it must be in the relation between the proclamation of civic ties, duties, and obligations in the civic festival of the Great Dionysia and the questioning, challenging plays produced in the festival that an understanding of the tragic moment will lie.

Rather than simply reflecting the cultural values of a fifth-century audience, then, rather than offering simple didactic messages from the city's poets to the citizens, tragedy seems deliberately to make difficult the assumption of the values of the civic discourse. And it is precisely this unsettling force of the tragic texts that makes certain critics' assertions of the necessarily simple, clear, and straightforward nature of texts for performance quite so insufficient. Indeed, it would seem more appropriate to claim that it is exactly the refusal to accept the simple, clear, and straightforward that constitutes the extraordinary force of the tragic dramas of Athens. . . .

Anthropologists regularly analyze the "sacred time" of a festival as a period of inversion—men dressed as women, slaves becoming masters, the carnival. The social order is reversed. Fifth-century Athenian tragedy's depictions of society collapsing in violence and disorder, and comedy's fulfillments of desires and fantasies, have often been understood precisely through such a sense of the ritual reversal of the norms (as if Aristophanic comedy merely fulfilled the repressed desires of everyday life, as if tragedy merely expressed the feared possibilities of collapse into social disorder). But the combination of the preplay rituals and the performances of the texts of fifth-century theater—which together make up the Great Dionysia—offer a more unsettling and problematic process, a more complex dialectic between the proclamation of social norms and their possibilities of transgression. For tragedy and comedy do not simply reverse the norms of society but inculcate a questioning of the very basis of those norms, the key structures of opposition on which "norm" and "transgression" rest. If ritual is designed to leave the structural positions of society legitimized, the tragic texts seem designed to leave an audience with a question (as often as not about the legitimation of social positions). It is here in the potential *undermining of a secure and stable sense of norm* (and thus of transgression) that the most unsettling thrust of tragedy may be located. . . .

The special circumstances of the City Dionysia festival, then, bring the special license of comedy, with its obscenity and lampoons, and the special license of tragedy, with its images of society collapsing. The two faces of Dionysos form the one festival. The tensions and ambiguities that tragedy and comedy differently set in motion, the tensions and ambiguities that arise from the transition from tragedy to comedy, all fall under the aegis of the one god, the divinity associated with illusion and change, paradox and ambiguity, release and transgression. Unlike the displays of civic rhetoric we have seen in such set pieces as Perikles' funeral speech or in Demosthenes' political rhetoric, the Great Dionysia, Dionysos' festival for the city, offers a full range of Dionysiac *transgression*, from the intellectually and emotionally powerful and dangerous tragedy, through ironic and subtle questioning, to the obscene, scatalogical, uproarious comedy. The drama festival, plays and ceremonies together, offers not just the power and profundity of a great dramatic literature but also the extraordinary process of the developing city putting its developing language and structure of thought at risk under the sway of the smiling and dangerous Dionysos.

Tragedy must be understood, then, in terms of the festival of which it is a constituent part and the silence of critics on the preplay ceremonies is indicative of a general unwillingness to consider both the extended context of the tragic texts and the particular difficulties involved in reading this literature of transgression and impasse. The tragic festival may at first sight seem to have little to do with our expectations of the Dionysiac religion under whose name it takes place. But in the interplay of norm and transgression enacted in the festival which both lauds the *polis* and depicts the stresses and tensions of a *polis* society in conflict, the Great Dionysia seems to me an essentially Dionysiac event.

Kurt A. Raaflaub

Tragedy and Democracy

Kurt A. Raaflaub, Robinson Professor of Classics and History at Brown University and Co-director of the Center for Hellenic Studies in Washington, D.C., was born and educated in Switzerland, and came to Brown in 1978. He has published numerous books and articles on Greek and Roman history, concentrating most recently on the development of Hellenic government and political theory. In the following passage from the article "Contemporary Perceptions of Democracy in Fifth-Century Athens," Raaflaub seeks to show how tragedy can be used to further our understanding of Athenian politics and history.

That (and why) we are justified in perceiving and interpreting Greek tragedies as important manifestations of political thought, does, I hope, no longer need elaborate explanation. . . . To put it simply, it was not the purpose of tragedy to reenact myth for its own sake but to interpret through the medium of myth contemporary problems for the benefit of the community and in the context of an important communal event. Contemporary concerns were, of course, manifold, not just

From Kurt A. Raaflaub, "Contemporary Perceptions of Democracy in Fifth-Century Athens," *Aspects of Athenian Democracy, Classica et Mediaevalia Dissertationes* XI. Copyright © 1990. Reprinted by permission of Kurt A. Raaflaub and Museum Tusculanum Press, University of Copenhagen.

political. But in a world that was increasingly politicized, tragedy necessarily assumed a political dimension and function as well. Usually, the poet avoided any direct involvement in political decisions; rather he analyzed indirectly an important problem that occupied the minds of his fellow citizens. By separating it from its actual context and transferring it into a mythical setting, and by translating it into mythical and dramatical action, he was able to make his audience aware of the background, complexities and possible consequences of that problem. Through such alienation aspects that were easily overlooked or suppressed in the struggles of everyday politics could be discussed more objectively and profoundly and presented to the audience in a way that facilitated identification and understanding. In doing this, the tragic poet assumed a traditional role that was expected of him, namely that of the poet as the moral and political educator of his community—a role that is distinctly visible even in the Homeric epic and emphasized most strongly in the *Frogs* of Aristophanes.

Accordingly, we should expect the tragedians to have taken a strong interest in the wide range of problems and tensions created by democracy. And indeed they did. Their concern for such issues is pervasive (matched only by that for problems connected with Athens' aggressive foreign policy and imperialism); it suffices to mention Aeschylus' *Suppliants, Eumenides* and *Prometheus,* and Sophocles' *Antigone* and *Oedipus.* However, despite all the scholarship that has been devoted to tragedy as a literary genre and to the individual plays, the task of interpreting them politically still is only partially accomplished. Some plays that obviously deal with major political issues (such as the *Eumenides* or *Antigone*) have, of course, attracted much attention in this respect too. . . . [But] I am convinced that much is yet to be learned from tragedy about the Athenians' perceptions of democracy and their attempts to cope with the problems caused by it. . . .

Relatively few tragedies deal with Athenian myths and events located on Athenian soil. Among those are the suppliant myths which, as we learn from the funeral orations, played an increasingly important role in Athenian ideology. Their dramatization must have had a special meaning for the audience and served a special purpose on the part of the poet precisely because the audience's identification with the dramatic action could be expected to be closer than usual. I consider it no accident, therefore, that the three preserved examples focus almost entirely on political issues, two of them intensively on democracy. Two are presented by Euripides in their pure Athenian version (the *Heraclidae* and the *Suppliant Women*), while Aeschylus' *Suppliants*, although transposed into a different myth and city (the Danaids and Argos), so obviously depicts Athenian situations and concerns that the audience undoubtedly was supposed and able to recognize that both the myth and the problems treated through it were their own.

Euripides' *The Suppliant Women*, performed 424–20, reflects the impact of the Peloponnesian War and the beginnings of the crisis of democracy. The fierce competition among the Athenian leaders, unleashed by the death of the "first man" and branded by Thucydides (2.65) as most disastrous for Athenian policies, was in full swing. Accordingly, the poet presents a comprehensive critique of democracy of which the constitutional debate is only one part. The play deals with the aftermath of the disastrous expedition of the "Seven Against Thebes": consciously risking war, Theseus and the Athenians intervene in Thebes on behalf of the mothers of the fallen heroes and rescue their bodies for burial in Attic soil.

There are some close correspondences between this suppliant play and the earlier one, the *Heraclidae*, which was performed at the outset of the war and gave strong though conditional support to Pericles' policy. It endorsed the decision to insist on the absolute sovereignty and liberty of the city and to refuse to yield to the ultimatum of a foreign power. On the other hand, it reminded the citizens that their greatest successes in the past had been achieved when they were protecting those in need of help and defending the ideals of Greek liberty and the unwritten panhellenic *nomos* that stood above the laws and decrees of the individual *polis*. Accordingly, in this new war too, the poet told his audience, they would only be able to succeed if they kept fighting for a just cause and avoided the danger of *hybris* and injustice.

The same principles are stressed in the *Suppliants*. But doubts and pessimism that already in the final scenes of the earlier play had marred the spirit of optimism are now all-pervasive: in every respect the reality is radically different. In going to war against Thebes, Adrastus has blindly sacrificed sound judgement (*euboulia*) to bold enterprise (*eupsychia*), yielded to the greed and *hybris* of his hotheaded followers, disregarded the warnings of seers and thereby caused disaster for his city (152–61, 214–18, 232–37). Theseus too is harshly criticized by the Theban herald for wanting to intervene in another city in matters that do not directly concern his own. Much of Thucydides' collective character portrait of the Athenians (1.70) is anticipated here: their tendency to let anger, pride or hope influence important decisions, to neglect the safety of their own person, to subordinate the interest of the family to that of the state, to sacrifice peace and prudence in rash decisions (476–510). Hyperactivism and interventionism (*polypragmosyne*) are typical of the Athenians who toil incessantly for their *eudaimonia* (576f.). But, we may add on the basis of later and more general remarks, they are unable to enjoy their fortune because every victory induces them to reach for the stars, and hope to gain all makes them despise a partial success (728–30, 736–44).

These characteristics are directly connected with democracy. In realizing how intimately constitution and policies depend on each other, Euripides again anticipates Thucydides. His critique of democracy focuses on two crucial problems: the quality of the leaders and the competence of the *demos*. In the center stands the constitutional debate which was discussed above. It emphasizes, on the positive side, sovereignty, liberty and equality of the *demos* and the strong institutional foundations of these achievements (404–8, 429–41; cf. 352f.), on the negative side, the excesses of demagoguery and the inability of the *demos* to control policies and politicians or even sufficiently participate in politics (411–25; cf. 481–5). As in a triptych, this central piece is flanked by two supplementary passages. In the earlier one, Euripides lashes out at the selfish and overambitious young leaders who drive their cities into ruinous wars without thinking of the common good (232–37), and at the citizens who, if rich, are useless for the community because they are consumed by greed, if poor, by jealousy and hatred: an easy prey for bad leaders; the only hope for the survival of the community rests with those in the middle (238–45). By contrast, in the second supplementary piece towards the end of the play, the poet indicates how these evils might be tackled: by strengthening the sense of community in all citizens and carefully preparing the young for their political responsibility. This, I think, is the reason why the dead heroes, brought back to Athens, are praised as models of courage and civic excellence (857–908). Together with Theseus, whose portrait was bound to recall the memory of Pericles, those heroes are presented as good and unselfish leaders, offering a positive counterpart to the selfish demagogues criticized earlier in the play. What is said explicitly of courage (911–17) is true for other parts of *politike arete* ["political virtue"] as well: it can be learned and must be taught from early on. "Things

learned in youth are often stored till old age; therefore give sound training to the young!" (916f.). Protagoras would have agreed!

Finally, in the *Phoenician Women* (probably performed shortly after the oligarchic *intermezzo* of 411 [see Part VII]), Euripides addresses
the problem of factionalism and the detrimental consequences for the
community of extreme ambition and selfishness among the elite. The
play offers an impressive example of how freely the poet could vary the
mythical storyline and adapt it to his needs: Iocasta here has survived
the revelation of her incestuous marriage to Oedipus, and the conflict
of the brothers is reduced to an elementary struggle for power. Eteocles
is depicted as a selfish tyrant, obsessed by hunger for power. While his
mother stresses the blessings of moderation and equality (528–44), he
considers those values empty words; what counts is only power, the
greatest goddess of all (499–525). Polyneices, although initially relying
on a just cause, forced to fight against his will, and in favor of a compromise (154f., 369f., 435–42, 469–93), at the end does not renounce
the use of power either (626–35). Facing the alternative of holding
power or saving Thebes, both brothers choose war and consciously accept the risk of ruining their city (559–85).

Euripides obviously takes issue here with attitudes that were rooted
in sophistic theories of power, common among an influential group of
young aristocrats and oligarchic leaders towards the end of the war, and
critically analyzed by Thucydides and Plato. Several attempts have been
made to establish direct connections between the play and contemporary politics by identifying Polyneices with Alcibiades or the two brothers with democracy and oligarchy. According to Jacqueline de Romilly's
plausible interpretation, the poet analyzes, obviously under the influence of the events of 411, in more general terms the fundamental problem that in their struggle for power the leaders push their claims to the
extreme, set their own interests above those of the community and end
up ruining it. The ideal of equality, set against such tendencies by Iocasta, certainly is a democratic value but, more importantly and generally, it opposes the aspirations to exclusive power by individuals or small
groups and aims at getting all citizens involved for the sake of the common good. As in the *Suppliants* and, half a century earlier, in Aeschylus'
plays, the solution lies in strengthening the sense of community. The
negative example of the two brothers finds its shining counterpart in
Creon's son Menoeceus who, defying his father's orders (962–76), sacrifices his life and saves the community (991–1018).

Euripides' social and political thought has often been criticized as shallow and trendy. The two plays discussed here seem to me to indicate, on the contrary, that his concerns about democracy were serious and that they caused him not only to address the problems connected with it comprehensively and prominently in his plays but also to try to establish the general principles that were essential for the survival and success of the community. Unlike, for example, the historians, he had the opportunity to communicate to a mass audience of his fellow citizens his thoughts and worries about their constitution and politics, and he seems to have used this opportunity intensively and responsibly.

Paul Cartledge

Dramatic Women

Paul Cartledge, Reader in Greek History and Fellow of Clare College, Cambridge University, has written extensively on Greek history and literature, including an extensive study of an important Spartan king: *Agesilaos and the Crisis of Sparta*. In the following selection from *The Greeks*, Cartledge raises questions about the roles of women in Athenian society and tragedy, focusing on Sophocles' characterization of Antigone.

What's in a name? Apparently a very great deal. Lysimakhe ("she who dissolves the battle"), chief priestess of Athena Polias in 411, would have smelled just as sweet by any other name, but she would not have been immortalized in the title of a play—as she was in Aristophanes' punning *Lysistrata* ("she who dissolves armies"). Perhaps he felt he could not use Lysimakhe's real name for the make-believe heroine of an irreverent sex-war comedy, but on the other hand he did feel the need to write such a comedy about the identities of and relations between men and women; indeed, more than one, since this was a theme to which he returned in the late 390s with his *Ekklesiazousai* or "Women attending the Assembly" (as in real life they could not).

This raises a point often but contradictorily commented upon since antiquity. In everyday life actual Athenian women were supposed to be neither seen nor heard of in public, but twice a year, at the Lenaia and Great Dionysia play festivals in honour of Dionysos, fictitious women took conspicuous roles on the Athenian civic stage (though impersonated by men). One of the functions of Aristophanic comedy, as indeed of all comedy at all times and in all places, was to laugh at and thereby somewhat diminish (male) anxiety or fear. Tragedy, however, as interpreted by the great Athenian dramatists, would appear to have had the opposite function: to bring into question out in the open, and thereby set at risk, all the society's most deeply held traditional norms (*nomoi*), including those affecting the role and status of women. Indeed, the Athenian tragedy we know about is in some sense a more female than male theatre. The dynamics of male-female relationships at Athens, not to mention Athenian misogyny, are in play in numerous surviving tragedies, notably the *Oresteia* trilogy of Aeschylus (458 B.C.) and the *Medea* of Euripides. But perhaps no other extant tragedy more centrally or acutely points up the "problem of women" within the context of the *polis* than Sophokles' *Antigone*, staged in 441 and so written within a decade of Perikles' citizenship law [Ar. *Const.* 26, Part I].

Interpretations, readings, and reworkings of this play have been legion—hence George Steiner's book-title *Antigones*. One that both corroborates the view of tragedy's function expressed above and slots neatly into the discourse of woman as polarized "other" may be worth summarizing here. Sophokles, it is argued (by Sourvinou-Inwood), pits an individual woman (and a "bad" one, labouring under inherited pollution as a product of her father Oedipus' incest with his own mother, who is thus both Antigone's mother and grandmother) against a man, Kreon, who stands for the male citizenry of the city of Thebes (a kind of anti-Athens, used symbolically as an English playwright might use France). A woman, moreover, who violates the norm (*nomos*) that women should be invisible, confined within the domestic household, and have nothing to do with the public, male space of politics; and who does so in flagrant contravention of *nomos* in another sense, the law decreed by Kreon that traitors shall not be given the proper burial rites that allow a corpse's shade to descend in peace to the underworld of

Hades. A woman, therefore (according to the cultural "logic" of the Greek city), who must herself die a "bad" death—suicide by hanging.

Or is her death really "bad"? On Sourvinou-Inwood's reading, it is not. For it is Antigone (or rather the principle for which she stands, and in the name of which she buries her formally traitorous brother Polyneikes) who wins the *agōn* ["struggle"] with Kreon, and she with whom Sophokles is inviting the audience to side. Although she has indeed flouted Kreon's temporal and secular decree, yet she has obeyed the traditional "unwritten," divine law that kinsmen must give due burial to dead relatives, whatever the circumstances of their death. To rephrase that reading in terms of polar oppositions, we could say that Sophokles has privileged the "gods v. mortals" rubric above both the "men v. women" and the "citizen v. non-citizen" polarities, not to mention such cultural sub-polarities as "public v. private" and "outside v. inside."

Whether or not that reading is the (or a) right one, or true to Sophokles' intentions, can never be known. But, if it is, it has to be said that Sophokles was taking an unconventional line on both treason and political power. In the conservative view of a Thucydides, at least, Antigone would surely have been guilty of gross *atasthaliē* ["recklessness"] or *hubris*, the violent transgression of society's recognized status-barriers. Indeed, her very name Antigone might, on this reading, be construed to mean "anti-procreation," that is, stiff-necked resistance to what were normatively deemed to be the female roles in Greek society, lawful marriage and legitimate motherhood.

Jeffrey Henderson

Comic Politics

Jeffrey Henderson, Chairman and Professor of Classical Studies at Boston University, has published numerous works on Aristophanes, including an edition (with commentary) of the *Lysistrata*, and is currently preparing the new edition of Aristophanes for the Loeb Classical Library series. In the following selection, Henderson argues that Aristophanes' works can inform us not only about Aristophanes' opinions, but also about the standards of the Athenian *demos* which judged the dramatic competition.

Aristophanic comedies typically depict Athens in the grip of a terrible and intractable problem (e.g., misconceived warfare, bad political leaders, an unjust jury-system, dangerous artistic or intellectual trends) which is solved in a fantastic but essentially plausible way, often by a comic hero(ine). The characters of these heroic plays fall into two main categories, sympathetic and unsympathetic. The sympathetic characters—the hero(ine) and his/her supporters—are always fictitious creations embodying ideal civic types or representing idealized versions of ordinary, marginal or powerless Athenians. The unsympathetic characters embody disapproved civic behavior (political, social, artistic, religious or intellectual) and usually represent specific leaders or categories of leaders. The sympathetic characters advocate positions allegedly held by political or social minorities (e.g., women) or by ordinary, disempowered citizens (e.g., small farmers). But these are shown winning out against the unsympathetic characters, who represent the current social or political hegemony. Characters or chorus-members representing the demos as a whole are portrayed as initially sceptical or hostile to the sympathetic character(s), but in the end they are persuaded. As for those who are responsible for the problem, they are exposed, then disgraced or expelled, and Athens is recalled to a sense of her true (traditional) ideals and is thus renewed.

In the (thoroughly democratic) comic view, the people are never at fault for their problems: they have merely been deceived by bad leaders or entranced by unworthy celebrities. By such portrayals the comic poets often tried to persuade the actual demos (sitting among the other spectators) to rethink or even change its mind about the way it is running the polis or about issues that had been decided but might be changed, to discard dangerous novelties, and to be more critical of its leaders. Aristophanes at least once succeeded: after the performance of *Frogs* in 405, he was awarded a crown by the city for the advice given by the chorus-leader in that play and subsequently adopted by the demos.

The use of satire and partisan criticism within a plot addressing itself to important issues of national scope was thus a democratic adaptation of such predemocratic traditions as carnival, komos and iambic poetry. That the comic festivals were state-run and not privately organized is striking evidence of the openness and self-confidence of a full democracy: the demos was completely in charge, so it did not fear attacks on its celebrities or resent admonition by the poets. On the contrary, the institution of Old Comedy performed functions essential to any democracy: public airing of minority views; promotion of the concept of society as inclusive and suprapolitical; and criticism of those holding power. In this function, the Old Comic festivals were organized protest. But like tragedy, comedy also articulated and explored civic ideals: through their comic fantasies and inversion of the norms, the poets identified the shortcomings of the status quo by holding it up against a vision of things as they ought to (or used to) be. This vision is normally crystallized by viewing the status quo through the eyes of ordinary people or people ordinarily excluded from public power, like women, and before an inclusive audience.

Still, many modern scholars (in contrast to their ancient counterparts) are often astonished by the extent of comic outspokenness on political issues and the degree of vilification in comic attacks on individuals, and often imagine that such criticisms could not have been intended, much less taken, at all seriously: if comedy was not merely an innocuous festive activity detached from the real world, then there must have been some special exemption, legal or cultural, for comic outspokenness. Neither alternative is satisfactory: certainly the comic festival was not a political meeting, but neither was it a purely festive "time out of time": it was rather a special opportunity for the whole polis to look at itself in a critical way, with serious matters often on the agenda. Moderns, in whose world art, religion, humor and politics are largely separate activities, find it hard to grasp the different situation of fifth-century Athens, where such dichotomies did not exist. There, festival and state were inseparable and included one another; the Athenians expected their poets to be "teachers" on all matters affecting life and society; and as a rule they were much less inclined than we are to treat their political leaders with fear and reverence. Since the Athenian people were themselves the government, they tended to see their elite leaders more as advisors and competitors for public stature than as august representatives of "the state." Even the gods come in for their share of jesting. Indeed, the "right of every citizen to speak freely" (*parrhesia*) was a proud hallmark of the Athenian democracy, and the comic poets were particularly expected to demonstrate the reality of this right.

There was, however, an important difference between Athenian *parrhesia* and American freedom of speech that is relevant to comic speech: the Athenians did not recognize what we know as "protected speech" or "intellectual freedom," nor did their slander laws seek to protect the *individual* from harm. In Athens, any sort of speech could be (and often was) punished if (and only if) it could be construed as threatening the democratic polis or unfairly compromising the ability of any member of the demos to participate in democratic governance; otherwise it was not punished. Failure to appreciate this peculiarity of Athenian *parrhesia* has led some to think that comic outspokenness (particularly as regards the abuse of individuals) went beyond what would have been permitted in strictly political discourse and so must have been somehow exempt from the rules. But the comic poets in fact articulate themselves comfortably within the prevailing norms of *parrhesia*: their "improper" language aside, all the modes of comic caricature, criticism and abuse are found also in contemporary political and forensic oratory; and conversely, whatever strictly political speakers avoid the comic poets also avoid, which would not be the case if they enjoyed a special license to say whatever they wanted without fear of being taken seriously.

That comic advice *could* be taken seriously is demonstrated most prominently by the case of *Frogs* and by the case of the philosopher Sokrates: the Athenians seem to have taken to heart the criticisms Aristophanes made in *Clouds* of 423, however, exaggerated they may have been. As Plato reported in his *Apology*, Aristophanes' portrait of Sokrates may have been "nonsensical" but nevertheless was an important factor in the people's decision to condemn him to death in 399.

That comic criticisms were trenchant rather than innocuous is also suggested by their tendentiousness. It is not true, as some claim, that comic poets launched their satirical attacks against all prominent people and all popular policies indiscriminately. Aristophanes in fact shows strong and consistent biases against the left—radical populists (e.g., Kleon), innovators artistic (e.g., Euripides) and intellectual (e.g., Sokrates), unfair manipulators of democratic freedoms (e.g., professional litigators)—while entirely sparing from criticism, and championing the ideology of, conservative democrats. In addition, comic poets, like any other public voices, tried to avoid actionable slander (statements that might affect the political standing of a member of the demos) and did not criticize either the democratic constitution or the inherent rightness of the demos' rule. Nor did they speak ill of the (honorable) dead, compromise the integrity of the state religion, or violate sensitive social protocols by (for example) compromising the integrity of respectable women or girls. Following each festival there was an assembly in which anyone who had a legal complaint could come forward.

Aristophanes, for example, was twice prosecuted by the politician Kleon, once for slandering the demos and its officers in front of visiting foreigners (in *Babylonians* of 426) and once for slandering Kleon himself (in *Knights* of 424). In the first instance the demos decided not to hear the case. In the second the poet and the politician settled out of court (Aristophanes subsequently boasted that he had not abided by the agreement). The demos could also punish comic poets by authorizing smaller stipends or by enacting laws restricting comic freedoms. One of these was enacted in 440, when Perikles led Athens to war against her own ally Samos, and another in 415, in the aftermath of the scandal involving parody of the Eleusinian Mysteries of Demeter. It is perhaps relevant that three of the men condemned in this affair seem to have been comic poets.

The comic poets thus seem to follow the operative rules for public voices: to avoid annoying (1) the demos or (2) anyone who might persuade the demos that he had been attacked in a manner threatening to democratic ideals or processes. In other words, all public advice, criticism and abuse had to be expressed in terms of the rules governing *parrhesia*, which safeguarded the discourses proper to the hegemonic ideology of the democracy. If the criticism and abuse we find in Old Comedy and in Athenian oratory often seems outrageous by our standards, it is because we differ from fifth-century Athenians in our definition of outrageous, not because orators and comic poets were held to no standards.

To control the empire Athens relied on a large fleet of triremes, warships designed for ramming enemy vessels and powered by 170 oarsmen in three tiers. Pictured is a reconstruction (not at full power). (Photo by Alexandra Guest, courtesy of the Trireme Trust)

The Popularity of the Athenian Empire

As the state perhaps most responsible for Hellas' victory over the Persian empire, the Athenians had some claim on the gratitude of their fellow Greeks (a fact the Athenians liked to emphasize). As the creators of demokratia, the Athenians potentially could position themselves as the champions of the demos in other cities. Nonetheless, Thucydides suggests that the other Greek states, many ruled by oligarchies, resented Athens' imperial position, and that the Athenians themselves realized (and accepted) this. The question of whether Athenian rule was actually "popular" is complex and perhaps tied closely to the conflict between "democratic" and "oligarchic" factions in Hellas (see Part VII), as well as to ancient (and modern) views of justice, autonomy, and the rule of the weak by the strong.

Sources

Thucydides

Comments on Athens' Popularity

In the passages below, Thucydides suggests that feelings in Greece before and during the Peloponnesian War ran very much against the Athenians, whereas the Spartans were able to claim that they fought to "free" Hellas.

[Athenian ambassadors at Sparta in 432 attempt to counter criticisms leveled against Athens by the Corinthians, and to dissuade the Spartans from war.]

[75]   Surely, Lacedæmonians, neither by the patriotism that we displayed at that crisis [i.e., the Persian Wars], nor by the wisdom of our counsels, do we merit our extreme unpopularity with the Hellenes, not at least unpopularity for our empire. That empire we acquired by no violent means, but because you were unwilling to prosecute to its conclusion the war against the barbarian, and because the allies attached themselves to us and spontaneously asked us to assume the command. And the nature of the case first compelled us to advance our empire to its present height; fear being our principal motive, though honour and interest afterwards came in. And at last, when almost all hated us, when some had already revolted and had been subdued, when you had ceased to be the friends that you once were, and had become objects of suspicion and dislike, it appeared no longer safe to give up our empire; especially as all who left us would fall to you. And no one can quarrel with a people for making, in matters of tremendous risk, the best provision that it can for its interest.

[76]   You, at all events, Lacedæmonians, have used your supremacy to settle the states in Peloponnese as is agreeable to you. And

From R. Crawley (translator), *Thucydides*.

if at the period of which we were speaking you had persevered to the end of the matter, and had incurred hatred in your command, we are sure that you would have made yourselves just as galling to the allies, and would have been forced to choose between a strong government and danger to yourselves. It follows that it was not a very wonderful action, or contrary to the common practice of mankind, if we did accept an empire that was offered to us, and refused to give it up under the pressure of the strongest motives, fear, honour, and interest. And it was not we who set the example, for it has always been the law that the weaker should be subject to the stronger. Besides, we believed ourselves to be worthy of our position, and so you thought us till now, when calculations of interest have made you take up the cry of justice—a consideration which no one ever yet brought forward to hinder his ambition when he had a chance of gaining anything by might. And praise is due to all who, if not so superior to human nature as to refuse dominion, yet respect justice more than their position compels them to do.

We imagine that our moderation would be best demonstrated by the conduct of others who should be placed in our position; but even our equity has very unreasonably subjected us to condemnation instead of approval. [77]   Our abatement of our rights in the contract trials with our allies, and our causing them to be decided by impartial laws at Athens, have gained us the character of being litigious. And none care to inquire why this reproach is not brought against other imperial powers, who treat their subjects with less moderation than we do; the secret being that where force can be used, law is not needed. But they are so habituated to associate with us as equals, that any defeat whatever that clashes with their notions of justice, whether it proceeds from a legal judgment or from the power which our empire gives us, makes them forget to be grateful for being allowed to retain most of their possessions, and more vexed at a part being taken, than if we had from the first cast law aside and openly gratified our covetousness. If we had done so, not even would they have disputed that the weaker must give way to the stronger. Men's indignation, it seems, is more excited by legal wrong than by violent wrong; the first looks like being cheated by an equal, the second like being compelled by a superior. At all events they contrived to put up with much worse treatment than this from the Mede, yet they think our rule severe, and this is to be expected, for the present always weighs heavy on the conquered.

This at least is certain. If you were to succeed in overthrowing us and in taking our place, you would speedily lose the popularity with which fear of us has invested you, if your policy of today is at all to tally with the sample that you gave of it during the brief period of your command against the Mede. Not only is your life at home regulated by rules and institutions incompatible with those of others, but your citizens abroad act neither on these rules nor on those which are recognised by the rest of Hellas.

[78] Take time then in forming your resolution. . . . [For the conclusion of this speech and the Spartan response, see Part VI.]

[In the following passage (2.8) Thucydides sums up feelings in Greece just as the Peloponnesian War began.]

The good wishes of men made greatly for the Lacedæmonians, especially as they proclaimed themselves the liberators of Hellas. No private or public effort that could help them in speech or action was omitted; each thinking that the cause suffered wherever he could not himself see to it. So general was the indignation felt against Athens, whether by those who wished to escape from her empire, or were apprehensive of being absorbed by it. . . .

[Hermocrates of Syracuse attempts to prevent the Sicilian city of Camarina from joining the Athenians in 415/14.]

[6.76] Camarinæans, we did not come on this embassy because we were afraid of your being frightened by the actual forces of the Athenians, but rather of your being gained by what they would say to you before you heard anything from us. They are come to Sicily with the pretext that you know, and the intention which we all suspect. . . . [T]he same policy which has proved so successful in Hellas is now being tried in Sicily. After being chosen as the leaders of the Ionians and of the other allies of Athenian origin, to punish the Mede, the Athenians accused some of failure in military service, some of fighting against each other, and others, as the case might be, upon any colourable pretext that could be found, until they thus subdued them all. In fine, in the struggle against the Medes, the Athenians did not fight for the liberty of the Hellenes, or the Hellenes for their own liberty, but the former to make their countrymen serve them instead of him, the latter to change one master for another, wiser indeed than the first, but wiser for evil. . . .

[The Athenians respond to Hermocrates' charges.]

[82]   Although we came here only to renew the former alliance, the attack of the Syracusan compels us to speak of our empire and of the good right we have to it. The best proof of this the speaker himself furnished, when he called the Ionians eternal enemies of the Dorians. It is the fact; and the Peloponnesian Dorians being our superiors in numbers and next neighbours, we Ionians looked out for the best means of escaping their domination. After the Median war we had a fleet, and so got rid of the empire and supremacy of the Lacedæmonians, who had no right to give orders to us more than we to them, except that of being the strongest at that moment; and being appointed leaders of the king's former subjects, we continue to be so, thinking that we are least likely to fall under the dominion of the Peloponnesians, if we have a force to defend ourselves with, and in strict truth having done nothing unfair in reducing to subjection the Ionians and islanders, the kinsfolk whom the Syracusans say we have enslaved. They, our kinsfolk, came against their mother country, that is to say against us, together with the Mede, and instead of having the courage to sacrifice their property as we did when we abandoned our city, chose to be slaves themselves, and to try to make us so.

[83]   We, therefore, deserve to rule because we placed the largest fleet and an unflinching patriotism at the service of the Hellenes, and because these, our subjects, did us mischief by their ready subservience to the Medes; and, desert apart, we seek to strengthen ourselves against the Peloponnesians. We make no fine professions of having a right to rule because we overthrew the barbarian single-handed, or because we risked what we did risk for the freedom of the subjects in question any more than for that of all, and for our own: no one can be quarrelled with for providing for his proper safety. If we are now here in Sicily, it is equally in the interest of our security, with which we perceive that your interest also coincides. We prove this from what the Syracusans cast against us and from what you somewhat too timorously suspect; knowing that those whom fear has made suspicious, may be carried away by the charm of eloquence for the moment, but when they come to act follow their interests.

Now, as we have said, fear makes us hold our empire in Hellas, and fear makes us now come, with the help of our friends, to order safely matters in Sicily, and not to enslave any but rather to prevent any from being enslaved. . . .

Thucydides

The Mytilenian Debate

The great city of Mytilene on the island of Lesbos revolted from Athenian control in 428/7. After retaking the city, the Athenians debated what should be done to the Mytilenians. At first they voted to execute the entire adult male population. But by the next day some Athenians regretted their decision, so another assembly was held at which the following speeches, according to Thucydides, were delivered.

[3.36]. . . . An assembly was therefore at once called, and after much expression of opinion upon both sides, Cleon, son of Cleænetus, the same who had carried the former motion of putting the Mitylenians to death, the most violent man at Athens, and at that time by far the most powerful with the commons, came forward again and spoke as follows:—

[37] "I have often before now been convinced that a democracy is incapable of empire, and never more so than by your present change of mind in the matter of Mitylene. Fears or plots being unknown to you in your daily relations with each other, you feel just the same with regard to your allies, and never reflect that the mistakes into which you may be led by listening to their appeals, or by giving way to your own compassion, are full of danger to yourselves, and bring you no thanks for your weakness from your allies; entirely forgetting that your empire is a despotism and your subjects disaffected conspirators, whose obedience is insured not by your suicidal concessions, but by the superiority given you by your own strength and not their loyalty. The most alarming feature in the case is the constant change of measures with which we appear to be threatened, and our seeming ignorance of the fact that bad laws which are never changed are better for a city than good ones that have no authority; that unlearned loyalty is more serviceable than quick-witted insubordination; and that ordinary men usually manage public affairs better than their more gifted fel-

From R. Crawley (translator), *Thucydides III*.

lows. The latter are always wanting to appear wiser than the laws, and to overrule every proposition brought forward, thinking that they cannot show their wit in more important matters, and by such behaviour too often ruin their country; while those who mistrust their own cleverness are content to be less learned than the laws, and less able to pick holes in the speech of a good speaker; and being fair judges rather than rival athletes, generally conduct affairs successfully. These we ought to imitate, and not be led on by cleverness and intellectual rivalry to advise your people against our real opinions.

[38] "For myself, I adhere to my former opinion, and wonder at those who have proposed to reopen the case of the Mitylenians, and who are thus causing a delay which is all in favour of the guilty, by making the sufferer proceed against the offender with the edge of his anger blunted; although where vengeance follows most closely upon the wrong, it best equals it and most amply requites it. I wonder also who will be the man who will maintain the contrary, and will pretend to show that the crimes of the Mitylenians are of service to us, and our misfortunes injurious to the allies. Such a man must plainly either have such confidence in his rhetoric as to adventure to prove that what has been once for all decided is still undetermined, or be bribed to try to delude us by elaborate sophisms. In such contests the state gives the rewards to others, and takes the dangers for herself. The persons to blame are you who are so foolish as to institute these contests; who go to see an oration as you would to see a sight, take your facts on hearsay, judge of the practicability of a project by the wit of its advocates, and trust for the truth of an affair not to the fact which you saw more than to the clever strictures which you heard; the easy victims of new-fangled arguments, unwilling to follow received conclusions; slaves to every new paradox, despisers of what is common; the first wish of every man being that he could speak himself, the next to rival those who can speak by seeming to be quite up with their ideas by applauding every hit almost before it is made, and by being as quick in catching an argument as you are slow in foreseeing its consequences; asking, if I may so say, for something different from the conditions under which we live, and yet comprehending inadequately those very conditions; very slaves to the pleasure of the ear, and more like the audience of a rhetorician than the council of a city.

[39] "In order to keep you from this, I proceed to show that no one state has ever injured you as much as Mitylene. I can make al-

lowance for those who revolt because they cannot bear our empire, or who have been forced to do so by the enemy. But for those who possessed an island with fortifications; who could fear our enemies only by sea, and there had their own force of gallies to protect them; who were independent and held in the highest honour by you—to act as these have done, this is not revolt—revolt implies oppression; it is deliberate and wanton aggression; an attempt to ruin us by siding with our bitterest enemies; a worse offence than a war undertaken on their own account in the acquisition of power. The fate of those of their neighbours who had already rebelled and had been subdued, was no lesson to them; their own prosperity could not dissuade them from affronting danger; but blindly confident in the future, and full of hopes beyond their power though not beyond their ambition, they declared war and made their decision to prefer might to right, their attack being determined not by provocation but by the moment which seemed propitious. The truth is that nothing so tends to make a people insolent as sudden and un-looked-for good fortune: in most cases it is safer for mankind to have success in reason than out of reason; and it is easier for them, one may say, to stave off adversity than to preserve prosperity. Our mistake has been to distinguish the Mitylenians as we have done: had they been long ago treated like the rest, they never would have so far forgotten themselves, human nature being as surely made arrogant by consideration, as it is awed by firmness. Let them now therefore be punished as their crime requires and do not, while you condemn the aristocracy, absolve the people. This is certain, that all attacked you without distinction, although they might have come over to us, and been now again in possession of their city. But no, they thought it safer to throw in their lot with the aristocracy and so joined their rebellion! Consider therefore! if you subject to the same punishment the ally who is forced to rebel by the enemy, and him who does so by his own free choice, which of them, think you, is there that will not rebel upon the slightest pretext; when the reward of success is freedom, and the penalty of failure nothing so very terrible? We meanwhile shall have to risk our money and our lives against one state after another; and if successful, shall receive a ruined town from which we can no longer draw the revenue upon which our strength depends; while if unsuccessful, we shall have an enemy the more upon our hands, and shall spend the time that might be employed in combating our existing foes in warring with our own allies.

[40] "No hope, therefore, that rhetoric may instil or money purchase, of the mercy due to human infirmity must be held out to the Mitylenians. Their offence was not involuntary, but of malice and deliberate; and mercy is only for unwilling offenders. I therefore now as before persist against your reversing your first decision, or giving way to the three failings most fatal to empire—pity, sentiment, and indulgence. Compassion is due to those who can reciprocate the feeling, not to those who will never pity us in return, but are our natural and necessary foes: the orators who charm us with sentiment may find other less important arenas for their talents, in the place of one where the city pays a heavy penalty for a momentary pleasure, themselves receiving fine acknowledgments for their fine phrases; while indulgence should be shown towards those who will be our friends in future, instead of towards men who will remain just what they were, and as much our enemies as before. To sum up shortly, I say that if you follow my advice you will do what is just towards the Mitylenians, and at the same time expedient; while by a different decision you will not oblige them so much as pass sentence upon yourselves. For if they were right in rebelling, you must be wrong in ruling. However, if, right or wrong, you determine to rule, you must carry out your principle and punish the Mitylenians as your interest requires, or give up your empire and cultivate honesty without danger. Make up your minds, therefore, to give them like for like; and do not let the victims who escaped the plot be more insensible than the conspirators who hatched it; but reflect what they would have done if victorious over you, especially as they were the aggressors. It is they who wrong their neighbour without a cause, that pursue their victim to the death, on account of the danger which they foresee in letting their enemy survive; since the object of a wanton wrong is more dangerous, if he escape, than an enemy who has not this to complain of. Do not, therefore, be traitors to yourselves, but recall as nearly as possible the moment of suffering and the supreme importance which you then attached to their reduction; and now pay them back in their turn, without yielding to present weakness or forgetting the peril that once hung over you. Punish them as they deserve, and teach your other allies by a striking example that the penalty of rebellion is death. Let them once understand this and you will not have so often to neglect your enemies while you are fighting with your own confederates.

[41]   Such were the words of Cleon. After him Diodotus, son of Eucrates, who had also in the previous assembly spoken most strongly against putting the Mitylenians to death, came forward and spoke as follows: —

[42]   "I neither blame the persons who have reopened the case of the Mitylenians, nor approve the protests which we have heard against important questions being frequently debated. I think the two things most opposed to good counsel are haste and passion; of which the one usually goes hand in hand with folly, the other with coarseness and narrowness of mind. As for the argument that speech ought not to be the exponent of action, the man who uses it must be either senseless or interested: senseless if he believes it possible to treat of the uncertain future through any other medium; interested if wishing to carry a disgraceful measure and doubting his ability to speak well in a bad cause, he thinks to frighten opponents and hearers by well aimed calumny. What is still more intolerable is to accuse a speaker of making a display in order to be paid for it. If ignorance only were imputed, an unsuccessful speaker might retire with a reputation for honesty, if not for wisdom; while the charge of dishonesty makes him suspected, if successful, and thought, if defeated, not only a fool but a rogue. The city is no gainer by such a system, since fear deprives it of its advisers: although in truth, if such are to be our speakers, it would be better for the country if they could not speak at all, as we should then make fewer blunders. The good citizen ought to triumph not by frightening his opponents but by beating them fairly in argument; and a wise city without over-distinguishing its best advisers, will nevertheless not deprive them of their due, and far from punishing an unlucky counsellor will not even disgrace him. In this way successful orators would be least tempted to sacrifice their convictions to popularity, in the hope of still higher honours, and unsuccessful speakers to resort to the same popular arts in order to win over the multitude.

[43]   "This is not our way; and, besides, from the moment that a man is suspected of giving advice, however good, from corrupt motives, through grudging him the gain which after all we are not certain he will receive, we thus deprive the city of its certain benefit. Plain good advice has thus come to be no less suspected than bad; and the advocate of the most monstrous measures is not more obliged to use deceit to gain the people, than the best counsellor is to lie in order to

be believed. The city and the city only, owing to these refinements, can never be served openly and without disguise; he who does serve it openly being always suspected of serving himself in some secret way in return. Thus what with the magnitude of the interests involved, and the view taken of our motives, we orators are obliged to look a little further than you who judge offhand; especially as we, your advisers, are responsible, while you, our audience, are not so. For if those who gave the advice, and those who took it, suffered equally, you would judge more calmly; as it is, you visit the disasters into which the whim of the moment may have led you, upon the single person of your adviser, not upon yourselves, his numerous companions in error.

[44] "However, I have not come forward either to oppose or to accuse in the matter of Mitylene; indeed, the question before us as sensible men is not their guilt, but our interests. Though I prove them ever so guilty I shall not, therefore, advise their death unless it be expedient; nor though they should have claims to indulgence, shall I recommend it, unless it be clearly for the good of the country. I consider that we are deliberating for the future more than for the present; and where Cleon is so positive as to the useful deterrent effects that will follow from making rebellion capital, I who consider the interests of the future quite as much as he, as positively maintain the contrary. And I require you not to reject my useful considerations for his specious ones: his speech may have the attraction of seeming the more just in your present temper against Mitylene; but we are not in a court of justice, but in a political assembly; and the question is not justice, but how to make the Mitylenians useful to Athens.

[45] "Now of course communities have enacted the penalty of death for many offences far lighter than this: still hope leads men to venture, and no one ever yet put himself in peril without the inward conviction that he would succeed in his design. Again, was there ever a city rebelling that did not believe that it possessed either in itself or in its alliances resources adequate to the enterprise? All, states and individuals, are alike prone to err, and there is no law that will prevent them; or why should men have exhausted the list of punishments in search of enactments to protect them from evildoers? It is probable that in early times the penalties for the greatest offences were less severe, and that, as these were disregarded, the penalty of death has been by degrees in most cases arrived at, which is itself disregarded in like

manner. Either then some means of terror more terrible than this must be discovered, or it must be owned that this restraint is useless; and that as long as poverty makes men bold by necessity, or plenty ambitious through insolence and pride, and the other conditions of life remain each under the thraldom of some fatal and master passion, so long will they continue to lead men into danger. Hope also and cupidity, the one leading and the other following, the one conceiving the attempt, the other suggesting the facility of succeeding, cause the widest ruin, and, although invisible agents, are far stronger than the dangers that are seen. Fortune, too, powerfully helps the delusion; and by the unexpected aid that she sometimes lends, tempts men to venture with inferior means, and more especially communities, as the stakes played for are the highest, freedom or empire, and as individuals when acting in masses irrationally magnify the objects that they strive for. In fine, it is impossible to prevent, and only great simplicity can hope to prevent, human nature doing what it has once set its mind upon, by force of law or by any other deterrent force whatsoever.

[46] "We must not, therefore, commit ourselves to a false policy through a belief in the efficacy of the punishment of death, or exclude rebels from the hope of repentance and an early atonement of their error. Consider a moment! At present, if a city that has already revolted perceive that it cannot succeed, it will come to terms while it is still able to refund expenses, and pay tribute afterwards. In the other case, what city think you would not prepare better than is now done, and hold out to the last against its besiegers, if it is all one whether it surrender late or soon? And how can it be otherwise than hurtful to us to be put to the expense of a siege, because surrender is out of the question; and if we take the city, to receive a ruined town from which we can no longer draw the revenue which forms our real strength against the enemy? We must not, therefore, sit as strict judges of the offenders to our own prejudice, but rather see how by moderate chastisements we may be enabled to benefit in future by the revenue-producing powers of our dependencies; and we must make up our minds to look for our protection not to legal terrors but to careful administration. At present we do exactly the opposite. When a free community, held in subjection by force, rises, as is only natural, and asserts its independence, it is no sooner reduced than we fancy ourselves obliged to punish it severely; although the right course with freemen is not to

chastise them rigorously when they do rise, but rigorously to watch them before they rise, and to prevent their ever entertaining the idea, and, the insurrection suppressed, to make as few responsible for it as possible.

[47]   "Only consider what a blunder you would commit in doing as Cleon recommends. As things are at present, the people in all the cities is your friend, and either does not revolt with the oligarchy, or, if forced to do so, becomes at once the enemy of the insurgents; so that in the war with the hostile city you have the masses on your side. But if you butcher the people of Mitylene, who had nothing to do with the revolt, and who, as soon as they got arms, of their own motion surrendered the town, first you will commit the crime of killing your benefactors; and next you will play directly into the hands of the higher classes, who when they induce their cities to rise, will immediately have the people on their side, through your having announced in advance the same punishment for those who are guilty and for those who are not. On the contrary, even if they were guilty, you ought to seem not to notice it, in order to avoid alienating the only class still friendly to us. In short, I consider it far more useful for the preservation of our empire voluntarily to put up with injustice, than to put to death, however justly, those whom it is our interest to keep alive. As for Cleon's idea that justice and expediency are both combined in punishment, facts do not confirm the possibility of such a combination.

[48]   "Confess, therefore, that this is the wisest course, and without conceding too much either to pity or to indulgence, by neither of which motives do I any more than Cleon wish you to be influenced, upon the plain merits of the case before you, be persuaded by me to try calmly those of the Mitylenians whom Paches sent off as guilty, and to leave the rest undisturbed. This is at once best for the future, and most terrible to your enemies at the present moment; inasmuch as good policy against an adversary is superior to the blind attacks of brute force.

[49]   Such were the words of Diodotus. The two opinions thus expressed were the ones that most directly contradicted each other; and the Athenians, notwithstanding their change of feeling, now proceeded to a division, in which the show of hands was almost equal, although the motion of Diodotus carried.

Thucydides

The Melian Dialogue

In the summer of 416 the Athenians sent out an expedition to the island of Melos in the southern Aegean. Thucydides chose to provide a detailed account of the negotiations supposedly resulting from the Athenians' demand that the Melians join their empire. The dialogue he records (as other Thucydidean speeches) has provoked great debate over Thucydides' personal responsibility for the views expressed, his potential sources, and what, if anything, the passages can tell us about Athens' (and Thucydides') attitudes toward the empire.

[5.84]. . . The Athenians also made an expedition against the isle of Melos with thirty ships of their own, six Chian, and two Lesbian vessels, sixteen hundred heavy infantry, three hundred archers, and twenty mounted archers from Athens, and about fifteen hundred heavy infantry from the allies and the islanders. The Melians are a colony of Lacedæmon that would not submit to the Athenians like the other islanders, and at first remained neutral and took no part in the struggle, but afterwards upon the Athenians using violence and plundering their territory, assumed an attitude of open hostility. Cleomedes, son of Lycomedes, and Tisias, son of Tisimachus, the generals, encamping in their territory with the above armament, before doing any harm to their land, sent envoys to negotiate. These the Melians did not bring before the people, but bade them state the object of their mission to the magistrats and the few; upon which the Athenian envoys spoke as follows:—

[85] ATHENIANS: Since the negotiations are not to go on before the people, in order that we may not be able to speak straight on without interruption, and deceive the ears of the multitude by seductive arguments which would pass without refutation (for we know that this is the meaning of our being brought before the few), what if you

From R. Crawley (translator), *Thucydides V.*

who sit there were to pursue a method more cautious still! Make no set speech yourselves, but take us up at whatever you do not like, and settle that before going any farther. And first tell us if this proposition of ours suits you.

[86]   The Melian commissioners answered: —

MELIANS: To the fairness of quietly instructing each other as you propose there is nothing to object; but your military preparations are too far advanced to agree with what you say, as we see you are come to be judges in your own cause, and that all we can reasonably expect from this negotiation is war, if we prove to have right on our side and refuse to submit, and in the contrary case, slavery.

[87]   ATHENIANS: If you have met to reason about presentiments of the future, or for anything else than to consult for the safety of your state upon the facts that you see before you, we will give over; otherwise we will go on.

[88]   MELIANS: It is natural and excusable for men in our position to turn more ways than one both in thought and utterance. However, the question in this conference is, as you say, the safety of our country; and the discussion, if you please, can proceed in the way which you propose.

[89]   ATHENIANS: For ourselves, we shall not trouble you with specious pretences — either of how we have a right to our empire because we overthrew the Mede, or are now attacking you because of wrong that you have done us — and make a long speech which would not be believed; and in return we hope that you, instead of thinking to influence us by saying that you did not join the Lacedæmonians, although their colonists, or that you have done us no wrong, will aim at what is feasible, holding in view the real sentiments of us both; since you know as well as we do that right, as the world goes, is only in question between equals in power, while the strong do what they can and the weak suffer what they must.

[90]   MELIANS: For our parts then we think it expedient — we speak as we are obliged, since you enjoin us to let right alone and talk only of interest — that you should not destroy the privilege so useful to all of being allowed in danger to invoke what is fair and right, and even to profit by arguments not strictly valid if they can be got to pass current. And you are as much interested in this as any, as your fall would be a signal for the heaviest vengeance and an example for the world to meditate upon.

[91]   ATHENIANS: The end of our empire, if end it should, does not frighten us: a rival empire like Lacedæmon, even if Lacedæmon was our real antagonist, is not so terrible to the vanquished as subjects who by themselves attack and overpower their rulers. This, however, is a risk that we are content to take. We will now proceed to show you that we are come here in the interest of our empire, and that we shall say what we are now going to say, for the preservation of your country; as we would fain exercise that empire over you without trouble, and see you preserved for the good of us both.

[92]   MELIANS: And how, pray, could it turn out as good for us to serve as for you to rule?

[93]   ATHENIANS: Because you would have the advantage of submitting before suffering the worst, and we should gain by not destroying you.

[94]   MELIANS: So that you would not consent to our being neutral, friends instead of enemies, but allies of neither side.

[95]   ATHENIANS: No; for your hostility cannot so much hurt us as your friendship will be an argument to our subjects of our weakness, and your enmity of our power.

[96]   MELIANS: Is that your subjects' idea of equity, to put those who have nothing to do with you in the same category with peoples that are most of them your own colonists, and some conquered rebels?

[97]   ATHENIANS: As far as right goes they think one has as much of it as the other, and that if any maintain their independence it is because they are strong, and that if we do not molest them it is because we are afraid; so that besides extending our empire we should gain in security by your subjection; the fact that you are islanders and weaker than others rendering it all the more important that you should not succeed in baffling the masters of the sea.

[98]   MELIANS: But do you consider that there is no security in the policy which we indicate? For here again if you debar us from talking about justice and invite us to obey your interest, we also must explain ours, and try to persuade you, if the two happen to coincide. How can you avoid making enemies of all existing neutrals who shall look at our case and conclude from it that one day or another you will attack them? And what is this but to make greater the enemies that

you have already, and to force others to become so who would otherwise have never thought of it?

[99]   ATHENIANS: Why, the fact is that continentals generally give us but little alarm; the liberty which they enjoy will long prevent their taking precautions against us; it is rather islanders like yourselves, outside our empire, and subjects smarting under the yoke, who would be the most likely to take a rash step and lead themselves and us into obvious danger.

[100]   MELIANS: Well then, if you risk so much to retain your empire, and your subjects to get rid of it, it were surely great baseness and cowardice in us who are still free not to try everything that can be tried, before submitting to your yoke.

[101]   ATHENIANS: Not if you are well advised, the contest not being an equal one, with honour as the prize and shame as the penalty, but a question of self-preservation and of not resisting those who are far stronger than you are.

[102]   MELIANS: But we know that the fortune of war is sometimes more impartial than the disproportion of numbers might lead one to suppose; and for us to submit is to give ourselves over to despair, while action still leaves us hope of maintaining ourselves.

[103]   ATHENIANS: Hope, danger's comforter, may be indulged in by those who have enough and to spare, if not without loss at all events without ruin; but its nature is to be extravagant, and those who go so far as to put their all upon the venture see it in its true colours only when they are ruined; but so long as the discovery would enable them to guard against it, it is never found wanting. Let not this be the case with you, who are weak and hang on a single turn of the scale; nor be like the vulgar, who when visible hopes fail them in extremity, turn to invisible, to prophecies and oracles, and other such inventions that delude men with hopes to their destruction.

[104]   MELIANS: You may be sure that we are as well aware as you of the difficulty of contending against your power and fortune, unless the terms be equal. But we trust with the help of the gods that our fortune may be as good as yours, since we are just men fighting against unjust, and that what we want in power will be made up by the alliance of the Lacedæmonians, who are bound, if only for very shame, to come to the aid of their kindred. Our confidence, therefore, after all is not so utterly irrational.

[105]   ATHENIANS: When you speak of the favour of the gods, we may as fairly hope for that as yourselves; neither our pretensions nor our conduct being in any way contrary to what men believe of the gods, or practise among themselves. Of the gods we believe, and of men we know, that by a necessary law of their nature they rule wherever they can. And it is not as if we were the first to make this law, or to act upon it when made: we found it existing before us, and shall leave it to exist for ever after us; all we do is to make use of it, knowing that you and everybody else, having the same power as we have, would do the same as we do. Thus, as far as the gods are concerned, we have no fear and no reason to fear to have the worse. But when we come to your notion about the Lacedæmonians, which leads you to believe that shame will make them help you, here we bless your simplicity but do not envy your folly. The Lacedæmonians, when themselves or their country's laws are in question, are the worthiest men alive; of their conduct towards others much might be said, but no clearer idea of it could be given than by shortly saying that of all the men we know they most indubitably consider what is agreeable honourable, and what is expedient just. Such a way of thinking does not promise much for the safety which you now unreasonably count upon.

[106]   MELIANS: But it is for this very reason that we now trust to this interest of theirs to prevent them from betraying the Melians, their colonists, and thereby losing the confidence of their friends in Hellas and helping their enemies.

[107]   ATHENIANS: Then you do not imagine that interest goes with security, while justice and honour cannot be followed without danger, a thing which the Lacedæmonians generally court as little as possible.

[108]   MELIANS: But we believe that they would be more likely to face even danger for our sake, and with more confidence than for others, as our nearness to Peloponnese makes it easier for them to act, and our common blood insures our fidelity.

[109]   ATHENIANS: Yes, but what an intending ally trusts to, is not the goodwill of those who ask his aid, but a decided superiority of power for action; and the Lacedæmonians look to this even more than others. At least, such is their distrust of their home resources that it is only with numerous allies that they attack a neighbour; now is it

likely that while we are masters of the sea they will cross over to an island?

[110]   MELIANS: But they would have others to send. The Cretan sea is a wide one, and it is more difficult for those who command it to intercept others, than for those who wish to elude them to do so safely. And should the Lacedæmonians miscarry in this, they would fall upon your land, and upon those left of your allies whom Brasidas did not reach; and instead of places which are not yours, you will have to fight for your own country and your own confederacy.

[111]   ATHENIANS: Some diversion of the kind you speak of you may one day experience, only to learn, as others have done, that the Athenians never once yet withdrew from a siege for fear of any. But we are struck by the fact, that after saying you would consult for the safety of your country, in all this discussion you have mentioned nothing which men might trust in and think to be saved by. Your strongest arguments depend upon hope and the future, and your actual resources are too scanty, as compared with those arrayed against you, for you to come out victorious. You will therefore show great blindness of judgment, unless, after allowing us to retire, you can find some counsel more prudent than this. You will surely not be caught by that idea of disgrace, which in dangers that are disgraceful, and at the same time too plain to be mistaken, proves so fatal to mankind; since in too many cases the very men that have their eyes perfectly open to what they are rushing into, let the thing called disgrace, by the mere influence of a seductive name, lead them on to a point at which they become so enslaved by the phrase as in fact to fall wilfully into disgrace more disgracing as the companion of error, than it would have ever been if of fortune. This, if you are well advised, you will guard against; and you will not think it dishonourable to submit to the greatest city in Hellas, when it makes you the moderate offer of becoming its tributary ally, without ceasing to enjoy the country that belongs to you; nor when you have the choice given you between war and security, will you be so blinded as to choose the worse. And it is certain that those who do not yield to their equals, who keep terms with their superiors, and are moderate towards their inferiors, on the whole succeed best. Think over the matter, therefore, after our withdrawal, and reflect once and again that it is for your country that you

are consulting, that you have not more than one, and that upon this one deliberation depends its prosperity or ruin.

[112] The Athenians now withdrew from the conference; and the Melians, left to themselves, came to a decision corresponding with what they had maintained in the discussion, and answered, "Our resolution, Athenians, is the same as it was at first. We will not deprive of freedom a city that has been inhabited these seven hundred years; but we put our trust in the fortune by which the gods have preserved it until now, and in the help of men, that is of the Lacedæmonians; and so we will try and save ourselves. Meanwhile we invite you to allow us to be friends to you and foes to neither party, and to retire from our country after making such a treaty as shall seem fit to us both."

[113] Such was the answer of the Melians. The Athenians now departing from the conference said, "Well, you alone, as it seems to us, judging from these resolutions, regard what is future as more certain than what is before your eyes, and what is out of sight, in your eagerness, as already come to pass; and as you have staked most on, and trusted most in, Lacedæmonians, fortune, and hopes, you will also be most deceived."

[114] The Athenian envoys now returned to the army; and the Melians showing no signs of yielding, the generals at once betook themselves to hostilities, and drew a line of circumvallation round the Melians. . . .

[Thucydides goes on to report, along with other events, that the Melians made two successful attacks on parts of the Athenian lines. His account of the affair then concludes as follows.]

[116]. . . Reinforcements afterwards arriving from Athens in consequence, under the command of Philocrates, son of Demeas, the siege was now pressed vigorously; and some treachery taking place inside, the Melians surrendered at discretion to the Athenians, who put to death all the grown men whom they took, and sold the women and children for slaves, and subsequently sent out five hundred colonists and inhabited the place themselves.

Analysis

G. E. M. de Ste. Croix

The Character of the Athenian Empire

G. E. M. de Ste. Croix, former Fellow and Tutor in Ancient History and now Honourable Fellow, New College, Oxford University, is perhaps best known for his massive volumes on *The Origins of the Peloponnesian War* and *The Class Struggle in the Ancient World*, although he has published many articles on a wide range of topics in ancient history. In the following selection, de Ste. Croix argues that Athens' empire was actually popular among the common citizens (the *demos* as opposed to the aristocrats) of the allied/subject states, and that Thucydides' characterization of the unpopularity of the Athenians is belied by his own reports of events.

Was the Athenian empire a selfish despotism, detested by the subjects whom it oppressed and exploited? The ancient sources, and modern scholars, are almost unanimous that it was, and the few voices . . . raised in opposition to this harsh verdict—which will here be called "the traditional view"—have not succeeded in modifying or even explaining its dominance. . . .

The real basis of the traditional view, with which that view must stand or fall, is the belief that the Athenian empire was hated by its subjects—a belief for which there is explicit and weighty support in the sources (above all Thucydides), but which nevertheless is demonstrably false. The first section of this paper will therefore be devoted to showing that whether or not the Athenian empire was politically

From G. E. M. de Ste. Croix, "The Character of the Athenian Empire," *Historia* 3. Copyright © 1954–1955 G. E. M. de Ste. Croix. Published by Franz Steiner Verlag.

oppressive or economically predatory, the general mass of the population of the allied (or subject) states, far from being hostile to Athens, actually welcomed her dominance and wished to remain within the empire, even—and perhaps more particularly—during the last thirty years of the fifth century, when the [hybris] of Athens, which bulks so large in the traditional view, is supposed to have been at its height.

By far the most important witness for the prosecution, in any arraignment of Athenian imperialism, is of course Thucydides; but it is precisely Thucydides who, under cross-examination, can be made to yield the most valuable pieces of detailed evidence of the falsity of his own generalisations. Before we examine his evidence, it will be well to make clear the conception of his speeches upon which some of the interpretations given here are based. . . . [T]here can surely be no doubt that some of the speeches in fact represent what the speakers would have said if they had expressed *with perfect frankness* the sentiments which the historian himself attributed to them, and hence may sometimes depart very far from what was actually said, above all because political and diplomatic speeches are seldom entirely candid.

Now Thucydides harps constantly on the unpopularity of imperial Athens, at least during the Peloponnesian War. He makes no less than eight of his speakers accuse the Athenians of "enslaving" their allies or of wishing to "enslave" other states, and he also uses the same expression in his own person. His Corinthian envoys at Sparta, summarising the historian's own view in a couple of words, call Athens the "tyrant city." Thucydides even represents the Athenians themselves as fully conscious that their rule was a tyranny: he makes not only Cleon but also Pericles admit that the empire had this character. It must be allowed that in such political contexts both "enslavement" and "tyranny"—and their cognates—are often used in a highly technical sense: any infringement of the *eleutheria* ["freedom"] of a city, however slight, might be described as "enslavement"; and terms such as ["tyrant polis"] do not necessarily imply (as the corresponding English expressions would) that Athens was an oppressive or unpopular ruler. However, it will hardly be denied that Thucydides regarded the dominance of Athens over her allies as indeed oppressive and unpopular. The speech he puts into the mouths of the Athenians at Sparta in 432 admits that their rule is "much detested by the Hellenes" and that Athens has become "hateful to most people." At the outbreak of the war, says Thucydides, "people in general were strongly in favour of Sparta, especially as she professed herself the liberator of Hellas. Every individual and every city was eager to help her by word and deed, to the extent of feeling that personal participation was necessary if her cause were not to suffer. So general was the indignation felt against Athens, some desiring to be liberated from her rule, others dreading to pass under it." In the winter of 413–12, when the news of the Athenian disaster in Sicily had become known, Thucydides would have us believe that all Hellas was astir, neutrals feeling that they ought to attack Athens spontaneously, and the subjects of Athens showing themselves ready to revolt "even beyond their capacity to do so," feeling passionately on the subject and refusing even to hear of the Athenians' being able to last out the summer.

This is what Thucydides wanted his readers to believe. It is undoubtedly the conception he himself honestly held. Nevertheless, his own detailed narrative proves that it is certainly false. Thucydides was such a remarkably objective historian that he himself has provided sufficient material for his own refutation. The news columns in Thucydides, so to speak, contradict the editorial Thucydides, and the editor himself does not always speak with the same voice.

In the "Mytilenean Debate" at Athens in 427, Thucydides makes Diodotus tell the assembled Athenians that in all the cities the demos is their friend, and either does not join the Few, the [*oligoi*], when they revolt, or, if constrained to do so, at once turns on the rebels, so that in fighting the refractory state the Athenians have the mass of the citizens [the *plethos*] on their side. . . . It is impossible to explain away the whole passage on the ground that Diodotus is just saying the kind of thing that might be expected to appeal to an Athenian audience. Not only do we have Thucydides' general statement that throughout the Greek world, after the Corcyraean revolution of 427, the leaders of the popular parties tried to bring in the Athenians, as [the *oligoi*] the Spartans; there is a great deal of evidence relating to individual cities, which we must now consider. Of course, the mere fact that a city did not revolt from Athens does not of itself necessarily imply fidelity: considerations of expediency, short-term or long-term, may often have been decisive—the fear of immediate Athenian counter-action, or the belief that Athens would ultimately become supreme. But that does not alter the fact that in almost every case in which we do have detailed information about the attitude of an allied city, we find only the Few hostile: scarcely ever is there reason to think that the demos was not mainly loyal. The evidence falls into two groups: for the 450s and 440s B.C. it is largely epigraphic, for the period of the Peloponnesian War it is mainly literary. We shall begin with the later period, for which the evidence is much more abundant.

The revolt of Lesbos in 428–7, in which Mytilene was the ringleader, is particularly interesting, because it is only at the very end of Thucydides' account that we gain any inkling of the real situation. At first, Thucydides implies that the Mytileneans were wholehearted and that only a few factious citizens, who were proxenoi of Athens, cared to inform the Athenians of the preparations for revolt. We hear much of the determined resistance of the Mytileneans and of their appeal to Sparta, and we may well be astonished when we suddenly discover from Thucydides that "the Mytileneans" who had organised and conducted the revolt were not the main body of the Mytileneans at all, but only the governing oligarchy, for no sooner had the Spartan commander Salaethus distributed hoplite equipment to the formerly light-armed demos, with the intention of making a *sortie en masse* against the besieging Athenian force, than the demos immediately mutinied and the government had to surrender to Athens [Thuc. 3.27–8]. . . .

We now have to examine the movements in the Ionian cities after the Sicilian catastrophe, in 412 and the years following, when Thucydides, in the statement quoted earlier, attributes to the subjects of Athens a passionate desire to revolt, even beyond their capacity to fulfil. . . . The events at Samos are particularly interesting: the Samian demos, after at least two if not three "purges" of [those "powerful" or "noble"], remained faithful to Athens to the bitter end, and were rewarded with the grant of Athenian citizenship. At Chios, although Thucydides speaks in several places of "the Chians" as planning to revolt from Athens early in 412, it is perfectly clear from two passages that it was only the Few who were disaffected, and that they did not even dare to disclose their plans to the demos until Alcibiades and a Spartan force arrived. The leaders of the pro-Athenian faction were then executed and an oligarchy was imposed by force, under the supervision of the Spartan commander Pedaritus; but this had no good results. When the Athenians invested the city, some of the Chians plotted to surrender it to them, but the blockade eventually had to be abandoned [Thuc. 8.5–7, 9, 14, 21, 24, 38, 73]. . . .

At Thasos, the extreme oligarchs in exile were delighted when the Athenian Dieitrephes set up a moderate oligarchy, for this, according to Thucydides, was exactly what they wanted, namely, "the abolition of the democracy which would have opposed them" in their design of making Thasos an oligarchy independent of Athens. The demos was not easily crushed, however, and the island remained in a very disturbed condition until Thrasybulus brought it back into the Athenian alliance in 407. That the Thasian demos should have been friendly to Athens is all the more remarkable when we remember that the island had revolted, about 465, as the result of a dispute with Athens about its [marts] and gold mine in Thrace, had stood a siege of over two years, and upon surrendering had been given terms which have been described as "terribly severe"—a sequence of events which has often been cited as an example of Athenian aggression. After describing what happened at Thasos in 411, Thucydides makes the very significant comment that what occurred there was just the sort of thing that did happen in the subject states: "once the cities had achieved [*sophrosyne*]"—he means, of course, oligarchies of a moderate type— "and impunity of action, they went on to full independence." We must not fail to notice that Neapolis on the mainland opposite, apparently a colony of Thasos, refused to join the island in its revolt, stood a siege, and finally co-operated in force in the reduction of Thasos, earning the thanks of the imperial city, expressed in decrees recorded in an inscription which has survived [Thuc. 1.100–1, 8.64]. . . .

Only at Ephesus, and perhaps (during the Ionian War) Miletus, among the cities about which we have any information, is there no visible trace of a pro-Athenian party. We may remember that Ephesus was always a centre of Persian influence: for example, its large donation in gold to the Spartan war-chest, probably in 427, recorded in an inscription found near Sparta, consisted of a thousand darics, the equivalent of four Attic silver talents or a little more.

We can now go back to the 450s and 440s B.C., a period for which, as mentioned above, the evidence on the questions under discussion is predominantly epigraphic. The revolt of Erythrae, from 454 or earlier to 452, was almost certainly due to the seizure of power by a Persian-backed tyranny. Miletus was also in revolt from at least 454 until 452/1; but during this period she was apparently under the control of a close oligarchy or tyranny, which seems to have driven out an important section of the citizen body (perhaps with Persian support), and was sentenced in its turn to perpetual and hereditary outlawry about 452, when the exiles returned and the city was brought back into the Athenian empire. The probable absence of Colophon from the tribute quota-lists of the second assessment period (450/49 to 447/6), and the Athenian decree relating to that city of (probably) 446, certainly point to a revolt about 450; but the known Persian associations of this inland city, the fact that it was handed over to the Persian Itamenes in 430 by one of two parties in a [*stasis*] (presumably of the usual character—oligarchs against democrats), and the Colophonian oath to preserve democracy—perhaps newly introduced, or at any rate restored—in the treaty made with Athens in 446 or thereabouts, strongly suggest that the revolt was the work of oligarchs receiving Persian support. The revolt of Euboea in 446 may well have been mainly the work of the Hippobotae, the aristocrats of Chalcis, for the Athenians drove them out on the reduction of the island and probably gave their lands to cleruchs, but inflicted no punishment beyond the taking of hostages, as far as we know, on the other Euboeans, except that they expelled the Hestiaeans (who had massacred the crew of an Athenian ship) and settled an Athenian colony on their lands. The revolt of Samos in 440/39, after certain Samians who "wished to revolutionise the constitution" had induced the Athenians to set up a democracy, was certainly brought about by exiled oligarchs, who allied themselves with the Persian satrap Pissuthnes, employed a force of seven hundred mercenaries, and worked in conjunction with the ["most powerful men"] remaining in the city. Here again there is no evidence of general hostility to Athens among the Samians, although once the oligarchs had got a firm grip on the city, and had captured and expelled the democratic leaders, they put up a stout resistance to Athens and were no doubt able to enforce the adherence of a considerable number of the common folk. [For Erythrae and Colophon see Part II.]

It is significant that in this early period, whenever we do have information about the circumstances of a revolt, we find good reason for attributing it to oligarchs or tyrants, who could evidently rely on Persian assistance wherever the situation of the city permitted. This is precisely the state of affairs we have already seen to exist later, during the Peloponnesian War. In some cases, both early and late, the bare fact of a revolt is recorded, without detail. Some of these revolts may have been wholehearted, but we certainly cannot assume so just because we have no evidence. Surely the reverse is true: surely we may assume that the situation we find in virtually all the towns for which we do have sufficient information existed in most of the remainder. The mere fact of the coming to power of an oligarchy in an allied city immediately upon a revolt from Athens, as evidently at Eretria in 411, tends to confirm that the democratic party in that city was pro-Athenian. . . .

In the light of all the evidence which has been cited above, we can understand and accept Plato's explanation of the long life of the Athenian empire: the Athenians, he says, kept their [*arche*] for seventy years "because they had friends in each of the cities." . . . [*Epist.* 7.332c]

Now Melos is, for most people, the characteristic example of Athenian brutality. The cruel treatment of the conquered island was certainly indefensible. There are, however, certain features in the affair, often overlooked, which may at least help us to see the whole incident in better proportion. Although we have no record of any recent hostilities between the two states, we know that earlier the Melians had not remained neutral in the war, as so many people, obsessed by the Melian Dialogue, seem to think. Doubtless in 416 the Melians, when confronted with a large Athenian armament, said they would like to be regarded henceforth as neutrals. In the Dialogue, Thucydides appears to make the Athenians concede that they are committing what would nowadays be called "unprovoked aggression." Just before he begins the Dialogue, however, Thucydides tells us that during the war the Melians had at first remained neutral, but that when the Athenians used violence towards them and plundered their lands, [they "assumed an attitude of open hostility"]. Epigraphic evidence allows us to go further still: it puts the original Athenian attack on Melos in quite a different light. The inscription found near Sparta, to which reference has already been made, records two separate donations by Melos to the Spartan war-funds. . . . The Athenian ravaging expedition . . . [of 426] . . . was doubtless sent in retaliation for the assistance the Melians had given to Sparta. At any rate, Thucydides says expressly that after this the Melians ["assumed an attitude of open hostility"]. Diodorus describes Melos as the one firm ally of Sparta among the Cycladic islands in 426. It is particularly interesting to observe that in 416 the Athenian envoys were not permitted by the Melian authorities to address the assembled people but were made to state their case "before the magistrates and the few"—a circumstance upon which

Thucydides allows the Athenians to make scornful comment. Melos put up a stout resistance to Athens, it is true, but so at first did Mytilene, where, as we have seen, the majority had no great desire to fight Athens. As we learn from Thucydides that at the end of the siege there was treachery inside Melos, it seems likely that the Melian commons did not entirely share the passion for neutral autonomy so eloquently expressed by their oligarchs.

On the question of atrocities in general, it should be emphasized that very few acts of brutality are recorded against the Athenians during the war: the only serious ones are those at Melos and Scione and those (less shocking) at Torone and Thyrea. All these were to a greater or less extent sanctioned by the Greek laws of war, even if they shocked some of the more humane Greeks of the time. The essential point is that the Athenians were certainly no more brutal, on the whole, in their treatment of the conquered than were other Greek states of their day; and the behaviour of the demos (in striking contrast with that of their own oligarchs) under the greatest test of all, civil strife, was exemplary: Aristotle's reference to the "habitual clemency of the demos" was well deserved, in particular by their conduct in 403, to which Aristotle and others pay tribute. The Argives enslaved the whole population of Mycenae and destroyed the town on capturing it about 465 B.C. In the Peloponnesian War, we are told by Thucydides, the Spartans began the practice of butchering all the traders they caught at sea—Athenians and their allies and, in the early part of the war, even neutrals. The Spartan admiral Alcidas slaughtered most of the prisoners he had taken from the Ionian states during his expedition in 427, although apparently they were not in arms. The Spartans in the same year, to gratify their implacable Theban allies, killed every one of the surviving defenders of Plataea in cold blood and enslaved their women. When the Helots were felt to be specially dangerous, apparently in 424, the Spartans secretly and treacherously murdered two thousand of the best of them. The Spartans massacred all the free men they captured on the fall of Argive Hysiae in 417. The men of Byzantium and Chalcedon slaughtered the whole multitude of prisoners (men, women and children) they had taken on their expedition into Bithynia in c. 416/5. After Aegospotami, in 405, all the Athenian prisoners, perhaps three or four thousand in number, were put to death by the Peloponnesians under Lysander, who during the same campaign killed all the men and enslaved the women and children of at least one city he took by storm, and enslaved all the inhabitants of at least one other. The close oligarchies which Lysander installed at this time in the Aegean and Asiatic cities executed their political opponents wholesale, as did Lysander's *protégés* the Thirty at Athens, and the victorious revolutionaries and counter-revolutionaries at Corcyra, Argos and elsewhere. It is necessary to emphasize all this, because isolated Athenian acts of cruelty have been remembered while the many other contemporary atrocities have been largely forgotten, and the quite misleading impression has come to prevail that the Athenians, increasingly corrupted by power, became ever harsher and more vindictive as the war progressed. In reality, this impression is probably due mainly to the Mytilenean Debate and the Melian Dialogue, in both of which our attention is strongly focussed upon the character of Athenian imperialism, as Thucydides conceived it. . . .

An overwhelming body of evidence has now been produced to show that the mass of the citizens in the allied or subject states were loyal to Athens throughout the whole period of the empire, until the final collapse in the Ionian War, and could on occasion give proof of a deep devotion to the imperial city, which can only be compared with the similar devotion of contemporary oligarchs to Sparta. This judgment holds, whatever the character of Athenian imperialism may have been and whatever verdict we ourselves may wish to pass upon it. The evidence is all the more impressive in that it comes mainly from Thucydides, who, whenever he is generalising, or interpreting the facts rather than stating them, depicts the subjects of Athens as groaning under her tyrannous rule. A subsidiary conclusion of no small importance which has emerged from this survey is that Thucydides, generally (and rightly) considered the most trustworthy of all ancient historians, is guilty of serious misrepresentation in his judgments on the Athenian empire. He was quite entitled to disapprove of the later empire, and to express this disapproval. What we may reasonably object to is his representing that the majority of its subjects detested it. At the same time, it must be laid to Thucydides' credit that we are able to convict him of this distortion precisely because he himself is scrupulously accurate in presenting the detailed evidence. The partiality of Thucydides could scarcely have been exposed but for the honesty of Thucydides.

Donald W. Bradeen

The Popularity of the Athenian Empire

Donald W. Bradeen, late Professor of Classics and Ancient History and Department Head at the University of Cincinnati, wrote numerous articles on Greek history and epigraphy, and with M. F. McGregor published the volume *Studies in Fifth-Century Attic Epigraphy*. In the following piece, Bradeen attempts to counter the arguments of de Ste. Croix, maintaining that Thucydides' views about the Athenians' popularity are not in conflict with his own narrative.

G. E. M. de Ste. Croix [has expressed the] position, in sum, that the Empire remained popular with "the mass of citizens in the allied or subject states," who "were loyal to Athens throughout the whole period of the empire, until the final collapse in the Ionian War;" a corollary to this is that Thucydides "is guilty of serious misrepresentation in his judgment on the Athenian Empire." The reason for this misrepresentation de Ste. Croix finds in Thucydides' oligarchic political outlook and his sympathy for the anti-Athenian Few among the allies. This is an intriguing thesis and the article is both interesting and impressive as it ranges far beyond this basic position by defending not only the Athenians and their Empire but also the demagogues and even the subjugation of Melos. In a way much of its appeal comes from the fact that de Ste. Croix sets out to prove his case against Thucydides primarily with evidence from Thucydides himself; as he puts it, "the news columns in Thucydides, so to speak, contradict the editorial Thucydides, and the editor himself does not always speak with the same voice." Now the attraction here stems from the fact that most of us ancient historians have a sympathy for Athens and her Empire; no matter how impartial we try to be, our whole training as classicists, and possibly our political bent as well, incline us that way. We want to justify Athens' treatment of her subjects, but in the way of such a justification stands the judgment of Thucydides, for whose work we have a great respect. But now if we can prove from Thucydides himself that his judgment is wrong, then the obstacle is removed, and if it be true that the majority of the subjects approved of the Empire, then here is our justification. . . . I hope to show that his argument is based upon three general assumptions which are questionable, to say the least; that there are several serious omissions in the presentation of the case; and that what appears to be a mass of corroborative evidence consists for the most part of ambiguous situations interpreted from de Ste. Croix' point of view.

First we should discuss the basic assumptions underlying de Ste. Croix' case; the first two of these may best be analyzed together. One seems to be that Thucydides was a partisan oligarch who allowed his political convictions to distort his picture of the entire situation; the second is that the speeches in his history can be lumped with his expressed personal opinions as the "editorial" Thucydides. Objections may be raised to the former on two counts. . . . [There] is no doubt that Thucydides was an aristocrat and that he disapproved of the "radical" democracy. But, . . . the main objection to de Ste. Croix' assumption is rather this: Was Thucydides the kind of man who would allow political views to distort seriously his historical judgment? This may seem to be only a matter of opinion, but it certainly is difficult to see behind the history an author who was either of the two things implied in this assumption. For on this basis he must have been either a fool who, with many times the evidence we have now, could not see the "truth" which we can now discover, primarily from the evidence he gives us, or else a completely dishonest man who deliberately painted a false picture. De Ste. Croix obviously thinks of him as the former, for he calls him "an exceptionally truthful man and anything but a superficial observer" who deceived himself because ". . . political and social influences, at the end of the fifth century exceptionally powerful, drove the historian to look at the whole Greek world in terms of that relatively small section of the Athenian citizen body to which he himself belonged. . . ." It may again be only a matter of opinion, but I cannot conceive that Thucydides, with the experience he must have had with the differences of opinion among the classes at Athens, was so blind as to think that the oligarchs' beliefs were those of "all the Greeks" or "every state and private citizen." . . .

[Another] assumption which I wish to re-examine is that in almost every subject city the *demos*, in a political sense, represented the majority and was, more or less by definition, pro-Athenian. De Ste. Croix states that "it would be perverse in the extreme to pretend" otherwise, but I am not so sure, in these days of "People's Democracy." The one time when we have definite figures, the *demos* at Samos, in a political sense, seems to number 300 in 412/11. Of course this means very little, as the situation was complicated by the presence of Athenian troops and ships, but this is a condition which, in a lesser degree, we cannot ignore at any period of the Empire. We must certainly take into account the ever-present threat of the Athenian fleet and the amount of military and civil control which the Athenians exercised over her allies. This definitely was not negligible. Aristotle may well be exaggerating when he speaks of seven hundred Athenian officials abroad in the fifth century, but even back near the middle of the century we have epigraphic proof of the presence of *phrourarchoi*, *episkopoi*, and *archontes* ["garrison commanders," "inspectors," and "magistrates"—see inscriptions in Part II] in the allied cities. It would be naive to think that these would not use their influence wherever possible to encourage pro-Athenian democratic elements, whether these had the support of the majority of the citizens or not. It seems to me quite conceivable that in most cases the majority was not sympathetic with Athens or even with a democracy, at least in the sense of rule by an urban *demos*. In fact, many of the subject states could not have had an urban *demos* of the type which Athens had, and we surely must make a distinction here between agricultural towns and commercial cities. Certainly in the Chalkidike, for instance, most of the population was rural, with that traditional rural conservatism which would have been satisfied with the oligarchic constitution of their ancestors, whether they were under a democracy or not. . . .

There was little chance, then, in the smaller cities of the Empire, for a democracy of the Athenian type, but what of the larger commercial cities, like Chios, Miletos, Mytilene, or Samos, which as centers of trade and usually possessing their own fleets, would have had a class equivalent to the *thetes* at Athens? Here, if anywhere, we should expect to find a pro-Athenian *demos*, eager for democracy. De Ste. Croix thinks that he can see one at Mytilene in Thucydides' account of the revolt of 428/7: towards the end, when that city was besieged by the Athenians and the Spartan commander gave shields and spears to the *demos* for a last-ditch sally, these men refused to obey and demanded that food should be brought out and shared equally or they would negotiate with the Athenians; this forced the government to surrender the city. Now this was the act of men driven by hunger and despair, not by any love for or loyalty to Athens. Diodotos presents it in this latter light when he has a case to plead, and so does de Ste. Croix, but this is not proving Thucydides' judgment wrong by the "news columns" in Thucydides, but by a distortion of them. I suggest that the important aspect of the situation at Mytilene is not the fact that the *demos* acted as it did in 428/7, but rather that the government was an oligarchy to the end and that the *demos* acquiesced in this, and in the revolt, so long. To me there can be only one reason for this—the people preferred autonomy under an oligarchy to the closer subjugation to Athens which a democracy would bring with it. For surely the setting up of a democracy would be possible only through the armed intervention of Athens, which would entail an Athenian garrison and probable loss of the fleet. It is true that de Ste. Croix denies the existence of an autonomous group of allies, either *de jure* or *de facto*. The question is debatable, but whether he be right or wrong, it is sufficient for our purposes here to note that the Mytileneans had, besides their oligarchic government, two things which would set them apart from most of the other allies— freedom from tribute and a fleet of their own; these could easily be equated with autonomy, at least in the popular mind. Now it is among the rowers in this fleet that one would expect to find the democratic Athenian sympathizers, but such was apparently not the case, since the Athenians threw into prison the crews of the ten Mytilenean ships at Athens when they suspected the revolt. And certainly long before this, if there had been any real desire for a democracy among the Mytilenean *demos*, the Athenians could have found a chance to support them against their oligarchs. Although the editors of *The Athenian Tribute Lists* have shown that the Athenians certainly did not impose democracy, one can hardly deny that they would have been sympathetic with a real "grass-roots" movement in any subject state. Therefore, it seems, the people of Mytilene did not have a desire for democracy and were so far from being pro-Athenian that they supported their own oligarchy; one of the main reasons for this must have been their preference for what at least seemed to them to be autonomy.

Much the same may be said of the *demos* in other large cities of the Empire, particularly Samos, Miletos, and Chios. . . .

But now we come to another point. We have analyzed above in Mytilene the first and most impressive piece in what de Ste. Croix calls "an overwhelming body of evidence . . . that the mass of citizens in the allied or subject states were loyal to Athens." The rest of this evidence consists mainly of an analysis of the revolts of the 'fifties and 'forties, of Brasidas' campaign in Thrace, and of the campaigns in Ionia after the defeat of the Sicilian expedition. But these are ambiguous situations and what de Ste. Croix offers is not evidence but a reinterpretation of what must have happened, granting always that his analysis of the political situation is right, Thucydides' wrong. But I submit that this is not legitimate evidence, since Thucydides' account is reasonable in itself and agrees in general with his conclusions. There is really no need to analyze in detail all of this "evidence;" one could write an expanded account of it on the basis that Thucydides was right which would not only be consistent but would also be likely to be far nearer the truth, since it would be backed by the main source for the period and also would take into account the military situation and the presence of Athenian garrisons. These were far more numerous than de Ste. Croix cares to admit, and one of the weaknesses of his case is that he continually ignores them. . . . The fact is that neither the Thracian nor Ionian campaigns, carried on during the course of the war, are really fair tests of Athens' popularity, for there were always extraordinary military pressures which distorted the situation. A garrison within a city, or the approach of a fleet, could insure in most cases the support of the majority, whose main interest was to be on the winning side, not necessarily of the war as a whole but of the local struggle at the moment. Furthermore, the propaganda during the war, as Thucydides points out in his analysis of the Corcyrean revolution, stressed Athens and democracy, Sparta and oligarchy, and this had certainly complicated matters, especially by 412. As for the evidence for the revolts of the earlier period, most of which is epigraphic and quite ambiguous, it seems to show that most of the uprisings were led by oligarchs, who were therefore obviously anti-Athenian, as we might expect, but it proves nothing as to whether the majority of the citizens supported the revolts or not. We have no way of telling whether the democrats who appear during or after the revolts are really representative of the majority or are only a few who took advantage of the situation to get in power as pro-Athenians; the latter seems definitely to have been the case in Samos in 440. . . .

To most . . . Greeks freedom was the most important of blessings, and this was the basis of the opposition to Athens. As Grote saw long ago, it was an emotional, not a rational, opposition. We may now think that the majority in the cities must have been far better off under a democracy, guided by Athenian overseers and protected by Athenian garrisons, that the imposition of Athenian coinage over the whole Empire was an economic blessing which they should have recognized, that Athenian juries must have acted more justly in trying allies than many of their own courts, and that the tribute was little to pay for the advantages which the Empire offered. We may even be right in this from a rational, historical point of view, but this is no reason to rewrite the history of Thucydides. For to the subject citizens, the carrying of the tribute and "first fruits" to Athens each spring, the forced appearances before a foreign court, the prohibition against coining their own silver, and the presence of Athenian garrisons and overseers were all signs of their loss of freedom and autonomy. When the chance came to try to win these back, they usually took it, whatever material advantages they threw away by so doing.

Charles W. Fornara

The Chalcis Decree and the "Popularity" of the Athenian Empire

In the following passage Charles W. Fornara uses the text of the Athenian decree concerning Chalcis (see Part II, "Regulations for Chalcis") to demonstrate both the invasive nature of Athenian rule and the unlikelihood of Athenian "popularity" in the empire. In the earlier portion of this

© 1977 by The Regents of the University of California. Reprinted from *Classical Antiquity*, vol. 10, pp. 49–53 by permission.

article Fornara argues that lines 52–57 of the decree contain a grant of immunity from paying Chalcidian taxes to Athenians residing in Chalcis.

The fact that [the Chalcis decree] assures us of the presence in Chalcis of Athenian citizens is surprising only because their number was evidently significant enough to procure them a specific tax exclusion. However, the few scraps of evidence we possess are entirely consistent with that assumption. Oinias son of Oinochares [an Athenian] of the deme Atene owned property in the Lelantine plain [in Euboea], though, to be sure, there is nothing to prove that his family possessed the estate prior to 446. More important is Lysias' assertion (34.3) that "when we acquired our walls and ships and money and allies, we did not cast about for a way to reject any Athenian but even made a grant of *epigamia* with the Euboeans." The privilege of such intermarriage-rights, *epigamia*, would of course legalize the inheritance by Athenians of Chalcidian property; and the date, though vague, is not to be discounted, for it is the conventional expression for the early part of the Pentacontaetia. In addition, it is certain that a large group of Athenians resided in Eretria by the mid-fifth century, though the archaeological evidence for Chalcis is less clear. Andocides' statement that the Athenians possessed more than two-thirds of Euboea is an exaggeration; nevertheless it points in the same direction, suggesting the gradual acquisition of Euboean property. It should occasion little surprise. Fifth century grants of *enktesis*, the right to ownership of foreign property, are conspicuously rare in the case of Athens; I count but five fifth-century instances in J. Pečirka's special study of the subject. But that the Athenians were recipients of the privilege in far greater measure than they conferred it lies in the very nature of things. Their imperial status compelled such homage. The fact is corroborated in general by pseudo-Xenophon, who chances to speak in 1.19 of the Athenian possession of property abroad as one factor making the Athenians efficient sailors. But the surest confirmation of all is provided by Aristoteles' decree of 378/7, the so-called "Charter of the Second Athenian Confederacy." The stelai there mentioned (lines 25ff), which were to be destroyed, probably were as Brunt has stated, "fifth-century covenants under which [the right of land ownership] was granted to Athenians in the territory of those cities." Certainly the prohibition expressed in lines 35–41 speaks for itself: "From the time of the archonship of Nausinicus no Athenian shall be permitted whether by private or public means to acquire house or property in the territory of the allies either by right of purchase or by means of inheritance or in any other fashion." The need for the prohibition betokens abuse; and it would be naive to believe that the Athenians had been unwilling or unable to procure the right to purchase Greek property during their heyday or that friendly governments would not have conferred that privilege in order to curry favor and retain office. Euboea, by its proximity, must have been particularly vulnerable.

Our sentence in the Chalcis decree, then, is of particular value in attesting the presence of Athenian property-holders in Chalcis and, beyond that, Athenian advocacy of the interests of these citizens after the rebellion of 446. Before this time, Athenian property-holders will have been subject to regular Chalcidian taxation. But the rebellion provided a golden opportunity which the Athenians used to make their fellow-citizens in Chalcis tax-exempt. The egotism of the action may appear to some too thorough-paced to be worthy of credence. Let these, however, consider the implications of that other clause of exemption appearing in lines 54f: ["and any to whom has been given immunity from taxes by the *demos* of the Athenians"]. These people, presumably bound by commercial ties to Athens, must have received the reward because they became partisans of Athens during the rebellion, for otherwise no conceivable reason would impel the Athenians to grant *ateleia* ["immunity from taxes"] of any sort to the metics of another city. However, the novelty and implications of the privilege conferred are as astonishing as the minimal interest they have excited. Perhaps the explanation is that the formula of *ateleia* occurs in other Athenian decrees. Yet the difference could not be greater. On those rare occasions when the Athenians conferred *ateleia* on their benefactors, it was at least a magnanimous gesture to the extent that they gave away something they prized themselves. Here, in contrast, they are being munificent with income not their own. That the Athenians honored their non-resident friends by freeing them from Chalcidian taxation—not by granting them privileges in Athens—is a notable example of Athenian imperialism in the mid-fifth century, for it implies the ultimate interference in the management of local affairs. Indeed, we must reach forward all the way to Roman times for a parallel. . . .

That the number of Athenians and other Chalcidians granted tax immunity was considerable is apparent from the reassessment [of the annual tribute] of Chalcis. The reduction from 5 to 3 T., too small to reflect the imposition of a cleruchy, is large enough considered as a reflection of the diminution of the Chalcidian tax-rolls, though naturally Athenian state-confiscation of the property of leading rebels is also a factor. Now what was decreed for Chalcis was almost certainly applied also to Eretria, which probably had its tribute halved, and to the rest of Euboea, excepting, of course, Hestiaia. Such being the case, it is probable that analogous measures were taken by the Athenians elsewhere when the opportunity arose. Now this kind of behaviour, documented by lines 52–55 of the Chalcis decree, is an example of the kind of practical ways the Empire helped and bought its friends as well as aided its own citizenry, and the implications, so far as the "popularity" of this empire is concerned, should be obvious. Abuse of the privilege of owning property in foreign states, immunization from local taxes for Athenian carpet-baggers and alien partisans, will have provoked and fanned a discontent utterly transcending any benefits accruing to Athenian-supported governments. Because it is invidious, this is the kind of pinch all people find intolerable and unjust, whatever their political convictions and ideological preferences.

This observation, though self-evident, seems necessary in view of some unrealistic assessments of the Athenian Empire now *en vogue.* Thus, in a celebrated essay, G. E. M. de Ste. Croix sought "to show that the mass of the citizens in the allied or subject states were loyal to Athens throughout the whole period of the empire, until the final collapse in the Ionian War, and could on occasion give proof of a deep devotion to the imperial city, which can only be compared with the similar devotion of contemporary oligarchs to Sparta." Such words as "loyalty" and "devotion" are completely improper; they reveal a distorted perspective. Greek communities in the Hellespont, Ionia, the Aegean, Euboea and elsewhere were not a United States with Athens a kind of nerve-center serving as their capital. They will have reserved their devotion for their own localities. Some citizens may have admired Athens, others envied her, and still others hated that city. But the political friendship of one state for another is cemented not by devotion but by a *quid pro quo.* It is not to be compared with the loyalties a national will feel for his own country, much less with the affection a modern scholar will feel for Pericles' "Golden Age."

But there is no need for the rehashing of the old arguments. The evidence from Thucydides, especially his three infamous episodes of Book III, proclaims an era when loyalty to one side or another had ceased to be a matter of political persuasion and had become one of survival. After 427 B.C. no doubt could exist in the minds of the ruling faction of a given city that a seizure of power by the other faction, whether by defection or internal revolution, would entail for themselves confiscation and proscription. The fact, therefore, to take one example supplied by de Ste. Croix, that "Sane and Dium, small as they were, and surrounded by cities now in alliance with Brasidas, held out, even when their lands were ravaged" cannot be attributed to "devotion" to Athens. Communities do not risk destruction because they have transferred their ultimate loyalties to another nation—though governments may do so, having cause to fear violence from within and without should they lose their power. Prior to 431, however, a different climate prevailed. The alternative to subjection to Athens was autonomy, not subjection to a foreign oligarchy, and what must have chafed the allies, whatever the nature of their governments, were limitations imposed upon them. And even if it were true that "any infringement of the *eleutheria* ["freedom"] of a city, however slight, might be described as 'enslavement,'" the point is not that this is a comparatively trivial "technical matter" but, totally to the contrary, that the Greeks felt so strongly about the abrogation of their freedom to the slightest degree that they defined it in terms of overpowering emotional impact. To conclude, then, our sentence in the Chalcis decree documents one aspect of the exploitation by Athens of its subjects presupposed by Thucydides in his general remarks about Athens and its popularity. Athenian acquisition of the property of foreign states and the spoliation of local tax-rolls were features of imperial Athens not the less significant because of their accidental preservation in this obscure sentence of [the regulations for Chalcis].

This relief, discovered on the acropolis and sometimes called the "Mourning Athena," depicts the goddess leaning on her spear as she apparently reads an inscribed list of Athenians killed in battle. (German Archaeological Institute)

The Causes of the Peloponnesian War

When war broke out between Athens and Sparta in 431, neither side could have envisioned a conflict, or rather a series of conflicts, which would last twenty-seven years and end in the dissolution of the Athenian empire. Sparta undoubtedly wished to force some concessions out of Athens regarding the Peloponnesian allies and perhaps to prevent further Athenian aggrandizement, whereas Athens (to judge by Pericles' strategy of allowing Sparta to ravage Attica) hoped simply to maintain the status quo by wearing the Spartans out. The war itself led to radical changes in Athens (where two oligarchical revolutions occurred) and Sparta (where their economy and foreign and domestic policies were influenced by new Aegean and Persian entanglements). The causes of the war have been debated endlessly, a fact which probably would have surprised Thucydides, who wrote the first portion of his history in an effort to put the issue to rest.

Sources

Aristophanes

Comic (?) Explanations

Aristophanes produced his play *Peace* at the Dionysia of 421, just before the Peace of Nicias which ended the first phase of the Peloponnesian War. In the following passage, the Chorus of farmers asks Hermes where the goddess Peace has gone. The *scholia* (explanatory notes or commentary on words or passages added to the margins of texts in antiquity and thereafter) on *Peace* 605 provide two interesting (if confused) quotations of the early third-century B.C. historian Philochorus. Both selections may shed light on the "Megarian Decree," a measure or measures ca. 432 by which the Athenians excluded the Megarians from the harbors of the empire and *agora* (marketplace) of Athens. Some scholars have felt that the decree demonstrated an Athenian attempt to ruin Megara economically by keeping her goods out of Athens or the empire, and that the measure was a principal cause of the Peloponnesian War. For the reference to the famous sculptor Pheidias, see the passage from Plutarch later in this section.

Peace

CHORUS-LEADER [*to Hermes*]: But where can this goddess have been, to be away from us all this long time? Friendliest of gods, do explain this to us.

HERMES: "O indigent peasants, mark well my words," if you want to hear how it was that she vanished. What started it all in the first place was Pheidias getting into trouble. Then Pericles became frightened he might share Pheidias' fate—for he was afraid of your character and your hard-biting temper—and before anything terrible could happen to *him*, he set the city ablaze by dropping into it a tiny spark of a Megarian decree: and he fanned up so great a war that all the Greeks were in tears with the smoke, both those over there and those over here; and as soon as the first vine had reluctantly begun to crackle, and the first wine-jar received a knock and kicked out in vengeful anger at another jar, there was no longer anyone who could put a stop to it, and Peace was disappearing.

TRYGAEUS: Well, by Apollo, I'd never been told that by anyone before, nor had I heard how she [Peace] was connected with Pheidias.

CHORUS-LEADER: No more had I, not till now. So that's why she's so fair of face—because she's a relation of his! There's a lot of things we don't realize!

Scholia on *Peace* 605 and 606

Pheidias: (The historian) Philochoros says these things (happened) when Pythodoros was archon [i.e., 432/1, scholars emend this to read "Theodoros," who was archon in 438/7]: "And the gold statue of Athena was set up in the great temple, having 44 talents weight of gold, with Pericles acting as commissioner (for the project), but Pheidias as builder. And Pheidias after completing (the statue) was judged to have cheated in reckoning the ivory for the scales (of the serpent). And fleeing into Elis, it is said that he contracted to build the statue of Zeus in Olympia, but that having completed this he was killed by Elians." When Skythodoros [unknown, emended to "Pythodoros," archon 432/1] was archon, who was seventh (archon) from this (named above), concerning the Megarians (Philochoros) says, "And they denounced the Athenians to the Lacedæmonians saying they had been unjustly excluded from the agora and the harbors of the Athenians. For the Athenians decreed these things, with Pericles making the motion, accusing them (the Megarians) of working the land sacred to the gods." [606] Certain ones say that when Pheidias the sculptor was thought to have cheated the city and had been exiled, Pericles having become fearful through his commissionership of the furnishing of the statue and his knowledge of the theft composed the bill against Megara and brought on the war in order that he would not have to undergo the normal scrutiny after office (*euthynae*), since the Athenians were occupied by the war, accusing the Megarians of working the sacred meadow of the goddesses.

Acharnians

Acharnians, our oldest extant play of Aristophanes, won the first prize at the Lenaea festival in 425. In this indictment of the war with Sparta and call for peace, the hero Dicaeopolis ("Just City") makes a private truce with the Spartans. In the passage included here, Dicaeopolis explains to the Chorus of Acharnians (residents of a large Athenian deme) why Sparta does not deserve all the blame for the war.

But friends — for there are only friends here listening —
why blame these things entirely on the Spartans?
It was men of ours — I do not say our polis;   515
remember that, I do not say our polis —
but some badly-minded troublemaking creeps,
some worthless counterfeit foreign currency,
who started denouncing shirts from Megara
and if they spotted a cucumber or a bunny   520
or piglets, cloves of garlic, lumps of salt,
it was Megarian, grabbed, sold off that very day.
Now that was merely local; small potatoes.
But then some young crapshooters got to drinking
and went to Megara and stole the whore Simaétha [a famous   525
    prostitute].
And then the Megarians, garlic-stung with passion,
got even by stealing two whores from Aspasia.
From this the origin of the war broke forth
on all the Greeks: from three [sluts].
And then in wrath Olympian Pericles   530
did lighten and thunder and turn Greece upside-down,
establishing laws that read like drinking-songs:
"Megarians shall be banned from land and markets
and banned from sea and also banned from shore."
Whereupon the Megarians, starving inch by inch,   535
appealed to Sparta to help make us repeal
the decree we passed in the matter of the whores.
But we refused although they repeatedly asked.
And then it came to a clashing of the shields.

Scholion on *Acharnians* 532

"Establishing laws:" Imitating the composer of drinking songs. . . .
[There follows a quotation of Timocreon of Rhodes, whose drinking
song Aristophanes apparently uses to spoof Pericles' law.] When Pericles composed the decree he moved that "The Megarians shall have
no share of the agora or the sea or the mainland." And Pericles
charged that the Megarians had farmed the sacred meadow.

Thucydides

The Truest Cause

In the following passages Thucydides suggests that the growth of Athenian
power led to Sparta's decision to begin the war: although other reasons for
the conflict were expressed openly, Athens' increasing strength constituted the "truest cause, though least expressed in public."

[1.23]. . . . [All these (calamities just listed)] came upon them with the
late war, which was begun by the Athenians and Peloponnesians by
the dissolution of the thirty years' truce made after the conquest of Euboea [446/5]. To the question why they broke the treaty, I answer by
placing first an account of their grounds of complaint and points of difference, that no one may ever have to ask the immediate cause which
plunged the Hellenes into a war of such magnitude. The truest cause I
consider to be the one which was formally most kept out of sight. The
growth of the power of Athens, and the terror which this inspired,
made war a necessity to Lacedæmon. Still it is well to give the grounds
alleged by either side, which led to the dissolution of the treaty and the
breaking out of the war.

Passage on page 284 from *Aristophanes' Acharnians*, 513–539, ed. and trans. Jeffrey
Henderson (Newburyport, MA: Focus/R. Pullins Co., 1992), pp. 49–50
From R. Crawley (translator), *Thucydides*.

[In 435 the naval powers of Corinth and Corcyra came to blows over the city of Epidamnus, and Corcyra subsequently (433) sought the alliance of the Athenians. According to Thucydides, the Corcyreans' arguments in Athens included the following.]

[33] 'Now there are many reasons why in the event of your compliance you will congratulate yourselves on this request having been made to you. First, because your assistance will be rendered to a power which, herself inoffensive, is a victim to the injustice of others. Secondly, because all that we most value is at stake in the present contest, and your welcome of us under these circumstances will be a proof of good will which will ever keep alive the gratitude you will lay up in our hearts. Thirdly, yourselves excepted, we are the greatest naval power in Hellas. . . . But it will be urged that it is only in the case of a war that we shall be found useful. To this we answer that if any of you imagine that that war is far off, he is grievously mistaken, and is blind to the fact that Lacedæmon regards you with jealousy and desires war, and that Corinth is powerful there,—the same, remember, that is your enemy, and is even now trying to subdue us as a preliminary to attacking you. . . .

[35] 'If it be urged that your reception of us will be a breach of the treaty existing between you and Lacedæmon, the answer is that we are a neutral state, and that one of the express provisions of that treaty is that it shall be competent for any Hellenic state that is neutral to join whichever side it pleases. . . .

[36] And if any of you believe that what we urge is expedient, but fear to act upon this belief, lest it should lead to a breach of the treaty, you must remember that on the one hand, whatever your fears, your strength will be formidable to your antagonists; on the other, whatever the confidence you derive from refusing to receive us, your weakness will have no terrors for a strong enemy. You must also remember that your decision is for Athens no less than for Corcyra, and that you are not making the best provision for her interests, if at a time when you are anxiously scanning the horizon that you may be in readiness for the breaking out of the war which is all but upon you, you hesitate to attach to your side a place whose adhesion or estrangement is alike pregnant with the most vital consequences. For it lies conveniently for the coast-navigation in the direction of Italy and Sicily, being able to bar the passage of naval reinforcements from thence to Peloponnese, and from Peloponnese thither; and it is in other respects a most desirable station. . . .'

[In reply to the Corcyreans' speech, the Corinthian ambassadors at Athens first criticize Corcyra's earlier policy of not making alliances, and the fact that as a Corinthian colony the Corcyreans have never paid Corinth due honor. To this they add the good offices performed by Corinth for Athens in the past, and then continue as follows:]

[42] 'Weigh well these considerations, and let your youth learn what they are from their elders, and let them determine to do unto us as we have done unto you. And let them not acknowledge the justice of what we say, but dispute its wisdom in the contingency of war. Not only is the straightest path generally speaking the wisest; but the coming of the war which the Corcyræans have used as a bugbear to persuade you to do wrong, is still uncertain, and it is not worth while to be carried away by it into gaining the instant and declared enmity of Corinth. It were, rather, wise to try and counteract the unfavourable impression which your conduct to Megara has created. For kindness shown at a time of need has a power of removing previous causes of complaint quite disproportionate to its amount. And do not be seduced by the prospect of a great naval alliance. Abstinence from all injustice to other first-rate powers is a greater tower of strength, than anything that can be gained by the sacrifice of permanent tranquillity for an apparent temporary advantage. . . .'

[44]. . . When the Athenians had heard both out, two assemblies were held. In the first there was a manifest disposition to listen to the representations of Corinth; in the second, public feeling had changed, and an alliance with Corcyra was decided on, with certain reservations. It was to be a defensive, not an offensive alliance. It did not involve a breach of the treaty with Peloponnese: Athens could not be required to join Corcyra in any attack upon Corinth. But each of the contracting parties had a right to the other's assistance against invasion, whether of his own territory, or that of an ally. For it began now to be felt that the coming of the Peloponnesian war was only a question of time, and no one was willing to see a naval power of such magnitude as Corcyra sacrificed to Corinth; though if they could let them weaken each other by mutual conflict, it would be no bad preparation for the struggle which Athens might one day have to wage with Corinth and the other naval powers. At the same time the island seemed to lie conveniently on the coasting passage to Italy and Sicily.

[45] With these views, Athens received Corcyra into alliance, and

on the departure of the Corinthians not long afterwards, sent ten ships to their assistance. They were commanded by Lacedæmonius, the son of Cimon, Diotimus, the son of Strombichus, and Proteas, the son of Epicles. Their instructions were to avoid collision with the Corinthian fleet except under certain circumstances. If it sailed to Corcyra and threatened a landing on her coast, or in any of her possessions, they were to do their utmost to prevent it. These instructions were prompted by an anxiety to avoid a breach of the treaty. . . .

[The Athenian "defensive" force ultimately assisted Corcyra against the attacking Corinthians (at Sybota, 433). Wary of Corinthian reprisals, the Athenians ordered Poteidaea (a Corinthian colony but tribute-paying member of the Athenian empire) to expel its Corinthian magistrates, surrender hostages, and pull down part of its walls (1.56–57). However, after negotiations with the Athenians failed and Spartan assured the colony of its assistance, Poteidaea revolted from Athens. Both the Athenians and Peloponnesians sent forces to the scene of the revolt.]

[66] The Athenians and Peloponnesians had these antecedent grounds of complaint against each other: the complaint of Corinth was that her colony of Potidaea, and Corinthian and Peloponnesian citizens within it, were being besieged [by the Athenians]; that of Athens against the Peloponnesians that they had incited a town of hers, a member of her alliance and a contributor to her revenue, to revolt, and had come and were openly fighting against her on the side of the Potidaeans. For all this, war had not yet broken out: there was still truce for a while; for this was a private enterprise on the part of Corinth.

[67] But the siege of Potidaea put an end to her inaction; she had men inside it: besides, she feared for the place. Immediately summoning the allies to Lacedæmon, she came and loudly accused Athens of breach of the treaty and aggression on the rights of Peloponnese. With her, the Æginetans, formally unrepresented from fear of Athens, in secret proved not the least urgent of the advocates for war, asserting that they had not the independence guaranteed to them by the treaty. After extending the summons to such other of the allies as might have complaints to make of Athenian aggression, the Lacedæmonians held their ordinary assembly, and invited them to speak. There were many who came forward and made their several accusations; among them the Megarians, in a long list of grievances, called

special attention to the fact of their exclusion from the ports of the Athenian empire and the market of Athens, in defiance of the treaty. Last of all the Corinthians came forward, and having let those who preceded them inflame the Lacedæmonians, now followed with a speech to this effect: —

[68] 'Lacedæmonians! the confidence which you feel in your constitution and social order, inclines you to receive any reflexions of ours on other powers with a certain scepticism. Hence springs your moderation, but hence also the rather limited knowledge which you betray in dealing with foreign politics. Time after time was our voice raised to warn you of the blows about to be dealt us by Athens, and time after time, instead of taking the trouble to ascertain the worth of our communications, you contented yourselves with suspecting the speakers of being inspired by private interest. And so, instead of calling these allies together before the blow fell, you have delayed to do so till we are smarting under it; allies among whom we have not the worst title to speak, as having the greatest complaints to make, complaints of Athenian outrage and Lacedæmonian neglect. Now if these assaults on the rights of Hellas had been made in the dark you might be unacquainted with the facts, and it would be our duty to enlighten you. As it is, long speeches are not needed where you see servitude accomplished for some of us, meditated for others — in particular for our allies — and prolonged preparations in the aggressor against the hour of war. Or what, pray, is the meaning of their reception of Corcyra by fraud, and their holding it against us by force? what of the siege of Potidaea? — places one of which lies most conveniently for any action against the Thracian towns; while the other would have contributed a very large navy to the Peloponnesians?

[69] 'For all this you are responsible. You it was who first allowed them to fortify their city after the Median war, and afterwards to erect the long walls, — you who, then and now, are always depriving of freedom not only those whom they have enslaved, but also those who have as yet been your allies. For the true author of the subjugation of a people is not so much the immediate agent, as the power which permits it having the means to prevent it; particularly if that power aspires to the glory of being the liberator of Hellas. . . .'

[After the Corinthian speech urging Sparta to war with Athens, Athenian ambassadors at Sparta on other business replied (see Part V above). According to Thucydides, they ended their speech as follows.

Afterwards the Spartan King Archidamus responded with a seemingly prophetic speech outlining the difficulties this war would bring on Sparta.]

[78] . . . ['W]hile it is still open to us both to choose aright, we bid you not to dissolve the treaty, or to break your oaths, but to have our differences settled by arbitration according to our agreement. Or else we take the gods who heard the oaths to witness, and if you begin hostilities, promise to try to follow your example somewhat closely.'

[79]　Such were the words of the Athenians. After the Lacedæmonians had heard the complaints of the allies against the Athenians, and the observations of the latter, they made all withdraw, and consulted by themselves on the question before them. The opinions of the majority all led to the same conclusion; the Athenians were open aggressors, and war must be declared at once. But Archidamus, the Lacedæmonian king, came forward, who had the reputation of being at once a wise and a moderate man, and made the following speech:—

[80]　'I have not lived so long, Lacedæmonians, without having had the experience of many wars, and I see those among you of the same age as myself, who will not fall into the common misfortune of longing for war from inexperience or from a belief in its advantage and its safety. This, the war on which you are now debating, would be one of the greatest magnitude, on a sober consideration of the matter. In a struggle with Peloponnesians and neighbours our strength is of the same character, and it is possible to move swiftly on the different points. But a struggle with a people who live in a distant land, who have also an extraordinary familiarity with the sea, and who are in the highest state of preparation in every other department; with wealth private and public, with ships, and horses, and heavy infantry, and a population such as no one other Hellenic place can equal, and lastly a number of tributary allies—what can justify us in rashly beginning such a struggle? wherein is our trust that we should rush on it unprepared? Is it in our ships? There we are inferior; while if we are to practise and become a match for them, time must intervene. Is it in our money? There we have a far greater deficiency. We neither have it in our treasury, nor are we ready to contribute it from our private funds.

[81]　Confidence might possibly be felt in our superiority in heavy infantry and population, which will enable us to invade and devastate their lands. But the Athenians have plenty of other land in their empire, and can import what they want by sea. Again, if we are to attempt

an insurrection of their allies, these will have to be supported with a fleet, most of them being islanders. What then is to be our war? For unless we can either beat them at sea, or deprive them of the revenues which feed their navy, we shall meet with little but disaster. Meanwhile our honour will be pledged to keeping on, particularly if it be the opinion that we began the quarrel. For let us never be elated by the fatal hope of the war being quickly ended by the devastation of their lands. I fear rather that we may leave it as a legacy to our children; so improbable is it that the Athenian spirit will be the slave of their land, or Athenian experience be cowed by war.

[82] 'Not that I would bid you be so unfeeling as to suffer them to injure your allies, and to refrain from unmasking their intrigues; but I do bid you not to take up arms at once, but to send and remonstrate with them in a tone not too suggestive of war, nor again too suggestive of submission, and to employ the interval in perfecting our own preparations. The means will be, first, the acquisition of allies, Hellenic or barbarian it matters not, so long as they are an accession to our strength naval or pecuniary—I say Hellenic or barbarian, because the odium of such an accession to all who like us are the objects of the designs of the Athenians is taken away by the law of self-preservation—and secondly the development of our home resources. . . .'

[After describing the Spartan character and recommending further negotiations, Archidamus ended.]

[85] . . . Last came forward Sthenelaidas, one of the Ephors for that year, and spoke to the Lacedæmonians as follows:—

[86] 'The long speech of the Athenians I do not pretend to understand. They said a good deal in praise of themselves, but nowhere denied that they are injuring our allies and Peloponnese. And yet if they behaved well against the Mede then, but ill towards us now, they deserve double punishment for having ceased to be good and for having become bad. We meanwhile are the same then and now, and shall not, if we are wise, disregard the wrongs of our allies, or put off till to-morrow the duty of assisting those who must suffer to-day. Others have much money and ships and horses, but we have good allies whom we must not give up to the Athenians, nor by law-suits and words decide the matter, as it is anything but in word that we are harmed, but render instant and powerful help. And let us not be told that it is fitting for us to deliberate under injustice; long deliberation is rather fitting for those who have injustice in contemplation. Vote therefore, Lacedæmonians,

for war, as the honour of Sparta demands, and neither allow the further aggrandisement of Athens, nor betray our allies to ruin, but with the gods let us advance against the aggressors.'

[87] With these words he, as Ephor, himself put the question to the assembly of the Lacedæmonians. He said that he could not determine which was the loudest acclamation (their mode of decision is by acclamation not by voting); the fact being that he wished to make them declare their opinion openly and thus to increase their ardour for war. Accordingly he said, 'All Lacedæmonians who are of opinion that the treaty has been broken, and that Athens is guilty, leave your seats and go there,' pointing out a certain place; 'all who are of the opposite opinion, there.' They accordingly stood up and divided; and those who held that the treaty had been broken were in a decided majority. . . .

[88] The Lacedæmonians voted that the treaty had been broken, and that war must be declared, not so much because they were persuaded by the arguments of the allies, as because they feared the growth of the power of the Athenians, seeing most of Hellas already subject to them.

[After a long digression describing Athens' growing power after 479 and down to the Samian War (see Part II), Thucydides continues.]

[118] After this, though not many years later, we at length come to what has been already related, the affairs of Corcyra and Potidaea, and the events that served as a pretext for the present war. All these actions of the Hellenes against each other and the barbarian occurred in the fifty years' interval between the retreat of Xerxes and the beginning of the present war. During this interval the Athenians succeeded in placing their empire on a firmer basis, and advanced their own home power to a very great height. The Lacedæmonians, though fully aware of it, opposed it only for a little while, but remained inactive during most of the period, being of old slow to go to war except under the pressure of necessity, and in the present instance being hampered by wars at home; until the growth of the Athenian power could be no longer ignored, and their own confederacy became the object of its encroachments. They then felt that they could endure it no longer, but that the time had come for them to throw themselves heart and soul upon the hostile power, and break it, if they could, by commencing the present war. And though the Lacedæmonians had made up their own minds on the fact of the breach of the treaty and the guilt of

the Athenians, yet they sent to Delphi and inquired of the god whether it would be well with them if they went to war; and, as it is reported, received from him the answer that if they put their whole strength into the war, victory would be theirs, and the promise that he himself would be with them, whether invoked or uninvoked. . . .

[At another conference the Peloponnesian allies voted for war (432). Further negotiations ensued, however, with the Spartans at one point bidding the Athenians to "drive out the curse" (on the Alcmeonid family, including Pericles on his mother's side: see Part III).]

[139]   To return to the Lacedæmonians. The history of their first embassy, the injunctions which it conveyed, and the rejoinder which it provoked, concerning the expulsion of the accursed persons, have been related already. It was followed by a second, which ordered Athens to raise the siege of Potidaea, and to respect the independence of Ægina. Above all, it gave her most distinctly to understand that war might be prevented by the revocation of the Megara decree, excluding the Megarians from the use of Athenian harbours and of the market of Athens. But Athens was not inclined either to revoke the decree, or to entertain their other proposals; she accused the Megarians of pushing their cultivation into the consecrated ground and the unenclosed land on the border, and of harbouring her runaway slaves. At last an embassy arrived with the Lacedæmonian ultimatum. The ambassadors were Ramphias, Melesippus, and Agesander. Not a word was said on any of the old subjects; there was simply this: — 'Lacedæmon wishes the peace to continue, and there is no reason why it should not, if you would leave the Hellenes independent.' Upon this the Athenians held an assembly, and laid the matter before their consideration. It was resolved to deliberate once for all on all their demands, and to give them an answer. There were many speakers who came forward and gave their support to one side or the other, urging the necessity of war, or the revocation of the decree and the folly of allowing it to stand in the way of peace. Among them came forward Pericles, son of Xanthippus, the first man of his time at Athens, ablest alike in counsel and in action, and gave the following advice: —

[140]   'There is one principle, Athenians, which I hold to through everything, and that is the principle of no concession to the Peloponnesians. I know that the spirit which inspires men while they are being persuaded to make war, is not always retained in action; that as circumstances change, resolutions change. Yet I see that now as

before the same, almost literally the same, counsel is demanded of me; and I put it to those of you, who are allowing yourselves to be persuaded, to support the national resolves even in the case of reverses, or to forfeit all credit for their wisdom in the event of success. For sometimes the course of things is as arbitrary as the plans of man; indeed this is why we usually blame chance for whatever does not happen as we expected. Now it was clear before, that Lacedæmon entertained designs against us; it is still more clear now. The treaty provides that we shall mutually submit our differences to legal settlement, and that we shall meanwhile each keep what we have. Yet the Lacedæmonians never yet made us any such offer, never yet would accept from us any such offer; on the contrary, they wish complaints to be settled by war instead of by negotiation; and in the end they drop the expostulatory tone, and appear here with the commanding tone. They command us to raise the siege of Potidaea, to let Ægina be independent, to revoke the Megara decree; and they conclude with an ultimatum warning us to leave the Hellenes independent. I hope that you will none of you think that we shall be going to war for a trifle if we refuse to revoke the Megara decree, which appears in front of their complaints, and the revocation of which is to save us from war, or let any feeling of self-reproach linger in your minds, as if you went to war for slight cause. Why, this trifle contains the whole seal and trial of your resolution. If you give way, you will instantly have to meet some greater demand, as having been frightened into obedience in the first instance; while a firm refusal will make them clearly understand that they must treat you more as equals. [141]   Make your decision therefore at once, either to submit before you are harmed, or if we are to go to war, as I for one think we ought, to do so without caring whether the ostensible cause be great or small, resolved against making concessions or consenting to a precarious tenure of our possessions. For all claims from an equal, urged upon a neighbour as commands, before any attempt at legal settlement, be they great or be they small, have only one meaning, and that is slavery. . . .'

[Pericles goes on to detail the advantages the Athenians possess over the Peloponnesians in terms of organization, finance, and naval power. He concludes the address as follows:]

[144]   'I have many other reasons to hope for a favourable issue, if you can prevail on yourselves not to combine schemes of fresh con-

quest with the conduct of the war, and to keep out of wilful dangers; indeed I am more afraid of our own blunders than of the enemy's devices. But these matters shall be explained in another speech, as events require; for the present dismiss these men with the answer that we will allow Megara the use of our market and harbours, when the Lacedæmonians suspend their alien acts in favour of us and our allies, there being nothing in the treaty to prevent either one or the other: that we will leave the cities independent, if independent we found them when we made the treaty, and when the Lacedæmonians grant to their cities an independence not involving subservience to Lacedæmonian interests, but such as each severally may desire: that we are willing to give the legal satisfaction which our agreements specify, and that we shall not commence hostilities, but shall resist those who do commence them. This is an answer agreeable at once to the rights and the dignity of Athens. It must be thoroughly understood that war is a necessity; but that the more readily we accept it, the less will be the ardour of our opponents, and that out of the greatest dangers communities and individuals acquire the greatest glory. Did not our fathers resist the Medes not only with resources far different from ours, but even when those resources had been abandoned; and more by wisdom than by fortune, more by daring than by strength, did not they beat off the barbarian and advance their affairs to their present height? We must not let them leave us behind, but must resist our enemies in any way and in every way, and attempt to hand down our power to our posterity unimpaired.'

[145] Such were the words of Pericles. The Athenians, persuaded of the wisdom of his advice, voted as he desired, and answered the Lacedæmonians as he recommended, both on the separate points and in the general; they would do nothing on dictation, but were ready to have the complaints settled in a fair and impartial manner by the legal method, which the terms of the truce prescribed. So the envoys departed home, and did not return again.

[146] These were the charges and differences existing between the rival powers before the war, arising immediately from the affair at Epidamnus and Corcyra. Still intercourse continued in spite of them, and mutual communication. It was carried on without heralds, but not without suspicion, as events were occurring which were equivalent to a breach of the treaty and matter for war.

Plutarch

Pericles and the War

In the 420s, Aristophanes joked about Pericles' involvement in provoking the Peloponnesian War. His jokes, and the stories upon which they may have been based (if Aristophanes did not entirely invent the idea himself), became the foundation for an elaborate tradition linking the war directly to Pericles (and his mistress or wife, Aspasia). Here, Plutarch draws on Thucydides and this tradition in his account of the war's beginning.

(29)   A few years later [after the Samian revolt], when the clouds were already gathering for the Peloponnesian war, Pericles persuaded the Athenians to send help to Corcyra in her war with Corinth and so bring over to their side an island with a powerful navy at a time when the Peloponnesians had all but declared war on them. And yet when the people had agreed to this measure, Pericles sent a squadron of no more than ten ships under Lacedaemonius, the son of Cimon, as if his object were to humiliate him because Cimon's family was on especially good terms with the Spartans. . . .

In consequence, Pericles was sharply criticized for the paltry size of the force he had sent. It was felt that it was too small to help the Corcyraeans in their hour of need, but that at the same time it provided those enemies of Athens who were accusing her of interference with an invaluable pretext, and he therefore reinforced it later with a larger squadron which arrived after the battle.

This action enraged the Corinthians and they denounced the Athenians at Sparta. The Megarians also joined them to complain that they were being shut out and driven away from every market and every harbour which the Athenians controlled, contrary to the common rights of the Greeks and the articles of peace entered into upon oath.

From Plutarch, *The Rise and Fall of Athens*, translated by I. Scott-Kilvert, pp. 195–199 (London/New York: Penguin, 1960). Reproduced by permission of Frederick Warne & Co.

The people of Aegina also considered themselves oppressed and out-raged and secretly bemoaned their grievances to the Spartans, as they did not dare to accuse the Athenians openly. At this point, too, Poti-daea revolted, a city which, although a colony of Corinth, was subject to Athens, and the siege on which the Athenians then embarked fur-ther hastened the outbreak of the war.

In spite of all this a succession of embassies was sent to Athens, and Archidamus, the Spartan king, strove to placate his allies and bring about a peaceful settlement of most of their grievances. In fact, it seems likely that the Athenians might have avoided war on any of the other issues, if only they could have been persuaded to lift their em-bargo against the Megarians and come to terms with them. And since it was Pericles who opposed this solution more strongly than anyone else and urged the people to persist in their hostility towards the Megarians, it was he alone who was held responsible for the war.

(30)   It is said that a Spartan mission arrived in Athens to discuss this very subject and that Pericles took refuge in the pretext that there was a law which forbade the tablet on which the Megarian decree was inscribed to be taken down. 'Very well, then,' one of the envoys named Polyalces suggested, 'there is no need to take it down. Just turn its face to the wall! Surely there is no law forbidding that!' This was neatly put, but it had no effect on Pericles, who seems to have harboured some private grudge against the Megarians. However, the charge which he brought against them in public was that they had appropriated for their own profane use the territory of Eleusis, which was consecrated to Demeter and Persephone, and he proposed that a herald should be sent first to them and should then proceed to Sparta to complain of their conduct. Pericles was certainly responsible for this decree, which sets out to justify his action in humane and reasonable terms. But then the herald who was sent, Anthemocritus, met his death at the hands of the Megarians, so it was believed, and thereupon Charinus proposed a decree against them. This laid it down that henceforth Athens should be the irreconcilable and implacable enemy of Megara, that any Megarian setting foot in Attica should be put to death, and that the generals, whenever they took the traditional oath of office, should swear besides this that they would invade the Megarid twice in each year, and that Anthemocritus should be buried with honours beside the Thriasian gates, which are now known as the Dipylon.

On their side the Megarians denied that they had murdered Anthemocritus, and threw the blame for the Athenians' actions upon Pericles and Aspasia, quoting those famous and hackneyed verses from Aristophanes' *Acharnians:*

> *Some young Athenians in a drunken frolic*
> *Kidnapped Simaetha, the courtesan, from Megara.*
> *The Megarians were furious, primed themselves with garlic*
> *Just like their fighting-cocks, then came and stole*
> *Two of Aspasia's girls to get their own back.*

(31)   The real reasons which caused the decree to be passed are extremely hard to discover, but all writers agree in blaming Pericles for the fact that it was not revoked. . . .

However, the most damning charge of all, and yet the one which finds most support, runs somewhat like this. Pheidias the sculptor had been entrusted, as I have mentioned, with the contract for producing the great statue of Athena. His friendship with Pericles, with whom he had great influence, earned him a number of enemies through sheer jealousy, while others made use of him to test the mood of the people and see what their temper would be in a case in which Pericles was involved. They therefore persuaded Menon, one of the artists working under Pheidias, to seat himself in the market-place as a suppliant and ask for the protection of the state in return for laying information against Pheidias. The people granted the man's plea and a motion for Pheidias's prosecution was laid before the Assembly. The charge of embezzlement was not proved, because from the very beginning, on Pericles' own advice, the gold used for the statue had been superimposed and laid around it in such a way that it could all be taken off and weighed, and this was what Pericles now ordered the prosecutors to do. . . .

(32)   About the same time Aspasia was put on trial for impiety. She was prosecuted by Hermippus the comic poet, who also accused her of procuring free-born Athenian women for Pericles and receiving them into her house. A decree was also introduced by Diopeithes, the diviner, to the effect that anybody who did not believe in the gods or taught theories about celestial phenomena should be liable to prosecution, and this was aimed to cast suspicion on Pericles through Anaxagoras. The people took up these slanders only too readily, and while they were in this mood a bill was passed on Dracontides' initiative directing that the accounts of the public funds that Pericles had

spent should be deposited with the prytanes, and that the jurors should pronounce their verdict on his case with ballots which had lain on the altar of the goddess on the Acropolis. However, this clause of the decree was amended by Hagnon, who moved that the case should be tried in the usual way, but before a body of 1,500 jurors, no matter whether it was to be termed a prosecution for embezzlement or bribery or malversation.

Pericles contrived to beg off Aspasia by bursting into floods of tears during her trial, so Aeschines tells us, and making a personal appeal to the jurors, but he was so alarmed for Anaxagoras's safety that he smuggled him out of the city. Pericles had already fallen foul of the people on the occasion of Pheidias's trial and he dreaded the jury's verdict on his own case, and so now that the war was threatening and smouldering, we are told that he deliberately fanned it into flame. He hoped in this way to dispel the charges against him and make the people forget their jealousy, since he knew that as soon as any great enterprise or danger was in prospect, the city would put herself in his hands alone because of his great authority and prestige. These are the motives which are alleged for his refusal to allow the people to give way to the demands of Sparta, but the true history of these events is hidden from us.

Analysis

Donald Kagan

The Causes of the War

In a concluding chapter from his *The Outbreak of the Peloponnesian War,* Donald Kagan first disputes Thucydides' contention that the growth of Athenian power led "inevitably" to war with Sparta, based on his view that Athens' power did not grow between 445 and 435. He then confronts

From Donald Kagan, *The Outbreak of the Peloponnesian War.* Copyright 1969. Used by permission of the publisher, Cornell University Press.

those who see the causes of the war in impersonal forces such as economic factors, and Dorian/Ionian or oligarchic/democratic hostility. Finally, in the passage presented here, Kagan emphasizes the series of events just before 431, especially the miscalculations of the Corinthians and Pericles.

The unpersuasiveness of all theories of inevitability is best demonstrated by a resumé of the events that led to the war. At each step it is clear that the decisions were not preordained, although, of course, the options narrowed as time went on. Our analysis of the years between the wars shows that the theory that peace between Athens and Sparta could not last must be imposed on the facts from the outside; it does not arise from the evidence. The internal quarrel at Epidamnus had no relation to the outside world and need not have affected the international situation in any way. Corinth's decision to intervene was in no way the necessary consequence of previous conditions. Corinthian control of Epidamnus was not necessary for Corinth's economic well-being, her security, even her prestige. Corinth decided that the affair at Epidamnus would provide a splendid opportunity for revenge on its traditional enemies, the Corcyreans. The Corinthians could have chosen to refuse the Epidamnian appeal; had they done so there would have been no crisis and no war. To be sure, they knew in advance that intervention would probably mean war with Corcyra, and they did not flinch from the prospect, for they were confident that they could defeat Corcyra with the help of their Peloponnesian allies.

When some of their friends tried to dissuade them from their course out of fear that Corcyra would obtain the help of Athens and so bring on a larger war, the Corinthians ignored their counsel. They did not do so because they wanted a war with Athens, but because they expected that Athens would not fight. They were led to this belief by their interpretation of the informal detente between the Peloponnesians and the Athenians. Their interpretation was not correct, because Corcyra and its navy presented special problems not easily and obviously dealt with by the unspoken understanding that each side would be permitted freedom of action in its own sphere of influence. Sparta and Sicyon, at least, understood the danger, and the Corinthians should have too. They proceeded with their dangerous policy because they miscalculated the Athenian response. Their miscalculation arose not from a traditional hatred of Athens caused by a commercial rivalry, but rather from a combination of irrational hatred for the Corcyreans and wishful thinking, which led them to expect from Athens the response that they wanted. Had reason prevailed, the Corinthians would have accepted the Corcyrean offer of arbitration, which would have left them in a better position than when they first became involved at Epidamnus. The crisis would have ended before it ever involved either Athens or Sparta, and the war would have been averted.

By the time Athens became involved in 433, her freedom of action was somewhat limited. Corcyra was at war with Corinth. If Athens remained aloof, the Corinthians might win and attach the Corcyrean fleet to the Spartan alliance and challenge the unquestioned naval supremacy that was the basis of Athenian security. Once it became clear that Corinth would not retreat, the Athenians had no choice but to meet the challenge. It is clear, however, that the Athenians did not seek a confrontation with Corinth for commercial, imperial, or any other reasons; the conflict was forced on them. They first tried to limit their commitment in the hope that Corcyra would win with its own forces.

When the Battle of Sybota blocked this resolution, they did what they could to localize the conflict and avoid involving Sparta. The preparations they made for a likely conflict with Corinth were calculated to avoid giving the Corinthians a valid pretext for demanding Spartan assistance. Two of these measures, the ultimatum of Potidaea and the Megarian Decree, were errors in judgment by Pericles. In the case of Potidaea, he reacted too vigorously to the threat that Corinthian machinations might produce rebellion in the empire and gave the impression of Athenian tyranny and aggressiveness. In the case of Megara, again his reaction was greater than the situation required. He intended to punish Megara for helping the Corinthians in the Battle of Sybota and to issue a warning to them and to any other friends of Corinth to stay out of the affair and prevent its spread. The action was probably unnecessary, for Sparta seemed to be exercising a restraining hand on most of her allies; yet the decree had a very serious effect on the internal politics of Sparta. It appeared to be an attack on an ally of Sparta launched without sufficient provocation, and it reinforced the impression of Athens as a tyrant and an aggressor. Pericles misjudged the stability of the political situation at Sparta and unintentionally gave the war party a goad with which it could drive Sparta and its allies to war. If his judgment had been better and, perhaps, if the Athenian irritation with the Megarians had been less, he might have taken a gentler tone, avoided provocative actions, and allowed the friends of Athens and peace to keep their control of Spartan policy. If he had, there might not have been a majority of warlike ephors to promise help to Potidaea and to cooperate with the Corinthians in stirring up the war. Had the Athenians shown more restraint, there is a possibility that even after the Battle of Sybota a general war could have been prevented.

All this is not to say that there were no existing forces or conditions that helped bring on the war. The perfectly ordinary civil war in a remote and unimportant town on the fringes of the civilized world could hardly have led to a great war *ex nihilo.* Certainly there needed to be a solid core of suspicion and mutual distrust in Athens and Sparta. Another crucial factor originating long before the outbreak of the crisis was the deep and emotional hatred between Corinth and Corcyra. Still another was the organizational weakness of the Spartan alliance, which permitted a power of the second magnitude to drag the hegemonal power into a dangerous war for its own interests. Connected with that was the constitutional weakness of the Spartan executive, which divided the real responsibility for the formulation and conduct of foreign policy and permitted unpredictable shifts back and forth between policies in a rather short space of time. Such weaknesses made it difficult to restrain outbursts of passion and to follow a sober, cautious policy in times of crisis. After the death of Pericles, the Athenian constitution would show a similar weakness, but so long as he was alive Athens was free of this problem.

It is also true that the machinery of diplomacy was too rudimentary to preserve peace in time of crisis. The Thirty Years' Peace was open to varying interpretations, as are all diplomatic agreements, but it provided only one, rather clumsy, means for settling disagreements. It authorized the submission of all disputes to arbitration, but it made no provision for consultation before minor differences reached the level of disputes needing arbitration. By the time arbitration is required, disputants are often so hostile that they refuse to use it. When disputes reach the level of arbitration, they have become public issues and aroused powerful emotions not easily controlled.

All these may be considered as remote or underlying causes of the war. They may be seen as contributing to the situation that made war possible, but all of them together did not make war necessary. For that, a complicated chain of circumstances and decisions was needed. If any of its links had not been present, the war would not have come.

It is customary to apply the metaphor of the powder keg or tinder-box to international situations that are deemed the inevitable forerunners of war. The usual way of putting it is that the conflicting interests and passions of the contending parties provided the inflammatory material, and the final crisis was only a spark that had sooner or later to fall and cause the inevitable conflagration or explosion. If we were to apply this metaphor to the outbreak of the Second Peloponnesian War, we should put it this way: The growth of the Athenian Empire and Sparta's jealousy and fear of it provided the inflammable material that ignited into the First Peloponnesian War. The Thirty Years' Peace poured water on that flame and extinguished it. What was left of the flammable material was continually cooled and dampened by the mutual restraint of Athens and Sparta in the decade 445–435. To start the war, the spark of the Epidamnian trouble needed to land on one of the rare bits of flammable stuff that had not been thoroughly drenched. Thereafter it needed to be continually and vigorously fanned by the Corinthians, soon assisted by the Megarians, Potidaeans, Aeginetans, and the Spartan war party. Even then the spark might have been extinguished had not the Athenians provided some additional fuel at the crucial moment.

No one planned the Peloponnesian War, and no state wanted it, yet each of the three great states bears part of the blame for bringing it on. The Corinthians did not want war with Athens but a free hand against Corcyra. They were willing to risk such a war, however, because they hoped Athens would not really bring it on, because they counted on their proven ability to gain the help of Sparta in case of war, and because they were determined to have their way. Theirs is the greatest guilt, for they had the freest choice and sufficient warning of the consequences of their actions, yet they would not be deterred from their purpose.

The Spartans too deserve a share of the blame. They allowed their war party to frighten them with unfounded alarms of Athenian aggression and the Corinthians to blackmail them with empty threats of secession. They ignored the advice of Archidamus, which would have allowed them to avoid the war without any loss of power, honor, or influence. They rejected the opportunity to arbitrate specific disputes as specified in the treaty and were captured by the romantic vision of destroying the Athenian Empire, liberating Greece, and restoring Sparta to unchallenged primacy. They were quite right to go into the war burdened by a guilty conscience.

The Athenians, however, were not without guilt. To be sure, their security required that they accept the Corcyrean alliance and prepare for further conflict with Corinth. They need not, however, have behaved with such arrogance and harshness toward Potidaea and Megara. This frightened their rivals and lent plausibility to the charges of the Corinthians. In one sense, although probably not in the way they intended, the enemies of Pericles were right in fixing on the Megarian Decree as the cause of the war and on Pericles as its instigator. If he had not issued it, the Corinthians might not have been able to persuade the Spartans of the evil intentions of Athens and so to drive them to war. There is even some possibility that if he had been willing to rescind it at the request of the second Spartan embassy, the peace party might have returned to power and the war have been avoided. By that time, however, Pericles' war strategy dominated his thinking. It demanded a policy of firmness, and the Spartan offer was rejected. The political situation at Sparta made arbitration impossible; the intransigence of Pericles prevented any other solution.

All the statesmen involved suffered from what might be called "a failure of imagination." Each allowed war to come and even helped bring it on because he thought he could gain something at a reasonable cost. Each evolved a strategy largely based on past wars and expected the next war to follow his own plan. None seems to have considered the consequences of miscalculation. None had prepared a reserve plan to fall back on in case his original estimation should prove wrong. All expected a short war; none was ready even for the ten years of the Archidamian War, much less the full twenty-seven years that it took to bring the conflict to a conclusion. They all failed to foresee the evil consequences that such a war would have for everyone, victors and vanquished alike, that it would bring economic ruin, class warfare, brutality, erosion of moral standards, and a permanent instability that left Greece vulnerable to foreign conquest. Had they done so they would scarcely have risked a war for the relatively minor disputes that brought it on. Had they done so, we should admit at once, they would have been far better men than most statesmen who have faced similar decisions in the millennia since then. The Peloponnesian War was not caused by impersonal forces, unless anger, fear, undue optimism, stubbornness, jealousy, bad judgment, and lack of foresight are impersonal forces. It was caused by men who made bad decisions in difficult circumstances. Neither the circumstances nor the decisions were inevitable.

G. E. M. de Ste. Croix

Thucydides, the Megarian Decree, and the Origins of the Peloponnesian War

G. E. M. de Ste. Croix was firmly convinced that Sparta bore the brunt of the responsibility for the war, emphasizing in his *Origins of the Peloponnesian War* that Sparta invaded Athens in 431, not the reverse. Thucydides' account, he maintains, demonstrates the Spartan attempt to find some excuse to offer for their decision to break the peace and attack Athens (hoping thereby to prevent further Athenian aggrandizement). The Megarian decree, he argues, was not an economically motivated and intentionally provocative act of imperialism, but rather a relatively minor act (motivated by the Megarians' violation of sacred land), which the Spartans then chose to use as a pretext for war. In a detailed discussion, de Ste. Croix argues that the decree did not ban Megarian goods or prevent Megarian trade in the Athenian empire, but rather prevented Megarians themselves (as opposed to their proxies) from entering the Athenian agora or the harbors of the empire. In a concluding section, de Ste. Croix then attempts to sum up his analysis of the cause of the war.

In I 23.5 Thucydides says that he has begun by setting out the *aitiai* and *diaphorai*, 'the grounds of complaint (or 'charges') and differences'

From G. E. M. de Ste. Croix, *The Origins of the Peloponnesian War*. Copyright © 1972 Duckworth Publishing. Reprinted by permission of the publisher.

[between Athens and Sparta]. (The word *aitia* is the noun of the verb *aitiaomai*, the root meaning of which is 'accuse, blame'.) In §6 Thucydides goes on, 'In my opinion, *the truest explanation (prophasis)*, although it was least publicised, was that the Athenians becoming great and instilling fear into the Spartans compelled them to go to war. But *the openly expressed grounds of complaint (aitiai)* on each side, on the basis of which they broke the truce and turned to war, were these'. There follows an account of these *aitiai*, which for Thucydides seem to be specifically the two Athenian clashes with Corinth, first over Corcyra (I 48.3 ff.; 55.2) and then over Potidaea (56.1 ff.; 66.1; 67.1), although other complaints are mentioned on the part of Aegina, Megara and others (67.2–4).

What is the contrast Thucydides is drawing, between the explanation which was 'truest although least publicised', and the 'openly expressed grounds of complaint'? This question has been discussed over and over again, with an almost invariable failure to grasp the essential point. Virtually all recent writers have taken it for granted from the very start that the contrast is between an 'immediate cause' (or causes) and a 'more remote' or 'underlying cause', or (to put essentially the same idea a little differently) between a 'superficial cause' and a 'profound cause': the last is the way Momigliano puts it and Kagan begins his chapter on 'The Causes of the War' with the statement, 'It was Thucydides who invented the distinction between the underlying, remote causes of war and the immediate causes.' There have been many similar formulations. In fact, Thucydides does not try to distinguish, *either here or anywhere else in his work*, between immediate or superficial and underlying or profound causes, and it is extraordinary that such an intention should so often have been foisted upon him, sometimes with a good deal of grumbling about the supposed obscurity of his meaning, and even with accusations of paradox. . . .

I hope to show . . . that if Thucydides is correctly understood he makes it very clear that the Spartans had no genuine reason for claiming that Athens had broken the Thirty Years Peace (which still had rather more than half its course to run) and therefore no legitimate excuse for resuming the war. We must not ignore the existence of a sworn peace-treaty which neither side could lawfully break unless perhaps released from its oaths by a clear and open breach by the other side; any alleged but disputed breach had to be referred to arbitration before there was any resort to war. . . .

Now in I 23.4–6 Thucydides speaks of 'the Athenians and Peloponnesians' as beginning the war and breaking the Thirty Years Peace, and he adds that in order to explain why they broke the peace he has given by way of prelude (he is referring to I 24–66) an account of the *aitiai* and *diaphorai*, 'the grounds of complaint and differences.' Later (I 55.2; 66) he repeats that these were the *aitiai* the Athenians and Peloponnesians had against each other: the Corinthians complained that Athens had fought against them, as an ally of Corcyra, during the continuance of the Peace (I 55.2), and was now besieging their colony, Potidaea, with Corinthians and Peloponnesians inside it (66), and the Athenians that the Peloponnesians had caused Potidaea, a tributary ally of theirs, to revolt and had openly fought on the side of the Potidaeans (66). But we then have to ask whether one of the two sides took the initiative in breaking the Peace, declaring war and launching the first attacks—because if so, Thucydides will necessarily be concentrating on that side's actions when he gives his explanation of the outbreak of hostility. As we shall see, there can be no possible doubt about this, if we accept Thucydides' narrative: quite apart from the fact that the Corinthians first broke the Peace, it was the Spartan Assembly which (ignoring Athenian appeals to arbitration) declared, quite falsely, that the Athenians had broken the Peace and that the war should be renewed, the Peloponnesian League Congress which endorsed that decision, the Thebans who thereafter committed the first overt warlike act, and the Peloponnesians who made the first major assault. Pearson, who has given the best analysis known to me of Thucydides I 23.5–6, is therefore right to say, 'Since it was the Peloponnesians who opened hostilities, it is they, not the Athenians, who are on the defensive in the inquiry that Thucydides is conducting. . . . No *prophasis* ["explanation"] is offered for the Athenians, as they are not technically the aggressors and have no need to defend themselves.' . . .

Now in I 23.6 the *aitiai* are said to be 'the grounds of complaint expressed *on either side*, from which they broke the Peace and turned to war'. But we have already seen that the only complaint Thucydides mentions on the Athenian side is that Corinth had brought about the revolt of Potidaea (I 66); and although this *aitia* was a justifiable one, the Athenians were not proposing to make it an excuse for launching a war: they gave it as a necessary reply to the Corinthian allegation that Athens had attacked Potidaea (66). The only *aitiai* which were brought forward as an excuse for breaking the Peace and initiating a general war were those on the Peloponnesian side, and they were not valid, for Athens had not in fact broken the treaty in any way of which the Peloponnesians were entitled to complain, and if she had, they should have responded to her appeal to arbitration. For all practical purposes, then, just as the *prophasis* in 23.6 is the explanation of the *Peloponnesian* decision to go to war, the *aitiai* are 'the grounds of complaint openly expressed' *by the Peloponnesians* in their official decisions and propaganda—their formal decision that the Peace had been broken by Athens, their embassies to Athens in which this view was expressed (126 ff., esp. 139.1), and their justification of their action to the outside world. In all this official Peloponnesian propaganda the *aitiai* would of course be 'openly expressed' ('so that the Spartans might provide themselves with the best possible pretext for going to war', 126.1), and it is precisely in this context that the 'truest explanation' was *aphanestatē* ["least expressed in public"]. The Spartans could never afford to admit publicly that their 'grounds of complaint' were bogus and that their real reason for declaring war was fear of Athens' growing power: had they done so, they would have convicted themselves of breaking the oaths by which they had sworn to keep the Peace for thirty years. This solves a problem Andrewes has created for himself, when he says, 'It is not clear why Thucydides should be at pains to tell us, somewhat obscurely, that this was a conception which lay just below the diplomatic surface, an idea which could be freely expressed at Sparta but not by a Spartan at Athens.' The reality *did* lie 'below the diplomatic surface' and the fear of the growth of Athenian power as a reason for breaking the Peace *was* 'an idea which could be freely expressed at Sparta but not by a Spartan at Athens'—because it gave Sparta no valid pretext for her war: only the *aitiai*, had they been justified (as they were not), could have done that. When Andrewes says, 'There is one place only, Athens itself, where no one could usefully assert in public that Athenian expansion justified war,' he overlooks the fact that the Peloponnesians could never afford to advance that argument in public *anywhere*, for it provided no legal justification for a renewal of the war, in breach of the treaty! . . .

It has often been remarked that the power of Athens was hardly as great in 432 as it had been in some earlier years before the Thirty Years Peace, above all in 457–4, after the conquest of Boeotia and before the disaster in Egypt. I believe that for Thucydides, a Periclean through and through in foreign policy, the 'land empire' that Athens had acquired for a time in the 450s, including as it did Boeotia, was not really an asset to Athens. . . . And whatever we may think about the comparative strength of Athens in the mid-450s and in 432, she was certainly stronger in 432 than she had been at any time since the Thirty Years Peace. Her vital reserves of money were growing steadily once more; she had demonstrated her power to control her allies by crushing the revolt of Samos, the greatest naval power of them all (cf. Thuc. VIII 76.4); she was no longer the precarious mistress of Boeotia, an area she could never hope to dominate except temporarily, when internal divisions happened to be rife; and she now had a defensive alliance with Corcyra, the next strongest naval power in Greece after herself.

We must now ask ourselves what Thucydides means when he says in I 23.6 that fear of the growth of Athenian power 'compelled' (*anankasai*) the Spartans to go to war—a famous statement which, being generally misinterpreted, has probably done more than any other single passage to create the current misconception of the Athenians as the aggressors in 432–1. The compulsion-words in Thucydides (usually *anankē, anankazein, katanankazein, anankaios*) can often, of course, refer to actual compulsion, where the person compelled has no real liberty of action. Often, on the other hand, as in other writers, they imply no more than strong pressure and do not by any means exclude a large measure of choice by the person under constraint—and so it is here. Whenever people are placed, as they so often are, in situations where their only possible choice is between two or more evils, and they choose the least unpleasant alternative, Thucydides is prepared to speak of *anankē* ["compulsion, necessity"]. This is too often ignored: Sealey, for instance, simply takes it for granted that *anankasai* in I 23.6 must have the strict meaning of 'compel'; for support, the best he can do is to appeal to the translation of Henry Dale—hardly a powerful argument, and there is no other. The Spartans were not in any literal sense 'compelled' to declare war, certainly not without resorting to arbitration first, as Thucydides makes their own king point out (85.2).

It is important to realise too that Thucydides is not making any kind of moral judgment, on the Spartans or the Athenians. . . . 'He does not *blame* the Athenians here,' Pearson [writes] 'because he is not concerned with praise or blame, like some later Greek historians, but with explaining the Spartan point of view. He wants to give their *prophasis* for going to war, their motive, excuse, or occasion, and, as he tells us again later, this was really *fear*— the fear of a worse alternative to war. . . . There is compulsion upon them only in so far as they are compelled to choose between two disagreeable alternatives'. Nor does Thucydides attribute to the Athenians (or Pericles) an imperialistic motive driving towards war. As de Romilly has said, 'The war is the result of an imperialistic development of Athenian power, not the expression of an actual imperialistic ambition.'

What Thucydides is saying, then, is in effect that the growth of Athenian power had placed Sparta in such a position that it was only natural, it was only to be expected, that being what she was (this qualification is essential) she would act as she did. Thucydides realised that human beings, especially when acting collectively, tend to react to certain situations in certain ways, which are more or less predictable. He would not have denied that they have a real power of choice: a large part of his History is centred upon climactic moments at which great decisions have to be made and the issue sometimes remains in doubt until the end. But he evidently believed that in some cases one can be reasonably certain, human nature being what it is, what choice will be made; and in such cases he is quite ready to speak of 'compulsion.'. . .

[De Ste. Croix now addresses the Megarian Decree(s)—Athens' reaction to the Megarians' alleged act of impiety (they were accused of working sacred land near Eleusis and then killing an Athenian herald sent to protest this: see sources above). The decree has been seized upon by some scholars as the true (and economic) cause of the war, and one (in their view) neglected by Thucydides.]

It is not surprising, therefore, that the form of retaliation [against the Megarians] the Athenians actually chose was milder: it was intended above all to humiliate the Megarians and impose indignity and inconvenience (and perhaps, as a secondary consideration, some financial loss) upon them, to the extent that Athens (*a*) could effect this without breaking the Thirty Years Peace, which forbade any resort to force, and (*b*) could expect obedience from her allies, whose co-operation was desirable but who would have nothing like the same interest in disciplining Megara. Even the limited form of retaliation the Athenians chose was claimed, as we know, to be a breach of the Peace, though entirely without justification, in my opinion. Pericles claimed, according to Thucydides (I 144.2), that the Athenian ban on the Megarians was no more contrary to the Peace than the Spartan practice of *xenēlasia* ["expulsion of foreigners"]; and I agree with the authors of [*The Athenian Tribute Lists:* see Suggestions for Additional Reading] that 'he can hardly be wrong on the fact.' Pericles and the Athenians probably did not care, or consider, whether the decree inflicted economic damage upon Megara or not, except in so far as it could be treated as a breach of the Peace if it went too far in this direction. In passing it the Athenians were not thinking in economic terms at all—or, for that matter, in strategic terms.

In short, the Megarian decree was something much more limited and very much less important *in itself* than has yet been realised. In itself it was just that 'little spark of a Megarian decree' which Aristophanes calls it in the *Peace* (line 609)—presenting a picture of it very different from the inflated one in the *Acharnians* (524–34), where his comic purpose required quite another emphasis. The decree became important only when the Megarians complained about it at Sparta. The vital point is that the Spartans were hard put to it to find any sort of plausible accusation against Athens of a breach of the treaty (the only state which had quite clearly broken the Peace being their own ally, Corinth) and naturally therefore jumped at this one, for two different reasons. First, the Megarian decree could be claimed (if with very poor justification) as a breach of the treaty; and secondly, many Athenians could easily be made to feel that the decree was too trivial a matter to go to war over, and once they gave way over this, further concessions could be extorted, as Thucydides (I 140.5) shows Pericles foreseeing. Thucydides makes Pericles inveigh repeatedly and emphatically against just such arguments as these by Athenian 'appeasers.' 'None of you must think,' he says, 'that we should be going to war over a triviality if we don't repeal the Megarian decree, when the Spartans emphasise that if we were to repeal it there need be no war. Don't allow yourselves to have any feelings of self-reproach, as if you were going to war on a minor issue. For this small thing involves the whole confirmation and trial of your resolution. If you give way, you will immediately be confronted with some greater demand' (Thuc. I 140.4–5). Here the Megarian decree is spoken of as if there were indeed people at Athens who considered it a mere 'small spark' (Ar., *Peace* 609), which ought not to be allowed to lead to war.

I should like to emphasise that the picture I have given of the Megarian decree, as a very minor matter until Sparta cleverly chose it as a test case of Athenian willingness to yield, is exactly the way it is presented by Thucydides, who does not even deign to mention it in its place, as he certainly ought to have done if it had really been an independent cause of the war, but refers to it *only* in the context of *Spartan and Megarian propaganda.* . . .

We are now forced to admit . . . that the exclusion from the Athenian Agora *could not have had a primarily commercial purpose,* although it may have had some minor commercial effects, if only by discouraging individual Megarian merchants from trading in Attica. The purpose of the exclusion from the Agora was surely to humiliate the Megarians, to put them in the same category as men convicted of disgraceful crimes or suspected of being carriers of pollution (*agos*). This ban would be most felt, appropriately enough, by those Megarians—a good proportion of them probably members of the governing oligarchy—who were likely to come to Athens for social, political or business reasons, for the Agora was the natural place in which to meet friends and acquaintances at Athens. . . . The Agora was also the place in which one might wish to take one's evening stroll. . . . To be banned from entering the Agora was a real humiliation. . . .

The predominant view among historians in recent years has been that Athens was the aggressor in the Peloponnesian war, and that she forced war on a reluctant Sparta. As I have made clear, I cannot accept that view at all. . . .

In so far as anyone can be held *immediately* responsible for the outbreak of the war which did so much to eat away the great achievements of fifth-century Greece, I think it is the Spartans (and their allies, in particular the Corinthians) who must bear the blame. We know from Thucydides (VII 18.2–3) that the Spartans themselves later realised they had been at fault in 432–1. It may well be that the Spartans and most of their allies conceived themselves as fighting to stop Athens from further aggrandisement, which might take place at their expense; but this, of course, does not excuse them from breaking the Thirty Years Peace and resorting to war.

It is a much more difficult task to allocate the ultimate responsibility for the war: as so often, our judgment is bound to be subjective, and it involves too many imponderables. All States, as Thucydides realised so well, always do what they believe to be in their own best interests; and all we can do is to hope that those interests will be intelligently assessed, and that they will coincide as far as possible with those of the majority of mankind.

We might begin by pointing out that the dynamic, explosive, volatile factor in the situation was Athenian democracy, the imperialistic democracy which struck fear into the hearts of all Greek oligarchs, at Sparta and elsewhere. During the Pentecontaetia Athens pursued her own imperial policy, although for some time — until after the ostracism of Cimon early in 461 — she was careful to avoid any direct conflict with the Peloponnesians. If Athens is to be given part of the blame for the eventual conflict of 432/1, it is above all those who controlled her policy between the years 461 and 446 who must presumably bear it. Precisely how the First Peloponnesian war broke out, *c.* 460, we do not know. At any rate, Athens and the Peloponnesians conducted very intermittent hostilities for some six years, *c.* 460 to *c.* 454, although very little happened after 457–6. I have argued that there is nothing definite to connect Pericles with the policy of creating a 'land empire' (by establishing control of the Megarid and of Boeotia and Phocis), which must have been a major bone of contention between Athens and Sparta. However that may be, the 'land empire' was certainly lost for ever in 446, although Athens did emerge from the

First Peloponnesian war with one very important gain: Aegina, conquered in 457, and expressly listed on the Athenian side by the Thirty Years Peace. After the Peace, the power of Athens gradually grew again, and her financial reserves were built up anew; this aroused alarm among the Peloponnesians. While Sparta was ready, in 440 and again in 432, to break the oaths she had sworn, as were some of her allies (in 432 the majority), Athens kept strictly to the terms of the treaty. It was no part of the policy of Pericles and those who, with him, guided Athenian policy in the years between 446/5 and 432 to provoke a renewal of the war with Sparta and her allies—a war which Athens could have little or no hope of winning. It may be said that Athens was inflexible in her policy and would make no concessions to the Peloponnesians in 432/1; but it is difficult to see what concession she could have made without giving an impression of fear and weakness which Sparta would have been likely to exploit immediately. Athens did in fact offer to repeal the Megarian decree (on which Sparta laid special emphasis) if the Spartans on their side would make a reasonable concession in return.

Sparta was a strongly conservative power, interested primarily in keeping the Peloponnese under control, and not often, until the late fifth century and the early fourth, venturing far outside it. We might well ask why the Spartans needed to break the Peace and fight in 432/1; and we might then be tempted to reply that the one compelling reason was Sparta's uniquely dangerous position as mistress of the Messenian Helots: she was the one Greek State which held in a degrading servile status a very large number of fellow-Greeks. Sparta could not take the risks which an ordinary Greek State might afford: she could not allow another city to reach a position of power from which it could threaten either herself or even her allies. It is probable that by the summer of 432 something like a majority of Spartans had already made up their minds to attack Athens, in spite of the powerful opposition of King Archidamus. And when in 432 Sparta's allies, led by Corinth, demanded action by Sparta against Athens, with a threat to secede if she did not act, the great majority of Spartans needed no further persuasion. Sparta had to fight to keep her League together, not only in order to keep open the one land exit from the Peloponnese, through the territories of Corinth and Megara, but even more because she needed to seal off the whole peninsula from the outside world. If a superior army ever invaded Laconia and Messenia (as in 370/69 and the years following), Sparta would lose control of Messenia and cease to be the strongest power in Greece. The Helot danger was the curse Sparta had brought upon herself, an admirable illustration of the maxim that a people which oppresses another cannot itself be free.

Socrates' connections with oligarchs like Critias and the problematic Alcibiades (as well as the views attributed to him by Plato) probably contributed to his conviction in 399. (© RMN/Musee Louvre)

Counter-Revolutions: Democracy versus Oligarchy

The prospect of a modern, western democracy undergoing an oligarchic revolution may seem remote (although it has happened as recently as 1967 in Greece). But one of the lessons of Athenian democracy surely must be the tenuous nature of popular rule—Athens itself endured two short-lived revolutions in 411 and 404/3. Debate about the propriety of democracy undoubtedly fueled the oligarchical movement to some degree, but the most detailed attacks on demokratia *post-date the revolutions themselves (much as expressions of southern "nationalism" in the United States continued or even increased after the Civil War). The Athenians of the late fifth and early fourth centuries inhabited a world which had not yet reached a consensus on the "best" form of regime, and for this reason they may have something to tell us about the origins, strengths, and weaknesses of democratic government.*

Sources

Herodotus

A Persian Debate on Forms of Government

After the death of the Persian Great King Cambyses in 522, the empire fell into the hands of a pretender who claimed to be Cambyses' brother but in reality was one of the Persian Magi. In this selection from Herodotus, a group of seven Persian noblemen debate the merits of monarchy, oligarchy, and popular rule after the overthrow of the false king (ca. 521). Most scholars doubt the historicity of this Persian debate, and associate the views here expressed with Greek political thought during Herodotus' own lifetime.

(3.80)   And now . . . the conspirators met together to consult about the situation of affairs. At this meeting speeches were made, to which many of the Greeks give no credence, but they were made nevertheless. Otanes recommended that the management of public affairs should be entrusted to the whole nation. "To me," he said, "it seems advisable that we should no longer have a single man to rule over us—the rule of one is neither good nor pleasant. You cannot have forgotten to what lengths Cambyses went in his haughty tyranny; and the haughtiness of the Magi you yourselves have experienced. How indeed is it possible that monarchy should be a well-adjusted thing, when it allows a man to do as he likes without being answerable? Such licence is enough to stir strange and unwonted thoughts in the heart of the worthiest of men. Give a person this power, and straightway his manifold good things puff him up with pride, while envy is so

From G. Rawlinson (translator), *The History of Herodotus, III*, Fourth Edition. Copyright © 1880 Scribner and Welford.

natural to human kind that it cannot but arise in him. But pride and envy together include all wickedness—both of them leading on to deeds of savage violence. True it is that kings, possessing as they do all that heart can desire, ought to be void of envy; but the contrary is seen in their conduct towards the citizens. They are jealous of the most virtuous among their subjects, and wish their death; while they take delight in the meanest and basest, being ever ready to listen to the tales of slanderers. A king, besides, is beyond all other men inconsistent with himself. Pay him court in moderation, and he is angry because you do not show him more profound respect—show him profound respect, and he is offended again, because (as he says) you fawn on him. But the worst of all is, that he sets aside the laws of the land, puts men to death without trial, and subjects women to violence. The rule of the many on the other hand, has, in the first place, the fairest of names, to wit, *isonomy* ["equality of rights"]; and further, it is free from all those outrages which a king is wont to commit. There, places are given by lot, the magistrate is answerable for what he does, and measures rest with the commonalty. I vote, therefore, that we do away with monarchy, and raise the people to power. For the people are all in all."

(81)   Such were the sentiments of Otanes. Megabyzus spoke next, and advised the setting up of an oligarchy:—"In all that Otanes has said to persuade you to put down monarchy," he observed, "I fully concur; but his recommendation that we should call the people to power seems to me not the best advice. For there is nothing so void of understanding, nothing so full of wantonness as the unwieldy rabble. It were folly not to be borne, for men, while seeking to escape the wantonness of a tyrant, to give themselves up to the wantonness of a rude unbridled mob. The tyrant, in all his doings, at least knows what he is about, but a mob is altogether devoid of knowledge; for how should there be any knowledge in a rabble, untaught, and with no natural sense of what is right and fit? It rushes wildly into state affairs with all the fury of a stream swollen in the winter, and confuses everything. Let the enemies of the Persians be ruled by *democracies*, but let us choose out from the citizens a certain number of the worthiest, and put the government into their hands. For thus both we ourselves shall be among the governors, and power being

entrusted to the best men, it is likely that the best counsels will prevail in the state."

(82)   This was the advice which Megabyzus gave, and after him Darius came forward, and spoke as follows:—"All that Megabyzus said against [rule by the people] was well said, I think; but about oligarchy he did not speak advisedly; for take these three forms of government—democracy, oligarchy, and monarchy—and let them each be at their best, I maintain that monarchy far surpasses the other two. What government can possibly be better than that of the very best man in the whole state? The counsels of such a man are like himself, and so he governs the mass of the people to their heart's content; while at the same time his measures against evildoers are kept more secret than in other states. Contrariwise, in oligarchies, where men vie with each other in the service the commonwealth, fierce enmities are apt to arise between man and man, each wishing to be leader, and to carry his own measures; whence violent quarrels come, which lead to open strife, often ending in bloodshed. Then monarchy is sure to follow; and this too shows how far that rule surpasses all others. Again, in a democracy, it is impossible but that there will be malpractices: these malpractices, however, do not lead to enmities, but to close friendships, which are formed among those engaged in them, who must hold well together to carry on their villanies. And so things go on until a man stands forth as champion of the commonalty, and puts down the evildoers. Straightway the author of so great a service is admired by all, and from being admired soon comes to be appointed king; so that here too it is plain that monarchy is the best government. Lastly, to sum up all in a word, whence, I ask, was it that we got the freedom which we enjoy?—did democracy give it us, or oligarchy, or a monarch? As a single man recovered our freedom for us, my sentence is that we keep to the rule of one. Even apart from this, we ought not to change the laws of our forefathers when they work fairly; for to do so is not well."

(83)   Such were the three opinions brought forward at this meeting: the four other Persians voted in favour of the last. [Darius went on to become the new Great King of Persia.]

On Stasis and the Athenian Oligarchs

During 427 violence erupted in Corcyra between the supporters of Athens and those whose sympathies lay with the Peloponnesians. Both sides sent forces to the island, but eventually the approach of a large Athenian force caused a Peloponnesian retreat. In a famous passage Thucydides describes the kind of civil strife, or *stasis*, that broke out between democratic and oligarchic factions in many cities during the Peloponnesian War. In the appended selections, Thucydides details the composition of the oligarchic movement at Athens in 411 and some of the events of their takeover.

[3.81 . . . The Corcyreans supporting Athens] slew such of their enemies as they laid hands on, dispatching afterwards as they landed them those whom they had persuaded to go on board the ships. Next they went to the sanctuary of Hera and persuaded about fifty men to take their trial, and condemned them all to death. The mass of the suppliants who had refused to do so, on seeing what was taking place, slew each other there in the consecrated ground; while some hanged themselves upon the trees, and others destroyed themselves as they were severally able. During seven days that [the Athenian general] Eurymedon stayed with his sixty ships, the Corcyræans were engaged in butchering those of their fellow-citizens whom they regarded as their enemies: and although the crime imputed was that of attempting to put down the democracy, some were slain also for private hatred, others for the monies owed to them by their creditors. Death thus raged in

From R. Crawley (translator), *Thucydides III*.

every shape; sons were killed by their fathers, and suppliants dragged from the altar or slain upon it; while some were even walled up in the temple of Dionysus and died there.

[82]   So bloody was the march of the revolution, and the impression which it made was the greater as it was one of the first to occur. Later on, one may say, the whole Hellenic world was convulsed; struggles being everywhere made by the popular chiefs to bring in the Athenians, and by the oligarchs to introduce the Lacedæmonians. In peace there would have been neither the pretext nor the wish to make such an invitation; but in war, with an alliance always at the command of either faction for the hurt of their adversaries and their own corresponding advantage, opportunities for bringing in the foreigner were never wanting to the revolutionary parties. The sufferings which revolution entailed upon the cities were many and terrible, such as have occurred and always will occur, as long as the nature of mankind remains the same; though in a severer or milder form, and varying in their symptoms, according to the variety of the particular cases. In peace and prosperity states and individuals have better sentiments, because they do not find themselves suddenly confronted with imperious necessities; but war takes away the easy supply of daily wants, and so proves a rough master, that brings most men's characters to a level with their fortunes. Revolution thus ran its course from city to city, and the places which it arrived at last, from having heard what had been done before, carried to a still greater excess the refinement of their inventions, as manifested in the cunning of their enterprises and the atrocity of their reprisals. Words had to change their ordinary meaning and to take that which was now given them. Reckless audacity became courage staunch to its associates; prudent hesitation, specious cowardice; moderation was held to be a cloak for unmanliness; ability to see all sides of a question inaptness to act on any. Frantic violence became the attribute of manliness; safe plotting, a justifiable means of self-defence. The advocate of extreme measures was always trustworthy; his opponent a man to be suspected. To succeed in a plot was to have a shrewd head, to divine a plot a still shrewder; but to try to provide against having to do either was to break up your party and to be afraid of your adversaries. In fine, to forestall an intending criminal, or to suggest the idea of a crime where it was wanting, was equally commended, until even blood became a weaker tie than party, from the

superior readiness of the latter to dare everything without reserve; such associations not having in view the blessings derivable from established institutions but being formed by ambition for their overthrow; while the confidence of their members in each other rested less on any religious sanction than upon complicity in crime. The fair proposals of an adversary were met with jealous precautions by the stronger of the two, and not with a generous confidence. Revenge also was held of more account than self-preservation. Oaths of reconciliation, being only proffered on either side to meet an immediate difficulty, only held good so long as no other weapon was at hand; but when opportunity offered, he who first ventured to seize it and to take his enemy off his guard, thought this perfidious vengeance sweeter than an open one, since, considerations of safety apart, success by treachery won him the palm of knowingness. Indeed rogues are oftener called clever than simpletons honest, and men are as ashamed of being the one as they are proud of being the other. The cause of all these evils was the lust for power felt by greed and ambition, and out of this the violence of parties once engaged in contention. The leaders in the cities, each provided with the fairest professions, on the one side with the cry of political equality of the people, on the other of an ordered aristocracy, sought prizes for themselves in those public interests which they pretended to cherish, and recoiling from no means in their struggles for ascendancy, dared and went through with the direst excesses; which were met in their turn by reprisals still more terrible, that, instead of stopping at what justice or the good of the state demanded, were only limited by the party caprice of the moment; unjust legal condemnations or the authority of the strong arm being with equal readiness invoked to glut the animosities of the hour. Thus religion was in honour with neither party; but the use of fair names to arrive at guilty ends was in high reputation. Meanwhile the moderate part of the citizens perished between the two, either for not joining in the quarrel, or because envy would not suffer them to escape.

[83] Thus every form of iniquity took root in the Hellenic countries by reason of the troubles. The ancient simplicity into which honour so largely entered was laughed down and disappeared; and society became divided into camps in which no man trusted his fellow. To put an end to this, there was neither promise to be depended upon, nor oath that could command respect; but all parties dwelling rather in

their calculation upon the hopelessness of a permanent state of things, were more intent upon self-defence than capable of confidence. In this contest the blunter wits were most successful. Apprehensive of their own deficiencies and of the cleverness of their antagonists, they feared to be worsted in debate and to be surprised by the combinations of their more versatile opponents, and so at once boldly had recourse to action: while their adversaries, arrogantly thinking that they should know in time, and that it was unnecessary to secure by action what policy afforded, often fell victims to their want of precaution.

[84] Meanwhile Corcyra gave the first example of most of the crimes alluded to; of the reprisals exacted by the governed who had never experienced equitable treatment or indeed aught but insolence from their rulers—when their hour came; of the iniquitous resolves of those who desired to get rid of their accustomed poverty, and ardently coveted their neighbours' goods; and lastly, of the savage and pitiless excesses into which men who had begun the struggle not in a class but in a party spirit, were hurried by their ungovernable passions. In the confusion into which life was now thrown in the cities, human nature, always rebelling against the law and now its master, gladly showed itself ungoverned in passion, above respect for justice, and the enemy of all superiority; since revenge would not have been set above religion, and gain above justice, had it not been for the fatal power of envy. Indeed men too often in the prosecution of their revenge set the example of doing away with those general laws to which all alike can look for salvation in adversity, instead of allowing them to subsist against the day of danger when their aid may be required. . . .

[In the winter of 412/11 the leaders of the Athenian fleet at Samos, at the instigation of the exiled Alcibiades (who promised to secure them Persian assistance against the Spartans), determined to replace the Athenian democracy with an oligarchy.]

[8.48]. . . The higher class, who also suffered most severely from the war, now conceived great hopes of getting the government into their own hands, and of triumphing over the enemy; and upon the return of the emissaries to Samos they formed their partisans into a club, and openly told the mass [of the Athenian forces] that the king would be their friend, and would provide them with money, if Alcibiades were restored, and the democracy abolished. The multitude, if at first irritated by these intrigues, were nevertheless kept quiet by the advantageous prospect of the pay from the king; and the oligarchical conspirators, after making this communication to the people, now reexamined the proposals of Alcibiades among themselves, with most of their associates. Unlike the rest, who thought them advantageous and trustworthy, Phrynichus, who was still general, by no means approved of the proposals. Alcibiades, he rightly thought, cared no more for an oligarchy than for a democracy, and only sought to change the institutions of his country in order to get himself recalled by his associates; while for themselves their one object should be to avoid civil discord. It was not the king's interest, when the Peloponnesians were now their equals at sea, and in possession of some of the chief cities in his empire, to go out of his way to side with the Athenians whom he did not trust, when he might make friends of the Peloponnesians who had never injured him. And as for the allied states to whom oligarchy was now offered, because the democracy was to be put down at Athens, he well knew that this would not make the rebels come in any the sooner, or confirm the loyal in their allegiance; as the allies would never prefer servitude with an oligarchy or democracy to freedom with either. Besides, the cities thought that the so-called better classes would prove just as oppressive as the commons, as being those who originated, proposed, and for the most part benefited from the acts of the commons injurious to the confederates. Indeed, if it depended on the better classes, the confederates would be put to death without trial and with violence; while the commons were their refuge and the chastiser of these men. This he positively knew that the cities had learned by experience, and that such was their opinion. The propositions of Alcibiades, and the intrigues now in progress, could therefore never meet with his approval.

[49]   However, the members of the club assembled, agreeably to their original determination, accepted what was proposed, and prepared to send Pisander and others on an embassy to Athens to treat for the restoration of Alcibiades and the abolition of the democracy in the city, and thus to make Tissaphernes [the Persian satrap] the friend of the Athenians. . . .

[Peisander visited Athens and began the preparations for revolution, arguing publicly that Persian assistance was necessary to win the war, and that this could only be secured under a more moderate form of government (8.53–54). After leaving Athens, his negotiations with the Persian Tissaphernes failed, but the oligarchic movement continued nonetheless.]

[67]   At this juncture arrived [back at Athens] Pisander and his colleagues, who lost no time in doing the rest [of the things necessary to install an oligarchy]. First they assembled the people, and moved to elect ten commissioners with full powers to frame a constitution, and that when this was done they should lay before the people their opinion as to the best mode of governing the city. Afterwards, when the day arrived, the conspirators enclosed the assembly in Colonus, a temple of Poseidon, a little more than a mile outside the city; when the commissioners simply brought forward this single motion, that any Athenian might propose whatever measure he pleased, heavy penalties being imposed upon any who should indict for illegality, or otherwise molest him for so doing. The way thus cleared, it was now plainly declared, that all tenure of office and receipt of pay under the existing institutions were at an end, and that five men must be elected as presidents, who should in their turn elect one hundred, and each of the hundred three apiece; and that this body thus made up to four hundred should enter the council chamber with full powers and govern as they judged best, and should convene the five thousand [i.e., the now restricted citizen body] whenever they pleased.

[68]   The man who moved this resolution was Pisander, who was throughout the chief ostensible agent in putting down the democracy. But he who concerted the whole affair, and prepared the way for the catastrophe, and who had given the greatest thought to the matter, was Antiphon, one of the best men of his day in Athens; who, with a head to contrive measures and a tongue to recommend them, did not willingly come forward in the assembly or upon any public scene, being ill-looked upon by the multitude owing to his reputation for talent; and who yet of any one man was best able to aid in the courts, or before the assembly, the suitors who required his opinion. Indeed, when he was afterwards himself tried for his life on the charge of having been concerned in setting up this very government, when the Four Hundred were overthrown and harshly dealt with by the commons, he made what would seem to be the best defence of any known up to my time. Phrynichus also went beyond all others in his zeal for the oligarchy. Afraid of Alcibiades, . . . he held that no oligarchy was ever likely to restore him, and once embarked in the enterprise, proved, where danger was to be faced, by far the staunchest of them all. Theramenes, son of Hagnon, was also one of the foremost of the putters down of the democracy—a man as able in council as in debate.

Conducted by so many and by such sagacious heads, the enterprise, great as it was, not unnaturally went forward; although it was no light matter to deprive the Athenian people of its freedom, almost a hundred years after the deposition of the tyrants, while it was not only not subject to any, but accustomed during more than half that time to rule over subjects of its own.

[69]   The assembly ratified the proposed constitution, without a single opposing voice. . . .

[70 . . . After replacing the boule of 500] . . . the Four Hundred entered the council chamber, and for the present contented themselves with drawing lots for their Prytanes, and making their prayers and sacrifices to the gods upon entering office, but afterwards departed widely from the democratic system of government, and except that they did not recall the exiles on account of Alcibiades, ruled the city by force; putting to death some men, though not many, whom they thought it convenient to remove, and imprisoning and banishing others. They also sent to Agis, the Lacedæmonian king, at Decelea, to say that they desired to make peace, and that he might reasonably be more disposed to treat now that he had them to deal with instead of the inconstant commons. . . .

[According to Thucydides, the leaders of the oligarchical movement claimed that the Athenian government should be limited to five thousand citizens (a fairly large number), but in reality wished to rule themselves (8.65–66). As the revolution progressed, some became unhappy with this state of affairs and insisted . . .] [89]   that the Five Thousand must be shown to exist not merely in name but in reality, and the constitution placed upon a fairer basis. But this was merely their political cry; most of them being driven by private ambition into the line of conduct so surely fatal to oligarchies that arise out of democracies. For all at once pretend to be not only equals but each the chief and master of his fellows; while under a democracy a disappointed candidate accepts his defeat more easily, because he has not the humiliation of being beaten by his equals. But what most clearly encouraged the malcontents was the power of Alcibiades at Samos, and their own disbelief in the stability of the oligarchy; and it was now a race between them as to which should first become the leader of the commons. . . .

[While dissatisfaction with the Four Hundred was growing in Athens, domestic politics were put on hold by a Peloponnesian assault on Athenian interests in Eubœa. When the Athenians were defeated there, the Peloponnesians] . . . effected the revolt of the whole of Euboea (except Oreus, which was held by the Athenians themselves), and settled generally the affairs of the island.

[96]   When the news of what had happened in Euboea reached Athens a panic ensued such as they had never before known. Neither the disaster in Sicily, great as it seemed at the time, nor any other had ever so much alarmed them. The camp at Samos was in revolt; they had no more ships or men to man them; they were at discord among themselves and might at any moment come to blows; and a disaster of this magnitude coming on the top of all, by which they lost their fleet, and worst of all Euboea, which was of more value to them than Attica, could not occur without throwing them into the deepest despondency. Meanwhile their greatest and most immediate trouble was the possibility that the enemy, emboldened by his victory, might sail at once against Piræus, which they had no longer ships to defend; and every moment they expected him to arrive. This, with a little more courage, he might easily have done, in which case he would either have increased the dissensions of the city by his presence, or if he had stayed to besiege it have compelled the fleet from Ionia, although the enemy of the oligarchy, to come to the rescue of their country and of their relatives, and in the meantime would have become master of the Hellespont, Ionia, the islands, and of everything as far as Euboea, or, to speak roundly, of the whole Athenian empire. But here, as on so many other occasions, the Lacedæmonians proved the most convenient people in the world for the Athenians to be at war with. The wide difference between the two characters, the slowness and want of energy of the Lacedæmonians as contrasted with the dash and enterprise of their opponents, proved of the greatest service, especially to a maritime empire like Athens. Indeed this was shown by the Syracusans, who were most like the Athenians in character, and also most successful in combating them.

[97]   Nevertheless, upon receipt of the news, the Athenians manned twenty ships and called immediately a first assembly in the Pnyx, where they had been used to meet formerly, and deposed the Four Hundred and voted to hand over the government to the Five Thousand, who were to be taken from the citizens serving as heavy infantry, decreeing also that no one should receive pay for the discharge of any office, or if he did should be held accursed. Many other assemblies were held afterwards, in which law-makers were elected and all other measures taken to form a constitution. It was during the first period of this constitution

that the Athenians appear to have enjoyed the best government that they ever did, at least in my time. For the fusion of the high and the low was effected with judgment, and this was what first enabled the state to raise up her head after her manifold disasters. They also voted for the recall of Alcibiades and of other exiles, and sent to him and to the camp at Samos, and urged them to devote themselves vigorously to the war. [Full democracy was restored not long after these events.]

Plato

Socrates and Athenian Democracy

The charges against Socrates in 399 included introducing new gods and corrupting the youth. Some of Socrates' younger associates, such as Alcibiades and Critias, had been involved in the oligarchic movement, and this fact undoubtedly contributed to the hostility toward the philosopher. Moreover, the famous oracle given to one of Socrates' associates to the effect that "no man is wiser than Socrates" had sent the philosopher on a quest to find a wise man. As he states earlier in his *Apology*, his questioning of others (and the inevitable exposure of their ignorance) made him unpopular. In the first selection below, Socrates explains why he will not follow the wishes of the majority if they ask him to give up his quest. In the second passage Socrates explains why he has avoided politics, providing an interesting counter to Pericles' views about the man who avoids state service (Thuc. 2.40: see Part I).

[I]f you said to me in this regard: "Socrates, we do not believe [your accuser] Anytus now; we acquit you, but only on condition that you spend no more time on this investigation and do not practise philosophy, and

Plato, *The Trial and Death of Socrates*, translated by G. M. A. Grube, 1975, Hackett Publishing Co., Inc. All rights reserved.

if you are caught doing so you will die;" if, as I say, you were to acquit me on those terms, I would say to you: "Gentlemen of the jury, I am grateful and I am your friend, but I will obey the god rather than you, and as long as I draw breath and am able, I shall not cease to practise philosophy, to exhort you and in my usual way to point out to any one of you whom I happen to meet: Good Sir, you are an Athenian, a citizen of the greatest city with the greatest reputation for both wisdom and power; are you not ashamed of your eagerness to possess as much wealth, reputation and honours as possible, while you do not care for nor give thought to wisdom or truth, or the best possible state of your soul?" Then, if one of you disputes this and says he does care, I shall not let him go at once or leave him, but I shall question him, examine him and test him, and if I do not think he has attained the goodness that he says he has, I shall reproach him because he attaches little importance to the most important things (30) and greater importance to inferior things. I shall treat in this way anyone I happen to meet, young and old, citizen and stranger, and more so the citizens because you are more kindred to me. Be sure that this is what the god orders me to do, and I think there is no greater blessing for the city than my service to the god. For I go around doing nothing but persuading both young and old among you not to care for your body or your wealth in preference to or as strongly as for the best possible state of your soul, as I say to you: "Wealth does not bring about excellence, but excellence brings about wealth and all other public and private blessings for men.". . .

(31c)   It may seem strange that while I go around and give this advice privately and interfere in private affairs, I do not venture to go to the assembly and there advise the city. You have heard me give the reason for this in many places. I have a divine sign from the god which [my accuser] Meletus has ridiculed in his deposition. This began when I was a child. It is a voice, and whenever it speaks it turns me away from something I am about to do, but it never encourages me to do anything. This is what has prevented me from taking part in public affairs, and I think it was quite right to prevent me. Be sure, gentlemen of the jury, that if I had long ago attempted to take part in politics, I should have died long ago, and benefited neither you nor myself. Do not be angry with me for speaking the truth; no man will survive who genuinely opposes you or any other crowd and prevents the occurrence of many unjust and illegal happenings in the city. A man who really fights for justice (32) must lead a private, not a public, life if he is to survive for even a short time.

The Aristotelian Constitution of the Athenians

The Revolutions of 411 and 404

In the following selections the author of the Aristotelian *Constitution of the Athenians* provides a brief history of the oligarchical revolutions of 411 and 404.

(29.1) As long as the war was evenly balanced, the Athenians preserved the democracy. But when, after the disaster in Sicily [in 413], the Spartan side was strengthened through its alliance with the Persian king, they were compelled to interfere with the democracy and set up the constitution of the Four Hundred [in 411], the speech introducing the decree was made by Melobius, and the motion stood in the name of Pythodorus of Anaphlystus. The many were persuaded especially by the thought that the King would be more likely to fight on their side if they based the constitution on a few men. (2) Pythodorus's decree was as follows. 'The people shall elect, in addition to the ten commissioners already in existence, a further twenty from the citizens over forty years old; these shall take an oath to draft such proposals as they believe to be in the best interests of the city, and shall draft proposals with a view to the city's safety. It shall be open also to anyone else who wishes to submit proposals, so that the committee may choose the best of all the proposals that are made.' (3) Clitophon moved that in other respects Pythodorus's proposal should be followed, but that the men elected should also search out the traditional laws which Cleisthenes had enacted when he set up the democracy, so that they might consider these too and deliberate for the best—his point being that Cleisthenes' constitution was not populist but very much like Solon's. (4) The men who were elected proposed first that it should be obligatory for the *prytaneis*

From Aristotle, *The Athenian Constitution*, edited and translated by P. J. Rhodes, pp. 73–75, 79–80, 85–86 (Harmondsworth: Penguin, 1984). Reproduced by permission Frederick Warne & Co.

to put to the vote all proposals that should be made for the safety of Athens. Then they suspended the prosecutions for illegal proposal, the denunciations and the summonses, so that those Athenians who wished might be free to deliberate on the matters laid before them; if on account of these matters anyone imposed a penalty, made a summons or brought a case into court, he should be liable to indication and delivery before the generals, and the generals should hand him over to the Eleven to be put to death. (5) After this they organized the constitution in the following way. It should not be permitted to spend Athens' revenues for any purpose other than the war; and all officials should serve without stipends for the duration of the war, apart from the nine archons and whatever *prytaneis* there might be, who should each receive three obols a day. Otherwise the whole control of the state should be entrusted to the Athenians best able to serve with their persons and their wealth, being not less than five thousand in number, for the duration of the war: this body of men should have full power to make treaties with whoever they wished. Ten men over forty years old should be chosen from each tribe, should swear an oath over sacred victims, and should draw up a register of the Five Thousand. . . .

(34.1) [The Five Thousand replaced the Four Hundred in 411.] The people soon took away their control of the state [in 410]. In . . . the archonship of Callias of Angele [406/5], the sea-battle of Arginusae was fought. After that, first, the ten generals who had won the battle were all condemned in a single vote, though some had not taken part in the battle and others had lost their own ships and had been saved by other ships: the people were deceived by those who stirred up their anger. Secondly, when the Spartans were willing to evacuate Decelea and make peace on the terms that each side should retain what it currently possessed, some were eager to accept but the masses were not: they were deceived by Cleophon, who prevented them from making peace by going into the assembly drunk and wearing his breastplate, and saying that he would not allow it unless the Spartans surrendered all the cities that they had taken. (2) The Athenians mismanaged affairs then, and not long afterwards they discovered their mistake. In the following year, the archonship of Alexias [405/4], they lost the sea-battle of Aegospotami, and as a result of that Lysander [of Sparta] became master of the city, and set up the Thirty in the following manner. (3) Peace had been made on condition that the Athenians should live under their traditional constitution. The democrats tried to preserve the democracy; of the notables those who belonged to the clubs and the exiles who had returned after the peace treaty were eager for oligarchy; those who did not belong to any club and who in other respects seemed inferior to none of the citizens had as their objective the traditional constitution: these last included Archinus, Anytus, Clitophon, Phormisius and many others, but their particular champion was Theramenes. Lysander gave his support to the oligarchs, and the people were intimidated and compelled to decide in favour of the oligarchy. The author of the decree was Dracontides of Aphidna.

(35.1)   In this way the Thirty were established, in the archonship of Pythodorus [404/3]. Having become masters of the city, they ignored the other resolutions about the constitution, but appointed five hundred councillors and the other officials from a short list of a thousand, and to support themselves chose ten governors of the Piraeus, eleven guardians of the gaol and three hundred attendants armed with whips; thus they gained control of the city. (2) At first they were moderate towards the citizens, and pretended that their aim was the traditional constitution. They took down from the Areopagus hill the laws of Ephialtes and Archestratus about the council of the Areopagus; and they annulled the laws of Solon which provided scope for disagreement, and the discretionary power which was left to jurors, in order to amend the constitution and leave no opportunity for disagreement. For instance, in the matter of a man's bequeathing his property to whoever he likes, the Thirty gave the testator full and absolute power, and removed the attached difficulties ('except when he is insane or senile, or under the influence of a woman'), so that there should be no way in for malicious prosecutors; and they did likewise in the other cases. (3) That is how they behaved at first. They eliminated malicious prosecutors, and those who curried favour with the people contrary to what was best and were harmful and wicked; and the city was pleased with these achievements, thinking that the Thirty were acting from good motives. (4) But when they had a firmer hold on the city they left none of the citizens alone, but put to death those who were outstanding for their wealth, birth or reputation, cunningly removing those whom they had cause to fear and whose property they wanted to plunder. Within a short space of time they had killed no fewer than fifteen hundred. . . .

[A group of Athenians defeated and deposed the Thirty, and a reconciliation was brought about with the help of the Spartan King Pausanias, who allowed democracy to be re-established.]

(41.1)   That final reconciliation took place subsequently. Meanwhile the people gained control of affairs and set up the present constitution, in the archonship of Pythodorus [404/3]: the people's taking political power seems justifiable, since it was the people themselves who achieved their return. (2) This was the eleventh of the changes in the constitution. . . . [and this] constitution has continued to that in force today, continually increasing the power of the masses. The people have made themselves masters of everything, and control all things by means of decrees and jury-courts, in which the sovereign power resides with the people; even the jurisdiction of the council has been transferred to the people. The Athenians seem to be right to follow this line, for it is easier to corrupt the few than the many, whether by money or by favours. (3) At first they decided not to pay stipends for attendance at the assembly. But when men were staying away from the assembly, and the *prytaneis* were trying various devices to bring the masses in to ratify the voting, first Agyrrhius provided for the payment of one obol, after him Heraclides of Clazomenae, the man known as 'king', raised it to two obols, and then Agyrrhius again raised it to three obols.

Analysis

Donald Kagan

The Revolutionary Movement

Modern scholars have little sympathy for the oligarchical revolutionaries who overthrew the Athenian democracy in 411 and 404. Nonetheless, in the following passage Donald Kagan attempts to place the movement within the historical context of fifth-century Greece, where democracy certainly was not considered the only reasonable or fair form of government, and where Athens constituted an exception to many norms of Greek politics. Some of the oligarchs, moreover, had legitimate concerns about the exhausted public finances, the nature of the democracy, and the war (they maintained) it had foisted upon Athens.

In 411 the Athenians entered the hundredth year since the expulsion of tyranny and the establishment of their freedom. For almost that entire period, since the reforms of Cleisthenes in 508/7, they had enjoyed a democratic constitution, moderate at first and more complete since the changes introduced by Ephialtes and Pericles toward the middle of the century. The passage of time and the growth of Athenian power and prosperity under the democracy had dampened almost all interest in trying to destroy it and replace it with oligarchy, the most common form of government among the Greeks. From time to time there were rumors of oligarchic plots, but none even reached the stage of action. Most Athenians of the upper class accepted the democracy, either vying for leadership within it or standing aloof from politics, although almost all leading Athenian politicians until the Peloponnesian War were of noble birth.

Yet hostility to the idea and reality of democracy did not disappear. Greek tradition, after all, was overwhelmingly aristocratic. The epics of Homer, the most widely known and influential works of all Greek literature, presented a world whose values were entirely aristocratic. It was for the nobles to make decisions and give orders and for the commoners to know their place and obey. The poems of Theognis of Megara reflected the bitterness of aristocrats whose world was overthrown by the political and social upheavals of the sixth century, and his words and ideas were remembered and had a powerful influence on enemies of democracy well into the fourth century, when they were quoted with approval by Plato. Theognis divided mankind into two distinct types: the good and noble and the bad and base. The distinction is based on birth and establishes a clear and firm tie between social status and virtue. The noble alone possesses judgment *(gnome)* and reverence *(aidos)*; therefore, the noble alone is capable of moderation, restraint, and justice. These are qualities enjoyed by few, and the many who are without them, who lack judgment and reverence, are necessarily shameless and arrogant. The good qualities, moreover, are acquired only by birth; they cannot be taught: "It is easier to beget and rear a man than to put good sense into him. No one has ever discovered a way to make a fool wise or a bad man good. . . . If thought could be made and put into a man, the son of a good man would never become bad since he would obey good counsel. But you will never make the bad man good by teaching."

The Theban poet Pindar, "the Voice of Aristocracy" as Werner Jaeger has called him, must have exercised an even greater influence on the Athenian upper classes. He lived past the middle of the fifth century, and his odes celebrated the athletic triumphs in the games that were so important in aristocratic culture. His message was much the same as that of Theognis: the nobly born were inherently superior to the mass of people intellectually and morally, and the difference could not be erased by education.

> *The splendor running in the blood has much weight.*
> *A man can learn and yet see darkly, blow one way,*
> *then another, walking ever*
> *on uncertain feet, his mind unfinished and*
> *fed with scraps of a thousand virtues. [Pindar Nem. 3.40–42]*

The capacity for understanding is innate. Only the natively wise can comprehend his poetry and other important things:

> *There are many sharp shafts*
> *   in the quiver*
> *under the crook of my arm.*
> *They speak to the understanding; most men need*
> *   interpreters.*
> *The wise man knows many things in his blood; the*
> *   vulgar are taught.*
> *They will say anything. They clatter vainly like*
> *crows against the sacred bird of Zeus. [Pindar Ol. 2.86–87]*

The implication of these beliefs is that democracy is, at the very least, unwise. To some, it would have seemed unfair and immoral as well.

In the fourth century, Plato and Aristotle must have been repeating old complaints when they pointed out the unfairness of democracy: "it distributes a sort of equality to equal and unequal alike"; democratic justice is "the enjoyment of arithmetical equality, and not the enjoyment of proportionate equality on the basis of merit." These views, appearing in philosophical works of the fourth century, show that the old idea of the natural and permanent separation between the deserving and undeserving classes distinguished by Theognis and Pindar lasted through and beyond the war. . . .

By the 420s time and change had altered the basis of distinguishing the classes. Whereas noble birth had been the criterion for Theognis and Pindar, the importance of money in shaping morality and political competence was emphasized by the author of the *Athenian Constitution* [of Pseudo-Xenophon (1.5), see Part I]. . . . There can be no doubt that the author and men of his class had thought carefully about what a good constitution, in contrast to democracy, would be. What they wanted was *eunomia*, the name Tyrtaeus had given to the Spartan constitution and that Pindar had applied to the oligarchy of Corinth. In such a constitution the best and most qualified men will make the laws. The good men *(chrestoi)* will punish the bad *(poneroi)*; only the *chrestoi* will deliberate about public affairs, "and they will not allow madmen to sit in the council or speak in the assembly. But as a result of these good measures the people would, of course, fall into servitude." The author understands, therefore, that bad government *(kakonomia)*, democracy, that is, is in the interest of the people, and he expects them to act in their own interest to preserve it. "But anybody who without belonging to the people prefers living in a town under democratic rule to living in one oligarchically has prepared himself for being immoral, well knowing that it is easier for a bad person to remain unnoticed in a town under democratic than in one under oligarchic rule." These words leave no doubt that the author and men like him regarded the overthrow of the democracy and its replacement by a better constitution as a moral obligation, but when he wrote, the democracy seemed secure and unshakable.

By 411 the practical problems facing the democracy, its failures, and its blunders intensified discontent with its institutions at the same time that they provided the opportunity to attack them. The removal from the scene of respected leaders such as Cimon, Pericles, and even Nicias and their replacement by the likes of Cleon, Hyperbolus, and even the nobly born but personally disreputable Alcibiades made democratic rule harder for noblemen to accept. The absence of strong, respected political leaders created and intensified divisions among the Athenians. In 411 the vacuum of leadership seems to have been filled increasingly by the *hetairiai*, the clubs that played an ever more important part in Athenian politics, especially among the enemies of democracy.

The members of these clubs, as well as others in the propertied classes, had borne and were still bearing unprecedented financial burdens. The costs of waging the war were higher than in the earlier years because of the existence of a Peloponnesian navy that threatened the Athenians' empire and food supply and required them to keep as large a fleet as possible at sea the year round. Meanwhile, the expenditure from the public treasury to civilians had not diminished but probably had increased. At the same time, public revenue was severely curtailed by rebellions of tribute-paying allies and the reduction of income from customs duties caused by the war's interference with commerce. The problem was made more intense by a reduction in the number of Athenians wealthy enough to assume the financial burden of religious and military services required by the state. On the eve of the war in 431, the number of Athenian men of hoplite census or above, the status required for eligibility to perform these liturgies, may have been as high as 25,000. By 411 the great plague and war casualties, especially the losses in Sicily, seem to have reduced that number to about 9,000. Neither figure is either precise or secure; yet any reasonable adjustment will still reveal a stunning diminution in the number of Athenians available in 411 to pay the state's expenses.

Those expenses must have been very high if the speeches that have come down to us under the name of Lysias are any indication. In one of them, a certain Aristophanes is said to have spent almost 15 talents on public services, including payments of the special war taxes, and service as trierarch. In another the speaker recounts his expenditures for the years 411/10 to 404/3, a total of almost 10 talents. His list provides us with evidence of the variety of public obligations imposed upon Athens' wealthier citizens: he produced tragic and comic dramas; paid for choral competitions, dancers, athletic contests, and trireme races; equipped six triremes for battle in seven years; and during that time twice contributed his share of the *eisphora* [property tax]. . . . There is good reason to think that the fortunes of many Athenian families were seriously reduced by public services during the Peloponnesian War. By 411, and especially in the years since the Sicilian disaster, the unprecedented expense would already have been strongly felt, and it would not take much imagination for the propertied classes to see that there would be similar and even greater demands in the future.

The moral standing of the democratic regime, the alleged foolishness of its policies and incompetence of their execution, the decline in the quality of leadership, and the heavy burden of public financial obligations were all problems of long standing for those Athenians skeptical of the democracy, although all of them were intensified in the years after Sicily. The new element in 411 was the dismal prospect for success or even survival in the war against the Peloponnesians. The dismay after the Sicilian disaster had quickly given way to determination and action. The Athenian response to rebellion in the empire had been remarkably successful and seemed to be on the point of stamping it out entirely. Had the Athenian forces been able to recover Miletus and Chios, the Persians might well have decided that the reports of Athens' imminent demise had been greatly exaggerated and withdrawn their support from the Peloponnesians, putting an end to Sparta's Aegean adventure and the threat to the Athenian Empire.

That opportunity, however, had been lost. . . . Instead, the rebellion had spread to the Hellespont and threatened the Athenian lifeline. The emergency reserve fund was gone, and the treasury was empty. Tissaphernes had healed the breach with the Spartans and promised to bring the Phoenician fleet into action against the Athenians. Finally, the Spartans had gained a foothold on the Hellespont and threatened to cut Athens' supply lines and win the war. The installation of *probouloi* [a special board created to advise the state, including Sophocles] in 413 had already changed the democratic constitution to a degree. In the face of these difficulties and dangers, it would not be surprising to find many Athenians in favor of further change in the domestic situation, some curtailment of democratic practices, a more efficient arrangement, and perhaps even a change of regime.

David Stockton

Violent Opposition

Among the works of David Stockton is a recent treatment of *The Classical Athenian Democracy*. In the following selection from that work, Stockton argues that real oligarchical sentiment (on a theoretical level)

From David Stockton, *The Classical Athenian Democracy*. Copyright © 1990 Oxford University Press. Reprinted by permission of Oxford University Press.

was in short supply in Athens and that the revolutionaries of 411 and 404/3 acted primarily on the basis of self-interest. The revolutions, in his view, help to demonstrate the depth of feeling most Athenians had for their democracy.

[Until] recently there was a widespread tendency to talk about oligarchs and an "oligarchic party" in post-Ephialtic Athens—for all that what had been in existence for some forty or so years before those reforms was not any sort of approach to an oligarchy but the broadly based Cleisthenic democracy. Yet our earliest contemporary witness, the "Old Oligarch" . . . who wrote his brief pamphlet at some indeterminate date in the 430s or 420s, evidently recognized that oligarchy or anything like it was a "non-starter" in his Athens. It was only in the wake of the massive disaster at Syracuse in 413 that anti-democrats could even begin to envisage the subversion of the democracy as a practicable objective; and even then those extremists had to take care to put down a thick smoke-screen to conceal their true objective so as to have any hope of securing the support of what we may call "moderate" Athenians. When we see the oligarchic revolutionaries of 411 themselves acknowledging the widespread unpalatability of oligarchy at Athens, who are we to question or contradict them? And the quick demise of their hopes, although they were led by able, well-organized, cunning, ruthless, and unscrupulous men in circumstances which could scarcely have been more favourable to their enterprise, further underlines the strength of the hold which the democracy had over the vast majority of citizens of all classes and conditions. Seven years later, the brief life of the narrow oligarchy of the Thirty, which had been imposed by her enemies on a defeated and helpless Athens, attests that same truth.

As some scholars have rightly insisted, it is misleading to seek to draw over-sharp distinctions between classes and sectional interests at Athens. Thucydides (2.65.2) observed that both rich and poor were united in their displeasure with Pericles in 430. . . . Nor is there much to support the superficially plausible view that the country-dwellers were against the war, in that they suffered more, and more directly, from the enemy incursions, while the city-dwellers were in favour of the war because they had no farms or orchards to abandon to sack, pillage, and neglect, and could themselves find ready overseas markets for their products or regular employment in the fleet and so on while enjoying all the material advantages of the "empire" which kept Athens rich and powerful. The country-dwellers constituted a majority of the citizen body, and hence could both influence public policy through their more numerous representatives on the *boulê* and determine it by their own personal votes in the *ecclêsia*, especially at the times when for periods of several weeks on end they were crowded within the girdle of the Long Walls during the yearly evacuations when they sought refuge from the enemy invasions. The reaction of the Acharnians, who lived among the foothills of Mt. Parnes on the northern edge of the central plain of Attica, was an eagerness to sally forth and engage the enemy rather than sit tight and watch while their properties were being overrun, . . . and though during the first invasion Pericles somehow contrived to prevent any meetings of the *ecclêsia* itself or other semi-formal gatherings while the enemy army was in Attica, it was not because he feared that a majority in the *ecclêsia* would be eager to come to terms but because he was worried that they might unwisely vote to take the field against a superior enemy. Only a few years later, when Aristophanes wanted to caricature the sort of Athenians most apt to be upset by his hero Dicaeopolis' private and personal peace-making activities, he picked these same Acharnians for the role [*Acharnians*, 425 B.C.]. . . . Every Athenian shared in the distress and privations consequent on the overcrowding within the Long Walls and from the Great Plague which carried off about one-third of Athens' hoplite strength and presumably at least as high a proportion of the other inhabitants. The prosperity of Athens was indivisible, with the country cultivators and craftsmen owing their well-being to the external power of Athens as much as did the "townees." (Indeed, the five demes which lay physically within the city walls sent fewer than thirty members to the Council of Five Hundred, the Peiraeus added a further nine, and three other demes which we can readily class as genuinely suburban contributed nine more, a total of forty-five or forty-six between them. That seems to show that the registered members of all these demes together constituted well under a tenth of the whole citizen body.) The rich also derived a considerable material advantage from the Athenian "empire" in that it gave them the opportunity to acquire profitable property holdings in the wide areas under their city's control. . . .

The events of 411 are excellent evidence of the strength of the hold which the democracy had at Athens. At a time of acute crisis and with the possibility of defeat staring the Athenians in the face after their appalling losses in Sicily; with the appearance in the Aegean of a powerful enemy fleet and a number of Athens' more important "allies" in revolt and affording ships, men, money, supplies, and bases to assist its operations; with the renewed activity of a Persia poised to intervene decisively with ships and subsidies; with a bankrupt treasury (the last "supreme emergency" special reserve of 1,000 talents had had to be released early in 412, and had been exhausted within one year); and with an anti-democratic movement ably led and cunningly and ruthlessly executed—with all that in their favour, the plotters clearly perceived that their only chance of succeeding lay in violence and intimidation, and above all in the lying pretence that they aimed at no more than a limited change designed to concentrate resources on the conduct of the war and to last only for the duration of the emergency. Within a few months the Four Hundred had collapsed, and the moderate régime of the Five Thousand which took their place endured for no more than a further eight months at most.

Nevertheless, 411 bred consequences which were to have a divisive and debilitating effect on Athens' conduct of a war which was not yet irretrievably lost. Knives were unsheathed as scores were settled; men were heavily fined, or wholly or partly deprived of their citizen rights. As Lysias subsequently wryly observed, to judge by the number of those alleged to have been members of the Four Hundred there must have been nearly a thousand of them! Athens was not only divided, she was also pickling a rod for her own back against the day when Sparta's final victory in 404 was to give frightened and embittered men the opportunity to get their revenge.

Under the command of the brilliant and charismatic Alcibiades, Athens' navy began to pull away from near disaster. The serious defeat which it inflicted on the Spartan fleet at Cyzicus restored confidence and eased the financial crisis a little. But the restoration of the full democracy shortly afterwards and the reintroduction of state payment for civilian services could not but exacerbate the financial difficulties, and Alcibiades' enemies had not been reconciled to him. For the moment he was too popular and successful to be attacked directly, but they could seek to hamper him: they starved him of money and reinforcements to follow up his victory at Cyzicus and secure the Hellespont, the life-line of Athens. Byzantium was not recaptured until the autumn of 408; and in the following spring the Persians at last came down off the fence and committed their vast resources to the whole-hearted support of Sparta. As Alcibiades' string of successes tailed off, the recollection of his erstwhile opportunism and self-centered treachery (he had taken himself off to Sparta when recalled from the early stages of the Sicilian expedition, and given her unstinted and expert help against his mother city, and then worked hand in glove with the Four Hundred in the early stages of their activity) became more vivid. After his failure to capture Andros, and the severe drubbing which his fleet received from the Spartan admiral Lysander in his absence, he was relieved of his command, and once again took himself off into exile. One last naval victory was won by Athens at Arginusae in 406, but the end was near.

Arginusae is a black mark on the Athenian democracy. Losses in ships and men had been heavy, and rightly or wrongly the conviction spread that many of the crews of the twenty-five warships which had gone down could have been rescued if only the *stratêgoi* ["generals"] had shown more energy and efficiency. Feelings ran high, and the eight men who had commanded at Arginusae were arraigned before the *ecclêsia*; two of them had made themselves scarce, but the other six (among them Thrasylus, one of the leaders of the "counter-revolution" on Samos in 411, and Pericles, son of the great Pericles) were condemned to death and their property escheated to the state. The nastiest feature of the proceedings was a departure from accepted practice which meant that the accused were tried *en bloc* without each being able to present an individual defence. By a curious coincidence, Socrates was one of the *prytaneis* presiding over the *ecclêsia*, and he stoutly objected to this irregularity. But the enraged assembly was not to be denied.

The incident shows the democracy in an ugly light. But sweeping condemnations are out of place. Athens' plight was desperate, and nerves were unstrung as the outlook grew bleaker and defeat more likely. The irregularities were untypical; and those who want to use them to condemn the whole system would do well to remember that instances of cavalier injustice are more frequently encountered under less broadly based systems. The "trial of the generals" pales into insignificance against the background of the murderous excesses of "the Thirty," to look no further afield than fifth-century Athens herself.

In the late summer of 405 the Spartan Lysander's doggedly correct strategy of attrition bore fruit when Athens' last fleet, incompetently commanded and dispirited, starved of money and supplies, was surprised and overwhelmed at Aegospotami: of its 180 triremes, a bare twenty managed to escape. As the noose was drawn tighter round the throat of her supply routes, Athens was starved into surrender within a matter of months.

Sparta had no love for democracies, and Lysander himself was all for very narrow oligarchies. Athens was obliged to readmit her exiles. Intimidated by Lysander and an occupying garrison in the Piraeus, the *ecclêsia* was constrained to authorize the establishment of a commission of thirty men to draft new laws. They were in control by about midsummer 404, and appointed a new Council of Five Hundred and a special commission of ten to supervise the dangerously radical port of Piraeus. They also packed the eleven-man "police commission" with their own sympathizers, headed by the thuggish Satyros. A number of citizens, among them generals and junior officers, had a little earlier formed a plot to try to stave off the extremists; they had been betrayed and arrested, and were now given a trumpery trial before the new Council and executed out of hand.

To begin with the Thirty masked their extremism. Their early destruction of the laws of Ephialtes can have been little more than symbolic, for it is plain that they would never have been content simply to return to the pre-Ephialtic system. Returned exiles, prominent among them Critias (one of the Four Hundred, who had taken himself off to Thessaly), were well represented among the Thirty; not surprisingly, some of the more active of the professional accusers who had been busy since 411 were put to death. During the autumn of 404, to safeguard their next moves, a Spartan garrison of 700 arrived in Athens; the cost of maintaining it fell on the Thirty, at whose request it had been sent, and was met by further condemnations and confiscations.

Theramenes had negotiated Athens' surrender and the peace treaty. Like Critias, he had been a member of the Four Hundred; but, unlike him, he had got out in time and had then played a prominent part in Athenian politics for the rest of the war. He is not an easy man to fathom; his shifts and changes earned him the sobriquet of "Mr Facing-both-ways," but whether he was simply a selfish opportunist or a flexible and realistic "moderate" it is now impossible to determine. Whichever he was, he set out to challenge Critias' dominance among the Thirty. His opposition to the invitation of the Spartan garrison, whose presence in Athens gave Critias and his friends the confidence to step up the tempo of terror and executions, had proved unavailing; and, to his objection that the government was too narrowly based, Critias responded by drawing up a list of three thousand citizens who alone should have full rights, including the right of trial before the Council: anybody not on that list could be executed without trial on the order of the Thirty. Theramenes still stubbornly maintained that three thousand were too few to constitute a secure basis for a lasting oligarchy; Critias countered by calling a general muster and then by a simple ruse separating all but the three thousand from their weapons, which were removed and stored under guard on the Acropolis.

Now free from any constraint; the Thirty extended their *pogrom* of murder and sequestrations yet more widely. Among their projects was one to single out thirty of the richest metics (resident aliens) for execution and give their property to each of themselves. Theramenes refused pointblank to have any part in it, and Critias moved in for the kill. Theramenes was arraigned before the Council of Five Hundred; and when his spirited defence threatened to win them over Critias, backed by a gang of armed men, formally struck his name from the list of the three thousand. The Council was too frightened to resist, and Theramenes was led off to be executed "by order of the Thirty." He made a good end: as he drained the fatal cup of hemlock, as if making a toast at a wine-party among friends, he tossed the last drop away saying, "Here's to the health of our dear Critias!" . . .

On top of crippling losses of life in battle against the enemy and in civil war, Athens had suffered terribly from disease and famine, violent disruption and brutal insecurity. Her citizens were stricken with all the despondency and disillusion that are the natural concomitants of losing a long war and a great empire. A yearning to forget the past, to try to pick up the pieces and get back to some sort of regular and reliable normality, was only to be expected. For all that, it is not so much the moderation of the settlement (which owed a great deal to Sparta's moderating influence over all the parties to it) but rather the honesty with which the amnesty was observed in the years that followed which constitutes an achievement of which any society could be justifiably proud. The Athenians were certainly not saints; and for decades to come we find men anxious to win favour or avoid unpopularity by dissociating themselves or their families from any part in the excesses of the anti-democrats. As many as sixty years later, Aeschines is heard insisting that his father, still alive at the age of ninety-four, had left Athens under the Thirty and helped in the restoration of the democracy. Their experiences in 411 and 404/3 had left the overwhelming bulk of the Athenians with a decided taste for their democratic system. Isocrates averred that, while the shortcomings of the earlier democratic politicians had made even the *dêmos* itself favourably inclined towards the ideas of the Four Hundred, the mad excesses of the Thirty had made everyone even more enthusiastic for democracy than the small band who had first seized Phylae [and then attacked the Thirty]. Plato, who was anything but a believer in or apologist for democracy, himself wrote that the rule of the Thirty (among whom two of his own close relatives had been prominent) had had the effect of making the democracy which had preceded it seem in retrospect like a Golden Age. Democracy was never again threatened during the next eighty years; and in 321 it was not any internal movement but the irresistible military might of Macedon which brought it down.

Kurt A. Raaflaub

A Hypothetical Debate About Democracy

In the following selection from his article on "Contemporary Perceptions of Democracy in Fifth-Century Athens," Kurt A. Raaflaub has collected views on democracy and oligarchy from various sources to reconstruct what no ancient work has provided us, a debate between an oligarch and a democrat on the merits and faults of their preferred forms of government.

In the last part of my paper I shall assemble the elements used at some point or other in the debate about democracy but scattered in various sources, in a "composite picture" by reconstructing a hypothetical de-

Kurt A. Raaflaub, "Contemporary Perceptions of Democracy in Fifth-Century Athens," in *Aspects of Athenian Democracy, Classica et Mediaevalia Dissertationes* XI. Copyright © 1990 Museum Tusculanum Press. Reprinted by permission of the publisher.

bate between oligarchs and democrats as it might have taken place in the last third of the fifth century. Although this may seem slightly frivolous, it offers a good way of combining and contrasting the arguments, of showing whether or not responses were available to any given criticism and how serious and specific such responses were, and of demonstrating how broad the range of arguments was and how far it exceeded those incorporated in the formal debates and comparisons discussed at the beginning of this paper. Only such arguments have been incorporated that are explicitly attested or can be claimed with certainty for the fifth century.

OLIGARCH: What is called *demokratia*, rule by the *demos*, really represents government by one part of the citizens only, namely the masses, the rabble. Such government is one-sided, partisan, serving only the interests of the ruling crowds. Thereby the upper classes, being a minority, are prevented from playing the kind of predominant role that befits their social status (Ps.Xen. *Ath. Pol.* 1.1ff.; 2.20). Indeed, it would not be exaggerated to say that the few, although being part of the community, are completely overpowered, virtually "enslaved," by the entire mass of citizens (Thuc. 4.86.4). As a consequence, it is unnatural and suspicious if someone who does not belong to the *demos* prefers to live in a democratic rather than an oligarchic city (Ps.Xen. 2.20).

DEMOCRAT: Well, the constitution is called *demokratia* for another reason, namely because power is not in the hand of a few but of the majority (Thuc. 2.37.1). Indeed, the *demos* is sovereign and lord (Eur. *Suppl.* 352, 406; *Cycl.* 119). But *demos* encompasses the entire city; democracy therefore means that all citizens make decisions and share political responsibility by voting in the assembly (Eur. *Suppl.* 349, 351f.; Herod. 3.80.6; Thuc. 6.39.1; Aesch. *Suppl.* 366–70, 483f., 601, 607, 964) and taking annual turns in holding office (Eur. *Suppl.* 406f.). No one is excluded; whoever has good advice to give has the right to do so and is praised for it (Eur. *Suppl.* 438–41). When it is a question of holding public responsibility, no one is turned away because he belongs to a certain class (whether high or low), and merit is certainly rewarded (Thuc. 2.37.1; 6.39.1). Thus in democracy everybody is not only allowed to participate but expected to contribute whatever he can as long as it is useful to the community (Ps.Xen. 1.2, 6; Thuc. 2.37.1; Eur. *Suppl.* 439). In fact, it is only in democracy that a citizen who does not participate in politics is considered not just

one who minds his own business *(apragmon)* but one who is useless
(Thuc. 2.40.2). But the oligarchs do not want the majority to be involved. They only share out the dangers; the profits they keep to
themselves (Thuc. 6.39.2).

OLIGARCH: It is not strange, then, that the *demos* wants no
share in those—certainly dangerous—offices like the generalship or
cavalry command in which competence is decisive for the safety or
danger of the entire people, but is keen to hold those magistracies
which are salaried and domestically profitable (Ps.Xen. 1.3)? At any
rate, what the oligarchs really want is that those who contribute most
to the needs of their city both financially and physically (i.e., the
wealthy ones and those fighting as hoplites) should be fully in charge.

DEMOCRAT: But this is precisely why it is justified that in
democracy the poor and the ordinary people should fully participate
in politics and have more power than the noble and rich; for it is the
ordinary people who man the fleet and bring the city her power
(Ps.Xen. 1.1). Moreover, even Aeschylus supports the view that those
who have to bear the consequences of decisions—particularly if these
are concerned with war and the safety of the whole community—
should share the responsibility for them *(Suppl.,* e.g., 365–69,
398–401). As a consequence, the citizens will not only feel goodwill
towards their leaders (Eur. *Suppl.* 349–51) but also devote all their
energy to the common good because they will know that they are
toiling not for a master but for themselves. Despite all this, in the
oligarchs' wonderful well-ordered state *(eunomia)* the many are
excluded from participation, government and power: inevitably, they
are enslaved by the few (Ps.Xen. 1.9; Thuc. 4.86.4). Thus participation in government and control of power by the people is the only
way to protect their liberty: democracy satisfies this elementary
need; democracy is freedom! (Ps.Xen. 1.8; Eur. *Suppl.* 352f., 404–8,
438–41; Thuc. 2.37.2; cf. again the classic formulation by Aristot. *Pol.*
1317a 40ff.).

OLIGARCH: Indeed, it is not difficult to define a well-ordered
state *(eunomia):* it is one in which the best establish the laws in their
own interest, determine the policy of their city, keep the lower classes
under tight control and do not allow crazy people to participate in
deliberation or discussion or even sit in the assembly (Ps.Xen. 1.9).
Democracy, on the other hand, is the model of a badly ordered state
(kakonomia) which they deliberately put up with because, as they say,

it preserves the power and freedom of the people (Ps.Xen. 1.7f.). However, what they call liberty, is crazy, excessive (Ps.Xen. 1.10–12 aims in the same direction; it is a frequent motive in the 4th century!), a nice cover word for anarchy and lawlessness. When they claim that nothing but free birth is needed to qualify for citizenship in democracy—by which they mean, of course, that only descent from citizen parents, no additional criteria are required—they describe as free what is not at all free. Men who have to earn their living and depend on others for their livelihood cannot possibly be called free. Really free are only those who have sufficient means to devote themselves to liberal occupations, a liberal education, and service to the community. Those are the truly free who deserve to be called "free citizens" and who alone should enjoy full citizen rights.

DEMOCRAT: On the contrary, by taking all citizens seriously in their capacity as free men, democracy offers them a supportive and humane environment and gives them the opportunity to develop their personality freely (Thuc. 2.41.1). In the democratic city social and political life is characterized by freedom, mutual respect and harmony (Thuc. 2.37.2). Such freedom is the hallmark not only of democracy as a constitution but also of its institutional elements, among which the right of each citizen to speak in the assembly undoubtedly is the most important (Eur. *Suppl.* 238–41).

OLIGARCH: It still is true that democrats tend to confuse insolence with democracy, lawlessness with liberty, impudence of speech *(parrhesia)* with political equality *(isonomia)* and licence to do whatever they want with happiness. In short, democracy is not known for its respect for law.

DEMOCRAT: Wrong! Except for one point: of course, democrats are proud of the freedom they enjoy to live as they like (cf. Thuc. 7.69.2; the argument is included in 2.37.1f.; the classic formulation is Aristot. *Pol.* 1317b 11–13). But otherwise, no constitution is so conscious of institutional safeguards, strict adherence to the rules (Thuc. 6.38.5) and, particularly, the accountability of office holders (Herod. 3.80.6). Indeed, democracy does respect the law; the citizens obey both the written and unwritten laws and those who happen to hold office (2.37.3). Moreover, it is precisely the fact that laws are published and thus common property of the community that fully establishes equality before the law and gives the poor a chance to stand up against the rich (Eur. *Suppl.* 429–37). Such equality among all citizens is the basic principle of democracy; it affects the selection for office — therefore the importance of the lot (Herod. 3.80.6) —, rotation in office (Eur. *Suppl.* 406–8), voting (ibid., 352f.), and speaking in the assembly (ibid., 438–41). It is only natural, therefore, that *demokratia* can easily be replaced by *isonomia* — the most beautiful name of all (Herod. 3.80.6) — or even *isegoria* (Herod. 5.78).

OLIGARCH: This is precisely what is so objectionable: democracy is neither an intelligent nor a fair system because it imposes the principles of such superficial equality on everybody and unfairly limits the opportunities of the wealthy. Political equality should be restricted to those who are really equal; one should not treat equals and unequals alike (Thuc. 6.38.5–39.1).

DEMOCRAT: But all citizens are equal in essential ways. It would not be just not to consider the same worthy of the same rights (Thuc. 6.38.5).

OLIGARCH: The fact is, of course, that they are not the same. Oligarchy means government by the noble, wealthy, educated, capable, experienced and morally superior (Ps.Xen. 1.5ff.); a system based on the rule of the best necessarily must be good (Herod. 3.81.3). Democracy, by contrast, is dominated by the poor, base, uneducated, incapable and irresponsible masses (Ps.Xen. 1.1ff.; Herod. 3.81.1f.). They even go so far as to consider the advice of the man on the street who, though incompetent, at least shows goodwill towards his peers, more advantageous and in their interest than the advice of the better ones or the clever intellectuals (Ps.Xen. 1.7; cf. Cleon in Thuc. 3.37.3). The fact is that those who make up the *demos* simply are not qualified to take on political responsibility, and even if they had the brains for it they would still lack the time for politics (Eur. *Suppl.* 417ff.). Where the *kakoi* ["bad"] dominate, evil necessarily creeps in and things must turn out badly (Herod. 3.82.4).

DEMOCRAT: Prejudices, prejudices! Protagoras, for one, would not agree with that. He insists that every citizen has in himself the seed of political skill. Without that, no community could survive, let alone prosper (Plato, *Prot.* 322b–d). That is why the Athenians listen to the specialist, whenever specialized knowledge in technical matters is required, and accept the advice of the wealthy in financial affairs and of the knowledgeable wherever that is useful, but when it comes to judging political arguments and deciding, they all claim competence and listen to every citizen's opinion (Plato, *Prot.* 319b–d,

322d–23a; Thuc. 6.39.1)—and rightly so! Individually, they may be inferior to the better ones but cumulatively, by adding up their talents and qualities, they are far superior even to the best. Simply put: in the many is all (Thuc. 6.39.1; Herod. 3.80.6).

OLIGARCH: What a crazy argument. No need to waste time refuting it! But Protagoras deserves a comment. Whether or not he intends his myth to be used in support of democracy, while emphasizing that every citizen has in himself the seed of [political skill or excellence] he also insists that such seed must be carefully developed and that education is of paramount importance (Plato, *Prot.* 323c–24d).

DEMOCRAT: No objection here! However, just as Athens is the education of Hellas (Thuc. 2.41.1), so democracy itself offers the best education to the citizen and encourages him to develop his personality freely in whatever direction he wishes, and to become as an individual versatile and as self-reliant (Thuc. 2.41.1) as the Athenians are collectively (Thuc. 2.36.3). Thus the Athenians do not need a rigorous educational system like the Spartans (Thuc. 2.39). In fact, every citizen is equally interested in the affairs of the state as in his own; even those who are mostly occupied with their own business are extremely well informed on general politics (Thuc. 2.40).

OLIGARCH: Which still does not save them from making terrible mistakes!

DEMOCRAT: Show me the system that doesn't! It might be pointed out, however, that this "crazy system" not only in the past has been responsible for remarkable successes (Herod. 5.78) but also, more recently, has made Athens the freest and greatest, most powerful and most self-sufficient city of all (Thuc. 6.89.5; 2.36.3). On the other hand, the leaders in democracy always belong to the noble or wealthy, and it is they who devise the policies for which democracy is hated (Thuc. 8.48.6). Actually, whenever the few take over from democracy they ruin their city through their fierce competition for the position of greatest influence; this inevitably leads to factional strife, eruption of violence, and even tyranny (Herod. 3.82.3; cf. Thuc. 6.89.3).

OLIGARCH: In democracy, by contrast, it is the collaboration, solidarity and friendship of the *kakoi* that harms the city and, in the long run, brings forward a strong man who might even exploit his popularity to set up a tyranny (Herod. 3.82.3). But there is no need to argue with extreme and theoretical scenarios; nothing could be worse than the political reality presented by democracy day in and day out. The *demos* is unruly, emotional and fickle, rushing into business like a mountain stream in the spring, unable to deliberate carefully and to keep the city on a straight course (Herod. 3.81.2; Eur. *Suppl.* 417ff.). For successes the masses take all the credit, failures they blame on their leaders (Thuc. 3.43). To win support for their proposals in the assembly, the politicians have to turn to flattery, and even a man with good advice to give has to tell lies if he is expected to be believed (Thuc. 3.42f.). The competition among the politicians is fierce; they use all tricks of rhetoric, overpower the masses with their cleverness and brilliance, and accuse each other of corruption and tyrannical aspirations. What they are really concerned with, is not the common good but their own profit and advancement, and their grandiose plans. They bask in their popularity and play to the whims of the masses until things go wrong. Then they blame the innocent for the harm they have done, get away with every crime and even convince the law courts to let them off scot-free.

DEMOCRAT: Well, to have good and responsible leaders is crucially important, indeed. If only there were a second Pericles! Some of them come pretty close to the ideal, though. On the other hand, the role of the *demos* is equally important, and the people's political experience and competence is easily underestimated. The average citizen is able to appreciate a good speech and recognize a clever argument (Thuc. 2.40). Moreover, every proposal is submitted to proper discussion; the worst thing is to rush into action before the consequences have been properly debated (ibid.; cf. 3.42).

OLIGARCH: Well, it still is true that it is easy to get something accepted that is new and sounds exciting; action follows immediately upon decision, and momentous decisions are made without sufficient knowledge of the issues involved (Thuc. 6.1). The whole city has taken on the characteristics of the democratic citizen: he is an innovator, quick to form a resolution and quick to carry it out, daring beyond his resources and against better judgement; eager to follow up a victory and reluctant to accept defeat; willing to sacrifice everything for the city and preferring hardship and activity to peace and quiet. As a result, the Athenians are the worst meddlers in other people's affairs you can think of. They seem incapable by nature either of living a quiet life themselves or of allowing anyone else to do so (Thuc. 1.70;

cf. Eur. *Suppl.* 476–510, 576f.). And all this is directly connected
with their democracy. Accordingly, their foreign policy is marred by
hasty decisions and tends to be interventionist, imperialistic, exploita-
tive and oppressive.

DEMOCRAT: Foreign policy is an entirely different matter
which requires its own debate. But no one should forget that the insti-
gators of such policies belong to that very elite that claims exclusive
rights in an oligarchy (Thuc. 8.48.6). Moreover, Athens has a tradition of intervening for the sake of helping the oppressed and saving
those in mortal danger. No city has a more impressive record of
achievement than democratic Athens. And all that has been won by
the very qualities of her citizens and their love for their city. Look
where all that has carried her . . .

Suggestions for Additional Reading

P. J. Rhodes' *The Athenian Empire* (*Greece and Rome* Survey 17, Oxford: Oxford University Press, 1985) provides an excellent introduction to the history of the empire and the problems in its study; *The Athenian Empire* by R. Meiggs (Oxford: Oxford University Press, 1972) is a thorough treatment of the subject. The new edition of Volume V of the *Cambridge Ancient History* (Cambridge: Cambridge University Press, 1992) provides up-to-date bibliography on most of the subjects treated here, as well as thoughtful accounts of the development of the Athenian democracy and empire. The most important documents for study of the period have been conveniently collected, edited, and translated by C. W. Fornara, *Archaic Times to the End of the Peloponnesian War* (Cambridge: Cambridge University Press, 1983). Meiggs' work and much of the *Cambridge Ancient History* are largely orthodox in their treatment of the dating of inscriptions and the development of empire, and many of the views expressed there took shape in the four volumes of *The Athenian Tribute Lists* (Cambridge, MA, and Princeton: American School of Classical Studies, 1939–53), edited by B. D. Meritt, H. T. Wade-Gery, and M. F. McGregor. Although this is a work for specialists, the third volume contains chapters on the development of the Athenian empire useful to those wishing to explore the foundations of the now conventional view of imperial history. For heterodox views see H. B. Mattingly, *The Athenian Empire Restored* (Ann Arbor: University of Michigan Press, 1996), and Fornara and Samons, *Athens from Cleisthenes to Pericles* (Berkeley: University of California Press, 1991).

The bibliography on Athenian democracy has exploded in the last two decades, especially in light of the recent 2,500 year anniversary of Cleisthenes' reforms. A conference in 1993 coinciding with this anniversary resulted in the volume *Dēmokratia* (Princeton: Princeton University Press, 1996), edited by J. Ober and C. Hedrick, which contains essays by numerous scholars (from various perspectives) and extensive bibliography. A fascinating and exhaustive account of Athens' reputation throughout the ages is provided by J. Roberts, *Athens on Trial* (Princeton: Princeton University Press, 1994). Several works have focused on the development of popular rule and possibly changing locus of sovereignty in the state. Apart from the works excerpted in Part I above, among those most useful to the student are M. Ostwald,

From Popular Sovereignty to the Sovereignty of the Law (Berkeley: University of California Press, 1986), and R. K. Sinclair, *Democracy and Participation in Classical Athens* (Cambridge: Cambridge University Press, 1988). V. Hanson's *The Other Greeks* (New York: Free Press, 1995) provides much needed balance, background, and context for Athens' political development. M. I. Finley's *Democracy Ancient and Modern* (New Brunswick, NJ: Rutgers, 1985) is a penetrating look at Athens' regime and its possible relevance for modern states.

For the study of Thucydides the *Historical Commentary on Thucydides* begun by A. W. Gomme and completed by K. J. Dover and A. Andrewes is still invaluable (Oxford: Oxford University Press, 1945–81), and can be useful even to the Greek-less reader (with a little effort). S. Hornblower, *A Commentary on Thucydides*, 2 vols. (Oxford: Oxford University Press, 1991–96), designed to be accessible to those who do not know Greek, provides extensive recent bibliography. K. J. Dover's *Thucydides* (*Greece and Rome* Survey 7, Oxford: Oxford University Press, 1973) provides an excellent introduction to the study of the historian, as does F. E. Adcock, *Thucydides and His History* (Cambridge: Cambridge University Press, 1963). On the funeral oration in particular see N. Loraux, *The Invention of Athens*, trans. A. Sheridan (Cambridge, MA: Harvard University Press, 1986).

As a historical figure Pericles has received perhaps less purely scholarly attention than he deserves. V. Ehrenberg's *Sophocles and Pericles* (Oxford: Blackwell, 1954) is still helpful; *A Commentary on Plutarch's Pericles* by P. Stadter (Chapel Hill: University of North Carolina Press, 1989), is most useful for readers of Greek. W. R. Connor, *The New Politicians in Fifth-Century Athens* (Princeton: Princeton University Press, 1971) places Pericles in the context of democratic political developments, especially emphasizing his precursive relationship to Cleon.

The study of Athenian art and architecture has provided some interesting perspectives on the empire and democracy. The Parthenon (built between 447 and 432) with its (possible) portrayal of the Panathenaic procession and giant gold and ivory statue of Athena stands at the center of the controversy. Many scholars have inferred from the account in Plutarch's *Pericles* (see Part II) that the building was financed, in large part, from the tribute paid by Athens' allies. This view has recently been challenged by L. Kallet-Marx, "Did Tribute Fund the Parthenon?" (*Classical Antiquity*, 8:1989, 252–66); in response it has been argued that Athena's treasury, from which most of the money for the Parthenon directly derived, also funded extensive military operations and must have contained both allied tribute and strictly Athenian money: see Samons, "Athenian Finance and the Treasury of Athena" (*Historia* 42:1993, 129–38). An excellent account of the Parthenon's aesthetic achievement and thematic possibilities may be found in J. Pollitt, *Art and Experience in Classical Greece* (Cambridge: Cambridge University Press, 1972).

The relationship of Athenian drama to politics and society at large has attracted much scholarship of late. Good places to start are the collections of essays edited by P. Euben, *Greek Tragedy and Political Theory* (Berkeley: University of California Press, 1986), and by J. Winckler and F. Zeitlin, *Nothing to Do with Dionysos?* (Princeton: Princeton University Press, 1990). For the sophists in Athens during this period see J. de Romilly, *The Great Sophists in Periclean Athens*, trans. J. Lloyd (Oxford: Oxford University Press, 1992).